# SELECTED PLAYS
# OF
# MICHEÁL mac LIAMMÓIR

Irish Drama Selections

*General Editors*
Joseph Ronsley
Ann Saddlemyer

# IRISH DRAMA SELECTIONS

ISSN 0260–7962

*All titles contain a Bibliographical Checklist. For details of plays, see the advertisement at the back of this book.*

# SELECTED PLAYS
# OF
# MICHEÁL mac LIAMMÓIR

Chosen and with an Introduction by

John Barrett

Irish Drama Selections

1998
COLIN SMYTHE
Gerrards Cross, Bucks.

THE CATHOLIC UNIVERSITY
OF AMERICA PRESS
Washington, D.C.

First published in 1998 by Colin Smythe Limited
Gerrards Cross, Buckinghamshire

**British Library Cataloguing in Publication Data**
A catalogue record for this book is available from
the British Library
ISBN 0-86140-154-9
ISBN 0-86140-155-7 pbk

**Library of Congress Cataloging-in-Publication Data**
mac Liammóir, Micheál, 1899–1978.
(Plays. Selections)
Selected plays of Micheál mac Liammóir / chosen and with an introduction by
John Barrett.
p.  cm. – (Irish drama selections. ISSN 0260-7962 : 11)
Includes bibliographical references (p.  ).
ISBN 0-8132-0888-2 (cloth). – ISBN 0-8132-0889-0 (pbk.)
1. Ireland – Drama.  I. Barrett, John.  II. Title.  III. Series.
PR6063.A25315A61998
822'.914 – dc21                    98-37909
                                   CIP

Produced in Great Britain
Printed by Redwood Book, Trowbridge, Wilts

# CONTENTS

# A Note on the Texts

Only two of mac Liammóir's plays in English have been previously published, *Where Stars Walk* (Progress House, Dublin, 1962) and *Ill Met by Moonlight* (James Duffy, Dublin, 1949) and, in a revised version (James Duffy, Dublin, 1954). It is the 1954 version of the play that is printed here. The texts of *The Mountains Look Different*, *The Liar*, and *Prelude in Kazbek Street* are based on prompt copies in the possession of the trustees of the mac Liammóir/Edwards estate.

# Acknowledgements

Thanks are due to my colleague Christopher Murray, to Ms. Mary Cannon, to the Curator, Special Collections Department, Northwestern University, Evanston, Ilinois, to Micheál Ó hAodha, and especially, to Richard Pine.

# Introduction

'I am a man of various tricky talents,' Micheál mac Liammóir[1] once said, 'the number and ill-sorted incongruity of which has often bewildered me and caused other people to ask me with increasing frequency why I wasn't doing any of a dozen things except the one on which I happened to be engaged at the time.'[2]

When he died in March 1978, Ireland lost the most versatile man of the theatre she has known. Actor, painter, playwright, scene and costume designer, poet (in the Irish language), prose writer, raconteur, linguist – mac Liammóir was a Renaissance man and a flamboyant one at that. To his individual achievements we must add a joint one, the founding of the Gate Theatre with his partner Hilton Edwards and the maintaining of high standards of production for fifty years. In these years mac Liammóir became something more than a well-known man of the theatre; he became a national institution – a focus both of affection and admiration and a recipient of many honours. He was made a Freeman of the City of Dublin and Trinity College conferred on him the honorary degree of Doctor of Literature.

It might seem that the biographer is well served with three volumes of mac Liammóir autobiography, *All for Hecuba* (1946), *Each Actor On His Ass* (1961) and the *roman-à-clef, Enter a Goldfish* (1977). But the accounts he gives are not always reliable and the reader should be aware of Hilton Edward's admonition to his friend: 'You exaggerate. You'll never learn not to exaggerate. It's in your blood.'[3]

Slightly more than exaggeration is the account mac Liammóir gives of his origins and place of birth. He claimed that he was born Michael Willmore in the suburb of Blackrock in the City of Cork on October 25th 1899, and that his father, an unsuccessful corn merchant, moved his family – his four daughters and his youngest, Michael – to London in 1906. This was accepted for years, but recent biographers have established that while he was indeed born on that date, it was at 150 Purves Road, Willesden, London, as Alfred Lee Wilmore, and that his first extended visit to Ireland was not until 1917.[4] Nor is there

xi

much evidence to support his claim that his mother was Irish; that there were Irish connections is probably true, but a stronger case can be made for an English Jewish background. It is understandable that one so passionately devoted to Ireland should wish to claim Irish birth and antecedents.

Not in dispute is the account of early unhappy schooldays (well described in *Enter a Goldfish*) when the the curly-haired seven-year-old, spoilt by older sisters, encountered the rough and tumble of the Willesden Council School. This caused him to retreat into himself and increased an already established weakness for 'play-acting'. He would, he tells us, spend long hours posturing and reciting in front of a mirror in the bedroom.

At the age of twelve, mac Liammóir secured a wider audience. In January 1911, he appeared with the young Noel Coward in a children's play, *The Goldfish*, in London. A role in *Peter Pan* followed (touring in 1911, 1912 and 1913), and his fame as a child actor – indeed, a child star – was established when he was chosen by Sir Beerbohm Tree to play the title role in *Oliver Twist*. The young Willmore became the darling of the women's illustrated magazines and was pampered and spoilt by the casts he appeared with. But not indefinitely. The moment that he had dreaded finally arrived; his voice broke and he had to turn his back on the stage.

The fear of growing old which mac Liammóir exhibited so strongly in his later life is the classic legacy of the child actor and it is an underlying concern in several of his plays. It is interesting to note that he creates very few older characters: where he does, they are free from bodily decrepitude and are vigorous and dominant. We can think of Finn in *Diarmuid and Gráinne* or Martin Grealish in *The Mountains Look Different* or Professor Prosper in *Ill Met by Moonlight*, who insists on his daily swim in the lake, even with a heavy cold.

Mac Liammóir tells us that in April 1914, at the age of fourteen, he spent some months in Seville with his Spanish relations and met a handsome cousin who helped him to discover his sexuality.[5] (Fictional Spanish relations, according to other members of his family). In August of that year with the outbreak of war, he returned home to London and was enrolled at the Willesden Polytechnic School of Art. He studied for a year before accepting the generous help of a patron and moving on to the more prestigious Slade School of Art. For the next thirteen years his creative energy was directed to painting and design.

It was in the autumn of 1914 that two of the most important events of his life occurred. The first was his triumphant declaration of his Irishness, which came about from a chance reading of Yeats's essay

on *Ireland and the Arts* (1901).
He was, he says, extraordinarily struck by this passage:

The Greeks looked within their borders and we, like them, have a history fuller than any modern history of imaginative events; and legends which surpass, as I think, all legends but theirs in wild beauty; and in our land, as in theirs, there is no river or mountain that is not associated in the memory with some event or legend; while political reasons have made love of country, as I think, even greater among us than among them. I would have our writers and craftsmen of many kinds master this history and these legends, and fix upon their memory the appearance of mountains and rivers and make it all visible again in their arts . . .[6]

Mac Liammóir tells us that in 'a rapture of joyful revelation'[7] he knew that his life would be changed from then on.

It was a change that determined the subject-matter of many of his early plays, *Diarmuid and Gráinne*, *Where Stars Walk*, *Ill Met by Moonlight*, but this was a later consequence. The immediate result was that he began to attend classes in Irish given by the Gaelic League in London and to immerse himself in Irish poetry, folklore and mythology. The metamorphosis from Albert Willmore to Micheál mac Liammóir had begun. It was very much a labour of love: Hilton Edwards has observed that 'it was Irish that was the language of his heart. In it all the diaries were written and all his stage directions on his acting scripts, leaving somewhat of a problem for his unfortunate understudy.'[8]

In this same autumn mac Liammóir became friendly with a fellow-student at the College of Art, Máire O'Keefe, 'a lanky mysterious girl with slanting blue-green eyes',[9] who was also (perhaps) a distant cousin. They quickly discovered that they had the same interests in art and literature (and Ireland) and soon they were inseparable companions. From 1914 to her premature death in 1927 they shared a platonic but intense relationship, and it is to her that he attributes the flowering of his talent. They shared too a belief in the mystic and paranormal: they were both convinced that they had lived their lives together in a previous existence and that this accounted for the extraordinary empathy between them. In *Enter a Goldfish* (where he writes in the third person and takes the name of Martin Weldon) mac Liammóir speaks of a vision that they shared:

'You did see it too, didn't you?', Martin murmured at the garden gate, just before leaving. 'Yes,' she answered, 'I saw it and remembered it, because that was where we first met. Oh, thousands of years ago, I suppose.'[10]

Prior relationships of this sort form the basis of *Where Stars Walk*.

In 1917 he came with Máire and her mother to Ireland – to visit the land he loved (and also, possibly, to avoid conscription). They rented a little house at Howth where Máire and Micheál would 'dream of the return of the Irish Gods to the Hill of Howth,'[11] and would go for long walks

lighting fires on the hill tops about Howth in all the four festivals in honour of the people of Faery, who were really, as the two celebrants did not forget, the ancient gods of Ireland.[12]

For three years they lived together in this fashion, while mac Liammóir struggled to earn money as a graphic artist, but in 1921 the doctors declared that Máire had consumption and recommended that she go abroad to recover. For the next five years they lived on the Continent, mostly in Switzerland, moving from one place to another, mac Liammóir selling his paintings and drawings wherever they travelled. Then on 7 January 1927, after a brief illness, Máire O'Keefe died. mac Liammóir tells us that this was the most traumatic moment of his life, a blow that shook his confidence. But though he was desolate, he was not abandoned:

a breath from nowhere would blow across my face. Perhaps it was the honeysuckle in the jar by my bed, or the scent of wet leaves outside the window, or the wind stirring in the trees, but I would feel certain she was there.[13]

In many of his plays mac Liammóir introduces mystical or paranormal incidents; it must be recognized that these are not the theatrical devices of Noel Coward, but derive from a genuinely held belief. In his autobiographical works he recounts many such incidents, such as when he was on board ship returning from America and became aware that his sister had died:

. . . I was back in my earliest youth, and by my side was my sister Christine, staring at me with sombre eyes through the tall summer grasses of a field by the river, or perched in a tree in the garden at home and whispering through the leaves: 'The dead come back, you know. Oh yes, you'll see one day.'. . . I had not seen her for ten years, but all that day she followed me through the boat, singing and laughing, whispering in my ear, keeping close to my side wherever I went. And by the evening I knew that she was dead.[14]

Thrown into deep depression by the death of Máire O'Keefe, mac Liammóir turned for support to his elder sister Marjorie, now married to the actor-manager Anew McMaster. As a consequence, he shortly found himself playing the humble part of Paris in *Romeo and Juliet*, somewhere in the south of England. This was in the spring of 1927 and marked a return to the stage after a gap of some thirteen years. In June of that year the McMaster Company crossed over to begin one of its excitingly unpredictable tours of Ireland, and in the same month in the town of Enniscorthy the company was joined by 'a sturdily-built young man in a tweed overcoat and cap, a promising English actor by the name of Hilton Edwards.'[15] There began a friendship and partnership that was to last until mac Liammóir's death in 1978, a lively blending of opposite personalities and complementary talents.

The first theatre they founded (with Professor Liam O'Bríain) was an Irish-speaking one, the Taibhdhearc, in Galway, and they opened on 27 August 1928 with Micheal's own first play, *Diarmuid agus Gráinne*. Hilton Edwards, without a word of Irish himself, directed it. In October the two partners founded the Dublin Gate Theatre, determined to give to Dublin theatregoers something more than the rather limited repertoire of Irish naturalistic plays that the Abbey was offering at that period. The Gate opened its doors with Ibsen's *Peer Gynt*, and this was followed by Eugene O'Neill's *The Hairy Ape*, mac Liammóir's *Diarmuid and Gráinne* (in his own translation) and Oscar Wilde's *Salomé*. Hilton Edwards summed up the contrast between the two theatres: '. . . the Abbey set out to show Ireland to herself and then to the world, we in the Gate began to show the world to Ireland',[16] a contrast more pithily described in Dublin circles as 'Sodom and Begorrah.'

When you think of Micheál mac Liammóir you tend to think in terms of style: elegant, bold, colourful, hyperbolic. He was, you might say, born under the sign of Cornucopia. This extravagance is found in all of his artistic endeavours and in his personal life as well. His habit of overstatement is well illustrated in the story told by one of his secretaries – one of the many mac Liammóir anecdotes that circulated around Dublin. Taking dictation from him one day in his garden, she began the letter: 'I am sitting here writing this outdoors and the garden is ablaze with colour.' She looked up, surprised, but saw only the same few dusty wallflowers in the corner. In his memoirs, on a number of occasions, he catches himself in the act of touching up the picture. He remembers the liner approaching New York on 'a morning bland with blue and gold and the sky-line painfully apparent.' It was Hilton Edwards who reminded him that the weather was overcast and that they had not seen the sky-line at all.[17]

A friend of mac Liammóir's once described his prose style as 'that of a herbaceous border', in its variety, profusion and colour. It can be argued that a temperament as expansive as his was better suited to the medium of prose than the more restricted form of drama. Denis Johnston was of this opinion and felt that his essays and volumes of autobiography were of a higher overall standard than his dramatic writings and, indeed, that he was one of the best prose writers to come out of Ireland in modern times.[18]

But there is an undeniable tendency to diffuseness in his work:

'It's going to be much too long, of course,' Hilton was saying. 'Much too long . . . and you're up to your old tricks again, of course. Never use one adjective when five will do: that's your motto. One of these days you'll die of a surfeit of words. Still, it's all part of the Baroque, I suppose, but do promise me you'll go easy with the twirls and the tendrils.'[19]

Mac Liammóir was a most commanding figure on stage; Cyril Cusack described him as 'without doubt the most beautiful presence ever to grace an Irish stage.'[20] His acting style, however, was not without its own share of twirls and tendrils. His early mentors belonged to the Victorian tradition and he favoured the declamatory in tone and gesture, deploring the modern method of acting as practised by 'young men of polite behaviour and weak lungs' with a 'fear of overstatement.'[21] This was certainly not one of his own fears.

It is difficult to point to any significant influence on mac Liammóir's plays. There is the general influence of l9th century melodrama and, in those plays of his that have a drawing-room context, the influence of Oscar Wilde is discernible; perhaps too, the more lateral influence of such West End writers as Noel Coward. But the structure and tone of his plays are very much his own.

All of mac Liammóir's plays, without exception, have a strong love interest. He confesses himself to be an incurable romantic, one who dreams of breathless encounters and quickening heartbeats:

It was always of Paris and Parisian intrigues that I dreamed among trees tall, elegant and still, under the golden afternoon light, the soft spring rains; a veiled figure with a little muff and a bustle like a puckered rose would pass a handsome bewhiskered man wearing yellow gloves and murmur: 'Demain à quatre heures alors, même endroit, il faut que je te voie, c'est très important . . .'[22]

In the wider sense of the term, too, his work exhibits an unabashed romanticism – not just in his writing, but in his designs, his painting and his drawing. He admits that 'the noble lady Romanticism' had him in thrall: 'wherever she casts those wonderful eyes of hers she views seas deluged with delight and awful forests full of darkness and mystery. Her robes are the colours of flame, and the hawk-headed gods walk by her side, with enchanted rings upon her fingers'.[23] The titles of his plays reflect a rather old-fashioned romanticism: *Ill Met by Moonlight*, *Where Stars Walk*, *The Mountains Look Different*, *Dancing Shadow*, *Slipper for the Moon*.

Perhaps, too, it was the romantic notion of spontaneity – the 'first fine careless rapture' – that led him in some of them to write in a way that is more careless than rapture.

Micheál mac Liammóir wrote ten original plays in English, three pageants, eight adaptations and fifteen or so variety sketches. This is a considerable output when we realize that he acted in over three hundred and fifty productions and that for most of these he designed both set and costumes.

After *Diarmuid and Gráinne* in 1928 there is a gap of twelve years before his next original work, *Where Stars Walk* in 1940. Between 1940 and 1954 seven of his ten plays were written and, after this, we have only the one-act *The Liar* in 1969 and the semi-autobiographical *Prelude in Kazbek Street* in 1973. Part of the reason for this decline in output was the series of one-man shows that he created and toured world-wide in the sixties: his celebration of Wilde, *The Importance of Being Oscar*, in 1960; *I Must be Talking to my Friends* in 1963 (a survey of Irish historical and literary figures); and his *Yeats* in 1965. This was, in a sense, a return to the cherished position of the child star – centre stage, the focus of attention and praise. These one-man shows, although they do not come within the scope of this study, are highly creative compilations and the linking passages, especially in *The Importance of Being Oscar*, are skilfully wrought.

Mac Liammóir's first work in English, *Diarmuid and Grainne*, a story from the Fenian cycle of the Irish sagas, opened on 18th November 1928. It was a project that had long been on his mind and he and Edwards often discussed it and mourned the fact that 'the day of mythical romanticism was at its lowest ebb in the theatre.'[24]. Because he wanted the play to be popular theatre, he discarded the idea of using verse; instead he aimed for a new type of prose dialogue that was more poetic and rhythmical than that prevailing. As he tells us in *All for Hecuba*:

It was a curious period for the dramatist, who, if he set his face against the expressionist movement that was creeping in from Russia and Germany and avoided modernism of style, found nothing else in the air but the conventional methods of the classics and the gramophones and cocktails, the witty regretful moods and tunes and libertines that Noel Coward had set free in Shaftesbury Avenue.[25]

The play has some fine moments, though a modern audience would find it hard to accept the high level of artificiality. It is curious that Lady Gregory should have praised the piece for its simplicity – 'beautifully staged and lighted; no plot, just the simple story of Finn and the Lovers. Simple language, a straight story, very moving. . . . A new departure.'[26] But mac Liammóir himself quickly came to recognize its shortcomings: '. . . in spite of much flattery and kindness, I began to dislike what I had written with intensity.'[27]

It was twelve years before his next play appeared. He had learnt a good deal about stagecraft in the interim and had gained the advantage of having his own company of actors to write for. *Where Stars Walk* received its premiere at the Gaiety Theatre on 19th February 1940 and was greeted by public and critical acclaim. He again turns to the Irish sagas, this time to the story of Etáin and Midhir in the earlier mythological cycle. In the saga, Etáin, a princess of the land of Faery, had become separated from her lover Midhir and had returned to earth to live in the court of a king, forgetting her unearthly past. Midhir appears in the court as a country boy, reawakens her consciousness and persuades her to return with him. They escape the perils of the court and fly off together in the guise of swans.

In the Programme Note to the play mac Liammóir expresses reservations about the audience's ability to accept another full-blown mythical heroic romance in the style of *Diarmuid and Gráinne*. He would, therefore, set the story of the immortal lovers in the context of contemporary Dublin; Etáin and Midhir become Eileen and Martin, maid and houseboy in a fashionable Dublin residence. This was a bold design and, for the most part, it works very well, as the trivial social life of Dublin of the 1940s is set against the vital and impassioned love of the young couple. The contrast is particularly pointed up by the introduction of a trio of effete dilettantes, Robert Twomey, Rex Dillon and Tommy Millington, satellites in the orbit of the glittering hostess, Sophia Sheridan. But a strategy that puts bores on stage is a dangerous one, and we may feel that, at the least, two of them would have sufficed.

Apart from this, the stagecraft of the piece is admirable. As an actor himself, mac Liammóir knew what worked in the theatre and was always capable of writing suspenseful scenes and strong curtains. He has a good feeling for the dramatic moment and knows how this must be earned, prepared for. The way in which he prepares us for the entrance of Martin is a good example; it involves the use of the planchette board, the playing of the harp and piano, the striking of the midnight hour, the knocking on the hall door ('it's just like the murder scene in Macbeth, dear'), and the smell of hawthorn. These are all introduced quite casually into the conversation, and yet by the time Martin actually appears we have been prepared for any manner of strangeness.

The play was a considerable success. It went on tour around Ireland in the same year. In 1947–48 it was presented by the company in Glasgow, in London, and then on a tour of Canada, finishing with a season at the Mansfield Theatre, New York. It was revived at the Gate Theatre in 1952 and again in 1978.

*Ill Met by Moonlight* (1946) is generally and rightly considered to be mac Liammóir's finest play. The setting is Connemara in the West of Ireland in a house called Brugh na Gealai (the fort of the moon), built on the site of a faery fort and owned by Professor Prosper, a folklorist (played by Hilton Edwards). He is visited on Midsummer's Eve by his nephew Robert Mallaroe and his bride, Catherine. But the faery spirits who lived in this fort long before human habitation call on Catherine to join them. The manservant Lee (played by mac Liammóir) explains it:

Them as lives in the air, or down under the ground maybe. Their blood begins to fail, you see, and if they sees a newly-married bride, they'll try to get a hold of her. For the sake of her sweet blood, do you understand me now?

Basically the plot is that of the changeling and the havoc that such a person wreaks, but the story here is strengthened by being placed in the broader context of Professor Prosper's psychic research. Yeats had used the changeling legend as the basis of his verse play *The Land of Heart's Desire* (1894), but, while Yeats's characters are 'dressed in the costume of some remote time', mac Liammóir places his in contemporary society. In a way that is similar to *Where Stars Walk*, he introduces the world of folk legend into a contemporary Irish setting:

'As the twilight comes down, as light gets uncertain, and things get distorted, or revealed in another way, they take on another personality, a haystack becomes a giant, a tree becomes a looming ghost, a far-off mountain seems glowing with flame . . . I tried a new trick, which is purely theatrical, of combining that world we've been talking about, the world Yeats rediscovered, the mythological world which he shrouded in twilight, with a pleasant modern commonplace world – to marry these two worlds was my experiment.'[28]

The modern commonplace world is mainly represented by the trio of comic servants and a conventional romantic sub-plot involving the Professor's daughter, Susan, and a neighbour, Charles Lushington Carew, who plays as named.

Again, there is much to admire in mac Liammóir's stagecraft. In acts two and three the gradual change in Catherine's behaviour is chillingly convincing, as we follow a series of well-placed indications, beginning with her sudden aversion to people who cut flowers:

'Filthy barbarians, sticking corpses upright in a pot!'

In the opening expository scene, too, his handling of material that is dense and intractable is masterly. He uses two informants (Lee and Bairbre) and two languages (Irish and English) and manages a particularly clever deployment of props. *Ill Met by Moonlight* is, I feel, the play to which mac Liammóir gave his fullest attention. It is the most original and the most thoughtful of his works and the most consistent; it is written without lapses or excesses of style or action. The play was revived in 1947, 1948 and 1949 (in a revised version) and again in 1969 and 1979, and it has also played on tour on many occasions. The text reproduced here is that of the revised 1949 production, published in 1954.

*The Mountains Look Different* (1948) is a strong melodrama again set in the West of Ireland. The central character, Bairbre, is a Connemara girl who had emigrated to London thirteen years previously and turned to prostitution. She has met and loved the innocent and unsuspecting Tom Grealish, whom she sees as her salvation, and, now married, returns with him to his father's Connemara home. Though the play is a highly moral one, the subject matter invoked the type of protest that had become virtually an initiation rite for the Irish dramatist. *The Irish Times* describes the scene:

. . . at the end of the second act two men left their seats and addressed the audience. They said they were protesting against *filth* being shown on a Dublin stage, and asked the audience to join with them in leaving the theatre.

A third man rose from his seat in the gallery. Shouts of *Sit down* and *If you don't like it, you can leave* then came from the audience. The man in the gallery was heard to say *Are you Catholics?*[29]

The strength of the piece lies in the gripping quality of the first two acts and in the characterization of the three central characters. Bairbre, especially, is a fine creation, moving as she does between hope for the future and despair about her past. There is a corresponding fluctuation in her dress and appearance and in her drinking and smoking habits; especially effective is the way in which she vacillates between the idioms and rhythms of her native Connemara and the harsher accents and idiom of the London street.

Her father-in-law, Martin Grealish, is a well-drawn and convincing character, apart from one major inconsistency. At his initial appearance he is described as 'a tall powerfully-built man of about sixty', and throughout the play he is seen as a vigorous – not to say violent – person. In act two, then, we are surprised to hear his son tell us:

Of course he's not a strong man at all, you know. Times he do be gasping like an old sheep and he only walking a mile or so out of this . . .

At his next appearance he is indeed seen to have laboured breathing, but after that it is forgotten. This is a good example of the type of inconsistency that bedevils many of mac Liammóir's plays. Presumably he had in mind the idea that Grealish's weakness might be contributory to his death – a factor, then, that would alleviate Bairbre's responsibility in it. If such was his design, he must have forgotten it; when a man is strangled so thoroughly that 'There's black marks on his throat', lesser bronchial complaints seem superfluous.

This is symptomatic of a general loss of control in the third act and there is a feeling that the piece has been somewhat hastily resolved. The play is always in the melodramatic mode (*Grealish begins to chuckle with sinister relish*), but in the first two acts this seems justified. In the final act, however, we find theatrical effects that are not supported by dramatic substance.

There is, moreover, a fundamental objection to the ending of the play. It becomes clear from Bairbre's account that she acted in self-defence ('he tried to force me') and we can see, even as she is led off by two strong Civic Guards, that there is not a jury in the land that will convict her. We can, of course, understand the playwright's dilemma. On the one hand he wishes to make the point that sin leads to sin (from promiscuity, to deceit, to murder), that we cannot escape from our past and so on; on the other hand, he does not want the audience to lose sympathy with his heroine. The moral forces at work in the play call for a charge of murder, while sentiment puts in a plea for justifiable homicide. But the audience is confused by this equivocation and finds it hard to accept Bairbre's final public atonement and confession of guilt.

In a reply to various critical attacks on the play mac Liammóir pointed out that it was based on the Greek model, beginning *in medias res* outside the dwelling house, observing the Unities, using Messenger, Chorus etc. and encompassing the notion of fate. He adds:

The play is a morality in the sense that, like the plays of Greece, it tells of sin and atonement, and I wrote it in this way because I wished to experiment with a modern theme in an approximation to a classic form.[30]

It seems that while he has adopted some of the trappings, he has missed the essential: the Greek plays are unequivocal.

Mac Liammóir's rural idiom in *The Mountains Look Different*, and in his other plays that have a country context, is very much his own creation. It is vigorous and colourful, yet restrained; and his intimate knowledge of Irish gives it authenticity. He was an admirer of Synge and in his Introduction to the Everyman Library edition of his plays had paid particular attention to the Gaelic influence on Synge's language:

. . . by translating to English so much that is commonplace in Gaelic syntax and idiom, it acquires in the process a most uncommon richness of flavour, a savage, salty tang, a sudden barbed yet kindly brilliance of images that falls upon the ear of an audience with all the delight of the unexpected.[31]

But he knew that Synge had mined this ore to exhaustion – linguistic barriers were erected and writers who followed him warned off:

. . . by its very position in time this speech, a freakish and eloquent hybrid, is doomed to the briefest existence... and what has proved one of the most potent attractions of modern dramatic literature in Ireland can but lead at last to a blind alley.[32]

In view of this warning it is strange – though it serves as another example of his inconsistency – that he should himself in *The*

*Mountains Look Different* fall so unregardingly, so grotesquely into the manner of Synge:

Three fine daughters I had, Matthew Conroy, and two of them praying nuns in Galway and the other married, a cross-eyed terror with a brood of screeching brats beyond in Boston. Five strapping sons I had, one of them a holy priest bent down on his two knees at the butt-end of Hong-Kong and three belted peelers and they steering the traffic of America. And the sole survivor of that crew, Tomas, ha? – to go lepping over to London for to get himself laced up with a strange one, a wife his father never laid an eye on no more than if she was a raging devil out of hell, and nothin with her...devil a red penny, do you hear me?

Despite its flaws, *The Mountains Look Different* proved to be popular in the theatre. After the Irish premiere, it transferred to the Citizen's Theatre, Glasgow. A version of the play in Irish, *Tá Crút Núa ar na Sléibhte*, translated by Liam O Bríain and designed by mac Liammóir, was produced at the Peacock Theatre in 1970.

Mac Liammóir favours a traditional, linear type of plot and, though he may experiment with subject-matter, in terms of formal structure he is generally conservative. But *The Liar*, his one-act play which had its premiere at the Dublin Theatre Festival in 1969, is a highly experimental work in this regard. On a long bench on the exposed deck of the Mail Boat he gathers a group of people who are emigrating to England, each with their fears and hopes, little lies and pretensions. The principal liar of the play is Martin Concannon, who has deceived both his wife and mother about the social status of the other. It is the unravelling of this deceit that is the mainspring of the plot.

There are two groups of people in the play – the trio of Martin, his wife Nonie, and his mother Cathy Concannon; and then the rest of the passengers, who are individualized to an extent but not named – a Young Woman, a Middle-aged Woman, an Older Woman, a Young Man, a Middle-aged Man, an Older Man. While they speak as individuals, they also form a stylized choric unit, the formal distinction of their ages emphasizing the universality of the piece. This chorus frames the action of the play and sets the mood of the piece with a quiet lyricism:

MEN AND WOMEN: Soon she'll be leaving the harbour,
                        we're all on board.
WOMEN:              And we'll be staring back at water

| | |
|---|---|
| MEN: | growing wider, |
| WOMEN: | dimmer |
| MEN: | darker |
| MIDDLE WOMAN: | under the last Wicklow star. |

But the play is not predominantly lyrical; more often the writing displays an humourous and shrewd perception of human nature. The play is structured on a series of interior monologues and this gives mac Liammóir greater latitude to express himself in the expansive way that he enjoys. There is, too, a strong autobiographical element in the play. The young Martin posturing before the mirror and acting out his many roles ('you're a play-actor! Nothing but an old playactor!') is recognizable as the young – and, indeed, not so young – mac Liammóir.

Mac Liammóir's last play, *Prelude in Kazbek Street*, is also to an extent autobiographical, though the subject of his homosexuality is dealt with far more openly in his later memoir, *Enter a Goldfish* (1977).[33] But the theatregoers who thronged to the Gate theatre in October 1973 to witness the Dublin Theatre Festival production of the play must have come in some expectation. And the play opens with a homosexual lovers' quarrel – a far cry indeed from *Diarmuid and Gráinne*. However, they quickly came to realize that there was going to be nothing intense or personal about the piece. The tone is for the most part light and humorous, and the problems of homosexuality are confined to the realms of formal discussion; they are contemplated rather than felt. The occasional protests against discrimination sound rhetorical as they do not arise from anything in the drama itself. In act one, for example, Serge Kovalesky speaks in indignation, but from no immediate cause:

If my sort of person is represented in a book or a movie as high or low camp, something that's both comic and contemptible, people will lap it up; if it's pornographic, it's acceptable permissiveness; but if it's given one shred of dignity or reality, God help us!

Kovalesky (mac Liammóir's persona in the play) is an inter-nationally celebrated Irish ballet dancer, in humbler times known as John Joseph Cassidy. At one point in the play he compares himself to Tamar, Queen of Georgia, whose custom it was to attract the attention of gentlemen travelling over the Kazbek Pass by appearing in her tower and waving a red scarf. She would seduce them, murder them, and then return to the tower, scarf in hand, to await the next victim. Serge sees this as an analogy of his own inconstant behaviour and in the course of the play we follow three such relationships: with the Frenchman Jean-Louis, the American William Vandamm, and the Englishman Robert Marshall.

The structure of the play depends solely on these three relationships and (unusually for mac Liammóir) is underplotted. The lack of action is compensated for by a great deal of humour and repartee and a certain amount of low comic action involving the favourite mac Liammóir device of the pair of comic servants, one of whom is countrified and ignorant (Andy) and the other who can instruct and reprimand (Mrs. Baty). We have, too, the familiar 'grotesque' or 'original' character – in this case Paco Gonzales.

In so far as the play has thematic impact, it is a play about loneliness, and we witness the double loneliness of Serge Kovalesky, as homosexual and as artist. Apart from Serge, the most memorable characterization is Madame Francisco Gonzales, who was formerly Marya Petrovna of the corps de ballet, but was born plain Maggie Kelly. In a way that is typical of mac Liammóir's whimsical humour, she offers a parallel to Serge's own situation. While the Marya Petrovna in her can soothe the Serge Kovalesky, the Maggie Kelly will take no nonsense from the John Joe Cassidy.

*Prelude in Kazbek Street* is a strange play. It is elegant and entertaining, but one feels that there is a deeper and sadder play contained within this material. There is a sense of disappointment that what could have been a serious contribution is pitched at the level of light comedy, with the characters not much above the soufflé socialites of his early work.

The five plays chosen for this volume (*Where Stars Walk* 1940, *Ill Met by Moonlight* 1946, *The Mountains Look Different* 1948, *The Liar* 1969 and *Prelude in Kazbek Street* 1973) have all in their different ways proved their worth in the theatre. Of the remaining four plays, *Home for Christmas* (1950) is a wellplotted and spirited seasonal farce, but *Dancing Shadow* (1941), *Portrait of Miriam* (1947) and *A Slipper for the Moon* (1954) are works that bear all the signs of hurried composition – loosely structured and written and full of inconsistencies.

Mac Liammóir's contribution to the Irish theatre was immense. He brought the best of European theatre to a Dublin stage which for too long had surrendered to provincialism. In so doing he provided new models for many Irish dramatists and an outlet for their work. His own work, for the most part, displays the same cosmopolitan outlook and he showed that it was possible to deal with Irish material in a more contemporary and sophisticated way than the Abbey had to offer. It is worth noting that two of mac Liammóir's plays are set in Europe, and all the other plays (except *Diarmuid and Grainne)* involve characters who are leaving Ireland, or who have returned home from abroad, or who are Europeans living in Ireland.

Micheál Ó hAodha, while admiring his many qualities, refers to him as 'a journeyman playwright'.[34] This is, I think, to undervalue both the imaginative quality of his work and its charm – so much a reflection of his own. It is true that he will be remembered pre-eminently as an actor but, while fewer and fewer of us can be grateful for those memories, all of us can continue to enjoy his writings and his plays. It is, I feel, a memorial very consciously bequeathed, for mac Liammóir more than anyone was aware of the fleeting quality of the art he loved :

On the sand we write our story: the stars shine overhead: we laugh and weep for a moment in this place or that, and then it is time for us to rise and move away to pitch our tents and paint our faces and evoke our gods elsewhere. . . . already the hampers are filled for the journey and all the clothes and props packed up. . . . Look! Here are the caskets of Portia in gold and silver and lead; the fishing-rod of Trigorin, the white seagull of Nina; here is Dorian's picture, Joan's armour, Napoleon's war-map, and the wheeled chair that belonged to Madame Desmermortes. This is the end of my story: here in a hat-box is Shylock's knife; here in a bottle is the blood of Oedipus.[35]

John Barrett

University College, Dublin.
February 1997.

# NOTES

1. The form he preferred in his later years and used in his last published work.
2. *An Oscar of No Importance*, (Heinemann, London, 1968) p.224.
3. *All for Hecuba*, (revised edition, Progress House, Dublin, 1961) p.354.
4. Micheál Ó hAodha, *The Importance of Being Micheál*, (Brandon, Dingle, l990), and Christopher Fitz-Simon: *The Boys*, (Gill and Macmillan, Dublin 1994).
5. *Enter a Goldfish* (Thames and Hudson, London, 1977) p.93.
6. *Ideas of Good and Evil 1896-1903* in *Essays and Introductions* (Macmillan, London, 1961) p.205.
7. *Enter a Goldfish* (Thames and Hudson, London, 1977) p.112.
8. *Enter Certain Players*, Edwards-mac Liammóir and the Gate 1928-1978, ed. Peter Luke (Dolmen Press, Dublin, 1978) p.86.
9. All for Hecuba, p.1.
10. *Enter a Goldfish* p.116.
11. *All for Hecuba* p.2.
12. *Enter a Goldfish* p.144.
13. *All for Hecuba* p.60.
14. *All for Hecuba* p.94. Other paranormal experiences are recorded in *Each Actor on his Ass* (Routledge and Kegan Paul, London, 1961) pp. 86,87; *Enter a Goldfish* p.129; pp 140-141.
15. *All for Hecuba* p.23.
16. *All for Hecuba* p.355.
17. *All for Hecuba* p.177.
18. In conversation with the author.
19. *An Oscar of No Importance* p.55.
20. *Evening Herald*, March 7th 1978. He continues: 'that very individual grace that was his, of stance and gesture, a voice mellifluous and carrying and a magnificence of presence which welcomed and lovingly embraced both audience and stage.'
21. *All for Hecuba* p.328.
22. *All for Hecuba* p.298.
23. *Drámaíocht Ghaeilge san am atá le teacht* in *Eire* (Cahill, Dublin 1940) p.40, trans. Brendan Devlin, in *Enter Certain Players* p.70.
24. Author's Programme Note on *Where Stars Walk*, 1978 revival.
25. *All for Hecuba* p.43.
26. *Lady Gregory's Journals* (ed. Daniel J. Murphy, Colin Smythe, Gerrards Cross, 1987) p.343.
27. *All for Hecuba* p.66.
28. Quoted by Richard Pine in his essay on mac Liammóir in *Enter Certain Players* pp.77, 78.
29. *The Irish Times*, 4th November 1948.
30. The complete text is given in the Prose section at the end of this volume.
31. *The Plays of John Millington-Synge* (Everyman Library edition, London, 1961) Introduction p.vi.
32. Ibid p.vii.
33. See chapter 4, p.94 and chapter 7, pp.174-176. The character of William Vandamm in the play is based on the Robert Hamnet of the memoir.
34. *The Importance of Being Micheal* p.134.
35. *Each Actor on His Ass* p.248.

# WHERE STARS WALK

## A Comedy of Dublin
## in the 1940s

> . . . how a Princess Edain,
> A daughter of a King of Ireland, heard
> A voice singing on a May Eve like this,
> And followed, half awake and half asleep,
> Until she came into the Land of Faery.
> Where nobody gets old and godly and grave,
> Where nobody gets old and crafty and wise,
> Where nobody gets old and bitter of tongue.
> And she is still there, busied with a dance
> Deep in the dewy shadow of a wood,
> (Or where stars walk upon a mountain-top.)

W.B. Yeats

# CHARACTERS

Sophia Sheridan
Robert Twomey
Rex Dillon
Tommy Millington
Sheila McCann
Mrs Dempsey
Eileen
Nigel Brunton
Martin

Where stars walk was first produced at the Gaiety Theatre, Dublin, on 19 February, 1940 with the following cast:

| | |
|---|---|
| SOPHIA SHERIDAN | Coralie Carmichael |
| ROBERT TWOMEY | Michael Golden |
| REX DILLON | Roy Irving |
| TOMMY MILLINGTON | Christopher Casson |
| SHEILA McCANN | Shelah Richards |
| MRS DEMPSEY | Maureen Delaney |
| EILEEN | Meriel Moore |
| NIGEL BRUNTON | Emerton Court |
| MARTIN | Micheál mac Liammóir |

The play was directed by Hilton Edwards.

The action of the play takes place in Sophia Sheridan's Dublin house in the early 1940s.

# ACT I

An evening in late April

# ACT II

Next morning

# ACT III

May Day Eve

*Author's Note*

This is my first play in the English language.

I had written a lengthy tragedy on legendary themes as well as two short comedies in Irish, and my Gate Theatre partner, Hilton Edwards, had filled my head with ambitions to write a new legend play about Midhir and Etáin. We talked of this for years in a series of long and increasingly vague conversations, for both of us, I think, realised that the day of mythical romanticism was at its lowest ebb in the theatre – not that it was dead, for fashions in art do not pass out of existence any more than the moon, or the tide, or the needles of the clock – and gradually I began to forget my immortal lovers and become more interested in the daily life of Dublin that laughed and whispered and cracked its derisive whips through the hours of my work in the theatre; and a little while after that a friend told me of a red-headed servant girl who had come into his house, and of how his wife had found her walking in her sleep in the midst of imaginary scenery and persons of great splendour.

My friend, his thoughts full of Freud and of Jung, had his own theories about it all, but I, in the middle of his talk, found myself remembering Etáin wandering in sleep through the corridors of Tara and dreaming of the immortal country she had forgotten, and presently, one event leading to another, I decided – again at my partner's suggestion – to combine it all in a species of modern comedy that might amuse the Dublin audience and leave me with enough of the unseen world partially to satisfy an incurable craving.

Micheál mac Liammóir

3

# Where Stars Walk

## PROLOGUE

*The curtain rises on darkness that is relieved only by a dim glow of reddish light on a woman's face. A harp plays a few mournful notes and a man's voice speaks.*

1ST MAN. There is no age in that country and no sorrow on any person.

2ND MAN. Do not go with this man, Etáin. Stay by my side in Tara.

1ST MAN. Do you not remember that country, Etáin? That smiling country that is beyond the end of the world?

WOMAN. I can remember so dimly. You are too far away.

2ND MAN. Etáin, do not listen to this man. Are you not happy with me? Have you not everything in the world to make you happy? Gold and silver and bronze on your hair, and the King of Ireland by your side?

WOMAN. I have been happy here.

1ST MAN. There in the hollow land there is no age. There is no sorrow in that country at the end of the world, and beyond the end of the world.

2ND MAN. Oh, do not go with him.

1ST MAN. Do you remember the land I have sung to you? There the hair of the people is yellow like the flag flower in the summer, their bodies are like the snow, their cheeks are coloured like the fox-glove.

WOMAN. There is no sorrow in that country at the end of the world and beyond the end of the world. Yet if I go back I must go as a shadow returning to shadows.

2ND MAN. Stay with me, Etáin.

1ST MAN. Do you remember the Country of the Young?

WOMAN. I remember you Midhir. (*The harp plays*) I remember you now. I will go back with you.

2ND MAN. Etáin!

3RD MAN. She is lost! Lost! Lost!

1ST MAN. Etáin.

5

WOMAN. Midhir!

2ND MAN. She is lost. (*The light on the woman's face seems to fade*).

SOPHIA (*sitting up suddenly*). There! Put on the light, Bob, there's an angel.

> (REX *puts on the lights and we see that we are in a large and quite normal-looking Dublin room with certain air of nonchalance and comfort. There is a profusion of early Spring flowers whose pale colours seem to melt into a large and lovely 'Primavera' that hangs over the grand piano. There are lazy-looking sofas and chairs and French windows leading onto a fair sized garden and the place is not distressingly overcrowded. If it were it would not suit* SOPHIA SHERIDAN, *to whom it belongs, and who has just demanded illumination. She is a large, lazy, graceful, dark-haired creature of about fifty-five, and when, with her subtle length of limb and her Italianate head, she troubles to look in, say, her late thirties, she easily does it. She continues to speak:*)

No, my dears, it's no good. Not even in a black-out.

TOMMY (*a nice fair-haired Protestant in rather endearing tweeds*). What's no good?

SOPHIA. Oh, all this. This sort of Celtic Twilight ending. It's not my stuff, anyway. I never thought Tommy's idea of putting out the lights would be much help and it wasn't. It's no good. I'm all wrong for the part. (*Pause*). There you are, you see. You know I'm all wrong and even Rex doesn't attempt to contradict me.

REX. Possibly, but I don't agree with you.

SOPHIA. Well, its true. No, I'm too wrong for words, whatever Tommy says. Besides what does Tommy know about it? He's only the author anyway. However, it's for a good cause, isn't it? That's one comfort.

BOB. (*He is nice too. You meet him every day in Ireland and everywhere else if it comes to that. If he were an actor you would unhesitatingly cast him as Horatio.*) Well, do you know, that's just where I'm a bit in the dark still. Is there a cause? Why are we doing it?

TOMMY: Well, really, Twomey! I think that's the most extraordinary question to ask. Weren't you at all the meetings? And what did you think it was for when Sophie asked you?

REX. It was really to give me a chance to produce a poetic play after all my Sunday night successes with little English drawing room comedies.

> (REX DILLON *is perhaps not so nice. Offensively like a*

6

*magazine cover in looks, he has just enough intelligence to be
irritating and not enough to be compassionable. But he's not
too bad and is useful, one would imagine, at Dublin parties,
combining a sense of balanced conversation with a perfect
understanding of the Irish kitchen and all its skeletons. He is
invited everywhere to the fury of all his hosts.*)

SOPHIA. Rex, don't be a fool. It's for the R.C.H.P.L.

BOB. The what?

SOPHIA. The Retired Cab Horses' Protection League. I fight for cab
horses all the time now. Life in Dublin is pointless unless you're
fighting for something. Well, I used to fight for the theatre before
I went to London, and in London I used to fight for parts, and
then I came home and fought for young poets. But people are so
ungrateful, my dear, especially poets. Either they get drunk at
your parties and seduce the servants, or they get sober and cut
you in the street. No, horses are much safer. Rex, give me a
cigarette, darling – (*as* REX *lifts the box.*) No, not that box, they're
Turks: there, thanks dear. (*As* BOB *lights it for her.*) Those are the
Virgins.

BOB. Sophie asked me to play in a charity show written by you. That's
all she told me.

SOPHIA. Bob, you know I told you the whole thing. Romantic play, aid
of cab horses. Be an angel and give me that holder, will you – no,
not the very long one – the rational one.

BOB (*as he does so*). I mean, I didn't know the cab horses part of it
was serious.

SOPHIA. Thanks, Bob. Deadly serious.

TOMMY. Well, I mean – really – why, here we are after a fortnight's
rehearsal and you're still wondering why we're doing it.

REX. Why does one do a play? Must there be a why? Anyway this one
is nothing to do with cab horses at all – the real reason is that
Sophie's bored in Dublin, and Sophie hankers after her old acting
days, though you did leave London in a huff, dear . . .

SOPHIA. Oh, I didn't; it was just that brute of a low-down little
producer man that drove me out with his insults – my dear, you've
no conception, you happy business boys who act in your spare
time because you like it – eleven o'clock in the morning he'd
begin on me and 'big black cow' was mildly flattering compared
with most of the things he called me.

REX. I suppose there's no such thing as a producer with decent
manners.

SOPHIA. Except you, darling. But then, you're such a ghastly producer.

7

No, don't be annoyed. I mean *I* think you're grand because you let me alone. But that scene in the wood where I meet the king is a mess, darling, you know it is. There's poor Bob as the King of Ireland, stuck up on a rostrum, balancing a spear, and me with my back to the audience from start to finish. And probably in a complete black-out when you're done with the lighting.

REX. No, no; you'll be in a lovely pale green haze.

SOPHIA. My poor face in a pale green haze! Never mind that – go on, Rex.

REX. Go on with what? Oh, of course . . . Well, Sophie thought she'd like to do something for the horses, and what could she do better than to act for them. And then up comes the Central Library Committee with a hall, and up comes Tommy with this play about Etáin and Midhir and . . .

TOMMY. And *what* a play! It's wrong from beginning to end.

REX. Badly dated, of course. But everything is, if you give it time.

BOB. Celtic Twilight Drama for Cab Horses. It's a period piece.

SOPHIA. Then what are you doing in it, painting your legs beige and going through all the agony of rehearsals if you're too modern to care about cab horses? All for the love of art?

BOB. No, all for the love of an artist.

SOPHIA. Who – me?

BOB. Of course. I'd do anything in the world for you.

SOPHIA. Except believe in my planchette. (*Offering box.*) Have a bit of fudge. Oh, I know you.

> (*Enter* SHEILA McCANN. *She is strangely and essentially a product of the Liffey banks. No other city breeds anything quite like her. She may have vague third cousins in Bloomsbury, in Montpàrnasse, or in Tunbridge Wells, but I don't think so. She has those prominent teeth that in Ireland generally indicate an uncontrollable humour and an endless suspicion of other people's intentions, and she is a mass of zip fastenings, boots, scarves, brooches, woollen gloves and rolls of scripts. She is generally laughing and always in a rage.*)

SHEILA. Am I late?

SOPHIA. Sheila McCann, have we ever had a rehearsal you weren't late for?

SHEILA. Do you mean to say you've done my scene without me?

REX. Yes, dear. I read you lines for you – both of them. Beautifully.

SHEILA. Thanks, Mr Dillon. I see I needn't inquire after your health. Radiant and rude. Do you mind if I take my hat off Sophie? It's a new one. Got any aspirin, anyone? I'm feeling, appalling.

8

SOPHIA. I'm afraid I haven't . . . I've some marvellous fruit salts, though. Would anyone like some?

REX. You've been working too hard, Miss McCann. How's the gossip and fashion column getting along? Thanks Sophie, I will have some fudge. (*He takes some and sits down near* SHEILA.)

SHEILA. How do you know I write a fashion and gossip column?

SOPHIA. Oh, don't be silly, Sheila. Everyone in Dublin knows that Dame Rumour is you, and that all that nonsense about me being a famous actress coming back to retirement in my native land came from you. I don't know what makes you hide it up. I think it's sweet of you to give me all that publicity. Of course you needn't have said all that blather about my emeralds and diamonds.

SHEILA. Well, it only wanted that. No use trying to help a friend, they all betray you.

SOPHIA. Sheila, do have a bit of ——

SHEILA. No, I won't have a bit of fudge. Poison to me.

TOMMY. Dame Rumour! Then was it you that wrote about me last week, saying I was going out on the Whitechurch bus to talk to my mountainy friends the Wee Folk who were helping me write my new play?

SHEILA. Yes, it was; and what are you going to do about it?

TOMMY. Well, I do think that was a bit thick. Making me a laughing stock like that.

SHEILA. Well, it's all out now. Betrayed right, left and centre.

REX. Writing a play for cab horses with the aid of the Wee Folk – crikey!

TOMMY. Absolute laughing stock!

SHEILA (*at* REX, *rather than to him*). What I want to know is how Mr Dillon found out about my job? God! How I dislike Dublin gossip. Can't blow your nose without everybody peering and prying. And will you for God's sake stop chewing that fudge stuff in my ear. It's like wet castanets.

BOB (*rising*). Well, do you know now, I don't want to break up a happy party, but ——

SOPHIA. Oh, it's so warm. . . . Open the windows a little, Bob. There's an angel.

(BOB *goes to window and opens it.*)

TOMMY. Wee Folk! Good heavens!

SHEILA. If you get a job in this town and make a success of it everybody feels insulted, that's what it means.

SOPHIA (*lazily*). Don't be such a fool, Sheila darling.

SHEILA. And don't you call me darling when you don't mean it. Even

9

if I have consented to help in this sugar plum of a play as a voice in the forest, I'm not an actress, and I don't want to be one, and I won't be called Darling by every Tom, Dick and Harry that tries to get round me and get publicity out of me, and then spits at me behind my back.

SOPHIA. I think it's very interesting of you to call me Tom, Dick and Harry.

SHEILA. Make it Sophia Lesbia Plurabella if you like. I'm going home.

BOB (*holding back curtains*). What a night. Look at those stars!

SHEILA (*as she goes to fire and pulls her hair about her head in the looking-glass*). Stars indeed!

SOPHIA (*purring loudly*). I love stars.

TOMMY. No, really, Sophie – imagine it: I've got a wonderful story, I work on it, I sweat blood, I finish it except for the very end of the last act – everything seems perfect, and then this nonsense about Wee Folk – oh, I don't know; I think the whole thing's a calamity.

SOPHIA. Oh, Sheila's paragraph went in a week ago. People have forgotten it already.

REX. It's going to be grand, Tommy. Second act's fine.

BOB (*coming away from the window*). What's wrong with it, Tommy?

TOMMY. Well, for one thing, there's the swans.

SOPHIA. Swans, darling.

TOMMY. Yes – swans.

SHEILA (*still at the mirror, her mouth full of hairpins*). Where do the swans come in? Sounds like Lohengrin to me.

REX. Pom-pom-pom-pom . . .

SHEILA. Tannhäuser.

REX. Sorry.

SOPHIA. No, it isn't, it's Meistersingers.

TOMMY. Well, you see, in the legend that my play is based on Etáin is an immortal, the wife of the god Midhir. She is banished from the Land of the Young and re-born on earth as a mortal woman. She marries the King of Ireland and completely forgets Midhir and that she was ever a goddess.

BOB. Yes, but you've got all that in the play.

TOMMY. Wait now; Midhir, her immortal lover, appears to her in Tara and begs her to go back with him to the Land of the Young. Now, how does she begin to remember her ancient life? How does she behave when she first recognises him, and how does she react when the knowledge comes to her that she is . . . well. *What* she is – an unearthly being, exiled on the earth, a wanderer, an alien.

SOPHIA. Well, I think I ought to do that part of her well enough.

10

BOB. Why? Do *you* feel an alien?

SOPHIA. Of course I do. Everyone who's ever acted feels an alien: especially with people outside the theatre of course, but you don't bother about that. But you're alien with your own people too: you're always suspecting they're bogus, or suspecting that they suspect you of being bogus, and one awful day you suspect yourself of being bogus and the fat's in the fire. It's like an elaborate spy game where you trust nobody and yourself least of all.

TOMMY. Well, that's more or less how I've come to feel. Worse, in a way, because lately I've grown alien even to the subject I've been working on – my characters aren't real, you see: they won't come to life.

BOB. There's nothing remotely real about legendary figures.

TOMMY. They're real enough to me. But when I write. . . .

SHEILA. Thought we were talking about swans.

TOMMY. I'm just coming to them. Now, her life with Midhir in the Land of the Young is before the play opens. My play begins with Etáin's re-birth as as mortal when she is married to the King of Ireland. She's living quite happily in Tara when one night a stranger comes to the Court.

SHEILA. Oh yes, with a harp on his back, like the Minstrel Boy.

SOPHIA. Go on, Tommy.

TOMMY. Well, a stranger comes mysteriously to the court and he sings to Etáin. Now this stranger is Midhir, her former lover, and when he sings to her she gradually begins to remember her old life, and she consents to go back with him to the Land of the Young. Well, the King tries to stop them going and strikes at them with his sword, but Midhir takes Etáin in his arms and they mount up through the air. The walls and the roof fly asunder and they float up into the night. That's the old story.

REX. Well, you haven't got that in the play, thank God – what a production!

TOMMY. They float up into the night . . . And all that can be seen after that are two white swans coupled with a golden chain, flying over Tara. Now, how on earth ——? (*Rises and goes to window.*)

SOPHIA. Oh, Tommy, it's superb. Is it too late to work it in for the end?

SHEILA. Oh, now she wants to dress up as the dying swan and float all over Beresford Hall with Tommy Millington and a Woolworth's lavatory chain. Sophie, you're perfect . . .

SOPHIA (*after a pause*). Sheila McCann, there are moments . . .

11

SHEILA. Oh, indeed, there *are* moments – Up the swans!

SOPHIA. Oh, you silly blithering ass, shut up. Throw a cushion at her Bob, a hard one.

BOB. I'd love to. (*Picks up cushion.*)

SHEILA. If you raise a hand against me you're no gentleman. That's what's wrong with Dublin nowadays. Nobody's got any manners.

REX. And is that your latest discovery, Miss McCann?

SOPHIA. Oh, but they use to have. Marvellous manners.

BOB. When was that, Sophie?

SOPHIA. Oh, I don't know – in the old days, you know, when we were oppressed. Grand it was, being oppressed. Only by the English, though. The English oppress one so much better than any other nation could. Sort of firmly unconscious. Oh dear . . . if it were only the swans that were the snag. If only I felt I could do you justice, my dear – because it *is* grand and I *do* love the part – but I'm just wrong for it. And I'm too old, though of course it's a marvel what you can do with lighting . . .

SHEILA. I never heard of any lighting that could make you look half your size.

SOPHIA (*after a pause*). You're perfectly right. And I ought to have marvellous red hair.

TOMMY. No. Gold! Etáin is gold as gold.

SOPHIA. Oh, well, gold if you like. But sort of red-gold-like a sunset, you know, a Stephen's Green sunset.

REX. Are you going to wear a wig, Sophie?

SOPHIA. The trouble with wigs is that they're apt to look so wiggy. I might get some lovely wistful thing to trail to my shoulders. Of course I'm pre-Raphaelite, at heart. Even with Communist shoulders and slacks I'm still pre-Raphaelite. (*She adds in a pensive Burne-Jones voice.*) Rosetti ought to have painted me.

SHEILA. Oh well, Elizabeth Arden seems to have made a pretty good shot at it.

SOPHIA. You know, there's no doubt you are a bit of a bitch, dear. I've been standing up for you to your friends for years, but they're appallingly right.

REX. Yes, we used to think you just tactless. But there's more to it than that.

SOPHIA. Oh well, it boils down to the fact that I'll have to wear a wig and try to look about twenty-five, that's all. Ah, my dear, that reminds me: my new maid: has anyone seen her?

BOB (*after a pause*). Yes, she let me in tonight, didn't she? Pasty face and red hair?

12

SOPHIA. That's it. She's got the most heavenly red hair. It's exactly the colour I want. When I look at it I'd like to tear it out in handfuls. Perhaps I could snip a little piece off when she wasn't looking and have it copied at Drago's. She's dopey enough not to notice.

SHEILA. What happened to that cracked old creature that used to cook for you? The one you had with you all your life – that's what you told us anyway – not obliged to believe it of course.

SOPHIA. If you mean my divine Mary Dempsey, she's still with me and she *has* been with me all my life. It's very silly of you to doubt everything you're told, Sheila. People will think there's been a great sorrow in you life if you go about doubting everything all over the place.

REX. But there has been a great sorrow in her life; hasn't there, McCann?

SHEILA. What do you mean?

REX. When the Irishwoman's Diary turned down your paragraph beginning 'Among other interesting people to be seen in the park any bright morning is Miss Sheila McCann whose . . .'

SHEILA (*rising*). If you don't shut up I'll make you. If you want to know what I dislike about you I'll tell you. You're such a busy little bee and such as nauseating coward that you've never dared to do anything in all your life that might discover you. You're pure Dublin, aren't you? The entire gamut, from Rathmines to Rathgar. You're a grand mixture of superiority and cautiousness, aren't you? You've never tried to act, not because you could if you did but because we might all come to see you – not that that's likely, God knows, but still ——

SOPHIA. Sheila, you have talent. Don't say a word, anybody ——

SHEILA. And don't you either, till I'm finished. Oh yes, I know I'm cross-grained and over-talkative. I'm probably irritable because I'm a virgin ——

SOPHIA. Sheila, what a terrible confession to make! At your age, really! Bob – somebody, stop her, quick!

REX. Stop her from what? Being a virgin?

SOPHIA. Don't be common, Rex.

SHEILA. It'd take a better man than you to do that, Mr Dillon. I say I know I'm irritable and cranky, but I don't sneer at people who do things.

SOPHIA. Oh Sheila, you do . . . you sneer at me.

SHEILA. Only because you don't do things any more. You've left the stage and just become a clever Dubliner.

SOPHIA. Oh, but I *do* things. I do Planchette. I get messages from the other world.

REX. That's very enterprising of you, Sophie.

SOPHIA. You shouldn't laugh at the other world. You might get stuck like it. And I do get messages.

BOB. How do they come through?

SOPHIA (*rising and going to a writing desk*). Look . . .

(*She shows them a small planchette.*)

You sit with it all alone – or you can do it with someone else if you like, but they must be sympathetic – and you ask it a question. And after a while it begins to move.

REX. Good God!

SOPHIA. It begins to move and finally it makes sort of scribbles, and then it writes the answer to your questions.

BOB. And does it always tell you what you'd like to know, Sophie?

SOPHIA. Oh, I know what you think. You think it's one's unconsciousness doing it all, and pushing your hands about and telling you what you *want* to believe. But it isn't. At least it isn't always. . . . Now tonight, just before you all came, it would do nothing but write 'Etáin' and then a lot of twisty things, where is it now – wait a moment, I'll find it for you. There are more things in heaven and earth than are dreamed of in Drumcondra, my dears. (*And she vanishes.*)

REX. I say, do you think our Darling Sophie is quite all right?

BOB. She's the most balanced woman *I've* ever known.

SHEILA. Yes, she'd be in her element on a high wire.

TOMMY. There may be something it it. I've known people do astounding things with tea-cups.

SOPHIA (*sweeping in and brandishing a sheet of paper*). Here you are, look! Look at all those squiggles.

TOMMY (*after a short pause*). But they're beautifully drawn!

REX. Clever girl, aren't you, Sophie?

SOPHIA. It wasn't I who did them, you idiot – it was the spirits.

TOMMY. But they're just like that carving stuff on the stones in New Grange.

SOPHIA. New Grange? Not the lunatic asylum place?

BOB. No, that's Grangegorman. New Grange is an ancient monument.

SOPHIA. Oh, I know. Pre-Celtic. Everything in Ireland is either Georgian or Pre-Celtic. Though all the Pre-Celtic things look very Celtic to me. Are these really like New Grange?

TOMMY. Yes, they are.

SOPHIA. There now – isn't that astonishing? And look at that word there – do you see? That's Etáin plain enough. (*Hands paper to*

BOB.)

BOB. Etáin. (*Pause.*) Here are some more words.

TOMMY. Good God, that's Irish. Wait a moment, give me that paper, will you?

> (*Snatches paper from* BOB).

Wait now – the letters are so twisted up I can't be sure, but it looks like '*Etáin 'na beatha or an talamh.*'

SOPHIA (*pause*). Well, what does that mean?

TOMMY. It means – '*Etáin on the earth.*'

BOB. That doesn't seem very lucid.

REX. Oh, fie, fie, fie, Bob, and you a Clongowes boy. I call that a very imperfect translation, Tommy.

TOMMY. Well, how would you translate it?

REX. 'Etáin is *living* on the earth' – isn't that it?

TOMMY. Sophie, may I keep this?

SOPHIA. Of course, my dear, if you want it. Why, if I get anything more like this it might help you to work out those swans.

REX. Oh, what a bit of luck for you, Miss McCann! Ancient Ireland comes to Rathmines . . .

SHEILA. Oh well, I've no objection to ancient Ireland. It's the new Ireland that's given me the willies. If the rehearsal's over and you're not going back over my bit, I'm going. Any of you sitting on my hat? Wouldn't put it past you. (*Searches here and there.*)

REX. By going back over your bit, do I understand you to mean when you say ''Tis daylight!' in the forest scene, or 'Hail, queen of Ireland!' in the last act. Because that's all you have to say.

SHEILA. Ah shut up, you disgusting little tadpole.

REX. Nasty, nasty. (*He sits at the piano*).

> (*They all begin to litanize together in tones rapidly accellerando.*)

SHEILA. Rex, you're worse than she is. (*Sheila rather roughly pulls her to her feet and peers at the first vacant chair.*)

SOPHIA. No, Pet, I'm not sitting on your hat. Nobody's sitting on your hat. Sheila darling, don't go yet. Let's all have a drink or something – SHEILA *is ominously muttering.* REX *plays the piano noisily*).

Ssh! Sheila darling, wozzums, not crossums stillums, izzums?

SHEILA. Is that intended to be funny or fascinating? Oh, very well, I'll have a drink. I give up the bloody hat.

REX. That's real big of you, McCann.

SOPHIA. Bob, ring the bell. No, don't ring the bell; it's broken. I'll have to shout. Everything's broken in (*she goes to the door*) this

15

house. Negligent of me, isn't it?) (*Opens the door and calls.*)
Eileen! Eileen, alannah! (*Comes back to sofa.*) Oh, when I think
of my lovely voice. In London the papers used to call it gold, and
in New York they said it was black velvet. In Dublin they said it
sounded rather tired. (*She sits down.*)

(MARY DEMPSEY, *an elderly, deep-bossomed carthorse of a
country woman with a rich baritone voice like the thunders of
Sinai, enters with mien most majestic. She stands with her
comfortable hands folded beneath her apron close to* SOPHIA.)

MARY. Did you ring, Miss Sophie?

SOPHIA. Don't be silly, darling, you know the bell's been broken for
weeks and if you had any sort of affection for me you'd have had
it mended ages ago. I shouted.

MARY (*with great toleration*). Ah well, you know best yourself, I
suppose you want a drink, Miss, do you?

SOPHIA. Yes, lots of drinks . . . Why didn't Eileen come?

MARY. I beg your pardon, Miss?

SOPHIA (*shouts*). I said, why didn't Eileen come?

MARY. Is it the new one? She wasn't able for it. Oh, I'm having
terrible trouble with that one, Miss.

SOPHIE. What are you blathering about?

MARY. What's that you say, Miss?

SOPHIA. I say, what are you blathering about?

MARY. She got a weakness, Miss.

REX. A weakness?

MARY. That's what she have, sir. Though I know no more than the
man in the moon what ails her rightly. She turned up the white
side of her eyes there a couple of minutes since and she's sitting
there without a stir out of her by the fire. 'Twas just before you
commenced roaring for her, Miss.

SOPHIA. Poor Eileen! Didn't you do anything for her?

MARY. I was just going to wet a sup of tea for her, Miss, when you
commenced roaring.

SOPHIA. I wish you wouldn't be so insistent about my roaring. She
must be ill, poor lamb. Like me.

MARY. What's that. Miss?

SHEILA (*shouts*). I said she was probably overworked.

MARY. Faith, she is not then. Is it Eileen? I declare to my God you'd
grow whiskers waiting for that one to put a stir out of herself. Oh,
I'll be charmed when the young chap arrives, Miss. Did anyone
answer you from the papers at all?

SOPHIA. Not yet. I only put it in last night.

16

REX. What's this, Sophie? Are you adding to the staff?

SOPHIA. I'm trying my luck with a houseboy. There's too much work for Mary and Eileen alone.

MARY. Well now, there wouldn't be, Miss, only for the young one there, sitting around scratching her elbows like the Queen of England and breaking the delph for a living. Oh, my, my, my, I said to myself when she walked in here that very first morning, there's the day-dreamy sort for you.

SOPHIA. Mary, we'd love something to drink.

MARY. Though God knows, I'd rather poor Eileen than that Maggie Cooney one out of Galway. I wouldn't like to tell a Christian person the way that one used to be capering around like a circus bee, and all them lads out of Portobello barracks looking for her to go to the pictures, how are you, plucking her eyebrows and plastering her lips and cracking the nuts in the door on Hallowe'en. Sure God help poor Eileen, she's quiet and decent anyway. But she's terrible idle. Sure 'tis a gift of God to be as idle as that, like the green hand. And them fainting fits. Fierce. Ah, maybe 'tis that little plancheen you do be tricking with, Miss. Ah, indeed now many's the time I noticed 'twas just when you'd be having a bit of sport with plancheen, Eileen would roll up the eyes in the kitchen and evil a sign of life out of her till I'd wet the tea.

SOPHIA. I do let you ramble on, don't I. Now you go and get those drinks and if Eileen's still feeling bad, hit her on the back and give her a drop of gin or an egg flip or something.

MARY (*going*). All the same now, there's something queer about that plancheen board with them little wheely things on it.

SOPHIA. Mary, open the curtains, will you? It's such a lovely night.

MARY. What's that, Miss?

SOPHIA. Open the curtains. It's a fine night.

(MARY *wades across the room and opens the curtains.*)

MARY: And every time you do play with plancheen she turns up the white side of her eyes and there she is without a move out of her and God knows what happens to the creature. Ah, for all I know she might be dead and buried . . . (*And she has gone.*)

BOB. Gin! What a remedy for hysterics!

SOPHIA. Deeply depressing, all this servant business. Here I am with all my worries, the cab horses and planchette and all this New Grange stuff and this show coming along, and then I'm told I overwork the servants. Oh, it isn't human.

TOMMY. What's that you were saying about a houseboy, Sophie?

SOPHIA. Oh yes, I'm going to have a houseboy if the Evening Mail can find me one. I think it's a grand idea. He'll have to be able to cook and do the fires and drive the car too. It'll be bliss to have someone to drive one about. One feels so regal. Do you think he'd look well in a dark blue uniform? Or perhaps green? Yes, bottle green with silver buttons.

SHEILA. Isn't it like you to worry yourself silly about his colour scheme before you've even engaged him.

SOPHIA. Well, I've put an advertisement in the Mail. I don't see what more I can do.

REX. And has no one applied for the job?

SOPHIA. Not yet. I suppose all the healthy young men of Ireland have left the country. Ireland is a land of adolescence and senility.

SHEILA. And which set do you belong to?

SOPHIA. Oh, the seniles, of course. Old age is an irresistible thought. The older you grow, the less you care about anything but essentials.

BOB. What do you consider essentials?

SOPHIA. Conversation and drink.

SHEILA. Wearing your larynx and your liver out. Still, that's better than neglecting them.

TOMMY. Now what does that remind me of – some line of poetry somewhere . . .

SHEILA. If your liver reminds you of poetry –

TOMMY. No, no, what Sophie was saying was about being old enough not to care any longer about anything but essentials. I've got it –
'For life moves out of a red flare of dreams
Into the common light of common days
Until old age brings the red flare again.'
(*The door opens slowly and* EILEEN *comes in. She is a young, slightly-built countrywoman with a mass of red hair and a pale but quite unremarkable face. She is carrying a tray laden with drinks.*)

EILEEN. Where will I put the tray, Miss?

SOPHIA. Eileen! I thought you were feeling ill?

EILEEN. I was, Miss, but I'm better now, thank God. Where will I put the beer, Miss?

SOPHIA. The beer? Oh yes – oh, put it down there. No, mind the flowers. That's right: there. Now, what'll you have. Sheila? There's gin and French and there's It and there's sherry and there's Irish.

REX. Don't have gin, McCann. It'll only make you cry.

SHEILA. Well, you haven't got to drive me home anyway – gin please,

Sophie.

SOPHIA. It or French, darling?

SHEILA. Haven't you any lime?

SOPHIA. No, darling. Never have it in the house. Subdues the passions. Hate it like poison.

SHEILA. No lime again. All right, then, It.

SOPHIA. There, chuck the It at her, Rex. What are you drinking, Bob?

BOB. I'll have a whisky thanks, Sophie.

SOPHIA. What are you waiting for, Eileen?

BOB. Thanks so much, that's perfect.

EILEEN. I thought maybe you'd like me to hand it round, Miss.

SOPHIA (*in a hoarse whisper*). She did that at her last place, you see. Grand, Eileen. Yes, you shall hand it round. Mr Twomey there, be careful. There we are. Now let me see, what next? Rex? (*Waves glass.*)

REX. Gin please, Sophie. I want to be just like la belle McCann.

SHEILA. Don't you wish you could? And do you mind not spilling things all over me, please? I'm up to my eyes in debt to the cleaners as it is.

SOPHIA. Tommy?

TOMMY. I'll just have some soda, please.

SOPHIA. How I love squirting soda . . . Oh look, that poor old bottle of sherry. No one ever wants sherry in this house. I must give a sherry party for my enemies one day and get rid of it once for all. There, take that to Mr Millington.

(EILEEN, *creeping gingerly about, hands a glass to* TOMMY.)

Now what'll I have? Gin, I suppose.

EILEEN (*handing drink to* TOMMY). Now sir.

TOMMY. Thank you.

EILEEN. Is that all now, Miss?

SOPHIA. Yes, dotey, that's all . . . Are you really better?

EILEEN. I am thanks, Miss. I think 'tis the stars.

SOPHIA. The what?

EILEEN. The stars, Miss. When the stars do be walking I do feel strange in myself. (*She smiles very sweetly at them all and goes out quietly.*)

BOB (*after a pause*). Well!

SOPHIA. Now, what did she mean by that?

REX (*with a flagrant imitation of* EILEEN'S *accent*). When the stars do be walking I do feel terrible queer in myself. Oh, Janey Mac, let me ou' a this!

BOB. You do collect peculiar servants, Sophie.

SHEILA. Who else would stay? Calls them darling and dotey and works them to death.

REX (*hand in pocket*). Oh, look what I've found. Aspirin (*He takes out a bottle.*) Two tablets left. Would you like to gobble them up, McCann?

SHEILA. No, I wouldn't.

REX. There's a stubborn girl. Cheer up, take them and soak them in your gin. Go on, you know you're dying to.

SHEILA. Oh, all right, all right! Pest. You're like a fox terrier without the charm. Come on.

(*She takes them.*)

I'm ill and nobody realises it, that's what it boils down to.

REX. When the stars do be walking I do feel queer in myself.

BOB. You know that was quite funny the first time you said it, Rex.

REX. Now, here's an extraordinary thing. Jameson always makes you hostile. Why is that? Now gin brings out the best in me. In fact all drink brings out the best in me. An hour or so in the Buttery and St Joseph himself couldn't hold a candle to me. (*He starts to pour out gin for himself.*)

SOPHIA. Have another gin, then. (*She sees the glass and bottle in his hand.*) Oh, splendid!

REX. Oh what a lot I've given myself. Never mind. It'll make my eyes sparkle.

SHEILA. Sophie, I've got to go home. May I ring for a taxi?

SOPHIA. Of course, darling. Oh, my dear, these taxi drivers are the ruin of romance. I thought someone here might give you a lift. And won't you have another drink? (*She sees that* SHEILA *has already done so.*) Oh!

SHEILA. Mr Dillon, you're sitting bang on my hat. Would you mind? Thanks. Flat as a pancake. Don't bother, it doesn't matter.

BOB. Sheila. I'm going now. I'll give you a lift. (*He rises.*)

SOPHIA. Must you go, Bob?

BOB. I'm afraid I must. Thanks so much, Sophie. I'll get my coat.

(*He goes to the door and exits into the hall.*)

TOMMY. Sophie, may I stay and talk for a bit?

SOPHIA. Of course, Tommy ——

REX (*helping himself to gin*). I didn't sit on her hat. It was always like that. She's one of those women whose hats are born crushed.

SHEILA. Flat as as pancake. Well, I don't care. No, it doesn't matter, Sophie. Dreary, depressing little – look at him, pouring out drinks for himself. It's like being in the room with Niagara. Yes, I will have a lift thanks, Mr Twomey. Nine o'clock tomorrow night again?

SOPHIA. Yes, nine o'clock, first, act, isn't it, Rex?

REX. What?

SOPHIA. Next rehearsal?

REX. Oh yes, yes, of course.

SHEILA. Goodnight, Sophie. (*She goes out into hall.*) Delightful evening.

REX. Oh, I am sorry. You all off? Yes, nine o'clock first act.

BOB. Sophie, *do* you know any Irish?

SOPHIA. Not a word, darling. Why?

BOB. I'm still thinking about that planchette . . . I can't . . .

SHEILA (*re-entering*). Bob Twomey, I have to get to Sandycove. Can't wait all night.

BOB. Sandycove? Good God!

SHEILA. Well, what's the matter with Sandycove? Oh! Not your direction, I suppose.

REX. Poor old Bob; lives in Sutton.

BOB. Oh no – it doesn't matter – no trouble at all. Goodnight, Sophie.

SOPHIA. Goodnight, precious.

(BOB holds the door open for SHEILA.)

SHEILA. My God, you'd think it was a crime to live in Sandycove. No pleasing anyone. God knows I never asked for a lift, did I? I don't care what I do, only I won't be harassed and bullied all the time. Delightful evening, Sophie, thanks again. (*She goes to door.*) That's what's wrong with Dublin these days. Nobody has any manners, that's what it boils down to.

(*She has gone.*)

REX. Be very tender with that one, Bob. Tender but firm.

BOB. Oh, I'll be firm all right. I don't much care for the look in her eye. Is that aspirin or gin, do you think?

SOPHIA. Just ingrowing McCann. Goodnight, Bob.

BOB. Say a prayer for me.

(*Gloomily he goes.*)

SOPHIA. There! He's going to drive her home after all. You never know. It might easily turn into a romance.

REX. Sophie, I must go.

SOPHIA. Of course, you must go, go on. Oh, I mean no; do stay. There's lots of gin left and I can easily go to bed.

REX. Sophie, you're extraordinarily pressing. I think you must have designs on me. But I must go. Goodnight.

REX. Like a lift, Tommy?

TOMMY. No – no – I'm staying for a bit.

21

REX. Oh! Goodnight.

SOPHIE. I'll let you out.

>(*She goes out.*)

REX (*deeply offended*). Romeo! I didn't think it of you.

>(*He goes.*)

TOMMY. Oh dear. (*He rises. His agitation grows.*) Oh dear, dear, dear. *What* a beastly mind. Tut, tut, tut.

>(*The sound of a door banging is heard, then* SOPHIE *comes back.* TOMMY *sits down and starts to play the harp.*)

SOPHIA. Well, that's that.

TOMMY. What?

SOPHIA. I said, that's that.

TOMMY. Oh yes. (*He plays on agitatedly.*)

SOPHIA. What's the matter with you?

TOMMY. Nothing. (*He stops playing and rises.*) Only I think it was probably – well, it would have been better for me to go.

SOPHIA. Why?

TOMMY. It's nearly midnight.

SOPHIA. I know. That's what's thrilling. We're going to do a bit of planchette. It always works better at midnight.

TOMMY. Um, planchette.

SOPHIA. Well, what's wrong with it?

TOMMY. Oh, nothing, of course, only ——

SOPHIA. What are you talking about?

TOMMY. I'm frightened of planchette. Oh, you can laugh if you want to. It's only a toy, but toys can open doors to things. (*He rises.*) Sophie, you *don't* know any Irish, do you?

SOPHIA. Certainly I do. *Lá breá* to you.

TOMMY. No, seriously.

SOPHIA. No, I don't, darling; why?

TOMMY. Well, there's a door opened by a toy. Oh, I know it's all rubbish, but that writing in Irish is difficult to explain.

SOPHIA. Then why try? It's wonderful to open doors. Now look here, are you going to play or are you not? Because if you're not, I shall play all alone and I'll probably go into a trance and frighten you to death. Now! (*She goes to the desk.*) Here we are, paper, that little table will do; there, that's right – put it just here, the pencil's sharp . . . Good! Now turn out the lights.

TOMMY. What do you want the lights out for?

SOPHIA. It's easier for the spirits.

TOMMY. But are we to sit in the dark?

SOPHIA. Plenty of light from the fire. Go on, Tommy. Put them out.

22

(TOMMY *puts out the lights.*)

SOPHIA. There! Now, sit down there on that. Here we go, No, just the tips of your fingers. Lightly, don't push. Now, Make your mind a complete blank.

TOMMY. That's a very difficult thing to do.

SOPHIA. Oh, not for me, my dear. My mind's always a complete blank.

TOMMY. You do underrate . . .

SOPHIA. Shut up, Tommy. No mental energy at all. Relax.

TOMMY. It's so difficult to relax.

SOPHIA. Sh!

(*A pause.*)

Tommy, you're pushing.

TOMMY. I'm not. You are.

SOPHIA. Don't contradict. The spirits don't like discord. Peace!

TOMMY. Oh, this is difficult!

(*A pause.*)

SOPHIA. (*In a whisper.*) It's moving.

TOMMY. Yes.

SOPHIA. Don't push.

TOMMY. I'm not.

SOPHIA. Well don't.

TOMMY. But I'm not, I tell you.

SOPHIA. Shut up. Peace. Harmony.

(*A pause.*)

TOMMY. My fingers are burning.

(*A pause.*)

Good, that's the fluid.

TOMMY. The what?

(*A pause.*)

SOPHIA. The spirit fluid. They're working through your fingers. Isn't it thrilling?

TOMMY. I don't think I like . . .

SOPHIA. Hold your tongue. Peace! Peace!

(*A pause.*)

TOMMY. It's stopped.

(*A pause.*)

SOPHIA. (*Whispering*) Wait!

TOMMY. My God!

SOPHIA. What is it?

TOMMY. It's so cold.

SOPHIA. Is it?

TOMMY. There!

23

(*This word is spoken in a gasp as the board suddenly moves over the paper with astonishing rapidity. A pause.*)

SOPHIA. I say! Did you push that time?

TOMMY. No.

SOPHIA. Honest, Tommy?

TOMMY. No, I didn't. I swear it. I – excuse me. (*He takes his fingers off the board and stands up mopping his face with his handkerchief.*)

SOPHIA. Tommy – what's the matter?

TOMMY. Nothing.

SOPHIA. But you're dripping. (*She takes hold of his hand.*) You're freezing.

TOMMY. No, it – first time, you see. It's a . . .

SOPHIA (*turns to the planchette*). Let's see what it says. (*She reads.*) Oh, just scribbles again – oh no, wait, here's a word. There, you see, it's the play again, 'Midhir'. That's plain enough. What's this – 'calls to you.' . . . 'Stars . . . walk.' (*She and* TOMMY *look at each other.*)

(*Twelve o'clock strikes. The door opens softly and* EILEEN *comes into the room.*)

EILEEN. Did you call me, ma'am?

SOPHIA. Why no, Eileen.

EILEEN. Or did the gentleman call me?

TOMMY. No.

EILEEN. I'm sorry, Miss. But somebody was calling me. I thought 'twas yourself or the gentleman. 'Twas a young man's voice, I think Miss.

SOPHIA. A young man's voice? (SOPHIA *looks at* TOMMY.)

EILEEN. Yes, Miss. (*She smiles.*) Maybe 'twas outside the house.

(*A loud knock is heard at the street door.*)

SOPHIA (*after a pause*). Answer the door, Eileen.

EILEEN. What, Miss?

SOPHIA. Answer the door. See who it is.

(*Three more knocks are heard.*)

EILEEN. If you please, Miss, I'd rather . . .

SOPHIA. Go along, Eileen. Open the door.

(*Several knocks are heard, and Eileen turns slowly and goes out of the room.*)

SOPHIA. Now, who on earth can that be at this time of night?

(*The knocking continues.*)

TOMMY. Yes, I ——

SOPHIA. Oh, shut up!

TOMMY. I beg your pardon?

SOPHIA. Not *you*, my dear. I'm sorry.

TOMMY. It's that wretched game of yours. It's upset your nerves.

SOPHIA. Nonsense. I'm not a nervous person.

> (*The knocking is repeated.*)

Oh, my God!

> (*More knocking.*)

It's just like the murder scene in Macbeth, dear.

TOMMY. Now there's no good getting into a panic.

SOPHIA. Panic yourself. Who's in a panic?

TOMMY. Like to smoke?

SOPHIA. No thanks. Oh, Tommy, why must people choose an hour like this to drop in? I loathe unconventional people so, don't you?

> (TOMMY, *laughs.*)

What are you laughing at? Me?

TOMMY. Eileen must have opened the door.

> (*Enter* MARY DEMPSEY.)

MARY. There's a young chap at the door, Miss, want's to see you.

SOPHIA. What does he want? Did he say?

MARY. He did not, Miss.

TOMMY. Good heavens, what a time for a chat.

MARY. I was wondering would it be the fellow from the Mail, Miss?

SOPHIA. Who?

MARY. The man from the Evening Mail.

SOPHIA. Good God Almighty – a reporter, my dear. Probably about my cab horses. Tell him to go to hell. (*She pokes the fire.*)

MARY. Oh, sure, I couldn't do that, Miss. He's not a gentleman, he'd never understand that sort of thing.

SOPHIA (*the poker poised in her hand like a sceptre*). What's he like?

MARY. Ah! he's a sort of a country chap, but he looks all right. My God, coming at an hour like this. 'Oh my, my, my,' I said to him. 'The lady'll never see you at all.' 'She will then,' says he, and walks into the hall, and he sweeping the old cap off of his head. 'Tell her,' says he, 'she'll not be sorry to see me.'

TOMMY. Evening Mail – what were you telling me tonight about the Evening Mail?

SOPHIA (*waving the poker*). The houseboy and chauffeur and all that – you know, bottle-green and silver buttons. You show him in, Mary. (*She puts the poker back in the fender.*)

MARY. Oh sure, whatever you say yourself, Miss. (*She moves towards the door.*)

SOPHIA. By the way, what happened to Eileen? I told her to answer the door.

MARY. I don't know what happened to her, Miss. She came runnin' through the hall past the kitchen and away with her up them stairs like a goat, 'twould dazzle you.

SOPHIA. I see . . . Oh well, you'd better tell your young man to come in. (*To* TOMMY.) I might as well see him, mightn't I?

TOMMY. Well, I don't know . . . I suppose so; yes. But I've never heard of such an hour to call about a job.

MARY. No sir. Such an hour. And clattering on the door there, pestering and pursuing decent people should be inside their beds.

SOPHIA. Where you should have been, my dear, ages ago ——

MARY (*at the door*). I beg your pardon, Miss?

SOPHIA. I said: Show the young man in.

MARY. Oh sure, whatever you say yourself, Miss Fly-by-night.
  (*She goes out.*)

TOMMY. Well, really Sophie, at this time of night ——

SOPHIA (*dreamily*). I adore new faces. The butcher boy, the woman who comes for the laundry – they all fill me with burning curiosity until I've seen them once. But isn't it grand to be so interested in people. I feel as though each new face may bring a revelation – it never does of course, but it always might. And it might come to you through a duchess or a dustman. What does it matter? One's always looking for something.

TOMMY. Ha! The black girl in search of her God, I suppose. (*He goes and sits at the piano.*)

SOPHIA (*quite seriously*). Oh no, not God exactly. But one of His works, perhaps, one of His vagaries.
  (TOMMY *plays a few chords softly on the piano.*)
  Tommy, why am I thinking about being a child tonight?

TOMMY. Why are you? You've said nothing about it.

SOPHIA (*pause*). I know, it's the smell of hawthorn.
  (TOMMY *stops playing suddenly.*)

TOMMY (*sniffs*). Hawthorn. Yes . . . Is it coming from the garden?

SOPHIA. Must be from someone else's garden – we haven't any hawthorn trees.

MARY (*entering*). Here's the young man, Miss.
  (MARTIN, *a young countryman in a clean, very shabby suit, enters in the shadow by the door. He seems curiously at ease and is swift in his movements, and the collarless shirt and the heavy western accent in which he speaks do not obscure a certain old-fashioned dignity. He looks out at the garden for a moment and the outline of his face is sharp and, in the moonlight, of an astonishing pallor. Then* MARY *switches on the lights and goes.*

26

MARTIN *turns and crosses to* SOPHIA, *standing before her, his cap in his hand.*)

MARTIN. Good evening, Madam.

SOPHIA. Good evening.

MARTIN (*turns to* TOMMY). Good evening, sir.

TOMMY. Oh-er-good evening.

MARTIN (*to* SOPHIA). This is terrible late for you, I'm afraid, Madam.

SOPHIA. Er – er – why yes, I suppose it is.

MARTIN. 'Twas very good of you to see me. (*To* TOMMY.) Wasn't it?

TOMMY. I think so.

MARTIN. I think so too. There's many ladies would have been nervous, seeing a stranger so late, wouldn't they?

SOPHIA. You know, I think you'd better explain to me what you want to see me about.

MARTIN. I'd like to explain it, Madam. I said nothing about it so far, I'd be in dread of pushing myself forward.

SOPHIA. Well, what is it?

MARTIN. 'Tis about myself coming here, Madam.

SOPHIA. You mean – you've come here to explain about yourself coming here?

MARTIN. That's the very thing I mean, but 'twas not the way you have it expressed, Madam.

SOPHIA. Oh?

MARTIN. No, I mean 'tis about myself coming here to stay. (*He smiles faintly, happily, as if he had come home.*)

SOPHIA. To stay?

MARTIN. You see, 'tis the way I'm idle presently, Madam, and I'd a notion you might be wanting someone.

SOPHIA. Well, I was looking for someone.

MARTIN. Oh, thanks be to God!

TOMMY. Rather a queer hour to call, though, isn't it?

MARTIN. Terrible queer, sir, right enough.

SOPHIA. So you are from the Mail?

MARTIN. The which, Madam?

SOPHIA. The Mail – The Evening Mail, you know.

MARTIN. I don't know, I'm sure, Madam.

TOMMY. But, my goodness gracious, you must know something – you want this job, it seems ——

MARTIN. I do sir.

SOPHIA. Oh, don't get fussed, Tommy. I want a houseboy, he wants a job. Don't you?

MARTIN. I do, Madam.

27

SOPHIA. What can you do?

MARTIN. I can do anything.

> (*He enumerates on his fingers.*)
>
> I can drive a car. And I can clean a car and keep it lovely. And I can do gardening. And I can cook.

SOPHIA. Go on.

MARTIN. Cook massive. And I wait at table – with white gloves on me, if you like that better – and can run messages, and I don't drink at all, Madam, only an odd time.

SOPHIA. I see. Can you dance a hornpipe?

MARTIN. I can. But will you require that?

TOMMY. Sophie!

SOPHIA. Probably, probably.

MARTIN. I can dance all right. And I can sing too.

SOPHIA. Well, I think you'd better come along to me and we'll see how we get on.

TOMMY (*rising*). But I say ——

SOPHIA. Don't interrupt me, I'm on the war-path. I'll try you for a week. Now, about wages ——

TOMMY. But what I mean is how did you hear about this?

MARTIN. I beg your pardon, sir?

TOMMY. How did you hear about this job? Did you see an advertisement in the Evening Mail?

MARTIN. I did not, sir. I never reads the papers.

SOPHIA. Then how on earth . . .

MARTIN. I think there's something puzzling you, isn't there, Madam?

SOPHIA. No, of course not. Only it's . . .

MARTIN. 'Tis the way I'm idle now a long time, you see, and I was passing by and I'd a notion I'd be wanted when I seen your house . . .

TOMMY. But you must have had some idea there was a job going here, or why on earth . . .?

MARTIN. I had, of course.

SOPHIA. There! That's what I mean. Oh, aren't they difficult? If you saw the advertisement in the papers ——

> (*She stops speaking.*)

MARTIN (*smiling, explanatory*). I never sees the papers, Madam. (*He looks upwards*).

> But I seen the house.

TOMMY. You must have seen a lot of other houses too.

MARTIN. I didn't mind them at all, sir.

SOPHIA. Because he knew this was the one house that'd give him a job. Don't cross-question him, Tommy, he's psychic. He must be. Oh. I wonder will he be all right, though? (*She gazes mournfully at* MARTIN.)

MARTIN. I'm sure I'll suit you Madam. All them things I told you I could do there's not a word of a lie in it. I can sweep and dust and garden and cook and drive and I'm terrible clean. Look at them hands, and the back of my neck is just as good, and me travelling the world for this job three days and nights.

TOMMY. For this job?

MARTIN. That's right, sir. 'Twas this house I set me heart on . . . Would you ever give me a try?

SOPHIA. It's raving mad, but I probably will. I almost certainly will . . .

TOMMY. Don't you think it might be better if he called again tomorrow?

SOPHIA. If you come back tomorrow, where would you sleep tonight?

MARTIN (*cheerfully*). Ah, I wouldn't mind, Madam. I'd sleep out under the sky. I've only fourpence in the world and I'd buy my breakfast with that and come back to you in the morning. I'll do that . . . I'll do that, if you like, Madam.

SOPHIA (*slowly, comfortably, as she looks at him*). I think you'd better stay.

 (TOMMY *protests mutely.*)

MARTIN. I'm very thankful to you, ma'm.

SOPHIA. I'll give you a week's trial. We can talk about wages to-morrow . . . I'll go and talk to Mrs Dempsey about a room for you. You'd better wait in the hall.

MARTIN. I will, Madam.

TOMMY. Sophie, do you mind if I have a talk to this man? I think I ought to have a word with him.

SOPHIA. Of course, if you think there's any more to be said. But I don't see *what*. By the way, what's your name?

MARTIN (*startled*). My name?

SOPHIA. Yes: what is it?

MARTIN. M – M – (*He stands, wide-eyed.*)

SOPHIA. What's the matter?

MARTIN. My name is M – M – Martin.

SOPHIA (*kindly*). I see.

 (*She goes out.*)

TOMMY (*after an awkward pause*). You can sit down, Martin.

MARTIN. Thank you sir.

 (*He sits down.*)

TOMMY. You know, I don't quite like all this.

MARTIN. 'Tis all right, sir.

TOMMY. I'd better be frank with you. If I had my way you wouldn't stay here tonight.

MARTIN (*steadily*). I know that, sir.

TOMMY. You wouldn't be engaged to work here at all.

MARTIN. I'm sorry you feel that way, sir. There is no harm in me at all.

TOMMY. I wonder.

MARTIN. I'm telling you the truth, sir.

TOMMY. What have you told us? Nothing except that you can do certain things in a house and with a car, and that you haven't any money.

MARTIN. I have fourpence, sir.

TOMMY. Very well; you've told us that you can do a few useful jobs, that you have fourpence in the world and that you want to stay here. What else have you told us?

MARTIN (*without a shade of insolence*). What else would you like to know, sir?

TOMMY (*with a little difficulty*). I don't want to be unjust to you just because you apply for this job in an odd way and, may I add, at an odd time. But I think you ought to understand how very odd it is, and how lucky you are – I wonder are just lucky? – that Mrs Sheridan – is well, a very exceptional lady.

MARTIN. I will be very lucky if she lets me stay here, sir. I knows that.

TOMMY. Very few women would engage you without a reference, or credentials or any sort of knowledge of what type of person you are.

MARTIN. The lady of this house likes me, sir. If she didn't like me she'd not let me stay.

TOMMY. Oh, it's hopeless to try to explain.

MARTIN. I think I'd understand better if you didn't explain anything at all, sir.

TOMMY. Listen . . . Oh good heavens, what can I say to you? First of all, what is all this about looking up at the house and thinking you'd get a job in it, and then coming in and finding the job you were looking for? You must have seen that advertisement in the Mail?

(*Pause.*)

Why, in God's name, don't you admit you saw it? There's no harm in having seen it.

MARTIN. I wish I'd said I had, sir. 'Twould have saved me a power of trouble ——

TOMMY. But didn't you?

30

MARTIN. I did not, sir.

TOMMY. Then what brought you here?

(*A pause.*)

It must have been something besides the mere look of the house.

MARTIN. That's true enough.

TOMMY. Then what was it?

MARTIN (*looking at him*). 'Twas my game with the stars, sir.

TOMMY. Game with the stars?

MARTIN. I'll tell you about it if you like, sir. When I was a little lad there'd be times I'd have a sort of dream. And it wasn't when I'd be in my sleep, but in my full waking. And I'd want to find something, or somebody . . . ah! I've a lot of it forgotten now, but I'd be walking in my dream down a road and my eyes raised sideways to the sky. And the stars'd follow me along and they like walking on the mountain tops beside me. And the brightest of them would stop suddin in their travels over an old tree or a bit of a rock, and I'd know then that what I was looking for was there. But I'd come out of the dream before I'd see the face.

TOMMY. The face?

MARTIN. The face I was trying to find. 'Twas a face . . . And 'twas always where the big stars stopped in their walking.

TOMMY. Well?

MARTIN. That was my star game, sir. And tonight I was walking this street, and I wondering what would I do when I felt the dream like it would be gathering up around me, and I thought, 'I'll find it there.' And sure enough the star stopped like in th' old dream, and I found I had stopped too, and there it was up in the high air and it sitting on the chimney pots. I opened the gate then, and I commenced walking up the path and I knew no more then till I heard myself beating hell out of the old knocker.

TOMMY. But there was no face?

MARTIN. Sure, the face turned into a job. Wasn't that a fine thing for me?

TOMMY. You seem to be a very lucky man.

MARTIN. I am, sir. I'm terrible lucky out and out. But I was certain sure I'd have the good fortune once I got the smell of the hawthorn.

TOMMY. You smelt the hawthorn too, did you?

MARTIN. I did , or course. Sure it near knocked me down and I coming in.

TOMMY. But what made you think *that* would get you a job?

MARTIN. Hawthorn is lucky for me, sir. When I'd get the sweet smell

31

rising up out of the trees I'd know I was in for spell of good luck
. . . Ah, but you think I'm a bad hat of course.

TOMMY. We seem to have wandered from the subject.

MARTIN (*sitting very straight and sane – a young man wanting a job, no
more*). Yes, sir.

TOMMY. Tell me, what was the difficulty about your name?

MARTIN. My name?

    (*He rises slowly, his eyes closing.*)

TOMMY (*watching him*). Yes. What did you say it was?

MARTIN (*with admirable fluency as he opens his eyes on to a normal
world*). Martin, sir. Martin Lydon.

TOMMY. I see.

MARTIN. Is there anything wrong, sir?

TOMMY. Oh – no . . . You haven't an impediment in your speech, have
you?

MARTIN. A which, sir?

TOMMY. An impediment – oh, what do you call it? Anything wrong
with your mouth?

MARTIN. There is not, sir. I never had a tooth drew out in all my life.

TOMMY. You never had a stutter or anything like that?

MARTIN. I had not, sir. I've a tongue like an eel.

TOMMY. Then why did you stutter when Mrs Sheridan asked you your
name?

MARTIN. I don't understand you, sir.

TOMMY. Yes, you do. When Mrs Sheridan asked you your name you –

MARTIN. I don't understand you, sir . . .

    (*Enter* SOPHIA *with* MARY DEMPSEY.)

SOPHIA. There now. Everything's fixed. Mrs Dempsey will give you
something to eat and show you where to sleep. Come in after
you've had your supper and I'll tell you what I want you to do
tomorrow.

MARTIN. Thank you, madam.

    (*He goes to the window and looks out at the garden.*)

MARY. This is the way, young fellow.

MARTIN (*turning at the window, the garden behind her*) That's a fine
airy night and the primroses pushing up out of the soil.

MARY. *This* is the way, young man.

MARTIN. You're very good, Mrs Dempsey. Thank you, madam.

    (*He goes.*)

MARY. Fly-by-night.

    (*She follows* MARTIN *out.*)

SOPHIA. He's got good eyesight.

TOMMY. Has he? What do you mean?

SOPHIA. The primroses are at the bottom of the garden. You can't see them from here at all after sunset.

TOMMY. Oh, he probably meant primroses in general.

SOPHIA (*staring out of the window*). Tommy ——

TOMMY. Yes?

SOPHIA. It doesn't matter. Give me a cigarette, will you?

TOMMY. Here. (*He offers her one.*)

SOPHIA. Thanks.

    (*He lights her cigarette.*)

  And now tell me why you disapprove of me.

TOMMY. I don't.

SOPHIA. Oh yes, you do.

TOMMY. I think you want a nurse to look after you.

SOPHIA. Do you mean about planchette?

TOMMY. No, I don't – though I think that's foolish too. Not foolish, perhaps – dangerous.

SOPHIA (*softly*). Yes, I believe it is a bit dangerous.

TOMMY. But this isn't about planchette. It's about this Lydon chap.

SOPHIA. Why, what's wrong with him?

TOMMY. I don't know. I'm not sure there's anything – wrong with him. But – I mean – do you think it's an ordinary sort of thing to do to have three words with any country gawk that chooses to walk into your house, and engage him with no references, no credentials, nothing whatever to recommend him ——

SOPHIA. Well of course it isn't ordinary ——

TOMMY. He doesn't seem to be very ordinary, either.

SOPHIA. I know. But nobody is really. That's one of the greatest secrets of life, Tommy. When you're as old as I am you'll discover that, and you'll stop writing plays about people like Midhir and Etán, because you'll discover that everyday people and everyday things can be just as mysterious and just as preposterous as anything in an ancient legend.

TOMMY. You've deliberately got me off the subject.

SOPHIA. Oh, Tommy!

TOMMY. I don't like the idea of his wandering about all over the house.

SOPHIA. If he wanders about at night he can't stay with me. Anyway, I've a feeling I shan't keep him.

TOMMY. You don't like him, then?

SOPHIA. Oh yes, I do. But I don't believe I'll keep him.

TOMMY. Why not?

SOPHIA. Don't know, really. I've a feeling he won't stay for long.

TOMMY. You felt that about that red-headed maid of yours.

SOPHIA. Eileen? Yes, and I still feel it about her – I feel it about them both. They're really only an incident in this house. They neither of them belong . . .

TOMMY. He wants to get something here, that's the feeling I have about him.

SOPHIA. Get something? Oh, there's not much for him to pinch here, if that's what you mean.

TOMMY. What about your jewellery?

SOPHIA. You mean the ones that Sheila wrote all that nonsense about in 'Irish Life'?

TOMMY. Yes, the emeralds.

SOPHIA. My dear, I'd better tell you the truth about those. They're all props.

TOMMY. Props?

SOPHIA. Yes, theatrical props, you know; fake, sham, paste.

TOMMY. Well!

SOPHIA. Yes, isn't it awful? Of course, they're very good fakes. I wore the emerald ones as Lady Macbeth at Stratford. Nemchinski was furious because the banquet scene was all in red and purple and he wanted me to wear some ghastly rubies that made me look like a rather go-ahead brothel in Port Said. But I smuggled my emeralds on to the stage every night in a drinking horn, dear, and I used to *pop* them on just before the curtain went up. He was very snappish about it. I suppose women are rather tiresome to have about a theatre.

TOMMY. Well! But everybody in Dublin thinks they're real, and you might just as easily be murdered for prop jewels as real ones.

SOPHIA. Thank you, Tommy, you're most reassuring. . . Oh, I am so tired.

TOMMY (*leaping to his feet*). I'm sorry. I ought to have gone ages ago.

SOPHIA (*yawning*). Oh, no; stay, darling, do stay. Stay forever – Oh! (*She yawns again.*) You know you're longing to.

TOMMY. No, I'm going home.

SOPHIA. Have I got circles under my eyes?

TOMMY. Yes, you have.

SOPHIA (*pause*). It is nice to live in Dublin again. That's the sort of answer you'd only get from a Dublin Protestant. 'Have I got circles under my eyes?' 'Yes you have.' The Catholic Irish or the true-blue English would never dream of such straight from the shoulder stuff as that. There'd be a thousand different evasions or contradictions or jesuitical convolutions from one lot, and an enormous endless bombardment from the other. 'Circles? Do you mean circles? Oh, but where? Darling, under your eyes? Oh, your *eyes*? Yes, but not *under* them. My deah! Let me have a teeny weeny peep! Oh, good heavens! I say, circles! No, you haven't! you can't have. I mean it isn't done.' And so on.

TOMMY. Well, you asked me, didn't you?

SOPHIA. Yes, Tommy, yes. I asked. And you gave me the one perfect answer.

(*She goes and looks in the glass.*)

Oh, my God! They're hanging round my knees.

TOMMY. What are?

SOPHIA. Circles?

TOMMY. You look marvellous. Oh look, may I leave my harp here?

SOPHIA. Of course you may.

TOMMY. I shall ring you up in the morning.

SOPHIA. What for?

TOMMY. To see if you're safe.

SOPHIA. Safe?

TOMMY. Well, I'm anxious about you.

SOPHIA. You needn't be.

TOMMY. I am, though. Don't come to the door.

SOPHIA. Of course I shall come to the door. I don't want two dangerous men prowling about the house all night.

TOMMY. It's no use trying to talk sense to you.

SOPHIA. Not a bit darling, so why waste your energy?

(SOPHIA *and* TOMMY *go out and the room is deserted for a few seconds. Then the door leading to the kitchen is opened and* MARTIN *enters alone. During this time the front door is heard to open and close.* MARTIN *stands looking about him. He gently touches the harp, the he goes to the window and stands looking out at the garden. A light wind begins to stir the branches of the trees.* SOPHIA *comes back. She does not see* MARTIN. *She takes up planchette board and sheets of paper, turns to sit on the sofa, then she sees* MARTIN *standing at the window.*)

SOPHIA. Oh!

MARTIN. Here I am, madam.

SOPHIA. You quite startled me.

MARTIN. I'm sorry, ma'am. 'Tis a bad thing a person to get a start.

SOPHIA. Were you there long?

MARTIN. One minute and a quarter, madam.

SOPHIA. Oh, I see.

MARTIN. 'Tis a grand, starry night.

SOPHIA. Marvellous.

MARTIN. And 'tis mild, too. 'Tis powerful mild, for a night in April.

SOPHIA. Yes. Oh look, the moon's rising.

MARTIN. 'Tis the old moon. She's only shell.

SOPHIA. Yes. A great amber shell . . . Did you get something to eat.

MARTIN. I did, thank you. And I seen my little room. 'Tis lovely. It has birds and flowers on the wallpaper.

SOPHIA. Really?

MARTIN. A paper with birds on it and flowers is grand. Only not when a person'd be sick.

SOPHIA (*laughing*). Why not?

MARTIN. Because if a person have a sickness, everything around him do come alive and commence to fight with him. The birds'd be screeching and the flowers'd be dropping their petals to scorch up his skin.

SOPHIA. Oh dear!

MARTIN. But I never had a day's sickness, thank God. 'Tis only my memory is bad. I hope you'll not be hard on me when I forget.

SOPHIA. Your memory's bad, is it? That's a pity.

MARTIN. Well now, I'd not say 'twas exactly bad. But 'tis queer. You see, madam, there's two sets of things to remember. 'Tis like the night and the day.

SOPHIA. I don't quite understand you.

MARTIN. Times it do be hard for me because I has to remember the night as well as the day. And there's times when the night and the day does be mingled. Most fellows can get along all right if they keeps their eyes opened and it daytime on all their duties. There's boots to clean and fires to blow and water to be boiled. But the stars has to be busy as well and I do have to remember the stars . . .

(*A pause. He stares away from her at the tree-tops.*)

SOPHIA (*a pause*). Martin, I think you'd better be off to bed.

MARTIN (*dutifully, turning to her*). Yes, madam. Will I turn out the lights, madam?

SOPHIA. Oh, just the big one. I'll turn out the rest.

(MARTIN *turns and watches her.*)

What are you waiting for?

MARTIN. I was wondering what you were doing with the door, Madam?

SOPHIA. The door? Oh you mean this! This is a planchette. It's a – well, it's a sort of toy.

MARTIN. A toy?

SOPHIA. Yes, a sort of toy.

MARTIN. I thought 'twas a little door, mind you. (*He turns out the light.*) Goodnight, Madam. (*He bows and goes.*)

SOPHIA (*pause*). Door! (*She smiles.*) Oh well.

>*(She prepares herself for planchette. Outside the house the wind is rising. There is a rustle of leaves. A church clock strikes the hour of one.)*

Dead as a doornail . . . I wonder if there's any truth at all in . . . Oh! (*She yawns.*) 'Red flare of dreams.'

>*(She rises and looks at herself in the mirror.)*

You go to bed, you silly doughfaced hag. Time you got your beauty sleep, by dear. (*She switches out the light on the mantelpiece.*) Wish I could learn that last speech . . . 'If I go back to the country of the Young I must go as a shadow . . .'

>*(She has gone. The room is lit only by moonlight and by the fire. The door leading to the servant's quarters opens slowly and EILEEN comes in. She walks towards the window and stands looking out into the garden. The moonlight falls on her. The door opens again slowly. A man's shadow is thrown on the wall.)*

EILEEN. Who are you?

MARTIN'S VOICE (*he does not answer her question but says*). Don't be afraid.

EILEEN. I'm not afraid.

MARTIN. Why are you here?

EILEEN. Why are *you* here? Why have you come?

MARTIN. I have come for you.

>*(The shadow grows larger as if it were coming into the room. EILEEN raises her head and stands proudly waiting as the curtain falls.)*

# CURTAIN

# ACT II

*The same room, next morning. A brilliant sun streams through the French windows. The room is tidy and the planchette table is in its place* MARY DEMPSEY *enters carrying a broom, a dust-pan and a brush. She goes to the hearth and kneels down.*

MARY: God bless us and save us, he'd have it all done right enough.
My, my, my. And the ash-trays all emptied. Not a speck. Now!
(*The telephone bell rings.*)
Yes, miss! (*She goes to the door and opens it.*) Was that herself
roaring now? I declare to God, I believe I'm going deaf. (*She goes
to the window to pull the curtains back.*) Oh, there's something
singing. (*She turns and sees the telephone.*) Oh, that old yoke! (*She
lifts the receiver.*) What is it? I can't hear a word, not a blessed
word. What's that? (*She inspects the telephone with disgust.*). God
bless us, I hate them old phones. Which? . . . Oh, is it yourself, Mr
Tommy? Aga . . . I'm grand, sir, thank be to God. How's yourself,
sir? . . . Which? . . . I'm sorry, sir I thought you were asking me
how was I . . . Mrs Sheridan! Is it Madam? . . . No, sir; no, Madam
didn't let a roar out of her yet . . . Oh, faith I know 'twas late
enough, sir, you're perfectly right . . . No, Madam never opens her
eyes till ten or eleven . . . Which? Sure, I know 'tis past eleven . . .
no, sir, oh, indeed I wouldn't go near her, . . . no, sir . . . do you
want to have me murdered? Sure, Madam'd have me evacuated
out of this if I went near her . . . no, sir, them's Madam's orders.
I'm not to put a foot near her until she commences roaring . . .
which? Oh, blast this old thing anyway. (*She shakes the receiver.*)
What's that? What? Murdered? (*A pause.*)
(EILEEN *Enters and stands quietly behind* MARY *watching her.*)
Ah, no, sir . . . Oh my God, no . . . sure who'd want to murder
poor Madam? . . . Ah, now, Mr Tommy, I'd do anything in the
world for you only that . . . no, I wouldn't dare go near her . . .
Very well, so Mr Tommy, maybe she'd be awake by the time
you'd be here . . . Oh, no . . . Which? I can't hear a word! Not a
blessed word! Good? Good which? (*Inspects the receiver.*) God

38

bless us, he's vanished. (*She hangs up.*)

EILEEN. Mrs Dempsey.

MARY (*starts*). What the – oh, 'tis yourself, is it?

EILEEN. 'Tis myself all right.

MARY. H'm! (*She goes to the fire and picks up the dustpan and brush.*)

MARY. Oh, nothing, nothing.

EILEEN. Ah, there is then. You were always great with me till today.

MARY. Maybe I was.

EILEEN. Then, what ails you now?

MARY. I don't want to talk to you.

EILEEN. But why not?

MARY. Which?

EILEEN. Why don't you want to talk to me?

MARY. Making a hare of me. Get along with your work now, if 'tis not too jaded you are to do it.

EILEEN. What are you talking about? What's wrong with you?

MARY. What's wrong with me, is it? Don't you know very well what's wrong with me?

EILEEN. I do not know.

MARY. How innocent you are! Oh God pity my foolishness that ever took you for a decent girl would have a bit of respect for herself.

EILEEN. What's that you're saying?

MARY. Listen to me, here, my girl. I'm saying that a young woman in service in the city should mind herself and not go trapesing around at night with the Devil knows who and the Devil knows where, like an old streeler.

EILEEN. You've no right to say that. What have I done?

MARY. Don't you know damn well what you have done?

EILEEN. I do not. I don't know what is it you have in your mind to be fighting and back-biting me all the morning and me without a word out of me trying to do my work.

MARY. Only for me being sorry for you I'd tell Madam all that I know about you, and I'd have you transported the way I did with that jade of hell out of Galway was here before you. Oh, my, my, my, and me thinking you were a decent respectable girl would never give herself a crick in the neck looking after any young chaps . . . And what notion ever overtook you to do it? Oh dear me, by all the saints you're a disgrace.

EILEEN. Young chaps, is it?

MARY. Now, mind you I'm not saying I know who 'twas. But if I could lay my hands on the young whipster, I'd throttle the life out of him and I'd force him to marry you if I'd to go down on my two knees in the mud to find him.

(MARY *continues to tidy the desk; she knocks a piece of paper onto the floor between the desk and the window.*)

EILEEN. I see. That's what you think of me. That I'd go carrying on with the first fellow that walks into this house for a job.

MARY. Oh, faith, you're wrong there. I don't think that at all.

EILEEN. What do you mean?

MARY. I may not know who 'twas you went rambling with but I know who 'twasn't.

EILEEN. And how do you know I went rambling at all?

MARY. When you'd see a bed hadn't been slept in nor the sheets on it turned down itself, what would you think? Ha? Tell me that.

EILEEN. So you went into my room, did you?

MARY. I did then. I went out to seven o'clock Mass this morning, and I called in to you to ask you would you get the fire in the kitchen lit agen I'd be back, and that I may drop down dead this minute if you'd been near that bed since the night before. (*Pause.*) Now, what do you say?

EILEEN. You are right about that . . . I wasn't in my bed last night.

MARY. And you wouldn't even have the decency to deny it.

EILEEN. Why would I deny it? 'Tis true.

MARY. Oh, my, my, my! May God forgive you.

EILEEN. But what you think isn't true. I know what you think. And it isn't true.

MARY. Ah, you were always a decent poor girl, Eileen. That's why I'm out with you now. If it was that strap Maggie I'd never put any pass on it. But to think of you forgetting yourself.

EILEEN. Forgetting myself? (*On her lips the phrase has a different meaning.*)

MARY. That's what had me upset.

EILEEN. But you've no cause to be upset.

MARY. If I could believe that now . . .

EILEEN. You can believe it or not, 'tis true.

MARY. I was thinking the fearfullest things.

EILEEN. There was no need for you to think anything at all.

MARY. Well, God be praised for that, anyway. What I was thinking was desperate. Aha, I'm telling you, my girl, there's no end to the desperate things would come into a decent woman's mind when she'd see a bed wasn't slept in. Doubts, suspicions, wicked notions, the Devil knows what I might be thinking only I wouldn't let myself . . . Oh, isn't it a terrible thing not to know what'd be in your mind against a person might be pure and innocent as the dribbled snow. But sure, my God, what the blazes were you doing?

EILEEN. What was I doing?

MARY. Or where were you at all?

EILEEN. I – I – (*Her eyes close.*)

MARY. Tell me now, where were you?

EILEEN. I can't remember.

MARY. You can't remember?

EILEEN. No.

MARY. Try, *a stór* try to remember.

EILEEN (*gazes out of the window.*) He took me out a long way away and the trees was all under blossom and the lambs crying out on the hills.

MARY. Who took you?

EILEEN. A shadow. 'Twas the shadow of the man that . . .

MARY. The man that came to this house . . . last night.

(*Her voice grows normal: she blinks and looks at* MRS DEMPSEY *and smiles as she explains.*)

The young fellow that's going to drive the car for Madam.

MARY. Martin, is it? Martin Lyden?

EILEEN. I never heard that name ——

MARY. It couldn't be Martin Lyden. I locked him in his room last night for fear —— (*she stops.*)

EILEEN. Why did you lock him in his room?

MARY. Because I didn't like him. Because I didn't want Madam to be robbed.

EILEEN. You locked him in his room?

MARY. I did then, and I'd do it again, till I know what class of a chap he is, or is he Christian or decent at all.

EILEEN. What time was it you locked him in?

MARY. 'Twas the moment he went up to his bed after him eating his supper, and I let him out this morning on my way out to Mass.

EILEEN. Then you had him shut up all night?

MARY. I had.

EILEEN (*with sudden fear*). You didn't lock him in his room. You didn't – you didn't.

MARY. Bedad I did so, and I put a press, ay and two presses agen the door.

EILEEN. Then he got out – some way or another . . . maybe the window.

MARY. Is it get out of that window? Faith he did not then, and the big

41

thick bar is on it. 'Tis a top room we put him in . . . listen! What's all this about him getting out? What makes you think he got out?

EILEEN (*with dread*). I don't know.

MARY. You do know. What makes you think he got out at all?

EILEEN. Because 'twas him took me out towards the mountains.

MARY. What?

EILEEN. 'Twas him took me out and I travelled the world with him till the day whitened.

(MARTIN *enters from the kitchen. He looks fixedly at* EILEEN *whose back is turned to him and then he goes to* MRS DEMPSEY.)

MARTIN. I have the car cleaned

MARY. Where's the key of the garage, young fellow?

MARTIN. Here.

MARY. Give it here to me.

(MARTIN *gives the key to* MRS DEMPSEY.)

MARTIN. There. Take care of it now.

MARY. Never fear.

MARTIN. And I've this room done out.

MARY. I seen it.

MARTIN. Is it all right?

MARY. 'Twasn't too bad.

(*A pause.*)

How did you sleep?

MARTIN. Tip-top.

MARY. Are you certain?

MARTIN. That's the third time you're after asking me that.

MARY. Ay, and maybe I'd ask you a fourth.

MARTIN. I slept grand.

MARY. I'm charmed to hear it.

MARTIN. Listen, what made you lock me up?

MARY. Which?

MARTIN. Why are you letting on you didn't hear me?

MARY (*turns violently to face* MARTIN). *You ignorant cábóg, for two pins I'd . . . How dare you stand there and tell me I'm not deaf?*

MARTIN. I'm sorry. 'Twas a ferocious thing to do right enough.

MARY. Oh, the ignorance! Oh my, my, my.

MARTIN. But what made you do it?

MARY. Do what?

MARTIN. Lock me up.

MARY. How well you can ask me that.

MARTIN. How well you wouldn't tell me why you did it.

MARY. Didn't I let you out this morning well enough.

MARTIN. You did. And if you let me out why wouldn't you tell me why you locked me in?

MARY. Ask the young one there. She'll maybe tell you more about it than I'd care to. Eileen, this is the new fellow, Martin Lydon. Fly-by-night. (*She sweeps out, a model of integrity.*)

> (MARTIN *goes over to* EILEEN *and stands behind her looking out into the garden. She does not speak or turn to him. Finally he breaks the silence.*)

MARTIN. Good morning to you.

EILEEN (*without turning round*). Good morning.

MARTIN. That's a grand day, thank God.

EILEEN. It is.

MARTIN. When you'd meet a person for the first time, wouldn't it be the decent thing to do to give him a look. I'd like to see your face.

EILEEN. Why do you not come round to the right side of me so?

MARTIN. I don't know.

EILEEN (*after a pause*). That's where my face is.

MARTIN. Yes, I know.

EILEEN (*after another pause*). Well?

> (*This is said with patience and sincerity in a low voice. There is no touch of coquetry.*)

MARTIN. I'd rather you turned round to see me. That's how we should meet.

> (EILEEN *turns round and they stand face to face. There is a moment's pause.*)

EILEEN. Oh!

MARTIN. What is it?

EILEEN. You look different now.

MARTIN. Different?

EILEEN. When you came into this room last night like a big shining shadow and the starlight falling down on you . . .

MARTIN. This room?

EILEEN. Where else?

MARTIN. I never was in this room with you before. But I remember another place.

EILEEN. You were never here with me?

MARTIN. I was never in this room with you. Never in all my life. That was only a dream.

EILEEN. Oh no!

MARTIN. 'Twas only a dream.

EILEEN. But you were here. You came in there at that door and we

43

walked out of this house and we followed the black roads that go out to the mountains and we counting the stars . . .

MARTIN. 'Twas only a dream you had.

EILEEN. Only a dream! But when we saw the hawthorn and the young fern and you called me by my name . . .

(*Over the two of them as they stand in the bright, early sunshine by the window, a slow change is creeping. They stand motionless with the archaic, rigid grace of Mycenean stone figures: their voices have gathered depth and a remote dreamlike passion. Something ancient and magical seems to quicken within them.*)

MARTIN. You have forgotten where we met before.

EILEEN. 'Tis you that have forgotten.

MARTIN. There's two memories in my head. One memory's about a dream I had last night, and 'twas of you, and you were standing her right enough, and we went walking out of this house together.

EILEEN. That was no dream. I stood here waiting for you, and you told me you had come to find me.

MARTIN. And the other memory I have . . .

EILEEN. What is it?

MARTIN. 'Twas a long time ago.

EILEEN. When you were a little lad, is it?

MARTIN. Ages ago. Too far away.

EILEEN. Tell me about your country.

MARTIN. I can't. I can't remember rightly.

EILEEN. You called me by my name last night.

MARTIN. Your name. What is your name?

EILEEN. My name is – (*She stands very proudly.*)

MARTIN. Tell me.

(*There is a knock at the front door.*)

(*They both start, and we see them again as before: two domestic servants with no trace of mystery or majesty about them. Their voices drop back from the slow chant they were beginning to assume to the complaisant sing-song of the countryside. They seem to have forgotten what they said a moment before.*)

EILEEN. What's that you were asking me?

MARTIN. What is your name?

EILEEN. Eileen.

MARTIN. Eileen.

EILEEN. You're Martin, aren't you?

MARTIN. Martin, that's right.

(*There is another knock at the front door.*)

EILEEN. There's that old door.

MARTIN. Is that your job or mine?

EILEEN. Which.

MARTIN. To open the door.

EILEEN. 'Tis mine. At least I'd imagine so.

MARTIN. Are you not certain?

EILEEN. My mind does always be in a fierce muddle in this house.

MARTIN. Is herself an old devil?

EILEEN. She is not then. She's a grand lady.

MARTIN. Why are you putting the two eyes through me that way?

EILEEN (*dreamily*). I was thinking . . . I don't know.

MARTIN. Go on.

EILEEN. I was thinking . . . I'd seen you some place before.

MARTIN. Maybe you have.

EILEEN. Wasn't it very queer me dreaming about you that way?

MARTIN. It was, mind you. You're sure you were dreaming?

EILEEN. I must have been.

MARTIN (*with increasing insistence*). You never seen me in this room before?

EILEEN. I mustn't have and you locked in your own place.

MARTIN. Don't forget that now.

EILEEN. But 'twas queer. Dreaming about you like that before ever I seen you . . .

MARTIN. I was dreaming too. . . .

(*There is another knock at the front door.*)

EILEEN. I must go. I'll be killed.

MARTIN. Who'll kill you?

EILEEN. Mrs Dempsey.

MARTIN. What do you care about Mrs Dempsey?

EILEEN. Oh, she have a terrible tongue.

MARTIN. What do any of the people in this house matter to you?

EILEEN. I don't know . . .

(*For a brief cobweb of a moment again the magic seems to descend.*)

MARTIN. You'll know one day. When the time comes you'll know what to do.

EILEEN (*with complete sincerity*). Yes.

(*There is another knock and* EILEEN *rushes out.* MARTIN *picks up a piece of paper from the floor.*)

MARTIN. Tut, tut, tut. I hates a dirty place. (*He replaces the paper on the desk.*)

TOMMY (*rushing in*). Lydon!

45

MARTIN. Yes, sir.

TOMMY. Is Mrs Sheridan up yet?

MARTIN. Muise I don't know sir is she. I have the boiler ready for her bath, sir.

TOMMY. But look here, don't you know if she's awake or not? Where's the cook?

MARTIN. She'll be in the kitchen, sir.

TOMMY. Call her, please, would you? And ask her is Mrs Sheridan awake.

MARTIN. Yes, sir.

TOMMY. Go on, go on.

MARTIN. Yes, sir. (*He goes out.*)

TOMMY. Crazy, absolutely crazy. Enough to drive anyone out of their mind.

MARTIN (*re-entering*). The cook's out, sir.

TOMMY. Oh, she's out, is she?

MARTIN. Doing a bit of marketing, sir. She's to put down a couple of ducks for lunch.

TOMMY. I don't care what's for lunch.

MARTIN. Ducks is grand, sir.

TOMMY. Really?

MARTIN. But I couldn't touch them myself. I wouldn't look at butcher's meat. Even a bit of poultry itself'd stick in my neck.

TOMMY. Deeply interesting.

MARTIN. It is, sir. I've a fierce stomach.

TOMMY. Look here, will you go up and knock at Mrs Sheridan's door?

MARTIN (*the modest male*). Well, now, sir, I wouldn't like, on my first morning. . . .

TOMMY. Oh, you wouldn't like to?

(*He examines the mantelpiece.*)

MARTIN Are you looking for something, sir?

TOMMY. No, nothing in particular. (*Suspiciously.*) Some pretty things here, aren't there?

MARTIN. There is, sir. Lovely.

TOMMY. Yes . . .

(*After a pause.*)

How did you sleep?

MARTIN (*a pause as he looks at* TOMMY, *laughing*). I slept grand, sir.

TOMMY. What are you laughing at?

MARTIN. I don't know, sir. But everyone seems terrible anxious to know how I slept.

TOMMY. Do you wonder at it?

MARTIN. Well now, I do a bit, sir.

TOMMY. Well, I'll tell you what I mean, Lydon. I don't like you and I
don't trust you. I don't know why but the feeling's there.

MARTIN. I'm sorry, sir. I likes you all right.

TOMMY. Oh, I can see what made Mrs Sheridan engage you. You're
just the sort of person it would amuse her to give a job to. You've
plenty of intelligence and plenty of cheek.

MARTIN. I haven't no cheek at all, sir.

TOMMY. You're bursting with cheek. If you weren't you'd never have
dared to come here at such an hour and ask for a job. You'd never
have told me that cock-a-bull story about . . .

(*A pause.*)

MARTIN. Yes, sir?

TOMMY. About following the stars and the face and . . . oh, I don't
know how I had the patience to listen to you. I knew there was
something wrong about you, and . . .

MARTIN. And something that made you frightened?

TOMMY. Ah! What's the use?

(*But he turns away from* MARTIN'S *eyes.*)

MARTIN. Maybe you're right, sir. Maybe there is something . . . wrong
. . . the way you'd look at me. But if you dared, sir, you'd look
closer and you'd see 'twas nothing wrong at all. 'Tis only
something you're looking for all the time yourself. Something
you're afraid to find.

(*He goes out very quietly.*)

TOMMY. Never in all my life . . .!

(*The telephone rings.*)

TOMMY. Oh my God! (*He takes up receiver.*) Hullo! . . . Yes . . . yes . . .
Oh, Mrs Sophia Sheridan . . . yes, she does live here . . . Well, I
don't know . . . no, I'm sorry, I don't know whether she's in or not
. . . Oh, dear no. You see, it's rather difficult to explain . . . who's
speaking, please? The Prattler? . . . oh, the London Prattler? Oh,
*really*? Well, now! . . . yes . . . yes. . . . Mr Grundon . . . what? Oh,
Mr Brunton, I'm sorry . . . well, I'm sure she'll see you if she's all
right, I . . . oh, no, she's not ill . . . not as far as I know . . . well, I
don't really know . . . .

(MARY DEMPSEY *enters.*)

MARY. Did you want to see me, sir?

TOMMY (*to phone*). Honestly I don't know.

MARY. Oh, very well, so. (*She starts to go.*)

TOMMY (*to* MARY). Come back here at once. I've got to talk to you
. . . (*To phone.*) Yes, Mr Brunton? (*To* MARY.) Oh, don't go, you

wretched creature . . . (*To phone.*) No, Mr Brunton, no, not you
. . . Well, then, all right ——

MARY. Do you want me here or do you not, sir?

TOMMY (*to* MARY). Yes, I do want you here badly . . . (*To phone.*)
Yes, Mr Brunton . . . Oh, I'm so sorry . . . you're where? Sir
Thomas who? Oh, *ffoulkes*! Yes, yes, of course – sorry. Sir
Thomas ffoulkes . . . Oh yes, about his Gaeltacht bead-making
industry. Yes, oh well you're just across the road . . . yes, almost
opposite. Oh, very well, if you think . . . right away? Oh, goodbye. (*He hangs up.*) More complications.

MARY. Which, sir?

TOMMY. Some wretched London society gossip-writer, Spring Show or
something, want to interview Mrs Sheridan. And by the way,
where is Mrs Sheridan?

MARY. In her bed, snoring, sir.

TOMMY. Are you sure?

MARY. Where else would she be?

TOMMY. Go up and see will you?

MARY. Oh, you need never feel anxious about Madam, Mr Tommy.

TOMMY. Possibly, possibly. Do go up and see is she is all right.

MARY. Now listen to me, Mr Tommy. I'd go upstairs this minute only
she'd murder me and she in her sleep ——
        (*There is knocking at the front door.*)
Now – ah! – was that herself roaring out for me?

TOMMY (*hopelessly, as he sits down*). No, it was someone at the door.

EILEEN (*entering with a card*). There's a gentleman at the door to see
madam.

TOMMY (*taking the card*). Oh heavens, it's that Brunton fellow from
the Prattler. You'd better tell him Mrs Sheridan is not in, I
suppose, Eileen – I don't know what to do. Tell him ——

MARY. Wait no, Mr Tommy, and I'll brave her. I'll brave he in her
room and I'll tell her there's a strange gentleman to see her, that'll
get her out of bed.

TOMMY. Oh do, for goodness sake! Let's know something definitive
anyhow.

EILEEN. What'll I tell the gentleman, sir?

TOMMY. Oh, tell him what you like.

BRUNTON (*appearing at the door*). God save all here! May I come in?
        (*He enters the room.*)

TOMMY. Oh – of course.

MARY. Holy Smoke, let me out of this. Excuse me, sir.
        (*She makes to Exit above* BRUNTON.)

BRUNTON. Of course, but, of course, I'll excuse you. I'm partly Irish myself, you know.

(BRUNTON *is marvellous. It doesn't matter whether he is tall or short, he gives an impression of bigness because he is so blonde and clean and pink-cheeked and happy. He's nicely dressed too, with that curious easiness of an Englishman's clothes, that does a good deal to tone down the alarmingly uneasy good health and spirits that send him jerking and spinning round the room to greet people and slap their backs until they're dizzy. An endless enthusiasm emanates from him; one feels that the unspeakable journey from Euston to Westland Row hasn't taken a feather out of him. Only Mr Wodehouse could really have understood him, but actually he's terribly fond of reading, especially of Anglo-Irish literature, and he thinks W. B. Yeats and the Joyce chappie absolutely tops.*)

MARY. Oh yes, sir.

(*She gets out of the room somehow.*)

BRUNTON. Do forgive my butting in, won't you?

TOMMY. Of course, – won't you sit down.

BRUNTON. Thanks.

EILEEN. Will I go away now, sir?

TOMMY. Yes, I suppose so.

EILEEN. Thank you, sir.

(*She exits.*)

BRUNTON. Are you Mr Sheridan?

TOMMY. Oh dear me, no. My name is Millington.

BRUNTON. How do you do?

TOMMY. How do you do?

BRUNTON. What a lovely day, isn't it?

TOMMY (*miserably*). I don't think so.

BRUNTON. No? Oh I think it's quite peerless. Do you often have days like this in Ireland?

TOMMY. Frequently. (*His mind is miles away.*) Oh yes, nearly all the time.

BRUNTON. I've fallen in love with Ireland. I arrived yesterday. Absolutely head-over-heels.

TOMMY. I'm so glad.

BRUNTON. Yes, I think Ireland's quite perfect. Of course you must be prepared to rough it, but if you are, Ireland is quite, quite perfect.

TOMMY. Good.

BRUNTON. Oh, I mean you've all such an understanding of living over here. Look at the way I came into this room. Priceless, you know.

49

I'd never dream of doing such a thing in England. English people are so stuffy, they simply wouldn't understand.

TOMMY. No.

BRUNTON. No. Do you know, old boy, England is just too dreary for words. Oh yes. All so different here. Of course you know what's wrong with London, don't you?

TOMMY. What's wrong with it?

BRUNTON. Oh, surely you know?

TOMMY. But I don't.

BRUNTON. Well, it's had it. (*There is a gloomy pause.*) Yes . . . And it's gone tatty. Simply tatty. There's only one word for it. Tatty.

TOMMY. Pity.

BRUNTON. Where's Mrs Sheridan?

TOMMY. That's what I can't tell you.

BRUNTON. How weird.

TOMMY. Yes, I know.

BRUNTON. You mean – you don't know where she is?

TOMMY. No.

BRUNTON. Why?

TOMMY. Why what?

BRUNTON. Why don't you know where she is?

TOMMY. I mean I just can't tell you where she is.

BRUNTON. Too weird for words.

TOMMY. She may be in bed.

BRUNTON. In bed. Do you mean in bed?

TOMMY. Yes.

BRUNTON. I say! What fun!

TOMMY. Fun?

BRUNTON. I mean it's so Irish. (*He laughs, irresistibly indulgent.*)

TOMMY. Is it?

BRUNTON (*after a pause*). Do you know, I don't believe you're Irish at all.

TOMMY. Well, I'm not, very.

BRUNTON. Ah! I knew it. Great reckless chaps with black curly hair and blue eyes put in with a sooty finger – oh, you know – not a bit like you.

TOMMY. I'm very Anglo, I'm afraid.

BRUNTON. Anglo?

TOMMY. You know, Protestant.

BRUNTON (*blankly*). Oh . . . sort of Oxford Groupish. *Where* is Mrs Sheridan?

TOMMY. Really, I don't know.

BRUNTON. She must be somewhere. More or less.

TOMMY. I know. As a matter of fact I'm rather anxious about her.

BRUNTON. So am I . . . I've got to sort of interview her about her little show in support of these comic cab horses, and it's simply got to by tonight.

TOMMY. I see.

BRUNTON (*after a pause*). I more or less represent the Prattler, you know. They're so frightfully thrilled about the horses. And then Mrs Sheridan was *such* a great artist. All we first-nighters wept like kids when she left the stage. What made her do it?

TOMMY. Oh – I think she'll tell you that herself better than I could.

BRUNTON. I haven't seen her since she played Hecuba. Very jolly she looked too, all sort of draped in sort of curtains.

TOMMY. Oh!

BRUNTON. I'm sort of starry-eyed about meeting her in the flesh, you know. Is she still a vegetarian?

TOMMY. I don't think so.

BRUNTON. What a pity. Of course her acting *is* pretty staggering, but she did look a teeny *weeny* bit pudgy as Hecuba. Do you know, I had a spot of tummy trouble last year and I lived on brussels sprouts for three months and I lost two pounds. Do you talk Erse?

TOMMY. Erse? Oh no, not much.

BRUNTON. I saw lots of it written up in the Post Office this morning. Looks a bit of a mess, actually. Still, I think it's fun to have one's own language, don't you?

TOMMY. I don't know, really.

BRUNTON. Oh, but you must have your language back. Of course you must. I mean why shouldn't you? It seems so cruel.

TOMMY. Does it?

BRUNTON. Well, it seems cruel to me. I mean, after all, the British have been pretty brutal to you over here, haven't they? Putting up your rents and forbidding you to keep a pig or two. Oh, it makes my blood boil. Of course, I'm the most sentimental chap ever born. That's my Irish blood, I daresay. I say, where is Mrs Sheridan?

(MARY DEMPSEY *enters in complete disarray.*)

MARY. Mr Tommy! Mr Tommy!

TOMMY. Yes, what is it?

MARY. Madam – she's ——

TOMMY. Where is she – what's happened?

MARY. She's not – she's not – oh, my God!

TOMMY. Mrs Dempsey, what's wrong?

MARY. She's not in her room, sir. She's not anywhere in the house, sir. Oh my God, suppose anything happened her? Oh, what'll I do? What'll I do?

TOMMY. Don't lose your head, now.

MARY. There was her empty bed and the blinds half up and her clothes all this way and that and she clean gone. Oh, Miss Sophie, Miss Sophie!

TOMMY. Was her bed slept in?

MARY. Oh 'twas, sir.

TOMMY. Well, what are we going to do? Wait a minute – Where's that Lydon fellow?

MARY. He'll be in the kitchen, sir.

TOMMY. Go and bring him here. Quickly.

MARY. I will, sir; I will – oh my God, if anything happened to poor Miss Sophie ——

SOPHIA (*enters, strolling in at the window*). If anything what, darling?

TOMMY (*seizing both* SOPHIE'S *hands*). Sophie!

BRUNTON (*rising*). Mrs Sheridan!

MARY. Oh Miss! Oh Miss Sophie! Oh, Miss, oh thank God!

SOPHIA. My dears! You make me feel like Grace Darling. What's wrong?

TOMMY. Sophie, what have you been doing?

MARY. Oh, where were you, Miss Sophie, where were you? Oh, thanks be to the blessed saints, you're safe.

BRUNTON. Sheer joy!

TOMMY. I thought you'd been murdered. Oh, forgive me – this is Mr Thornton.

BRUNTON. Brunton, old man, Brunton, do you mind? How do you do Mrs Sheridan?

SOPHIA. How do you do? Go on, Tommy, what's all the fuss about? My dear, what a lovely morning I've had. Wait till I extract this hat.

(*She goes to the mirror.*)

Oh, what a wind-blasted witch! Now tell me all about it, Tommy. (*To* MARY.) Mary Dempsey, *darling*, don't look so woebegone.

MARY. Oh, Miss Sophie . . .

BRUNTON. Now, Mary, don't start keening again, will you?

SOPHIA (*turning slowly round to have a good look at* BRUNTON). Do sit down, Mr Dunstan. Cheer up, Mary, and get me some breakfast. I'm starving.

MARY. I will, Miss. I will. Is it rashers, Miss?

SOPHIA. Oh, I don't care. Just food, dear. Food.

TOMMY. You haven't had any breakfast?

SOPHIA. I never do . . . but I'll have some now.

TOMMY. But it's nearly lunch time.

SOPHIA. Is it?

BRUNTON. Brunch! You must have brunch! Breakfast is such a dim
sort of meal for a woman like you.

SOPHIA. Ah! How right you are. Go away, Mary Dempsey, and get me
food and call it what you like. (*To* BRUNTON.) Who are you, Mr
Huntingdon?

BRUNTON (*with a beaming smile*). Brunton, do you mind awfully?

SOPHIA. Mr Brunton, who are you?

BRUNTON. Well, I'm ——

SOPHIA (*pointing a long clairvoyant finger at him*). A journalist!

BRUNTON. Well, yes, I am. Sort of, you know. Aha!

SOPHIA. H'm! Have you come to interview me?

BRUNTON. Well, if you'll let me. For the Prattler, you know.

SOPHIA. Oh I know. But what can the Prattler want with me? I don't
act any longer and I don't play golf. I don't use Pond's . . . I don't
go to London first nights and I don't sit on shooting sticks.

BRUNTON. Well, I'll tell you.

TOMMY. Please forgive me, Mr Brunton. Sophie, you've got to tell me
why you gave us all such a fright.

SOPHIA. Listen, Tommy. No one but a goose like you would get a
fright at all just because a brawny ex-actress chooses to take a
walk in Phoenix Park one morning and gets up early to do it.
What's wrong with it?

TOMMY. Phoenix Park? If you'd rung me I'd have driven you. What
did you want to go to Phoenix Park for?

SOPHIA. Mr Brunton, my following remarks will be truthful and are
therefore not meant for print. Well, Tommy, I couldn't sleep last
night, at least I couldn't sleep well, because when I did drop off I
had the strangest dreams.

TOMMY. You were dreaming too?

SOPHIA. I was. Well, the dreams got more and more vivid and more
and more . . . frightening isn't the word. They were just uncanny
and so terribly mixed up. But I woke finally just as the dawn was
breaking with such a brightness in my head – do you know what I
mean? So I got out of my bed and walked and walked.

TOMMY. Go on.

SOPHIA. It was marvellous. It was though I were walking on air. And
the story of Midhir and Etáin became so vivid, so living. And I
believe now, Tommy, that I can help you with the last act. I do.

Clear as daylight to me.

BRUNTON. Fascinating! She's too fascinating for words.

SOPHIA. Ah, there you are *still*, Mr Brunton. Oh! Do you know what I believe you'd love before you start that interview?

BRUNTON. What's that, Mrs Sheridan?

SOPHIA. A nice glass of lovely sherry.

BRUNTON. Oh, terribly kind of you.

SOPHIA. Yes, you would. And you shall have it too.

(*She goes to the door and shouts.*)

Eileen! Eileen! Now, not a word. Sherry it's going to be. Tommy, nice glass of sherry?

TOMMY. No thanks, Sophie. Oh, I'm so glad you're all right.

SOPHIA. Whatever made you think I wouldn't be? Oh, of course. The new house-boy. Seen my house-boy, Mr Brunton? (*She offers* BRUNTON *a cigarette which he refuses.*) He'd be lovely copy for you. Talks with a brogue.

BRUNTON. So do you, you know. Enchanting.

SOPHIA. Nonsense, I speak pure Hammersmith. I was at school there. (*She lights a cigarette.*)

BRUNTON. No, you have that heavenly Celtic burr. (*He pronounces it with a soft 'C'.*) Definitely.

SOPHIA. Oh wirra, wirra, wirra, do you think so? Eileen!

(EILEEN *comes in.*)

Oh, there you are.

EILEEN. Yes, Miss, here I am.

BRUNTON (*admiringly*). Oh!

EILEEN. What would you like to have, Miss?

SOPHIA. The bottle of sherry, my dear, and quickly too. Bring two glasses, one for Mr Millington.

EILEEN. Very good, Miss. I'm glad you're not murdered, Miss.

SOPHIA. Yes, isn't it grand, Eileen?

BRUNTON. Fabulous brogue; fabulous hair.

(TOMMY *rises.*)

TOMMY. Sophie, I'm going. I've to meet a man for lunch.

SOPHIA. Really, truly?

TOMMY. Afraid so. Goodbye, Mr Brunton.

BRUNTON (*with extraordinary depth of feeling*). Oh, goodbye, old man, goodbye.

TOMMY. Goodbye, Sophie.

SOPHIA. Farewell Thomas. Rehearsal tonight at nine.

TOMMY. Yes, of course. Goodbye, goodbye.

(*He Exits.*)

BRUNTON. And now, Mrs Sheridan, I want to hear all about the play. (*He takes out a notebook and prepares to take notes.*) And all about the Irish horses you're interested in. We all think it's so sort of splendid of you. Four-footed friends, you know ...

SOPHIA. Yes ... Now which would you like to hear about first? The play or the four-footed friends?

BRUNTON. Oh, the play, I think.

SOPHIA. Thank God.

BRUNTON. Why?

SOPHIA. Oh, it's only that I don't feel madly sporting today. I'd much rather tell you about the play. It's a quite lovely play; reaction from contemporary: all about Midhir and Etáin.

BRUNTON. What?

SOPHIA. Midhir and Etáin. They're two lovers in an old Irish story.
(EILEEN *comes in with a tray on which are two glasses and the bottle of sherry.*)

BRUNTON. I say, do go on. How do you spell them?

SOPHIA. Midhir. (*She spells the word.*) M-i-d-h-i-r – got that?

BRUNTON. Yes. Fascinating.

SOPHIA. And E-t-á with an accent *that* way, you know, -i-n.

BRUNTON. . . . -a- with an *acute* accent, Mrs Sheridan, -i-n, makes it look a bit foreign actually, doesn't it? How do you say them?

SOPHIA. Midhir and Etáin.
(EILEEN, *as she is putting down the tray, pauses for a moment, listening.*)

BRUNTON. Oh! It's Erse.

SOPHIA. What? Oh, yes, of course. Eileen, put the tray down there, will you?

EILEEN. Yes – yes, Miss. (*She settles the things on the tray.*) Will there be anything else you'd want, Miss?

SOPHIA. I don't think so.

EILEEN. Cook told me to tell you your breakfast was ready, Miss.

SOPHIA. Oh dear me, is it? I think I'll have it in here. You'll have some, won't you, Mr Pringle? After you've had some sherry. (*She starts relentlessly to pour out the sherry.*)

BRUNTON. Oh, no thank you. *Actually*, I'm lunching at the Shelbourne with the editor of the 'Irish Mirror'. Nice chap. Met him at Sir Thomas ffloulkes's. Damned entertaining about his peasant bead-masking. Oh, I say, what an endless glass of sherry. Really, I don't think I ——

SOPHIA. Nonsense! You must drink it to the dregs. And you should have something to eat too. Never lunch with a newspaper man on

55

an empty stomach, Mr Brunton, it might go to your head.

BRUNTON. Oh? Why? . . . Well, of course it's oh so kind and sweet of you, but really ——

SOPHIA. Well, we shall see. Bring in the brunch, Eileen.

EILEEN. The which, Miss?

SOPHIA. The rashers, you simple unsophisticated thing, the rashers.

EILEEN. I will to be sure, Miss.

> (EILEEN *goes out.*)

BRUNTON. Oh, that delicious Dublin brogue. Isn't it wizard?

SOPHIA (*with an admirable imitation of* BRUNTON). *Oh! too wizard for words. Crumbs! Now, now, drink up, Mr Brunton. My eye is upon you. I'm taking this little drop to keep you company.*

BRUNTON. *Slanter.*

SOPHIA (*half-choking*). I beg your pardon.

BRUNTON. Aha! I learnt that on the Mail boat coming over. *Slanter!*

SOPHIA. Oh yes, of course. Hey, Nonny nonny, Mr Brunton.

BRUNTON. Cheers! (*They drink and he gives a polite and slightly shuddering smile.*)

SOPHIA. Now to the play. Midhir and Etáin are lovers in the Land of the Young – that's a sort of fairyland, you see.

BRUNTON. Enchanting. (*He drinks another sip.*) Delicious.

> (*He pushes the glass from him with admirably controlled nausea.*)

SOPHIA. Etáin is banished from fairyland and is born on the earth as a mortal woman. Got that?

BRUNTON. Yes, yes, I'm waiting.

SOPHIA. She marries the King of Ireland and lives at Tara.

BRUNTON. I know, 'The harp that once,' Grand, grand.

SOPHIA. She has forgotten that she was ever an immortal, when one night – it is May Day eve and all the hawthorn is in flower – one night a stranger comes to Tara.

BRUNTON. Her lover!

SOPHIA. That's it. It's Midhir. And he begs her to go back with him to the Land of the Young.

> (MARTIN *and* EILEEN *enter, each carrying a tray of dishes, plates, a coffee pot, etc.*)

And for a long time Etáin doesn't recognise her lover. She can remember nothing at all – got that?

BRUNTON. Yes. (*He is writing feverishly.*)

MARTIN. Excuse me, Madam.

SOPHIA. Yes?

MARTIN. Where will we put the dishes, Madam?

SOPHIA. Anywhere you like, darling.

MARTIN *and* EILEEN *begin to arrange the trays.*)

BRUNTON (*as he writes*). Etáin – can remember – nothing – at all – of – her – former – life. Is that right?

SOPHIA. You know, what fascinates me so much is that non-recognition, that loss of memory. In the end, of course, the story grows more and more fantastic – Etáin return to Midhir and they go away together as two swans flying through the night.

(MARTIN, *who is bending over the tray slowly, slowly straightens up and looks at* EILEEN *who is settling the cups and plates.*)

BRUNTON. Two swans. Charming! Pavlova! Remember?

SOPHIA. Yes, yes. But it's not the swans that interest me so much. What I love is the thought of Etáin, the goddess, as an ordinary woman, unconscious of her immortality, face to face with her lover, and believing him to be a stranger; and then, you see, very slowly in occasional flashes, remembering . . .

(EILEEN *looks up slowly.*)

BRUNTON. Yes?

SOPHIA. That's what has been working in my mind for days now. Imagine this woman waking at night sometimes to hear a far-off music, watching the dawn break over the hills of Meath, or the stars shining down on Tara, and knowing somewhere within herself that she is divine . . . And then the darkness gathers again, and she forgets and is a normal human being.

(EILEEN, *with a slight effort, returns to the dishes on the table.*)

BRUNTON. Yes, yes.

SOPHIA. Until this stranger comes and sings to her. 'There the cheeks are like the foxglove and hair is like the flag-flowers in summer. There is no age there, and no sorrow on any person.'

(EILEEN *looks up again until her eyes meet* MARTIN'S.)

And then she begins to remember . . .

(EILEEN *begins to move towards* MARTIN, *her eyes on him.*)

Bit by bit, her ancient life, her immortal self, and then, at last, her lover's name, Midhir . . .

(EILEEN *falls in a faint on the ground.*)

SOPHIA (*rising*). Eileen!

MARTIN (*kneeling by* EILEEN). Don't be afraid. Madam. 'Twas only the light dazzled her. The darkness will gather again.

(*He looks up at* SOPHIA *and smiles.*)

Everything will be all right.

(*His hands touch* EILEEN'S *forehead.*)

# CURTAIN

# ACT III

*It is the first night of 'Midhir and Etáin'. The hour about half-past eleven; the room is softly and fully lit, and looks intriguing and romantic because there are lilies everywhere. A big fire burns on the hearth. The curtains are closed.*
MARY DEMPSEY, *carrying a tray of bottles, enters from the kitchen.*

MARY. Them's the usuals. There's the gin, the Jameson, the brandy, the syphons, the water, Oh my, my, my, the Italian – oh, by all the saints! Eileen! Martin!

MARTIN (*off-stage*). I'm coming.

MARY (*taking up two champagne bottles*). Oh the ignorance, 'twould kill you. Martin!

MARTIN (*entering with two more champagne bottles in his hands*). I have them. I have them.

MARY. Do you know what it is, you're a terrible man. Oh, dear me, and you so smart and quick in yourself till today, I declare I don't know what it is ails you at all. You're as dreamy as Eileen.

MARTIN. What's wrong with you now?

MARY. Them bottles, what else? Them's for the dining-room. Oh merciful heavens, you're a torment. Bring them back away out of my sight, and bring in the It.

MARTIN. The two bottles, is it?

MARY. You might as well, and look sharp about it. Go on, now.
(*Exit* MARTIN.)
The gin, the brandy, the Jameson, the syphons: ah, the guzzling gentry! Oh isn't it a fright to be drinking. 'Tis ruination, ruination . . . ah well. Martin! Where's that fellow at all? Martin!

MARTIN (*coming in with the bottles*). Here they are now. Where'll I put them?

MARY. Put one here and one over there. Did Eileen not come in?

MARTIN. She did. She's taking off her coat inside in the kitchen.

MARY. What did she say about the opera?

MARTIN. She didn't have time to tell me anything and you screeching

58

for me to bring in the It. Will we go ask her?

EILEEN (*coming in from the kitchen as she ties on her apron*). I seen the play. Is there anything I can do for the party?

MARY. Did you come back alone?

EILEEN. I did not. Mr Tommy's Lizzie was with me as far as the gate.

MARY. Why didn't you bring her in for a cup of tea so?

EILEEN. She'd go back to heat up a jar for Mr Tommy.

MARY. Isn't there enough jars here for twenty Mr Tommies?

EILEEN. 'Tis a hot jar for his bed she have to do.

MARY. Ah, the poor bachelors, they do have desperate cold feet. Is it a hot jar for that fellow and it the first of May tomorrow!

MARTIN. There's no more to do. Will we go back to the kitchen?

MARY. We will, why not, and Eileen can tell us all about – Oh my, will you look at them glasses, you'd think 'twas sweating they were. Run inside for a couple of teacloths, Martin, till we give them a rub.

MARTIN. I will.

(*Exit* MARTIN.)

MARY. How did you like the opera?

EILEEN. 'Twas all right.

MARY. Is that all you have to say about it?

EILEEN. I liked it all right. But 'twas hard to understand, mind you.

(MARTIN *comes back with the two cloths.*)

MARY. Give me that one, now you take that, my girl, and help polish them old glasses – hah! (*She breathes on one.*) Look at that now – just give a big breath – hah!

EILEEN (*taking a glass and blowing into it*). Hah.

MARY. No spitting, mind. Go on, now, what was hard to understand?

EILEEN. Oh, they talked queer, you know – and there was Madam all in green, she was lovely all right, but she'd long red hair on her ——

MARY. Madam with foxy hair? (*Tenderly.*) Ah the creature!

EILEEN. Oh she looked beautiful, and there was Mr Twomey as the King of Ireland, and some class of an old story it was, you know, like – like one you'd read – or – something like – you might hear . . .

(*She turns slowly to where* MARTIN *is standing at the window with the moonlight on him.*)

MARTIN (*softly*). Go on, Eileen.

EILEEN (*recovering her normal manner*). Oh, Mr Twomey! He was nearly in his pelt. He'd on a sort of train like, and crown on his head, and a big sword and his two chests all bare, Mrs Dempsey, and his legs – oh very sunburnt he looked, but still – !

MARY. My God, isn't that fierce?

EILEEN. Sure Lizzie Coughlan was disgusted. She said 'twas a disgrace to a Catholic city, legs and all that – oh!

MARY. What's a disgrace?

EILEEN. Oh, the big bare legs of him. Sure I wouldn't mind them myself at all, 'twas only what Lizzie Coughlan said.

MARY. What wouldn't you mind?

EILEEN (*shouting*). Mr Twomey's legs.

MARY. Ah never mind his legs, child of grace, get on with the play.

EILEEN. 'Tis all about a lady called Etáin . . . and the King of Ireland: that was Mr Twomey, and the lady have a *grá* for a . . . another king . . . (*She looks falteringly at* MARTIN.)

MARTIN. Go on.

EILEEN. Yes; Midhir, the other king's name was, and that was Mr Tommy, and he was all in green too, and he brought her away at the end of all, back to his own country.

MARY. And that's the whole of what was in it, ha!

EILEEN. And they talked terrible queer, mind you.

MARY. What way queer?

EILEEN. Och, I don't know; 'Treasure of my heart', and 'pulse of my soul', and all that. Oh, 'twas very Englishy all right. (*She gives a final polish to the glass she is holding.*) Will that do now?

MARY. It will. Come on now, they should be back soon. Martin, go and take off that white coat, Madam likes you to wear the dark one at night.

(*She starts to move off towards the kitchen.*)

Come on now, the pair of you. Sure them merry-makers'll be trooping down on us like a shower.

(*She has gone.*)

(*There is a pause.* MARTIN *walks over to* EILEEN. *She half-shrinks from him.*)

MARTIN. I'll want your answer tonight, you know.

(*A pause.*)

You're not frightened, sure you're not?

EILEEN. I'm not frightened, only ——

MARTIN. Go on.

EILEEN. 'Twas the play.

MARTIN. Did the play frighten you?

EILEEN. I never seen a play in all my life, only the pictures an odd time, and once I seen some pierrots in Lisdoonvarna, and they singing and cracking old jokes, 'twould break your heart laughing.

MARTIN. What was the play like?

EILEEN. 'Twas . . . (*She shakes her head.*) I can't tell you. Sure I couldn't make out the half of it. But I thought sometimes that I knew it all. I knew it like by heart, and I thought there were bits in it were wrong and that I'd know better myself the way to do it. . . . 'Twas like looking in a mirror and seeing everything a touch crooked.

MARTIN. I'll want your answer tonight.

EILEEN. Martin, I'm not frightened. I'm like lost . . .

MARTIN. Lost?

EILEEN. I feel sometimes when you'd be with me like I was two people. And you're two people as well. (*Her eyes grow brilliant.*) And if we were to go away out of this place together we'd know . . . . (*Her face clouds again. her voice grown normal.*) Was that Mrs Dempsey calling me?

MARTIN. 'Twasn't.

> (*The door bell rings.*)

EILEEN. That's the party. Open the door for them now.

MARTIN. I'll want your answer tonight.

> (*He goes out.*)
>
> (EILEEN, *smiling to herself, goes to the drink table, and stands there in an expected manner. She is longing to pour things for the party.*)

BRUNTON (*entering, is in evening dress and in the highest spirits*). I say, am I really the first to arrive?

MARTIN (*following* BRUNTON *in*). You are, sir. What'll you do now, sir?

BRUNTON. What shall I do? Oh – I see. Yes. Well, I think I shall wait. You see, I'm really just a gate-crasher.

MARTIN (*beaming at him*). Are your really?

BRUNTON. Well, sort of ——

EILEEN. Will you have a drink, sir?

BRUNTON. What? Oh – how sweet!

MARTIN. Yes, sir.

BRUNTON. Oh, but I mean, do you think one ought? Does one?

MARTIN. I don't know, I'm sure, sir.

EILEEN. Ah do, sir. I'll bring it to you.

BRUNTON. Well, perhaps one might. Very well then, give me some brandy. I say, what fun Ireland is.

> (EILEEN *starts to pour out the brandy.*)

EILEEN (*quivering with excitement*). Splash, sir?

BRUNTON. What? Oh – yes, yes. Definitely, splash.

(*The front door bell rings.*)

MARTIN. Excuse me.

(*He Exits.*)

EILEEN. There now, I hope you'll like it, sir. (*She brings the drink to* BRUNTON.)

BRUNTON. Oh thanks. The old Cruiskeen Lawn, is that right? Oh! You're the girl with the red hair who had the vapours, aren't you?

EILEEN. I beg your pardon, sir?

BRUNTON. The one that fainted that morning?

EILEEN (*ashamed*). I am, sir.

BRUNTON. Poor little thing. All gone now? Feeling all fit? Don't you be after doing it again, you know!

(BRUNTON'S *kind sympathy completely shakes* EILEEN'S *faith in herself in him and in the world. She hangs her head.*)

EILEEN. Yes, thank you, sir.

(*Enter* MARTIN, BOB TWOMEY *and* REX DILLON.)

MARTIN. Now gentlemen.

BOB. Oh my God, there he is again.

REX. Shut up.

BOB. Ah, there you are, Mr Brunton. May I introduce Rex Dillon, our producer?

REX. How do you do?

BRUNTON (*shaking hands*). I say, jolly nice work.

REX. Glad you liked it.

BRUNTON. Fascinating brogue. So say that again, Mr Dillon.

REX. Say what?

BRUNTON. 'Say fwot!' Love it so much. Wish I could do it. Do you know, Mr Twomey, I've been imbibing quite heavily. Brandy!

BOB. Oh, is Sophie back, then?

BRUNTON. No, she's going to make an entrance. Wasn't she lovely to-night? Wasn't she?

BOB. Marvellous. She always is.

BRUNTON. Spoke like an angel, and looked exactly three years old. Too much heaven! And what a wig! Like lovely sort of flames.

REX. Got a cigarette, Bob?

BOB. Here you are.

(*He takes out his cigarette case.*)

BRUNTON (*to* BOB *who offers him a cigarette*). No thanks. Never smoke . . . chest groggy. I say, I did think you looked super in your King of Ireland kit this evening. Are those legs really yours?

BOB. I beg your pardon?

BRUNTON. The colour, I mean. Superb tan.

REX. No, it's all false, Mr Brunton. It all comes out of a bottle. He's as white as the driven snow, really.

BRUNTON. Oh? Pity. I say, I do so love the way you talk.

MARTIN. Will we be wanting any more, sir?

REX. No, that'll be all right – your run along.

MARTIN. Come on, Eileen.

EILEEN (*crosses to* BOB). You did you part very nice, sir.

BOB. Thank you, Eileen.

EILEEN. Mr Tommy's Lizzie was giving you great praise. And Mr Tommy was great, sir.

BOB. Yes, wasn't he?

MARTIN. Come along out of that.

> (MARTIN *and* EILEEN *go out.* EILEEN *casting regretful glances at the bottles.*)

BOB. What will you drink, Brunton?

BRUNTON. Oh no, really – really I won't. I've got lots here. Mustn't be after getting stocious you know. Love that word!

BOB. You're a quick study . . . Rex?

REX. Oh, gin, I suppose. Wonder why Sophie never has a cocktail in the house?

BOB. She doesn't think they suit her . . .

BRUNTON. Tummy all gaga? Oh, poor darling.

BOB. No, I mean she doesn't think they suit her style. She belongs to the Countess Markiewiez period.

REX (*taking the drink from* BOB). Thanks, Bob.

BRUNTON. Countess Markiewiez period? Now what was that? Arm chairs?

BOB. No, revolutions.

BRUNTON. I say! Real ones?

> (BOB *pours out a drink for himself.*)

> Do you know I simply raved about that play tonight. Tell me, the man who played Mi – um – er – what's his name, the fairy king, wasn't that the author?

REX. Yes, that was Tom Millington. I think you met him here, didn't you, the first day you arrived?

BRUNTON. Oh, so I did. Nice fellow, so eager. I do like people to be eager, don't you. Especially women, of course. I mean, I think an eager woman is such an adorable thing, don't you?

REX. And such a rarity.

BOB. Especially in Dublin.

BRUNTON. Really? What a pity? However, I'm going back to England tomorrow.

BOB (*delighted*). Are you?

REX. Don't be so pleased about it, Bob. Extraordinary thing about Dublin, Brunton. You must forgive us. The only time you ever see unadulterated pleasure on a Dublin face is when you announce that you're going away. 'Are you really now? Isn't that grand?' It isn't rudeness exactly – it's a sort of congratulation on being able to escape.

BRUNTON. To escape? Oh, but fancy wanting to escape. If I were an Irishman, I should never want to escape.

BOB. Oh wouldn't you?

BRUNTON. Cynic. Don't tell me that you hate your native land.

BOB. I hate it passionately and I love it passionately.

REX. That's rather a hackneyed remark, Bob.

BOB. It's a hackneyed feeling. It's none the less real. Every remark you can make and every emotion you can feel about this country is bound to be hackneyed. Irish people say more and feel more about their country than any other people in the world.

REX. Yes, and live in it less.

BOB. Of course they live in it less. What has it to offer any of us apart from inspiration, frustration and intoxication?

REX. You're forgetting annihilation.

BOB. Ah, but I'm serious.

REX. Bob, you're in very bad mood for a party. Ireland hasn't had a chance. It's all a question of population.

BRUNTON. Yes, what a tiny population you have. But you've such compensations here. All your old fairy tales and all that, you know, sort of!

REX. Oh, plenty of fairy tales.

BRUNTON. No, I mean really. Where else in the world nowadays would you get people to listen to an enchanting old story like that one of Mr Millington's tonight? And the audience adored it. Of course all that come away to Fairyland sort of thing – it's all part and parcel of the Celt, isn't it?

REX (*accompanying himself on the piano*). Come, come away, come, come away, come – come – away! . . . No, I'll tell you something funny, Bob. The only place I've felt the real significance of the Midhir and Etáin legend since we started on this thing has been here in this house.

BOB. How do you mean?

REX. Well now . . . I can't explain why, but until three nights ago the whole idea was getting more and more real to me. But that was during the rehearsals here. There was a sort of – glamour's the word I suppose – yes, a sort of glamour growing up about it all that made me believe in it. And yet it didn't come from the play itself, because the moment we got into that hall and began fooling about with lights and costumes and rostrums and all the rest of it, it just became a dreary Celtic Twilight play in fancy dress. No: the real thing is here somehow – here in this house, and I can feel it again tonight. (*Suddenly.*) Did you notice that smell of hawthorn when that chap opened the door to us?

BOB. No, I don't think I did.

REX. I did. And there's a sort of expectancy in the house . . . what is it? A sort of ancient feeling, as though the pagan summer night were pressing its way into the house . . . as though . . .

BOB. You're getting fanciful, Rex.

BRUNTON. It's his Irish imagination. Steady up, old man.

REX (*smiling*). Yes, I'm sure it is. But I wish I knew why I kept thinking – here is where it's all going on, here is where it's really happening. It's here in the house.

BOB. What do you mean by 'it'?

REX. I wonder if an old story could repeat itself? I wonder if Etáin, the 'lost one' she was called, Tommy says – if she were to lose herself again, be like?

BRUNTON. I say, that sounds a bit Annie Besantish, doesn't it? Do you mean re-incarnation? You know – Madame Blavatsky and all that. Terribly phoney.

REX. I don't quite no what I mean.

    (BOB *laughs.*)

Oh, you can laugh. But Tommy's play seems to me to have set something in motion, something akin to itself and yet different . . .

BOB. My God, and you say I'm in a bad mood for a party.

BRUNTON. I say, is it going to be a real party? Any women – besides Mrs Sheridan, I mean?

BOB. No, it's not going to be a party. Just a drink and a bit of cold something, Sophie said. As for women – let me see – your friend, Miss McCann will be here. The one you were congratulating to-night.

BRUNTON (*dubiously*). Oh . . . yes, Jolly interesting mind. Not exactly what you'd call a *femme fatale*, is she?

REX. She may not be *fatale*, but she's fatal. Almost disastrous.

    (SHEILA MCCANN *enters escorted by a rather depressed* TOMMY.)

SHEILA. I always thought you were a pretty poor driver, Bob Twomey, but you're the answer to the maiden's prayer compared to this fellow.

TOMMY. Never again, never again. I'll never drive her again as long as I live.

SHEILA. Look at my face. Well, do you wonder at it? Isn't it well for me to be alive at all? When the head wasn't being bumped off me on the roof I was being hurled into the canal.

REX. Would you like to –

SHEILA. No, I would *not* like to wash my hands, or take my hat off, thanks. You'll have to find something else to sit on. Will anyone give me a drink? . . . Well?

REX (*prepares to pour out drink for* SHEILA). You've had more than enough, sweet one, but here you go. Gin again, of course.

SHEILA. Don't drown it with that other stuff. (*As* BRUNTON *gets* SHEILA'S *drink and carries it to her.*) Oh, hullo, John Bull, how are you since?

BRUNTON. Since when?

SHEILA. Oh my God! . . . Since you came tapping at my door in the dressing-room to praise me for playing a part I didn't play at all.

BRUNTON. No, rather embarrassing. Frightfully sorry.

SHEILA. Can't be helped. Well, how are you since then?

BRUNTON. Oh very fit, thanks. How are you, little lady?

SHEILA. Deeply depressed, thanks. It's gin and Celtic Twilight mixed. Too much for me.

REX (*to* BOB). Hear what he called McCann? Little lady!

BOB. God's own Englishman and the Irish war-maiden.

REX. No, but 'little lady' to McCann, really! Tommy?

(*He waves a bottle at* TOMMY.)

TOMMY. How do you think they liked the play, Bob?

BOB. Well . . . .

SHEILA. Yes, that's what Tommy thinks.

BRUNTON. Oh they liked it all right. Oh Lord, yes. Oh, definitely.

TOMMY. I had the feeling they loathed it. They liked Sophie of course. She was right, though, about being wrong, if you know what I mean. I could see that tonight.

BRUNTON. I say, I thought she was tops. Absolutely tops.

TOMMY. Oh, but you wouldn't know what I mean . . . English people may love the Celtic Twilight still I don't know: but here it reminds people of their nursery days.

REX. But I like being reminded of my nursery days.

BRUNTON. Well, I enjoy a play that gives you a bit of the creeps. Why, that bit at the end where the spooky chap – it was you, wasn't it? Put the cloak round her and it was all made like swans' wings.

66

That was very jolly. Very, very jolly. I say, was that your idea, Dillon?

REX. No, it was Sophie's. Came to her sudden-like in Phoenix Park.

BRUNTON. Yes, of course. Fabulous woman. What a loss to our stage ... I say, yes, I will have another spot.

(SOPHIA, *in a ravishing gown that drips all over her and is impossible to classify as evening, dinner, or anything else, appears at the door.*)

SOPHIA. Hullo, you bowsies, I'm starving. Sheila, give me a brandy ... Now, fancy seeing you, Mr Banting. Lovely surprise.

BRUNTON. Ah ha, Mrs Sheridan, magnificent, magnifi- – – –

SOPHIA. Wasn't it stupefying? Rex, you did very nicely. Ah my Tommy, cheer up, darling. *Don't* look so alone and palely loitering. (*To the room at large.*) He thinks they hated it, but they didn't. They loved the swans.

BRUNTON. I've just been telling him.

SHEILA. Here's your drink. Where's that henchwoman with the passion for handing things round? I don't want to be on my feet all night; they're persecuting me.

SOPHIA. Eileen – yes, where is she? Scream for her, Bob, I've no voice left. No, don't scream for her. Let's go and eat. I shall die if I don't eat.

EILEEN (*enters*). Did you call me, Miss?

SOPHIA. You know, you do give one the creeps, dotey. No, I didn't call, but I nearly did, if you take my meaning. One of these days, I'm going to wrap you up in a registered envelope and send you to Psychical Research.

EILEEN. Why no, Miss. Will I hand the drinks around?

SOPHIA. On the whole, do you know, I don't think so. No, you can do that after supper. Where's Martin?

MARTIN (*entering*). Here I am, Miss.

SHEILA. It's an organization, that's what it is. All this popping in on their cues like jack-in-the-boxes.

MARTIN. (*with unperturbed dignity*). The supper is served, Madam.

SOPHIA. Thank God we can eat. Come along – Sheila, my darling, we'll lead the way. There are lots of other people coming along later, but we won't wait for them, will we? Bob, I wish you were really that lovely colour you are in the play ... a sort of midnight tangerine ... I adore brown men, one feels so fragile beside them.

SHEILA. Fragile how are you! I'm the fragile one and nobody seems to realise it. (*As she goes.*) Can I bring my glass with me? Did your feet ever persecute you, Mr Brunton?

67

REX. Come along with me, McCann, and have something to eat. Your poor nerves are shattered . . . It's war, isn't it? Summer already . . . Come along.

> (REX *and* SHEILA, *with mutual dislike and difficulty, go out together.*)

EILEEN. Excuse me, Miss.

SOPHIA. Yes, Eileen?

EILEEN. Could I speak to you for a moment?

SOPHIA. Of course. Bob, drag Mr Brunton along with you, I'll be with you in a moment. You don't mind, Mr Brunton?

BRUNTON. Mind? Good heavens, no. (*to* SOPHIA.) You know, Mrs Sheridan, I'm going to miss all this when I get back to civilisation!

> (BRUNTON, BOB *and* TOMMY *go, presumably, into the dining room.*)

SOPHIA. Well, Eileen?

EILEEN. I wanted to thank you, Miss, for letting me go to see the play.

SOPHIA (*laughing*). Oh, that's very sweet of you, darling. Enjoy it?

EILEEN (*very gravely*). I did not, Miss.

SOPHIA. Oh? What was wrong?

EILEEN. 'Twas nearly all wrong, Miss. Ah, 'twas very showy and all that, but 'twas all different, some way.

SOPHIA. Different from how you'd imagined it?

EILEEN. 'Twas wrong. When Midhir was asking you to go back you were dreamy-like, you said grand things and you smiling. But it wasn't that way . . . till the end. 'Twasn't easy or dreamy to leave the earth behind. 'Twas terrible, a woman to struggle between two worlds and she not to know which was her own. 'Twas terrible to be lost, to be like in the darkness . . . and to hear the voices crying out all the time. And then his voice and it rising up out of her sleep, and the blackness of the world around her, and she waiting for the stars . . . (*She looks slowly upwards.*)

SOPHIA (*rising*). Do you know, Eileen – I think ——

EILEEN (*blinking: the maid servant again*). I'm sorry, Miss. I was forgetting. I want to thank you very much for letting me out to the play, miss; 'twas great.

SOPHIA (*there is a pause. Very gently she backs away*). Eileen, get the room tidy and leave some drinks out. You can go to bed then. You must be tired.

EILEEN. Thank you very much, Miss.

SOPHIA. Goodnight, Eileen.

EILEEN. Goodbye . . .

> (SOPHIA *looks at* EILEEN *curiously, and goes into the dining*

*room.*)

(EILEEN *begins to tidy the glasses and carries them out on a tray.*)

(MARTIN *comes in from the dining room. He turns down the lights, opens the windows, and draws back the curtains. He looks out.* EILEEN *comes back.*)

EILEEN. What are you waiting for?

MARTIN. You know well what I'm waiting for.

EILEEN. I don't believe I can do it, Martin. I don't believe I can do it at all.

MARTIN. Why were you talking that way to Madam?

EILEEN. What way?

MARTIN. Telling her what was wrong with that old play. What have it to do with Madam was it right or wrong?

EILEEN. I only said thank you for letting me out to see it.

MARTIN. You told her 'twas wrong. You told her 'twas not the way you remembered . . .

EILEEN (*slowly*). Yes – that's right. I did think it was wrong.

MARTIN. You should never have told Madam. When she came in just now she was all white like and she shaking and trembling. 'Go in there', says she, 'and talk to Eileen. There's something wrong', says she, 'and I can never put it right. But let you go in to her;' says she, ' 'tis the only thing we can do.'

EILEEN. The only thing they can do?

MARTIN. Aye. All them fine people and they writing their plays and they acting out other people's lives and making great stories out of other people's words, what can they do at the end of it all when yourself can see what's wrong but leave the likes of you and me together and let the real story live itself out again.

EILEEN. The real story . . .

MARTIN. The real story. That's what I'm telling you . . .

EILEEN. Martin, I'm afraid. Why did you come here? What brought you to this place?

MARTIN. If I told you that you'd never believe me.

EILEEN. Ah! I know! That time, that first time when your shadow came into this room before you, and it tall and black like a tree at night and it shining like a lamp before the altar of God, I know what you told me then. 'Twas for myself you came, you told me. And you brought me out under the sky where there were sweet smells and they rising up out of the grass, and little lights and they walking over the hills.

MARTIN. 'Twas them brought me back to you. The little lights and

69

they dancing.

EILEEN. You told me all the things I had forgotten. And I was sure then I'd never forget them again. And then, next morning, 'twas you that had forgotten.

MARTIN. I've not forgotten now.

EILEEN. But I'm afraid again . . .

(*With sudden passion.*)

What is it that's tearing me in two like the sea splitting the stones, or the wind and it raving through the world! Why did you come here? Why did you come back again to wake me from my sleep!

MARTIN. You knew I'd come back.

EILEEN. I knew it. The first thing I remembered in this life was the shadow of a face I could never find and 'twas you. I never saw you, and yet I knew you were there. I knew you were my life in some other place. I knew you'd come back to find me. I knew it when I was a baby, and I running on my two bare feet down the hill to school in the summertime. I knew it when I was a young girl and my mother coaxing me to a match I couldn't face. I knew it when I came to Dublin to hide myself away because I never believed you'd find me in the big city. And all that time I was stupid and slow because of dreams were twisting round in my head. But I was happy because there were things to do, roads to walk and dishes to wash and other girls to talk . . . until . . .

MARTIN. What?

EILEEN. Until she began with that play. And that little board thing she have to write things out on a paper. It wrote out messages for her, it wrote out —— 

MARTIN. It wrote out your secret. It wrote out that you'd come back that you were back again where I could find you. Well, I've come. I've come back for you. And now I'll never leave you.

EILEEN. M – Mart – Martin.

MARTIN. Do you think 'twas easy for myself? Do you think I didn't know it too all my life in that little place where I was a lad, and I was struggling day in day out with work in the fields, cutting turf and dragging stones and I waiting, and the two lives going round in my head, and I never knowing which life I belonged to . . . until I seen the stars in my dream and they walking over the mountain to the place where I'd find yourself. Well, I'm here. I've fought my way back through all the years . . .

EILEEN. The years . . .

MARTIN. And now I'm waiting for your answer.

EILEEN. If I could tear myself away I'd go with you, Martin, I'd walk out with you now to the end of the world.

MARTIN. To the end of the world and beyond the end of the world.

EILEEN. Say that again.

MARTIN. To the end of the world and beyond the end of the world.

EILEEN. That was what I remembered . . . That was how the words began to be right in the play, and they set me off, remembering it all. But I'll not go, Martin. I'm afraid to go. I'm used to this now, to this life where 'tis warm and safe and there's things to do and people to talk to.

MARTIN. You'll be with me and with your own people. What are these people to you?

EILEEN. Ah, if I could forget . . . Oh, Martin, I'm a stranger in both worlds. I'm lost, I'm alone, I don't know myself. My own face in the glass . . .

MARTIN. This world will fade again. It faded before and you a queen with gold and silver and bronze on your hair.

EILEEN. Don't make me remember ——

MARTIN. You can't forget! You remember it now. You remember that green night of spring when I waited outside the walls for you, the smell of the thorn trees and they under blossom, the lambs and they crying out in the hills . . .

(*The change is now almost complete. The domestic servants have vanished and we are back in the early world. The room is so full of shadow that we have forgotten it. We might as well be on the mountains already.*)

EILEEN. I saw your face and it like a star through the smoke of the torches. And the crowd there . . . the crowds of faces that tried to keep me back.

MARTIN. I was too strong for them.

EILEEN. There was music in that place and strong food and sweet drink on the table. An old man knocked over a cup of wine and the dogs lapped it up off the floor. And I could see that little thing, and I could see the face of my man when you sang a song to me about your own country where there was no sorrow.

MARTIN. There is no sorrow in that country and no age on any person.

EILEEN. I tried to remember it then. 'Twas all so dark.

MARTIN. There the hair of the people is of the colour of the flag-flowers in the summer, their bodies are white like the snow, their cheeks are like the foxglove.

EILEEN. 'And will you come to me?' you said. 'Will you come back to that country?'

MARTIN. Now you remember!

71

EILEEN. I remember . . .

> (*She turns to* MARTIN *and smiles.*)

I remember it now. The night of feasting, the harps and the wine, the battle in the air, your eyes like two candle flames, and I going back in your arms to our own people; to our own people.

MARTIN. You were lost again, but I found you. 'Twas a hard way for you and a hard way for myself but I found you.

EILEEN. Why did we come back (*She indicates the room, her poor black dress.*) like this?

MARTIN. What other way would I have found you? Only the poor people have remembered the likes of you and me.

EILEEN. Only the poor.

MARTIN. And will you leave it all now? Will you go back with me?

EILEEN. I will go back with you. I will go back . . . again . . .

MARTIN (*he puts his arm round* EILEEN'S *shoulders and leads her to the window*). Look! (*He points to the sky.*) The stars are walking over the edge of the world. Are you ready?

EILEEN (*looking round the room*). Goodbye. (*There is a pause.*) Let us go.

> (MARTIN *and* EILEEN *go into the moonlight together.*)
> (*The room is empty and flooded with light and shadow. Sounds of laughter from the dining room are heard. The door opens and* SOPHIA *and* TOMMY *enter.*)

SOPHIA. I'm sorry. I'm not in the mood for them. No . . . I wish they'd all go away.

TOMMY. Depressed?

SOPHIA. Not exactly . . . But the house is so lonely all of a sudden. So empty. Don't you feel how empty it is? Like a conservatory when someone's taken the flowers away.

TOMMY. What would cheer you up? Planchette?

SOPHIA. Oh no. That's all over. Whatever made me fool about with that sort of thing has left me. I shall have to find a new enthusiasm, Tommy. I've nothing now. I'm all alone in this house again. Just Mary Dempsey and me.

TOMMY. You've Eileen and Martin.

SOPHIA. No, they're gone. The house is empty . . . Oh, don't mind me, I'm just in a bad mood.

TOMMY. So am I. (*He goes and gets his harp.*) But with me it's the play. I've failed. I've missed it all. (*He idly touches the keys of the harp.*) Probably what I lacked was models. You see, in a modern play, you've living people all around you to model your characters on, but in a play about the ancient world where are you to look?

72

SOPHIA. Just what I'm beginning to wonder.

  (TOMMY *plays a few running chords.*)

Tommy, do you ever feel that what you're searching for among the clouds may be dancing before your eyes? And that it may escape and vanish without your ever discovering that for one moment . . . was so close?

TOMMY. I wonder? (*He starts to play the Etáin léitmotif almost unconsciously.*)

SOPHIA. What's that you're playing? Oh, of course, it's your play . . . where Etáin goes back.

TOMMY. Yes.

SOPHIA. Lovely. It really is like a woman leaving all this dross behind her. (*She rises and wanders to the window.*) It's like stars . . . stars walking over mountain tops. (*She looks up at the sky.*) Tommy! . . . Look!

TOMMY. What is it? (*He stops playing.*)

SOPHIA (*softly*). Come and look.

  (TOMMY *goes to the window and stands behind* SOPHIA *looking at the sky. A faint, whirring sound is heard, far away.*)

TOMMY (*slowly*). A swan. How lovely.

SOPHIA. Look . . . there are two of them.

# THE CURTAIN FALLS SLOWLY

# ILL MET BY MOONLIGHT

## A Play in Three Acts

*For Eithne and Hilton and for Another*

Ill met by moonlight, proud Titania!

*A Midsummer Night's Dream*

# CHARACTERS

PROFESSOR SEBASTIEN PROSPER, a folklorist
BAIRBRE, a young girl
SUSAN, a daughter
LEE, a man-servant
ROBERT MALLAROE, a husband
CATHERINE MALLAROE, a wife
HAMILTON, a lady's maid
CHARLES LUSHINGTON-CAREW, a guest

ILL MET BY MOONLIGHT was first produced at the Gaiety Theatre, Dublin, on 8 April 1946 with the following cast:

| | |
|---|---|
| PROFESSOR SEBASTIEN PROSPER | Hilton Edwards |
| BAIRBRE | Sally Travers |
| LEE | Micheál macLiammóir |
| SUSAN | Maureen Cusack |
| ROBERT MALLAROE | Liam Gaffney |
| CATHERINE MALLAROE | Eithne Dunne |
| HAMILTON | Ginette Waddell |
| CHARLES LUSHINGTON-CAREW | Thomas Ross |

The play was directed by Hilton Edwards
and the setting was by Molly McEwen.

The action of the play passes in Brugh na Gealaí, the home of Profesor Sebastien Prosper, in Connemara, on the eve of midsummer.

# ACT I

SCENE I: Sebastien's House

SCENE II: The same, three hours later

# ACT II

SCENE I: The same, twelve hours later

SCENE II: The same, a few hours later

# ACT III

The same, some hours later

# ACT I

## Scene I

SCENE: *We are in the library of* DR CATHERINE PROSPER'S *house in Connemara; a wide and irregularly built room where, if a visitor were to call from the outer world he would find, on advancing through the front door and archway that leads to this apartment, a stairway curving up from his right, a spacious fireplace on his left about which are several deep and well-worn chairs and a sofa of no mean comfort and, facing this, in the opposite wall, a huge pair of glass doors that lead to the garden, the last ravishing glances of which are discernible through the panes. The effect of the room, in spite of the presence of a portrait by Laurencin of a young and beautiful woman in an evening gown of the mid-twenties, is that of a great sea cavern, for its tall, sloping, dusky and uneven; but there are books everywhere, higgeldy-piggeldy, in certain places as high as the sloping bits of ceiling, and a dim and gorgeously-coloured tapestry bunched in folds like a curtain. At the foot of the stairs there stands, or rather seems to lean a little forward into the room with an elderly, ominous stoop, a big grandfather clock; and in a convenient position for the light from the window, a big desk, littered with papers, documents, pipes, spectacles, opened letters, magazines, parcels, paperweights and telephone, and other things of a similar nature. At this desk sits the famous* PROFESSOR *himself, comfortable, irascible, and completely at ease. Bearded, with a shock of brown hair with one thick white strand, his looks suggest to the informed a compromise between Serge de Diaghiliev and James McNeill Whistler, but at the moment he lacks the dandyism for which both these gentlemen were renowned, for he wears what looks like a camel-haired dressing-gown of uncertain age, pulls at an unlighted pipe, and has a small Swiss cow bell round his neck on a black ribbon.*

*When the curtain rises, he is making a note in a small red book, while close at his elbow, patient and beshawled, a young country woman in a scarlet petticoat stands regarding him with mild amusement. He finishes his note and mechanically rings the cow bell; the country woman continues to gaze and presently to laugh. He looks up angrily and rings the bell again.*

79

PROSPER. Well?

BAIRBRE. *O sea.**

    (*She begins to laugh helplessly.* PROSPER *rings the bell again and she laughs more than ever.*)

PROSPER. *Lean leat!*

BAIRBRE. *Well, séard rinne siad, fleasc mór de bhláthanna samhraidh* ⸻

PROSPER. *Fleasc?*

BAIRBRE. *Sea, fleasc* (*she gesticulates and illustrates a circle*), *agus salann bán, agus fuil an ghabhair scaipthhe air agus . . .*

PROSPER. *Fuil an ghabhair?* Ah! Goat's blood. (*He makes a note.*)

BAIRBRE. *Agus tháing an tsean-bhuime annsin gur chaith si thart ar a muinéal é, agus thug an fear chéile clamhta faoin ngiall di . . .*

PROSPER. *Clamhta?*

BAIRBRE (*nodding*). *Faoin ngiall.* (PROSPER *looks puzzled. She continues.*) *Agus amach léi annsin arais go dti an . . . go dti an dún sidhe.*

PROSPER. *Crioch?* (*He half-closes the book.*)

BAIRBRE. *Annsin bhi na ba a tabhairt bainne aris, an caorcaorthainn faoi bhláth, agus chuile short i gceart. 'S gurab é sin eachtra na hiarlaise as Brugh na. Gealaí go nuige seo.*

PROSPER (*haltingly*). *Cé'n focal sin?*

BAIRBRE. *Cén'n focal?*

PROSPER. *Iarlais?*

BAIRBRE. *Iarlais? Sea mhanam – iarlais iarlais, deile?*

PROSPER. *Bon Dieu,* what a language. (*Shouting to garden left.*) Lee! Lee! (*He reaches out his hand for a heavy green book whose pages he turns over muttering.*) *Iarlais . . . I . . . A . . . R . . . Lee!*

    (LEE *enters from the garden to the side of the professional desk. He is a dark-haired, dark-eyed, Connemara man of about thirty, dressed in conventional grey-striped trousers, incongruously clipped for cycling, a blue collarless shirt with the sleeves rolled up and a black unbuttoned waistcoat.*)

LEE. Yes, sir.

PROSPER. What is an iarlais?

    (LEE, *looks with mingled amusement and admiration at* BAIRBRE, *who remains impassive, wrapped in her shawl.*)

LEE. An *iarlais* is a bad old thing they (*the They in this sentence is lightly and imperceptibly accented*) leaves behind them in place of a good. And that's all trish-trash and lies as you knows yourself.

---

*For a translation of this and of the other Irish phrases in the play, see Appendix.

PROSPER. Mm! Brilliantly cleared up. Thank you, Lee. Officially translated, I take it that the word *Iarlais* means Changeling?

LEE. A changeling . . . It do, sir, it do.

PROSPER (*musingly*). It do, sir, it do. I often wonder, Lee if the Irish spoken by you woebegone relics of a bygone age in these desolate mountains is on a par with the incomparable mess you have made of the language of Shakespeare. Well, I've got the story I wanted out of your female bard. Tell them to bring her some food. Be off. (*He rings the bell at her.* BAIRBRE *laughs again*). Why the hell's she laughing?

BAIRBRE. *Ora' dhiabhail, an cluigin sin! Tá s´é glan as a mheabhair.*

LEE. 'Tis the little bell you have round your neck, sir. She says 'tis the way you're clean mad.

PROSPER. Mad? Nonsense. This bell saves my lungs. Be off! *Imigh leat.*

> (BAIRBRE *bobs a courtesy and starts to go through the archway, but is stopped by* PROSPER'S *voice. She returns to* PROSPER'S *side.*)

PROSPER (*continued*). No – wait. *Fan ort!* There's a point here I want cleared up. Let's run it through. (*He turns to the beginning of his notes.*) The newly married bride in this story walks out in the moonlight on Midsummer Eve, meets the fairies, and is stolen by them under the withered rowan tree at the corner of the house. *Caorcaorthainn* is rowan tree, isn't it?

LEE. 'Tis, sir. Same as the ones outside, sir. (*He glances out of the window.*)

PROSPER. The changeling who is left in her place returns a woman bewitched, who cuts up hell with the family, kills her old father-in-law, and on the same day seduces her husband's friend, who was probably best man at her wedding.

LEE. Ah, that was a bad little one. Sir, maybe you've forgotten . . .

PROSPER. Yes, that little girl, she had a busy day. *Enfin*, she was banished by a wreath of flowers . . . (*He indicates a word in the notebook.*) Isn't that it? . . . sprinkled with salt and goat's blood . . . thrown over her neck by her old nurse and by her husband giving her . . . where is it, ah, here . . . a *clamhta faoin* something -- can't read my own damn writing – what is the word?

LEE. I wouldn't know, sir.

PROSPER. Then ask the girl.

LEE. What'll I ask her?

PROSPER. Ask her what the husband gave his wife.

LEE. *Dhé* . . . I wouldn't like to do that, sir.

PROSPER. Bawdy rattleplate. Bairbre . . .

BAIRBRE. *Sea, 'dhuine uasail?*

PROSPER. *Céard*-um-*thug*-um – oh, go on, Lee.

LEE (*to* BAIRBRE). *Céard rinne an fear chéile sa scéal leis an iarlais chur amach as an áit?*

BAIRBRE. *Clamhta maith faoin ngiall thug sé dhi.*

PROSPER. That's it. What is it in English?

LEE. He gave her a good puck in the gob, sir.

PROSPER (*snorts*). Charming. (*Making a note.*) For 'Puck in the gob' read 'Poke in the snoot'.

LEE. Ah, whatever you say yourself, sir.

PROSPER (*his hands outstretched in appreciation*). Ah! (*Making a note.*) Good! Mischievous changeling banished by salt, blood and flowers, provided by nurse; poke in the snoot supplied by loving husband. Thank you, madam, you can go. (*He rings the bell*).

LEE. *Imigh leat, Bhairbre.*

BAIRBRE. *'Soirbhigh Dia dhaoibh!* (*She bows and goes towards the archway followed by* LEE.)

PROSPER (*returning to his notes*): So, with the transformation of bride to changeling, powers of the underworld are renewed with startling results. The cows give milk again, plump hens lay punctual eggs – I wish our hens would do the same – and the withered rowan tree springs into blossom. (*He glances out of the window left*). Yes . . . oh, it's the same old theme. Nothing new. Kidnapping in order to reinforce the ebbing powers of thee underworld. A sort of psychic bargaining. Always coupled with the earth's fruition. Where does it come from, this crazy idea? (*He begins to write in his book*).

> (BAIRBRE *goes out with many lingering glances at the incomprehensible Professor.*)

LEE (*returning*). Now, sir, let me remind you . . .

PROSPER (*looking up*). Lee!

LEE. Sir?

PROSPER (*still writing*). What are your intentions regarding that young baggage?

LEE. 'Tis herself have the intentions, sir; 'tis the dowry she's lacking.

PROSPER. I see. You'd like to marry her, I think, *hein*?

LEE. Well, now – if she'd a couple of pounds, I'd take her —— (*The telephone rings*).

PROSPER (*as he takes up the receiver*): H'm! What reckless impetuous romantics you people are! (*To phone.*) Hello! Yes! Sebastian Prosper speaking: Yes. Call from London? That means trouble.

Oh, yes, I'll hold on ... (*To* LEE) ... Incidentally, Lee you are a brazen and singularly unaccomplished liar. You and that slut are obviously in love, or rather, you are in that condition of physical vigour and mental apathy which people with means describe as being in love, and people without them, ironically enough, call wanting a place of their own. What the hell am I holding this thing in my hand for? (*He brandishes the receiver – to phone.*) Hello; Yes. Sebastian Prosper speaking. Who? Bloxham and what? Fawcitt? And who, pray, are they? What? You? My agents! No, you're not. My agents are ... who are my London agents, Lee?

LEE. Bloxham and Fawcitt, sir.

PROSPER. Yes, of course, My agents, my good man, are Bloxham and Fawcitt. What? Then why didn't you say so? Well, what is it? No, I didn't get a wire.

LEE. You did, sir. 'Tis there.

PROSPER. Will you allow me to get a word in edge or any other ways? (*to phone*): Then possibly I didn't read it. A lecture tour in America? No, certainly not. My subject, Bloxham, is fairies. In the Unites States of America, that is misleading. Sorry. (*He sneezes.*)

(*Precisely at this point,* SUSAN PROSPER, *the only daughter of the doctor, comes running downstairs in a tremendous hurry and a rather wrong sort of frock.* SUSAN *is about nineteen and would appear as outwardly charming as she inwardly is, if only her hair, which should be loosely clustered about her face, were not screwed on the top of her head in a desperate effort to appear grown-up; if only someone would tell her what not to wear, and if only she were not so cruelly puzzled by life. Not that she appears puzzled by anything at the moment. She is radiantly pleased and excited, as she dashes downstairs and crosses to her father's right side, fastening her dress as she comes.*)

SUSAN. Daddy, the car's coming! It's just turned the bend at Joyce's Bridge, a huge, tomato-coloured, terribly smart thing! Oh, Daddy ... (*She kisses him and runs towards the door.*)

PROSPER (*continuing to the phone*). Will you, for your own sake, if not for mine, stop calling me 'Daddy'? (*To* SUSAN.) I repeat, I am sorry I will not go to America. (*Realising his mistake, he goes back to the receiver.*) Go away, Susan! No, I will not go to America. When I'm starving I'll ring you. Goodbye. Susan! (*He puts down the receiver and stretches out his hand to her.*) What, precisely, is the cause of this delirium?

SUSAN. Delirium? They're arriving ... they've just turned round the bend . . . of course I'm delirious! Oh, Daddy . . . isn't it marvellous?

PROSPER. Who is 'they', what is tomato-coloured, and why marvellous?

SUSAN. Cousin Robert, of course, Oh, you can't have forgotten?

PROSPER. Nonsense, you have no cousin Robert . . . Susan! come here. Come here at once. (*He rings the cow bell violently*).

SUSAN (*patiently*): But Sebastian, you invited them yourself . . . it was all settled three days ago: you *can't* have forgotten. They telegraphed and you answered it.

PROSPER. Lee, what are you standing there for like a cow watching a train? Why did you let me answer it?

LEE. 'Twas a reply paid, sir.

PROSPER. H'm! *Il est bon diplomate,* this cousin of yours. Well, what have I answered?

LEE. You put 'Come if you dare', sir.

PROSPER. Well?

SUSAN. Well . . . I changed the wording a bit, nothing very much.

PROSPER. And who are you to tamper with a masterpiece?

SUSAN. I only changed the last word. You will be nice to them both, won't you? (*She runs back to the window.*)

LEE (*gloomily*): 'Tis bad luck a man to bring a young wife to the house at all, and they in the throes of marriage.

PROSPER. Hold this sacrilegious tongue, Lee. (*He rings his bell and* SUSAN *returns to his side*). Susan, would you have your father play the hypocrite?

SUSAN. Yes, I would. I don't want them to think us peculiar. (*She comes down and perches on the arm of a chair facing* PROSPER). Just because you're French and famous and we've wandered about all over the place, there's no need for them to think we're different from other people.

PROSPER. Well, are we?

SUSAN. Oh, we are, Sebastian, we're extremely peculiar. I feel it in my bones. I'm going to do my hair up while they're here and call you Daddy, and you can get up for breakfast and stop using bad language.

PROSPER. Susan, you pain me inexpressibly. What the bloody hell are you talking about?

SUSAN. There you go, you see. Oh, of course, it's all right *en famille*, it's like fishermen in a pub dropping into Irish after hours; but in front of nice refined people it sounds lousy, honest to God it does. (*A bell rings in the outer hall*).

LEE (*springing into action*). They're upon ye!

SUSAN. There they are! Oh, come on, Daddy – Lee! Lee!

LEE. I'll go open the door, Miss Sukey. (SUSAN *hastily rearranges a flower in her hair, as* LEE *dashes out of the room*).

PROSPER. Susan! Understand this: your cousin and his new wife are your affair – I have work to do. I leave you to entertainment of your *invités*. (*He sneezes*). 'This ancient method of ridding the house of a changeling . . .'

SUSAN. Oh, Daddy, what a swine you can be!

PROSPER. Kindly remember: the greater the truth, the greater the libel.

SUSAN. Oh God, please give me patience with a sub-human father. (*He rings his bell at her and returns to his work*).

    (SUSAN *turns from him to the archway and is confronted by* ROBERT MALLAROE *and his wife* CATHERINE, *who have been shown in by* LEE *just in time to hear the last passage of arms. They look suitably astonished, or rather,* CATHERINE *does, for she is new to this sort of thing.* ROBERT, *however, a pleasant, reassuring young man, gives her a pleasant reassuring pat on the shoulder and comes boldly towards* PROSPER, *drawing his wife after him by the hand.*)

LEE (*with a clarion call*). The married couple, God bless them. (*And he leaves them to it*).

ROBERT. Well Sebastian, this is grand! Catherine, this is my uncle. My wife, Catherine. (*After an ominous pause he resolutely adds*): Well, how are you, Sebastian?

PROSPER (*without looking up*). Robert Mallaroe, as the only son . . . most fortunately . . . of my beloved wife's brother Bob, I am fond of you in a dim and bloodtied sort of fashion, but I am not pleased to see you now. (*He sneezes.*)

CATHERINE. God bless you.

ROBERT. Sebastian, this is Catherine. (PROSPER *continues to write.*)

CATHERINE. How do you do, Uncle Sebastian. (*Catherine's voice is as lovely as her face: there is no doubt about that.*)

PROSPER (*looking up in a rage that dies a sudden death as he sees her kind and beautiful eyes smiling into his*): H'm! (*He changes his glasses and stares at her a moment*). You're a very lovely creature – what the devil did you marry *him* for?

CATHERINE. He asked me to.

PROSPER. Bloody cheek. (*He returns to his work*).

SUSAN (*in great happiness*). Daddy! (*and she continues in her visitor's voice*): Isn't he too French for words? Yes, Really, Daddy. Hullo,

Cousin Robert.

ROBERT. Hullo Susan. Come on . . . give me a kiss. (ROBERT AND SUSAN *peck at each other's cheeks.*)

SUSAN. You're Catherine. How do you do?

CATHERINE. You're Susan. How do you do?

SUSAN AND CATHERINE (*Together*): I've heard so much about you . . .

PROSPER. I've heard so much about you! Of course, I did not believe a word of it. *Ah mairde!*

CATHERINE (*with appalling fluency*): *Je vous en prie, Monsieur.*

PROSPER. H'm! You understand French?

CATHERINE. Even that sort.

PROSPER. German, too, I have no doubt.

CATHERINE. German, too. Linguistically speaking, you won't have a moment's privacy if we stay.

PROSPER. Ach so, Madame Berlitz! I shall take refuge in Irish.

CATHERINE. You're safe there. I don't know a word.

ROBERT (*to* PROSPER): You'll soon learn in Connemara, She has an ear . . .

PROSPER. And a cheek . . .

CATHERINE. And a hand. (*She extends it*). Are we on the same side? Are we going to be friends?

PROSPER. What am I suppose to do with this? Bite it?

CATHERINE. If you do, God help you. (PROSPER *kisses* CATHERINE'S *hand*).

SUSAN. Don't you mind Daddy, he'll adore you after dinner.

CATHERINE. Oh, long before then.

PROSPER. *Tout est possible* . . . 'a voice calling on the name of the victim.' (*He begins to write again*).

SUSAN. Changelings. Daddy's mad on them. Changelings and Shakespeare. Funny taste for a Frenchman, isn't it? Would you like to sit down, or shall I show you your room?

CATHERINE. Well . . . (*She looks, smiling and hesitating at* ROBERT).

ROBERT. You go up, darling. I know the way.

PROSPER. Who better?

LEE (*appears with several bags*): God look down on me.

PROSPER. What the hell is all this?

LEE. There's stacks more of it west at the door. Will I bring it above?

PROSPER. H'm. Take the lad's up. I like her. Chuck my nephew's out of the window.

ROBERT. Don't you dare. I brought them for my honeymoon.

PROSPER. Out of the window.

SUSAN. Oh, Lee, I wish you'd use the back stairs . . .

LEE. *Ara,* for God's sake – sure them's broke.

SUSAN. We have a back stairs, you know, but he hates them.

PROSPER. So you're going to honeymoon with me, hein?

CATHERINE. With you – Oh . . . well I rather thought . . . with him. (*She indicates* ROBERT). But here, yes, if you'll put up with us.

PROSPER. Put up with you? But, of course! I adore matrimony. Yes, do stay. Plastically, at any rate, you have many points. Your head's superb. I hope, Madame, that you are not one of those pampered, feather-brained young things (*He unties his tie*) who, like me nephew, here, seems to think nothing of upsetting the orderly ways of a household (*His shirt begins to come off*) where there is serious work to be done, who have no reverence for the most ordinary observances of family life (*He wrenches himself free of his sleeveless singlet*) and who seems to imagine there is a virtue in kicking over the traces of convention to an extent that is beyond the limits of common decency. (*His trousers are half off; he notices Catherine's amusement.*) What are you laughing at?

SUSAN. Daddy!

ROBERT. Hey!

PROSPER. I am more than adequately clothed, thank you. (*He steps out of his trousers and stands clad in shorts and white shoes.*) I now go down to bathe. If you care to join me, you can. Not you, Idleness, your wife. (*He goes through the garden doors.*)

SUSAN. Don't you mind Daddy. He's not really eccentric (LEE *begins to gather the baggage together*) you know – just a child of nature. Yes, that's what Daddy is.

CATHERINE. He's wonderful. Come along, Susan. (SUSAN *and* CATHERINE *begins to ascend the stairs.* LEE *is still gathering the bags.*)

SUSAN. Lee, hurry up with those things.

CATHERINE. Here he comes again.

PROSPER (*reappearing*). Lee! Am I to walk like Adam through my own beautiful garden? My dressing-gown, quickly!

LEE (*taking a dressing-gown from a chair at the desk*). Musha, how modest you are.

SUSAN. Daddy, go away and swim. Come along Catherine.

LEE (*shouting after them as he helps* PROSPER *into the dressing-gown*). The baggage'll be up after ye – Oh my God, your stomach's fierce.

PROSPER. I beg your pardon?

LEE. Ah 'tis slack as a turkey's neck. How it now the way I showed you – hup! (*He hits the Professorial stomach a sharp whack.*)

PROSPER. Lee, I am not a horse.

LEE. No, sir.

PROSPER. Take these bagatelles out of my sight and get back to your kitchen or wherever you belong . . .

LEE. Oh, begob, I'll get back where I belong sir. And I want to tell you one thing: you're in a desperate cranky old mood today sir, God forgive you. (*He takes up the rugs and the bags and begins to mount the stairs.*) Yourself knows the story in this house, Mr Robert; working on my two feet from morning to night I do be: I declare to my God I'm bandy-legged with the work, sure the Devil and Dr Foster wouldn't satisfy him! But I know what I'll do, sir. I've made my mind up, I'll give in my notice and I'll go off to America and begob when I'm gone they'll bloody well miss me, I can tell you that! (*And he is gone.*)

PROSPER. Silent O Moyle, be the roar of thy waters. (*He blows his nose.*) I've caught a real stinker.

ROBERT. That's a good bit of colloquial English for a Frenchman.

PROSPER. I was born in Alsace. I am a goose of Strasbourg. We are bi-lingual there like the people here. It helps with a third language. (*He sits on the side of the desk and lights a pipe.*)

ROBERT (*crossing to the mantlepiece where he finds a box of cigarettes*). May I?

PROSPER. Nothing I could say would stop you. (*As he nods and lights his own pipe.*) Tell me, Robert . . . where did you find that lovely creature?

ROBERT. Paris. I told you in my letter.

PROSPER. Never read letters. And what was she doing in Paris?

ROBERT. Acting.

PROSPER. Who to?

ROBERT. Oh, audiences.

PROSPER. Why must English people go to France to act?

ROBERT. She's not English, she's Irish.

PROSPER. H'm?

PROSPER. My dear Robert, in Paris the difference between Rathgar and Pimlico is a hair's breadth. Is she any good?

ROBERT. I don't think so. That's how we met . . . You see, I gave her a filthy notice for 'Lady from the Sea.' She smacked my face with a swing door in the Ritz Bar, and a week later I married her. It was an accident, of course. The swing door, I mean.

PROSPER. Ah. No mechanical sense. Women never have. So you are a journalist now, eh? You fail at folklore and philosophy – you take refuge in fiction. And it all ends in matrimony all over me.

ROBERT. It was her idea. She wanted to see Connemara – and to

88

meet you, incidentally. Why, God knows! I suppose it was that book of yours.

PROSPER. Which one?

ROBERT. 'Superstition and the Time Theory.'

PROSPER. Oh that. (*The grandfather clock whirrs softly.*) Ah, that . . . That reminds me (*He picks up his towel from a chair and moves towards the garden*): I'm going to bathe.

ROBERT. With that cold?

PROSPER. Soak it out of me.

ROBERT. Do you mind if I come down with you?

PROSPER. Of course . . . (*As they move away together*): The loss of the sense of time . . . it can account you know for so many of these so-called visionary experiences in places like this. Look at our servant here – Lee – he is terrified of the idea of anyone bringing a bride to this house. Now if, as you may imagine . . .

(*They have gone. The clock begins to chime. The amber colour sunshine shifts on the wall; the shadows deepen. As the clock reaches its fifth stroke,* EMMA HAMILTON, *an elderly woman in decent black and carrying a small black bag and a large book bound in brown paper, appears from the hall and trips with a sort of brisk hesitation into the room*).

HAMILTON (*seeing the departing figures in the garden*): Well, I must say!

(*Hearing the clock finishing nine strokes, she compares the time it tells to that of her own wrist-watch, and comes to the obvious conclusion that as her own watch is never wrong, the clock must be.*)

Fast! ts, ts, ts!

(*She leaves the brown paper book on the sideboard, turns the hands of the clock back to three minutes to nine, and closed the clock case. As she does this,* LEE *descends the stairs.*)

LEE (*aghast at the presence of an unknown female*): Musha, God be good to us!

HAMILTON. What? (*She turns and sees* LEE). Ah!

LEE. Who's that I see?

HAMILTON. My name is Hamilton – Emma Hamilton.

LEE (*coming down the stairs*): Well, begob you don't look like it.

HAMILTON. If you're referring to Lord Nelson, we're not related. Not remotely, we're not.

LEE. But who are you at all?

HAMILTON. I'm Miss Beatty's – I mean Mrs Mallaroe's maid.

LEE. And what were you doing with that clock?

HAMILTON. Putting it right. It was fast. Most misleading.

LEE. Well, you've no right to touch that. That's an old ancient clock.

HAMILTON. H'm! That's no reason for it to go fast. There's a time for everything.

LEE. Ah musha, there's no time at all in this house. (*As if to give the lie to this statement, the clock strikes nine again.*)

HAMILTON. There you are, you see. Nine to the tick. Now we can begin.

LEE. Begin what?

HAMILTON. To arrange things. Where am I expected to sleep?

LEE. You're not expected at all, sleeping or waking. (*He crosses to the desk and begins to fold up the Professor's clothes.*) And I want to tell you there's going to be holy murder when himself finds out about you.

LEE. Who's himself?

LEE. The Professor, who else?

HAMILTON. Ah, Professor Prosper – folklorist and psycho-something or other. I seen his photo once in the 'Bystander'. Where am I expected to sleep?

LEE. Ah, he's world-wide. And all for nothing. Do you know what he does be doing? Every bit of an old lying story he'd hear out of the country people, he'll be speckling it down. And then it do be printed out in a book. And the big bucks in London and New York do be giving him money – ay, and good money – out of the head of that. Aha! we do be filling up his two ears with all the trash and lies, about dreams and *piseogs*.

HAMILTON. What ogs?

LEE (*folding up a tie*): *Piseogs*. Them's superstitions. And spells and charms like would raise the hair on your head, my girl.

HAMILTON. I knew I shouldn't like Ireland. (*She shivers.*) We used to drop over sometimes to stay before Miss Catherine went on the stage. Primitive. That's what it was. Just like the people. And that was County Wicklow which is Piccadilly Circus, as you might say, compared to Connemara.

LEE. Miss Catherine, it is? Let me tell you 'tis a pity she came to this house at all the way she is.

HAMILTON. Why?

LEE. 'Tis bad luck, bringing a young bride here. Do you see them trees?

HAMILTON. Those blasted ones?

LEE. Never mind the name. Them was withered through herself coming back as a bride. I'm telling you.

HAMILTON. Who?

LEE. Herself, up there.

HAMILTON. What did her coming back as a bride have to do with the trees withering?

LEE. When a rowan tree do wither 'tis a sign their blood is thin. Do you see, now?

HAMILTON. Whose blood?

LEE. Them as lives in the air, or down under the ground maybe. Their blood begins to fall, you see, and if they sees a new-married bride, they'll try for to get a hold of her. For the sake of her sweet blood, do you understand me, now? One small speckle of her blood and she dancing with them will give new life to themselves and new life to their trees, the way they'll break out in blossom again. But if they fail to get her ——

HAMILTON. Well?

LEE. There comes the last blight on the trees . . . Ach, 'tis all lies, of course.

HAMILTON. You give me the creeps, you do. (*She pulls herself together.*) Where am I expected to sleep?

LEE. You'll get your sleep. We'll pop you in along with Bartley's Ellen Laith.

HAMILTON. What's Bartley's Ellen Lee?

LEE. 'Tis Irish. Ellen Laith means Grey Nelly.

HAMILTON. Well, I'm not going to be popped in along with Grey Nelly or Grey anyone else. Where's my mistress?

LEE. She's above.

HAMILTON. Above what?

LEE (*compassionately*): Ah, you're no better nor a Zulu, you creature.

SUSAN (*appearing on the stairs, followed by* CATHERINE): . . . and this part of the house was built earlier, you see – oh, there you are Lee. Oh! (*She sees* HAMILTON.)

CATHERINE. Hamilton! I'd forgotten all about you – I'm so sorry. Susan, this is Hamilton, who takes care of me; this is Miss Prosper, Hamilton.

SUSAN. How do you do?

HAMILTON. Thank you, Miss, I'm sure.

LEE. Ah! 'Tis the devil's own work man trying to get her some place to sleep. Will I pop her in with Bartley's Nelly, Miss Sukey?

CATHERINE. Bartley's Nelly?

HAMILTON (*joylessly*): Bartley's *Grey* Nelly, Miss.

SUSAN. There's a top room! Lee – show Miss, Miss ——

LEE. I will, Miss. (*He crosses to the stairs and glances back at*

HAMILTON.) God between us and all harm. (*He blesses himself piously.*) Folly me.

CATHERINE. You can finishing unpacking for me, too. Hammy. Lee will show you the room.

HAMILTON. Yes, Miss. (*She glances round the darkening room.*) Quite like Tolstoy, isn't it? The atmosphere, I mean?

LEE. Come on out of that, you wild devil. (*They go up.*)

CATHERINE. Well – that's that.

SUSAN. Fancy bringing a maid about wherever you go. You are lucky, Catherine.

CATHERINE. You try bringing Hamilton about wherever you go. No, you're the lucky one, Susan.

SUSAN. Me?

CATHERINE. Living here. In a place like this. It's wonderful. (*She goes to the window and looks out. Dusk is falling.*) It's the sort of place I've dreamed about. Often . . . what are those trees out there?

SUSAN. What? Oh, those are rowans. They withered the year before Lucy was drowned. They used to be lovely, Sebastian says.

CATHERINE. Oh! (*Looking at the portrait over the fire*): Lucy was your mother, wasn't she?

SUSAN. Yes. Wasn't she lovely? I wish I were like her. Do you know what the people here believe about her being drowned?

CATHERINE. No, what?

SUSAN. They believe the spirits stole her – the fairies, you know. (*A pause.*) Silly fools. It's because of this house being built on a ring.

CATHERINE. A fairy ring?

SUSAN. Yes, a bit of ground sacred to the earth spirits. The rowans began to wither, you see, and the people thought that was a sign.

CATHERINE. Of what?

SUSAN. That the fairies wanted to destroy the house, and that they dragged Lucy into the water so she could help them to get the place back to themselves, and then the rowans would flower again.

CATHERINE. But do people here, really believe that?

SUSAN. Oh yes. They're as superstitious, you wouldn't believe.

CATHERINE. They look so bare and wintry – starved somehow, poor things. They should be in full flower. Were you born here, Susan?

SUSAN. Oh yes. Upstairs. Yes, it's June now. This is the time for the rowan blossom. Catherine, what lovely things you've got. Is that from Paris?

CATHERINE. M'm? This? Oh, no, London. (*She turns reluctantly from the window.*)

SUSAN. I wish you'd give me some hints. I know my clothes are like mud. But what can I do in a place like Bruenagally? We did an American tour last year. Sebastian was lecturing and he took me along, and in Philadelphia, a lady asked who was the girl that looked like the family Bible, and it was me. Wasn't that awful? And not one of the men made a single pass at me. I was raging. I love men, too.

CATHERINE. Do you?

SUSAN. Sebastian says I'm an oversexed hag. Do you think I am?

CATHERINE. No, Susan, I think you're very sweet.

SUSAN. Its rotten being a famous man's daughter. People treat Sebastian like a monument and me like the old woman who keeps the keys. I adore being with him, of course, but I would love to get married. (*Pause.*) Catherine, can you keep a secret?

CATHERINE. Cross hearts.

SUSAN. Then I'll tell you something. I know a man I might be able to ensnare.

CATHERINE (*laughing*): You siren. What's he like?

SUSAN. That's the trouble. He's deadly.

CATHERINE. Oh dear. That's a snag. And do you love him?

SUSAN. Madly. Madly. With every fibre of my what do you call it.

CATHERINE. Being.

SUSAN. That's it. And I'm sure he loves me, but he's too well brought up to say so.

CATHERINE. What does he look like?

SUSAN. Pink. With lovely teeth. And I do love him. Really. Truly. He's just right for me.

CATHERINE. Darling. (*She is beginning to understand and like Susan.*) You're really serious about him.

SUSAN (*with passionate sincerity*): Yes, I am. Because he doesn't make me feel inadequate, you see. His name's Charles Lushington-Carew, and he lives in an enormous house near Lettertrack and he has horses and a yacht and two sisters with photos in 'The Tatler' and one of them uses Pond's Vanishing. And she's married to an English Peer. And they have their meals regularly and everything, oh it's heavenly. Well, this is the secret. I've invited him here to stay and signed the letter Sebastian. He'll be here for lunch tomorrow.

CATHERINE. You what?

SUSAN. Well, you see, he'd never have come for me, so I committed forgery. I'm an expert forger.

CATHERINE. Susan!

SUSAN. What's the matter?

CATHERINE. Well – I mean – oh dear! You have been neglected, haven't you?

SUSAN. I suppose I have. (*She glances at the picture over the mantlepiece.*) That's having no mother to guide me, you see. But I had to do something. How did you hook Robert, Cousin Catherine?

CATHERINE (*smiling*): I shut him in a swing door.

SUSAN. There you are, you see. We all have our methods. (*She runs to the desk and writes.*) Come and watch me copy this! 'Changelings: salt; goat's blood; wild flowers; Sebastian Prosper.' There! could you tell the difference?

CATHERINE. No, it's incredible. (*Her voice, however, is a little shocked by the promptings of good behaviour.*) I wonder what Uncle Sebastian will say when your young man arrives?

SUSAN. Oh, there'll be murder. But he'll calm down. Sebastian's all right. Let's have a cocktail, shall we? (*She goes to a table covered with drinks, books and glasses.*) There's some booze somewhere – yes, here we are!

CATHERINE. Clever girl, I'd love a cocktail. (*She glances at the notes on the desk.*)

SUSAN. If you mix everything up, it's a cocktail, isn't it? (*She is wildly pouring drinks into a silver shaker.*) Brandy, gin, Cointreau – don't know what this one is. (*She pours it in all the same.*) Vodka! We'll be absolutely debauched. (*She continues her work.*)

CATHERINE (*reading*): 'When the distant voice calls on the name of the victim . . .'

SUSAN. What? Oh! Are you interested in Daddy's stuff?

CATHERINE. Mm? Oh, heavens, yes. I'd never given a thought to psychic things you know, till I read his book.

SUSAN (*still shaking cocktails*): Psychic. You'd better not let him hear you saying that. He doesn't believe a word of it – not the psychic part, anyway. He thinks it's all nerves. He believes that people who lose all sense of time, see visions, hear voices, and all that sort of thing, are neurotics. You should read his 'Experiments in Vision and Neurosis'. There, (*she hands* CATHERINE *a drink.*) There's a beauty . . . I feel like an adventuress drinking cocktails with an actress. Here's to my darling new cousin.

CATHERINE. Here's to mine. (*They smile at one another and drink.*) Good God, what have you put in this?

SUSAN. Everything I could find. Is it wrong?

CATHERINE. Wrong? It's like the Last Trumpet. Well, goodbye! (*She drinks again.*)

(*The clock strikes.*)

SUSAN. Sebastian thinks time has a lot to do with vision, you know. He thinks time stops in the minds who are having visions and that what seems to take ages to happen, really goes by in a flash . . . Catherine, I wish you'd tell me what to do with my hair. (*She twists her head about in front of the mirror.*)

CATHERINE. 'Collective Hypnosis'. I remember. But how could time stop for a lot of people, all at once?

SUSAN. I don't know, but it does.

CATHERINE. Of course you could believe anything at all in a place like this.

SUSAN. If you lived in a place like this, you wouldn't want to think about time-theories. You'd want to think about clothes and theatres and scandals. You know, actresses and things. That's why it's so thrilling having you here (*A gong is beaten off-stage somewhere.*) That's dinner. Lee . . . Lee!

LEE (*coming downstairs, followed by* HAMILTON): I'm coming, I'm coming, sure God knows I've only the one pair of feet, haven't I? What is it you want now, Miss?

SUSAN. Dinner's ready. Will you get into a coat and dish it up? (*She drains her glass.*)

LEE. I will, to be sure, why not? Come along, Emma.

HAMILTON (*after a glance directed just over his head*): Everything is unpacked, Miss. I've done my level best. Is there anything else you require?

CATHERINE. No, thanks, Hammy. You settled in?

HAMILTON. Oh, yes, thank you, Miss. And I've got a view from my window. Some blasted trees and a small lake with two gentlemen bathing in it. Quite picturesque in its way. The lake, I mean. Good evening, Miss (*she gives* LEE *a rather dreadful glare as she crosses to the archway.*) That clock's fast again. Excuse me Miss. (*She goes.*)

LEE (*gazing after her*): If you'd hair on your chest that one'd blow it off, wouldn't she? Will she be eating the same food as ourselves, Miss Sukey?

SUSAN. Of course she will, you blithering lump.

LEE. I'd be in dread would she snap a bite out of me. I would, honest to God. (LEE *goes out stealthily.*)

SUSAN. What are you laughing at, Catherine?

CATHERINE. I don't know. I think it's the cocktail.

(SEBASTIAN'S *voice is heard outside, saying: 'And popular belief is always distorted . . .'.*)

95

SUSAN. Here they come! (*She rises and switches on a light by the fire.*) Now, not a word about Charles, Promise!

CATHERINE. CHARLES? Oh, your young man, of course. No, not a word! Cross hearts. (ROBERT and PROSPER *enter together.* ROBERT, *his coat over his arm is tying his tie as he crosses to the fireplace.* PROSPER *switches on the main lights at the archway.*)

ROBERT. Yes, I grasp that, but why the spite and malice? (*He reaches* CATHERINE.) Hullo, darling! Missed me?

CATHERINE. Terribly!

ROBERT. Forgive me, my lamb – forgive me, Susan – I'm red-hot on Sebastian's trail. Now, tell me why, Sebastian? Why?

PROSPER. You want a scientific explanation, Monsieur. *Bon*, I give it you. Excuse. (*He blows his nose with great thoroughness.*) The so-called changling of European folklore shows spiteful and malicious characteristics because, in reality, the temporary neurosis affecting the patient created by emotional stimulation and other causes, deadens the surface consciousness in charge but the animal self.

ROBERT. And the patient behaves like a person bewitched.

PROSPER. Precisely. As if she were somebody else. There's nothing supernatural about the damn thing at all. There's not one single shred of evidence of any force at work outside the ego of the patient himself.

CATHERINE. The patient?

PROSPER. And the stoppage of the sense of time in his brain. And sometimes, in rare cases, in the brains of those who share his hallucination.

ROBERT. You mean that time can stop for a whole group of people? All at once?

PROSPER. Yes. Rarely of course. But it can. One second suspended —— (*He holds up his finger.*)

SUSAN (*hoarsely*). Don't mind him, have another drink.

PROSPER (*to no one in particular*). You can give me one, too. Is this clear?

ROBERT (*dubiously*). Mm . . . but you've not accounted for the other phenomena in these cases; hens that stop laying eggs, cows that give no milk, flowering trees that wither. ——

PROSPER. Because they are never true. Or, if they are, neither I nor the author of the Golden Bough have come across one single case in which they were not obvious coincidence or the glibbest invention. (CATHERINE *hands him a drink.*) Thank you. Flowering trees, my aunt Fanny! (*He drinks.*) My God! Are you trying to kill me, you seductive hussy?

96

LEE (*appearing in the archway with a gong*). Your dinners boiled!

ROBERT (*after a second's stupefied silence*). Time for me to have a cocktail, Susan?

PROSPER. Cocktail! It's a bomb!

> (LEE *beats a tattoo on the gong.* PROSPER *rises and offers* CATHERINE *his arm, gathering up his dressing-gown to display two well-developed Alsatian calves.*)

SUSAN. Daddy! You can't sit down at the table with those legs!

PROSPER. Can't I? Watch me! Madame! (*He regally continues his walk with* CATHERINE *towards the archway.*)

SUSAN. Oh you're so mean, you might put your trousers on.

PROSPER. You have been drinking.

SUSAN. Well, if I have, who drove me to it?

ROBERT (*after a sip of his cocktail*). Crikey! Who made this? Lucrezia Borgia?

SUSAN. Oh, put them on, there's a darling. (*She whispers to him*): Do let's be like other people.

PROSPER (*breaking from* CATHERINE *and turning to the stairs*). Oh all right, all right – start without me – I hate soup anyway.

LEE. 'Tisn't soup at all, sir, 'tis some old class of patty.

> (*He goes out, beating meditatively on the gong.* SUSAN *switches out the light at the fire.*)

PROSPER. Look! A full moon rises. We celebrate the Eve of Midsummer. (*He goes upstairs.*)

SUSAN. There! Now he's messed up the partners.

ROBERT. Oh, we'll struggle in somehow. I say, you can put a sting in your cocktail, can't you? What do you call it? 'Journey's End'?

SUSAN. No, Bruenagally Brew.

CATHERINE. What's Bruenagally?

ROBERT. It's the name of the house, of course.

CATHERINE. Yes, but what does it mean?

SUSAN (*switching off the main light and leaving the room in moonlight*). The Fortress of the Moon.

CATHERINE. The moon . . . (*She takes a step slowly to the garden.*)

SUSAN. No, this way Catherine. (*They go through the archway.*)

CATHERINE (*with an effort*). Of course . . . (*They go out.*)

ROBERT (*outside*). Same old room.

CATHERINE'S Voice. And candlelight! That's perfect.

> (*The clock strikes the half. The big room is growing bright with moonlight.* BAIRBRE *emerges from the archway and makes for the garden door as* LEE *comes from the dining room with a salver in his hand.*)

LEE. *A Bhairbre! A Bhairbre ni Mhainin, bhfuil tú 'dhul abhaile?*

BAIRBRE. *Níl go fóilleach a mhanam. Thoir i dteach Mháire fhanfas mé anocht. Beidh mé 'dhul thart le tóin a' ti.*

> (CATHERINE *comes out of the dining room and crosses to the sofa. She takes up a little gold bag she had left behind and is about to return when she sees* LEE.)

CATHERINE (*with a little start*). Oh!

BAIRBRE (*in one breath*). Hullo goodnight, *a mham!*

> (*She runs out through the garden.*)

CATHERINE. Goodnight.

LEE. Were you looking for something, Miss?

CATHERINE. Just my bag, that's all. (*A bell rings in the dining room.*)

LEE. That'll be for the fish. Ah, the way they do eat here, Miss, dribbles and drabbles, 'twould put you astray I declare to God. (*He turns to go.*)

CATHERINE. Who was that little girl?

LEE. That's young Bairbre Mannin, Miss. She do be telling old stories like to himself.

CATHERINE. Stories about —— ?

LEE. All lies, Miss. Sure Bruenagally's full of lies. (*He points to* PROSPER'S *notes.*) Like that one there, Miss. All lies.

(*A thread of music is heard far away.* CATHERINE *looks up and then round at the picture of Lucy.*)

LEE. Is there anything wrong, Miss?

CATHERINE. I thought I – no, no, thanks so much.

LEE. Thank you, Miss. (*He goes out, with a glance to her over his shoulder.*)

CATHERINE. Bruenagally —— Midsummer ——

> (*She turns from the picture and goes towards the dining room, when suddenly a small voice calls from far away, 'Catherine!' She turns sharply, and whispers*):

Yes?

> (*The voice calls again, 'Catherine!' The sound of music increases.* CATHERINE *stands looking from the garden to the picture and back again as the silver light falls upon her. The voice calls again, 'Catherine! Catherine!' in accents that are at once mocking and dangerously seductive. Then with an effort, she draws herself together and almost runs into the dining room. The music continues.*)

# CURTAIN

# Scene II

SCENE: *The same. Three hours later.* CATHERINE *is sitting on the sofa by the fire with her feet up and* SUSAN *hovers near.* ROBERT *is walking up and down.*

SUSAN (*after a pause*). You look heavenly. I wish I looked pale and romantic when I felt lousy . . . I mean when I'm overwrought. I go bright purple, and my face hangs down to my feet. Honest to God it does.

ROBERT. That's your liver.

SUSAN. That's what Sebastian says. I think it's being thwarted. What would you do if you had dewlaps, Catherine?

CATHERINE (*lazily*). Commit suicide.

PROSPER'S Voice (*off-stage, from dining room*). Susan! Lee! Are you going to bring me that bloody brandy or must I send out a scout party for it?

SUSAN. *Komm' gleich!* That means 'Keep your shirt on' in German. I picked it up in Dublin in a restaurant called the Unicorn.

PROSPER (*off-stage*). Susan!

SUSAN. Coming, you irascible old brute! I've a good mind to make a clean breast of it, about Charles. He can sleep on it, then. Yes, I'll tell him now. Pray for me! (*She runs out.*)

CATHERINE. I'm feeling rather guilty.

ROBERT. Why?

CATHERINE. Isn't this where he writes?

ROBERT. Don't you worry about Sebastian. Darling, are you really feeling all right?

CATHERINE. Of course I am. (*But it isn't quite true.*)

ROBERT. Not sorry we came?

CATHERINE. Oh no. (*Her eyes wander round the room.*) Yes . . . Oh, Robert.

ROBERT. What is it?

CATHERINE. Nothing. I'm glad to see you there, that's all.

99

ROBERT. Paris, London, Holyhead, Dublin. Only four places. I want to make love to you all over the world.

CATHERINE. Please do.

ROBERT. Happy with me?

CATHERINE. You know I am.

ROBERT. Say it.

CATHERINE. I'm happy with you . . . my love.

ROBERT (*leaning back, his head on her breast*). Being in love makes your brain addled. The same old things we say over and over again. Millions of lovers, ever since time began, I suppose. 'Do you love me?' 'Yes.' 'Then say it.' 'Yes, I love you.' 'And I love you. Yes . . . ' Addled. Oh, isn't it grand to be addled! Our generation's so wise, knows everything, does everything, we understand all the abstractions of love and call it chemical reaction, suppression, repression, obsession, depression; we talk it and write it; we're witty and wise and fact-facing and hard-headed – until it touches us . . . And then what do we say?

CATHERINE. I love you.

ROBERT. Right first time! (*They laugh.*) Catherine! (*They kiss. Suddenly she begins to cry.*) What is it? Darling, what's wrong? Tell me . . . Sweetheart, you're not thinking about that . . . that there past of yours, are you? Don't think about it . . . Never again, never . . . (*She clings to him.*) I know. You had an affair before you met me. Before you even crushed me in the swing door. Well, you've told me, haven't you? And I haven't crushed *you* in a swing door, have I. What are affairs? I'm not an affair. I'm your husband. For life. Look at me. (*She stares at him. He blows her nose. But she is far away.*) Better?

CATHERINE. Keep close to me. Don't go away. Don't let me go away from you.

ROBERT. Darling – you're shaking like a —— What is it? Tell me.

CATHERINE. Something happened tonight ——

ROBERT. Here.

CATHERINE. Yes. Just after dinner began, you remember, I left the table to get my bag? Remember?

(*Somehow the mention of her bag comforts her: it is familiar anyway.*)

ROBERT. Well?

CATHERINE. It was half dark in here and I saw that man – what's his name – Lee – and there was a girl, a country girl in a shawl . . . And then they went out and I was alone and the moonlight was coming in from the garden. Falling on the floor like silver . . . And suddenly I thought I heard a voice calling . . .

HAMILTON (*calling – off-stage*). Miss Catherine! (HAMILTON *appears at the archway, a tray of drinks in her hands.*)

CATHERINE. No! . . .

HAMILTON. Oh, there you are, Miss.

ROBERT. Sh! Hamilton, what is it?

HAMILTON. Beverages, sir. Pardon the intrusion, I'm sure, Miss, but I didn't think that heathen was in a fit state to bring them in to you. Not the way he is now.

ROBERT. Oh, Lee.

HAMILTON. That's him, sir. (*She puts down the tray.*)

ROBERT (*pouring a brandy for* CATHERINE). What's wrong with him?

HAMILTON (*darkly*). We'll call it high spirits, sir. Yes . . . (*Having approved of the tray, she goes towards the Professorial desk.*) Can't find my volume, sir. Ulysses. Mislaid it – most provoking. Anything else you require, Miss Catherine?

CATHERINE. No, thanks, Hammy.

HAMILTON. It's a good thing that you both just take toast for breakfast, Miss. There's not an egg in the place. The hens won't lay, I'm told.

ROBERT. Oh?

HAMILTON. No, they won't lay. Like Bernard Shaw. St. Joan, I mean. And the cows are dry, if you'll pardon the expression. Mm . . . You look pinched yourself, Miss Pasty. You ought to be in bed.

CATHERINE (*with infinite patience*). Yes, I'm going soon. Goodnight, Hammy.

HAMILTON. On your own you ought to go, too. That's the worst of being married; never a wink 'till you're too worn out to want it. Look at Catherine of Russia. Oh, well. (*She plumps up the cushions and turns to go as* PROSPER *enters, with* SUSAN, *from the dining room.*)

PROSPER. On the contrary, you forger of your father's name, I shall be delighted to welcome your clandestine lover.

HAMILTON. Goodnight, Miss. (*She turns, and* PROSPER *sees her for the first time.*)

PROSPER. Well, Really! (*She trips up the stairs.*)

PROSPER. What, please, was that?

CATHERINE. That's Hamilton – she's my maid – I'm so sorry she startled you.

PROSPER. Startled me? She has unmanned me. (*He sneezes.*) Hamilton! Her Christian name, no doubt, is Emma?

CATHERINE. Well, yes, it is.

PROSPER. Emma Hamilton! It's blasphemy.

101

ROBERT. Sebastian, I'm dreadfully sorry, I do wish you had read my letter.

PROSPER. I have no leisure for light reading.

ROBERT. No; you see, I told you in it, I thought we'd be less trouble if we brought Catherine's maid,

PROSPER. A maid! (CATHERINE *has poured him a drink from the cognac bottle; she now offers it to him.*) Thank you, my dear, I need it. You call that goblin, that emanation from the combined imaginings of Kraft-Ebbing, Baudelaire and Edgar Allen Poë – a maid? (*The clock strikes three-quarters.* CATHERINE *sways and falls back in a faint. They crowd about her.*) What's wrong?

SUSAN. Catherine!

CATHERINE. I'm sorry – I'm dizzy or something . . . Uncle Sebastian, do you mind if I go up to bed?

ROBERT. Come on, you're worn out.

SUSAN. Of course, if you're tired, Catherine ——

PROSPER. Yes, you are tired. Run along. But don't let the Bitch of Endor upon you. (*He stops, troubled.*) Goodnight, run along . . . Now don't fan about there like a broody hen. And don't try to kiss me: I am of a passionate disposition and I reek with disease. (*He sneezes.*) Robert, take her away. (*He crosses to desk and takes up some papers.*)

CATHERINE. Goodnight.

ROBERT. Come on, darling. (*He leads her upstairs.*) We'll talk.

SUSAN (*regretfully*). I thought we'd – oh well . . . I hope you'll be all right in the morning.

CATHERINE. Oh, I'll be marvellous in the morning. (*She and* ROBERT *have gone.*)

PROSPER (*with ruthless imitation*). 'Oh, I'll be marvellous in the morning. Bla – bla – bla.' What a generation. Worse than my own. (*He walks across the room and pours himself a drink.*) My little Miranda, your father, Prosper, wishes to review this situation.

SUSAN. Oh dear!

PROSPER. Do not look resigned. It's not becoming. My work, Susan, is interrupted by these guests. My servant, Lee, is drunk.

SUSAN. Is Lee stocious again? I begged him not to.

PROSPER. He tells me it is because this is St. John's Eve, so he must celebrate. I am relieved that this is only one Saint's Eve instead of All Saints' Day. Nevertheless, I am distracted from my writing; I call for a cognac, then my unique daughter informs me she has become a forger and has invited my future son-in-law to lunch tomorrow. This is what we may call a nice bloody mess. Hein?

102

SUSAN. No, it's not. You'll be used to Catherine tomorrow, and when I'm off your hands, you'll love it. You've often told me all you wanted was to see me settled down with plenty of table cloths and sheets.

PROSPER. Ah, you are so like your mother sometimes, you bad girl. (*He embraces her. They cling to each other for a moment.*) One never gets used to people going away. Never. (*A pause.*) (*He speaks in a changed tone.*) This Charles, you like him, hein?

SUSAN. Yes, I do like him. And I love him as well. I swear it. That's a good thing, isn't it, Daddy? To like the person you love?

PROSPER. Yes, it's good, and it is not common. So, you love him, do you?

SUSAN. For ever and ever and ever. Hopelessly. Hopelessly.

PROSPER. For ever and ever? Yes . . . Hopelessly, no.

SUSAN. Well, that depends on you.

PROSPER. Of course it is ridiculous for you to marry Charles. Yet, perhaps it is perfect. He is a bloody fool, but he is a charming bloody fool. I think. He will give you the life you like. And I will give you a dowry and everything *comme-il-faut.* You are all right. Your manners are lousy, but this is, I think, my fault. Goodnight, Mademoiselle. I adore you. (*He kisses her hand and crosses to his desk.*) Hop it to bed.

SUSAN. *Bon soir,* papa. (*She runs off upstairs.*)

PROSPER (*muttering as he cons his notes*). 'The precise moment of metamorphosis from human being into changling. Does the change from mortal into this scum and froth of immortality begin at the moment when the patient imagines he hears the summoning voice calling him by name, or during the walk into the night air that so frequently accompanies the elaborate self-deception of his adventure.' (*The clock strikes twelve; a light is switched on in the outer hall.*) 'The scum and froth of immortality,' that's not bad . . . 'It is certain that most of the subjects of this particular hallucination believe themselves to be met in the moonlight by —— '

LEE (*entering in an obviously though not excessively bibulous mood*). Will I close up the house, sir?

PROSPER. Shut up.

LEE. I will to be sure, why not. (*He crosses to the garden door, singing.*)

    'Always close the house at night,
      For if you don't you'll get a fright . . .'

PROSPER. I said, 'shut up.'

LEE. Amn't I shutting up as fast as I can? Will I bring up ——

PROSPER. Shut up your mouth, not the house.

LEE. Oh, yes, sir.

PROSPER (*reading*). '. . . met in the moonlight by certain creatures of the underworld, who . . .' What are you standing there for?

LEE (*who has arrived at the small table by the fire and is fascinated by the bottles he sees there.*) Would it be any harm, sir?

PROSPER. '. . . whose purpose would appear to be the replenishment of their own ebbing powers . . .'

LEE. No harm, sir, thank you kindly. (*He fills a glass with great care and begins to drink.*)

PROSPER. '. . . and whose recovery can only be effected by the infusion of stolen human energies.'

LEE. Now, what in the name of God does that mean? 'Infusing of human energies'?

PROSPER. When your friends, the elementals – the gentry – steal a human person, why do you think they do it?

LEE (*after a gloomy pause*). That's their own business, isn't it? (*He drinks again.*)

PROSPER. Yes, but what you people believe about them is my business, do you see.

LEE. Believe, is it? Sure I don't believe in them at all. Don't you know as well as I knows myself the likes of that is only for old ones and childer. Is it me believe in the gentry? Ha! (*A chair or something is knocked over in the room above.*) Oh, merciful God, did you hear that, sir?

PROSPER. Yes, I have heard a chair, probably hurled at the head of Mr Robert Mallaroe by a not unjustifiably exasperated wife —— (*He rises, sorting his papers.*) Go to bed, Lee.

LEE. Ah, do you think would it only be a bit of decent scrapping, sir?

PROSPER. Go to bed, Lee. You have wasted long enough my time (LEE *spits abjectly in the palm of his left hand, dips the forefinger and little finger of his right therein, and crooks them over his left shoulder.*) And close the garden door, last night you have forgotten.

LEE. I will, and I'll wind the clock, sir.

PROSPER. Then wind it, Goblin, wind it. Let time march on, it must. (*He is halfway up the stairs when he collides with* HAMILTON *on her way down in a highly respectable dressing-gown.*) Ah!

HAMILTON. Oh, I beg your pardon, sir! (*He crosses her.*) Oh, dear! Bad luck to cross on the stairs, so they say. Excuse me, I'm sure.

PROSPER. What have the stairs got to do with it? Out damn spot! (*He goes.*)

104

HAMILTON (*as* LEE *begins to wind the clock*). 'Fair thoughts and happy hours attend on you.' That's Shakespeare, too. I do hope he didn't notice my negligée. (*She descends.*) Have you seen my James Joyce?

LEE. Who's that?

HAMILTON. Never heard of James Joyce, I suppose?

LEE. Would it be the pig dealer in Carna you mean?

HAMILTON. Pig dealer! He's a sewer-realist. Same as Salvador Daly. Oh, yes. Very graphic in parts, too. Most of what he writes you can't grasp, and what you can makes you wish you hadn't, if you take my meaning.

LEE. Why do you read what he writes, so?

HAMILTON. Well, it's culture. Like Jean Paul Sarter. Ten years ago I took the plunge into culture and I've never looked back. Never.

LEE (*awestruck*). God help you, that was a great misfortune.

HAMILTON. I don't believe you understand a word I'm talking about.

LEE (*fascinated*). Sure I do, of course . . . Ah don't worry, your secret's safe with me. God help us we all make mistakes. (*With fearful confidentiality.*) I suppose 'twas the way he left you in the lurch?

HAMILTON (*surveying him with growing distaste*). What a provincialist you are.

LEE. Ah not at all, I'm a Catholic. (*He turns away and puts the clock-key in its place.*)

HAMILTON. And what have you been doing with that clock?

LEE. Winding it, what else?

HAMILTON. It's fast again. (*She consults her own watch.*) I'll put it right. (*She turns the hand back to one minute before twelve.*)

LEE. God, you're cracked about time.

HAMILTON. Time is very important . . . There! Now, it's correct. Same as the BBC. (*The clock begins to strike. On the third stroke, a voice calls 'Catherine!'*)

LEE. *Seafóid!*

HAMILTON. Pardon.

LEE. I said *seafóid.* That's the Irish for blather. (*He opens the clock-face.*)

HAMILTON. You leave that alone. (*She tries to get his hand away, and thus it is, busy with their wrangle over time they do not observe that* CATHERINE *has softly descended the stairs and is walking slowly in the direction of the French windows.*)

HAMILTON (*continues*). Leave that alone, I tell you.

LEE. Ah, leave it alone, yourself.

HAMILTON. Interfering!

A VOICE (*close to the house*). Catherine!

LEE. Hush!

HAMILTON. What?

LEE (*slowly looking upwards*). Listen! (*As they gaze upwards,* CATHERINE *walks out into the garden.*)

HAMILTON. What is it?

LEE (*dully*). 'Tis nothing . . . Take your hand away from that clock. (*He taps her hand away: a grating noise issues from the clock and dies with a chuckle.*)

HAMILTON. Now, you've done it.

LEE. 'Tis yourself has done it.

HAMILTON. Me? What have I done?

LEE. You've stopped the time . . .

MANY VOICES (*outside the house*). Catherine! Catherine! Catherine! (*The voices end in a soft high laughter. The music grows louder.*)
(LEE, *after staring dumbly for a moment at* HAMILTON, *turns and looks out into the garden, where the moonlight is flooding.*)

# THE CURTAIN FALLS

# ACT II

## Scene I

*The scene is the same, twelve hours later. Brilliant sunshine streams through the open French windows.* PROSPER, *seated at his desk, is working away at his papers.* LEE *is inspecting a tray of coffee things near the sofa. The sound of men's voices is heard singing outside the house.*

MEN'S VOICES.  'Oró sé do bheatha abhaile
Oró sé do bheatha abhaile
Oró sé do bheatha abhaile
'Nois ar theacht an tsamhraidh.'

PROSPER. What is that singing, Lee?

LEE. That? (*He looks puzzled.*) That'll be the mountainy men working in the fields, sir. After all these years in their silence. Singing . . .

PROSPER. There! (*Throwing down his pen.*) I work no more today. The sun is too bright. It dazzles my eye – look at that sky!

LEE (*carrying the coffee tray towards* PROSPER *and glancing out of the window.*) Ah, the sun's splitting the trees. Isn't it a great wonder it wouldn't coax out the blossom?

BAIRBRE (*running in from the garden*). *A Laoi! A Laoi! Breathnuigh!*

LEE. *Céard é féin?*

BAIRBRE. *Tá'n chearc rua tharéis an ubh seo bhreith! Breathnuigh!* (*She holds out her hand with an egg in it.*)

LEE. *Th'anam ó'n diabhal, féach é sin!*

PROSPER. What is this, a local defence meeting?

BAIRBRE. *Go mbeannuigh' Dia dhuit, a dhuine uasail! Breathnuigh.* (*She shows* PROSPER *the egg.*)

PROSPER. *Bonjour!* What does she say? (*Seeing the egg*): Who is responsible for this?

LEE. The foxy hen is after laying it, sir.

PROSPER. Bravo! Give it to me! (*To* BAIRBRE): *Tabhair om! Tabhair!* (*She puts it into his hands.*) Ha! Aren't women wonderful, eh? (*He regards the egg with deep but abstract admiration*): Oh

107

mysterious and primeval egg, warm as milk and pale as honey. Mute mother of chickens chirping in the nest, or couching modest as marguerites *en cocotte*, or succulent in the casserole, lapped in the oils and wines of the South. Oh, immortal fragility, tender and brittle as a bubble of glass and containing all the secrets of perpetuity to say nothing of those of *omelettes, soufflés divers, et crêpes Suzette . . .* We can make anything in the world, now we have an egg from our own chickens. (*He rises.*) Bairbre, I feel good today. Something is in the air. Carry to this foxy chicken my homage and a small halo with my best regards. Where is my pipe of meerschaum? (*He begins to search among the things on the mantlepiece.*)

BAIRBRE. *Céard deir sé?*

LEE (*briefly*). *Bladar.*

BAIRBRE. *Ora dhiabhail! Tá sé glan as a mheabhair.* (*She runs away laughing towards the garden, colliding with* SUSAN *who is coming in wearing a striped dressing-gown, with a small turban twisted round her head. Her arms are full of flowers.*) *Dia dhuit. Miss Sukey.*

SUSAN. *Dia's Muire dhuit.* (BAIRBRE *goes out through the garden.*) Hullo, Sebastian.

PROSPER. What are you as this morning? A trick cyclist?

SUSAN. Just a mermaid. I had a bathe and then I picked these – smell, Sebastian!

PROSPER. I can't with this lousy cold. Wait. (*He sniffs.*) I haven't a cold. (*He sniffs the flowers.*) No, not a sniffle left. Ha! That's funny. Lee, cable at once the Christian Science Monitor and take to Ellen this egg.

SUSAN. An egg? (PROSPER *gives the egg to* SUSAN.)

LEE. 'Tis the foxy hen done it, Miss Sukey, isn't she the raving wonder?

SUSAN. After seven months! Crikey! Give it to Ellen and say we'll have hundreds of pancakes. (*She puts egg on tray in* LEE'S *hands.*)

LEE. Hundreds . . .? Oh yes Miss, God, it has me mesmerised! (*He goes out through the archway to the kitchen, carrying the egg with pride and awe on the tray.*)

PROSPER. I will smoke a pipe of peace. Where is my meerschaum?

SUSAN. I think we'll mix all these up together. (*She takes a big vase from the table and goes towards the garden.*) Did you see Catherine yet?

PROSPER. Who? (*He is still looking for his pipe.*)

SUSAN (*off-stage*). Catherine. (*And we can hear the water flowing from*

108

*the tap in the garden into the flower-jar.*)

PROSPER. Who is Catherine – what is she? (*A pause.*) Ah! We have visitors in the house. I knew there was somewhere a cloud in the sky! Susan!

SUSAN (*shouting from the garden*). Yes?

PROSPER. Why the devil do we have to make of this house a railway station, hein? Explain! (*He begins searching for something on the desk.* HAMILTON *appears on the stairs.*)

HAMILTON. Good morning, sir.

PROSPER. What did I tell you, hein? Good morning, Emma. Where is this bloody thing?

HAMILTON. Hamilton is the name, sir. Excuse me, sir, but have you seen Miss Catherine?

PROSPER. Have you seen my meerschaum? (SUSAN *comes back from the garden with a full vase of flowers and goes towards the table.*)

SUSAN. Good morning.

HAMILTON. Top o' the morning, Miss.

SUSAN. What?

HAMILTON. I said 'top o' the morning.' That's correct, isn't it? When you're in Rome, do as Rome does. Within reason, of course.

PROSPER (*choking*). Huh!

HAMILTON. Well, if you'd read the lives of the Roman Emperors you'd know what I was referring to. Have you seen Miss Catherine, Miss?

SUSAN (*arranging her flowers*). No – haven't you?

HAMILTON. Haven't you seen her, sir?

PROSPER (*sitting at desk*). What's she like? (ROBERT *comes in through the archway, and goes over to* PROSPER. *His mood is one of puzzled mystification.*)

ROBERT. Hullo, everybody. Anyone seen Catherine?

PROSPER. If this quite unimportant question continues, I shall go mad. What matters to me is my —— (*He finds his pipe on the desk.*) Ah, *ça y est!* I have found her.

ROBERT. Where?

PROSPER. *Voilà!* ROBERT. Oh, that!

PROSPER. And now I will help you. Can you, without entering a wilderness of descriptive detail, tell me: What are you looking for?

ROBERT. My wife.

PROSPER. Did you look under the bed? (*He lights his pipe.*)

ROBERT. It's no joke to lose your wife, Sebastian.

PROSPER. It would be for quite a lot of people.

109

SUSAN. Don't go bitching things up, Sebastian.

HAMILTON. I shall never get used to Ireland. Not ever I shan't. Miss Catherine! (*She exits through the archway, calling*): Miss Catherine! Miss Catherine! (*Her voice ascends an astonishing scale.*)

PROSPER. A voice calling on the victim, hein?

ROBERT (*sharply*). What made you say that?

PROSPER. It was a quotation. From myself.

ROBERT. What makes you —— ? Did Catherine say anything to you?

PROSPER. What about?

ROBERT. About something that happened last night – something . . . Sebastian, I'm anxious about her. Seriously.

PROSPER. But why? She has gone for a walk, that's all.

SUSAN. She may have gone to the village – I'll look for her (*Calling*): Catherine! Catherine! (*And she exits running through the archway.*)

> (HAMILTON'S *voice is heard calling somewhere and* SUSAN'S *voice is also heard farther off calling. They both call* '*Catherine*'.)

HAMILTON (*off-stage*). Miss Catherine! Miss Catherine!

> (PROSPER *begins to laugh.*)

ROBERT (*bitterly*). Awfully amusing, isn't it?

PROSPER. If you are so anxious when she goes for five minutes from your sight, why the hell don't you go and look for her?

ROBERT. It isn't five minutes – she wasn't there when I woke up this morning.

PROSPER. What?

ROBERT. I slept like a log – it's the air here, I suppose – but when I woke up she – she wasn't there, that's all.

PROSPER. You should not leave her lying about. She often vanishes like this?

ROBERT. No – Oh, I wouldn't be worried about it at all normally – she might be out for a walk or a bathe or anything. (*His voice grows serious.*) Only last night Sebastian, she told me something ——

PROSPER. Well?

ROBERT. It happened during dinner. She'd come in here to get a bag or something. And she heard, or she thought she heard, somebody calling her by name.

PROSPER. Oh!

ROBERT. Had you been telling her any of your fairy tales?

PROSPER. I don't tell fairy tales. I analyse them.

ROBERT. What do you make of it?

110

PROSPER. That she heard somebody calling her? Probably somebody was. Do you want to keep her on a chain?

ROBERT (*going restlessly to the garden door*). Sebastian, for a man whose life is one endless concentration on what he himself believes to be the non-existent, your intuition is dazzling. If you'd ever loved anyone yourself ——

PROSPER. Robert!

ROBERT. What?

PROSPER. Don't say things like that. In joke or seriousness. Don't say them.

ROBERT. I'm going to find her. (*He goes out through the garden.*) (PROSPER *turns and stares up at the picture over the fire, his hands clenched on the mantlepiece.*)

(*Far away we can hear the laughter of young girls. Abruptly then, standing at the garden door, is* CATHERINE. *She looks curiously round the room and begins to wander towards the middle of it. When she sees* PROSPER, *whose back is turned to her, she begins to laugh softly.*)

PROSPER (*turning*). So there you are!

CATHERINE. Yes; here I am (*A pause. She sweeps him a brief mocking curtsy. She laughs again, a faint, sweet, rather distressing laugh.*) The man who knows everything. Professor Sebastian Prosper. (*She laughs again.*)

PROSPER. What are you laughing at, Madame? Me?

CATHERINE (*lazily*). Yes, I think I am. To see you staring at that picture still. The old gentleman remembers.

PROSPER (*with an attempt at his usual bantering mood*). You're an impudent hussy.

CATHERINE (*going to him*). Do you know, Sebastian, I don't like calling me that. (*She touches his coat.*) Not a bit . . . Your cold all right?

PROSPER. It has gone.

CATHERINE. Good. Did you get my present?

PROSPER. Your present?

CATHERINE. I sent you an egg.

PROSPER. You?

CATHERINE. Yes. (*She smiles at him, with an indefinable, languorous defiance, her eyes half closed.*)

PROSPER. That was very charming of you . . . I thought it was one of my hens that laid it.

CATHERINE. Ah, but I put the idea into her head. (PROSPER *laughs.*) (*Her voice changes.*) What are you always staring at that picture

111

for? (PROSPER *faces her, his laughter freezes.*) Staring won't bring her back out of the lake, will it?

PROSPER (*startled by her knowledge of this*). Who told you —— ?

CATHERINE. Susan. (*Her voice is still languorous and veiled; the girl's name is spoken with a silky inflection.*) You don't believe what the people here think, do you?

PROSPER. What do you mean?

CATHERINE. The stories about the fairies taking her.

PROSPER. My beliefs, like my memories, are my own affair.

CATHERINE. Of course, Oh, be as secretive about things as you like. (*She rises and turns towards the garden.*) Funny thing, sunshine, isn't it? It dazzles the eyes. I suppose I shall get used to it. (*She shields her eyes with her fingertips.*)

PROSPER. You won't in Connemara. There's not enough of it.

HAMILTON'S VOICE (*off-stage, far away*). Miss Catherine! Miss Catherine!

PROSPER. I suppose you know that the entire ménage has been turned into a search party on your account. Your poor husband thinks you were lost. I think it rather a pity you weren't. (*He sits on the sofa.*)

CATHERINE. Do you!

PROSPER. Yes.

CATHERINE. I saw Robert in the garden quite close. He's still up there by the rowan trees, searching.

PROSPER. He didn't see you?

CATHERINE. I hid. He was quite frantic.

PROSPER. What did you hide for?

CATHERINE. It amused me.

PROSPER. What a tricky little sense of humour.

CATHERINE. Do you remember when Lucy used to hide?

PROSPER (*after a pause*). What's wrong with you?

CATHERINE (*turning sharply*). Wrong with me? What should be wrong with me?

PROSPER (*slowly*). I don't know.

CATHERINE (*coming to sit by his side*). Don't you like me?

PROSPER. Not overwhelmingly at the moment. You were all right last night.

CATHERINE. Was I?

PROSPER. But women are always all right at night.

CATHERINE. Everything is better at night, isn't it? Why must we have this stupid day? Look at that sun. Like a great staring wheel. Clack, clack, clack . . . Sebastian, why have you turned away from me?

112

PROSPER. I like the sun, you see.

CATHERINE. And Lucy liked the moon. (*She nuzzles against him like a kitten.*) You never understood that, did you?

PROSPER. You'd better let your husband know you are safe. (*He rises and moves away.*)

CATHERINE. Oh, there's time enough.

PROSPER (*turning*). Hein?

CATHERINE. Plenty of time for everything – now. Isn't there?

PROSPER. I will tell Robert for you that you are found. I am sure it does not interest you, but he is concerned about your hiding like that.

CATHERINE. He needn't be.

PROSPER. No. Hidden things always turn up in the end, don't they? (PROSPER, *with a curious glance at her, goes out through the archway. The men begin to sing in the fields again.* CATHERINE, *her body moving to the rythm of their song, walks through the room with an amused and appraising eye. Suddenly, as she comes in front of* SUSAN'S *flowers, she stops dead and backs away. The singing ceases.*) Hamilton! (*She goes over to the fireplace.*) Filthy barbarians, sticking corpses upright in a pot . . . Hamilton!

HAMILTON (*her voice coming from the hall*). Yes, Miss! Oh, Miss Catherine – oh! Well I must say. Where are you, Miss?

CATHERINE. Here —— (HAMILTON, *crossing from one side of the archway to the other without looking into the room.*)

HAMILTON. Where's here? (*She returns and seeing* CATHERINE, *she comes forward with what for her is a beaming smile.*) Why, there you are, Miss! Well! Wherever did you get to?

CATHERINE. Take those things and hide them under the grass.

HAMILTON. What?

CATHERINE (*pointing to the flowers with terror*). Those things there, those flowers – bury them away, do you hear me? I can't live with dying things.

HAMILTON. Bury the flowers? What's wrong.

CATHERINE. Will you do as I tell you?

HAMILTON. Oh, all right, Miss. (*She reluctantly crosses and takes up the flowers in their vase.*) Does seem a shame, though, they're as fresh as fresh.

CATHERINE (*with horror*). Fresh! (*She hides her face in her hands.*)

HAMILTON (*continuing*). Besides, we're not in our own place, you know, Miss.

CATHERINE (*uncovering her face*). I'm in my own place. Remember that. (HAMILTON *gapes at her.*) Don't stand there. Get out!

113

HAMILTON. Why Miss!

CATHERINE. Get out! And take those dying things with you. (*During this speech,* ROBERT *appears at the garden door.*)

ROBERT. Darling, there you are! Where have you been? I've been searching for you the entire ——

CATHERINE (*to* HAMILTON). Do you hear what I'm saying?

ROBERT. What's wrong?

HAMILTON. Got out of bed the wrong side, if you ask me. Talk about Scarlet O'Hara. Well!

ROBERT. Sweetheart, what is it?

HAMILTON. If she's a sweetheart, I'm de Valera. (*And stalks out through the archway, taking the flowers with her.*)

ROBERT (*going over to* CATHERINE). Catherine, what's the matter?

CATHERINE (*turning slowly and looking at him*). Why, it's Robert – Robert Mallaroe. And I am Catherine.

    (*She begins to laugh. She is standing so close to* ROBERT *that his arms slip around her, but he cannot see her eyes, because he is too busy kissing her hair.*)

ROBERT. Darling. (*There is a brief silence. Her face is indefinably secretive and still.*) I was so worried about you. Do you realise how you frightened me last night, you wicked thing?

CATHERINE. Did I? How?

ROBERT. The things you told me upstairs. Oh, now of course, we both know you were tired – it was simply nerves —— In the morning, things are all straightened out. Look at that sunshine. (*He crosses to the garden doors.*) Come and look at it.

CATHERINE. I don't want to.

ROBERT. What?

CATHERINE. I don't like it.

ROBERT. You don't like it?

CATHERINE. It makes my eyes ache. (*She curls up on the sofa, her eyes away from the light.*) Robert!

ROBERT. Yes? (*He comes to the head of the sofa and looks down at her, taking her hands, which are thrown above her head, in his.*)

CATHERINE. You'll stay with me Robert, won't you? If I can keep close to you . . .

ROBERT. You said that last night.

CATHERINE. Did I?

ROBERT. Do you think I want to chase you away?

CATHERINE. You might.

ROBERT (*after a pause, laughingly*). You look so funny upside down.

CATHERINE. You're just as upside down as me.

ROBERT. There (*He kisses her.*) What's the matter?

CATHERINE. Nothing – why?

ROBERT. Your lips are as cold as ice. You all right?

CATHERINE. Yes.

ROBERT. Now give me one the right way up. (*As he comes round to sit by her side, she shudders with a faint repulsion, which he doesn't see. He kisses her again.*) You been crying?

CATHERINE. Crying? No.

ROBERT. Your eyes are so bright. You look like . . . (*He pauses, stroking her face.*) 'Smooth as monumental alabaster.' I never realised what he meant, 'till now. But you're not monumental. You're like a flower . . . like a rose . . . Oh! Catherine, there's such a dreadful strain of exhibitionary possessiveness about loving someone so much. I want to show you off to the world! I want to say, 'This is my wife – look at her! This is what I mean by a woman.' Form of conceit, you know, really.

CATHERINE. Funny how coarse your hair is. It amuses me . . .

ROBERT. And that's probably why, in my heart, I'm glad you want to go back to the stage. (*Her hand drops from his hair: she sits up a little.*) When we go back to London . . .

CATHERINE. I don't want to . . . go back . . . to London.

ROBERT. You don't want to?

CATHERINE. No.

ROBERT. Oh, I don't mean yet, you know. We'll stay here for a little – as long as my uncle and Susan will put up with us – then Dublin for a week or so.

CATHERINE. Put up with us? (*She sits upright and looks at him coldly.*) What are you talking about?

ROBERT. Well, my sweet, one can't descend on people and take possession for ever.

CATHERINE (*rising and wandering to the centre of the room*). Can't one? (*Something in his phrase amuses her, she gives a short, soft laugh.*)

ROBERT. Surely not. I know I'm his nephew, but we don't own the place – I mean. We're not invaders, are we?

CATHERINE (*stopping dead*). Invaders?

ROBERT. Well, it would be an invasion to stay on indefinitely.

CATHERINE (*facing him*). There's nothing indefinite about it. And you used the word 'invasion,' I didn't.

ROBERT. My darling Catherine, what on earth . . .?

CATHERINE. Listen to me. I'm not going back – back to the stage. That's the first thing I want you to realise.

ROBERT. What?

CATHERINE (*moving to the foot of the stairs*). I'm not going back to the stage. I'm not going to Dublin and I'm not going to London. (*She turns and looks at him again.*) Have you grasped all that?

ROBERT (*incredulous and half-laughing*). Then what are you going to do?

CATHERINE (*her face expressionless*). I'm going to stay here. (*She begins to mount the stairs.*)

PROSPER (*off stage*). Lee! Lee, where are you? Lee!

ROBERT. Catherine! (*He stands at the foot of the stairs, looking up.*)

CATHERINE. I'm going to stay here. (*She disappears; we hear her laughter dying away.*)

PROSPER (*dashing in, waving a handkerchief*). There she goes! Lee Ah! Where is Lee, Robert, do you know? (*He rushes round the room.*) There! Spoil my rest, would you? Ruin my morning slumbers? Ah! Lee!

ROBERT. What's all this? What are you trying to do?

PROSPER. Catch her. Catch the fiend! Lee! (*He rings his bell.*) There she goes! She has formed for me an attachment I find importunate and embarrassing ... Lee! There – Ah!

ROBERT. There what?

PROSPER. The Bee, of course, imbecile! Lee!

LEE (*entering with a basket of turf*). In the name of God, what class of hopping is it you're up to now? *Hóra!* Mind yourself, you devil! (*For* PROSPER *has swiped at him in the chase.*) Cranky old ... ah, sweet bad luck to you anyway. (*He sets the tray down by the hearth.*) Yourself and your old bee.

PROSPER (*his hand suspended dramatically in mid-air*). Wait. (*He stalks the bee.*) Ca y est! (*He looks dismally round.*) She has flown.

ROBERT (*joining in the chase*). Wait. Sh.

PROSPER. Yes, sh! (*He steals forward after* ROBERT): She is going to reside ... Sh! Shut up, Lee.

LEE. I didn't open my mouth.

PROSPER. Well don't.

ROBERT (*successfully, with a handkerchief at the window*). There's your lady!

PROSPER. Ah, what a woman trap! Give her to me. Wait! (*He takes a small china bowl from the desk. The bee passes therin and is stoppered by the handkerchief.*) Ah, the soft and purposeful queen. Thank you, my dear Robert. Regard this cup – phew! What an exercise. I am quite exhausted – it contains this subtle buzzing piece of impudent and perfect intelligence. I was angry because she disturbed and then eluded me, you see? Now she is my prisoner, and I am full of tenderness. She shall not die. No. Back to your golden hive, intruder on the memories of middle age. Fly! (*The bee flies out of the window.* PROSPER *and* ROBERT *watch her go.*)

LEE. God save us. I think 'tis worse he's getting.

PROSPER. So! You have found your prisoner, too, I think?

ROBERT. Catherine? Oh, yes.

PROSPER. Take care she does not turn out a bee in the other sense.

ROBERT. Why do you say that?

PROSPER. This place is full of honey . . . If she puzzles you, let me know, will you? (*He goes to the door.*) Castor oil is sometimes useful on a summer's day. (*He goes.*)

LEE. God forgive him, he's terrible wayward. Ah, one of these fine days, he'll wake up and find myself gone west out of this. Ah well, here I am mending the fire . . . and the rocks cracking in the sun. Miss likes to have the place warm.

ROBERT. Nice to smell turf again when you've been away a long time.

LEE. Is that so, sir? Oh, I suppose 'twould be. Sure they're burning it now from Aran to Dublin. Burning up poor old Ireland on us, sod by sod – ah, they'll have it all burned away soon, and maybe the sooner the better.

ROBERT (*smiling*). You're a defeatist, Lee.

LEE. Is that a fact now? Ah, I would'nt be surprised. I've fierce delicate ankles. I was in persecution all winter, and when I'd have a sup taken, I'd get a roaring in my two ears like the Shannon. Did you ever have a roaring in your two ears, sir?

ROBERT (*dismally*). I've got one now.

VOICES (*singing in the hills far away*).

> A Una Bhán, ba rós i ngáirdín thu
> 'S be choinnlcoir óir ar bhord na bainríon' thu
> Ba cheiliúr is ba cheolúr ag gabhail an bhealaigh seo róm thu
> Agus 'se mo chreach mhaidne bhróach nár pósadh le do dhubh-ghrá thu

ROBERT. What's that singing?

LEE (*rising from the hearth*). That'll be the mountainy men in the fields, sir. Tis Una Bhán – after all these years in their silence. They're singing . . .

ROBERT. What do the words mean?

LEE (*translating laboriously.*

> 'Oh beautiful Una' – that's a young lady you see, sir –

'Oh beautiful Una, you were a rose in a garden

And you were a golden candlestick on the table of a queen

And you made a fine melodious music and you going the
road before me;

Ah, Una, wouldn't it be better for me to be without my
two eyes than ever to have seen your face.'

(*The voices die away.*)

ROBERT (*after a pause*). They're always melancholy.

LEE. Oh, very melancholy indeed sir. Songs about the women does
always be melancholy. (*He goes over to the garden door and looks
out.*) Such a day! 'Tis as though you'd be eating furze-blossoms.
This isn't like a real day at all. 'Tis like an old dream or
something. There's a taste in my mouth like gold.

ROBERT. Like gold.

LEE. I must be getting to my work. We've a great company today, sir.
Mr Slushing-Calamazoo is after arriving west at the door with a
mountain of luggage. He's inside in the parlour with Miss Sukey.

ROBERT. Mr Who?

LEE. Mr Slushing-Calamazoo, sir. Ah, he's a Protestant, sir. Very
respectable, but. And he's mad about the Irish language, sir. He
have us moidered. You wouldn't know what he'd be talking
about. Is Miss Catherine above, sir?

ROBERT. M'm? Oh, yes, she is; yes. (*He crosses to a chair and sits
down.*)

LEE (*crossing to above* ROBERT). She's a beautiful young lady, sir.
God bless her, she's massive. Ah, 'twould be a very cross man
would give that one a kick out of the bed. It must be a fine thing
to be married and have a place of your own. Have she a big place
of her own in Dublin or somewhere, I suppose?

ROBERT. Big place? Oh no, well, her people are dead, you see. She's
an actress.

LEE. An actress? (*A long pause while he ruminates on this.*) Oh, my
God! And she got married to your self, ha? An actress . . . Ah,
well, wasn't she right to try and better herself?

ROBERT. Oh – yes. (*He rises to hide his smile and takes a cigarette from
the mantlepiece and lights it.*)

LEE. An actress. God bless us! Acrobatin' around in a little tent, she
do be I suppose? Do she go bareback, sir? M'm! Ha, 'tis sad
altogether about the old one she have attending on her, sir.

ROBERT. Hamilton?

LEE (*darkly*). Hamilton is the name, sir . . . she . . . told me about her
trouble, sir. That was a desperate plunge to take. And once she

118

got going she never looked back, she said. Oh my . . . (*lusciously*): Ah now, there must be great temptations in the big world lying in wait for an old one itself in the big cities. The big cities is a fright. Were you ever in the town of Clifden, sir?

ROBERT. Yes.

LEE.. 'Tis given out 'tis worse nor Paris or France. (*He allows this to sink in.*) Would it be any harm to take a fag, sir?

ROBERT. No, go ahead.

LEE (*taking a cigarette from a box on the table*). I'll smoke this in the kitchen. Ah, many's the time I think of marriage. There's a nice girleen, Bairbre Mannin from beyond Lissbeg. Ah, but she haven't much. She picks up a bit from himself, telling him stories. Her father was a *seanchai*, you see.

ROBERT. What's a *seanchai*?

LEE. A *seanchai* is a liar by profession, sir. He's a man does by telling yarns about ghosts and fairies and the like, and the likes of Mr Prosper does pay money down for it. Isn't that a great wonder? Ah, she's a grand little girleen, but she have no money and she have no English, and all the same I'd like to marry her, amn't I the roaring fool?

ROBERT. Well, why don't you?

LEE. Begob, or, a day like this, I think I might marry anyone at all, sir, anyone at all . . . (*He breaks off.*) Sh!

SUSAN'S VOICE. He might be in here – we'll go and see.

CHARLE'S VOICE. I say, don't bother.

LEE. There he is now, sir – coming in on the floor before you – Mr Slushington-Cazew!

> (SUSAN and CHARLES *appear through the archway.* SUSAN *has changed her frock and is resplendent in a flowered georgette, a little too large for her.* CHARLES LUSHINGTON-CAREW, *whose name describes him perfectly, is charming. He is in his late twenties and in very choice tweeds, and is no different in any way from a thousand others of his type. Only his newly-found passion for the Irish language differentiates him from the majority of his fellows, and this is an invisible quality, as his struggle with Gaelic syntax has not acquired him a Fáinne and he has not quite succumbed to a kill.*)

SUSAN. Oh, he's not here! Cousin Robert, this is a great friend of my family's – Mr Lushington-Carew, Mr Mallaroe. (*The two men shake hands.*)

ROBERT. How do you do?

CHARLES. How do you do? Good morning, Lee. *Go mbeannuigh' –*

eh! *Dia – dhuit.* Got it!

LEE. The same to yourself, sir. 'Tis fresh and well you're looking, God bless you, I think you got very stout in the face, sir.

SUSAN. Oh stop oozing about, Lee. Go away! Do sit down, Charles.

CHARLES. Oh, thanks Susan. (*He sits.*) Well, well, this is splendid – *Connus tá tú, Lee?*

LEE. (*after a pause*). I agree with every word you say, sir. My soul, you've rocks of Irish. (*Going.*) Did you hear the news Miss Sukey? Mr Robert's Miss Catherine was founded.

SUSAN. I know that – hop it!

LEE. I will to be sure, Miss, why not? (*He goes towards the archway where he lingers, fascinated.*)

CHARLES. I say, I do wish you'd let me have a crack with Lee, now and then Susie, it's so frightfully good for my genders.

ROBERT. What's that?

CHARLES. Genders. Know anything about them?

LEE. Ah, genders is tricky little things, Mr Charles. Very tricky indeed, sir . . .

SUSAN (*bringing the tray with decanter and glasses*). Can't you forget genders? (*She hands glass to* CHARLES, *then one to* ROBERT *and then takes one herself.*)

LEE. I'll do my best, Miss. (*He goes away to the kitchen.*)

SUSAN. We're going to have lunch soon in the garden. Robert, I'm so glad Cousin Catherine was found – he lost her, you know.

CHARLES. I say, did you really? Who is she?

ROBERT. My wife.

CHARLES. Oh, bad show. Turn up again?

ROBERT. Oh yes, she's all right. She'd gone for a long walk, that's all.

SUSAN. You would like a drink, wouldn't you? I'm an awfully boozy hostess: I think new people are much less shy together if they're half seas-over, don't you? (*She hands round some sherry.*) There!

ROBERT. Thanks.

CHARLES. Susie! (*He raises his glass.*) You're looking very smart and grown-up.

SUSAN (*twisting round, the glasses in her hand*). Do you think so? Oh, it's just an old rag . . .

ROBERT. Very pretty old rag.

SUSAN (*sitting on the arm of* CHARLE'S *chair*). Do you think so too, Charles?

CHARLES. Absolute heaven. Know that old toast? '*Bean ar do mhian agat: Talamh gan cios agat.*' It means: 'May you get the woman of your desire and a . . . (SUSAN *chokes and puts down her glass. The*

120

*men rise.*) I say, Susie!

ROBERT. Gone the wrong way?

SUSAN. Oh, Charles! Are you proposing to me? Fancy saying it right out like that – in two languages – and you never mentioned a word when we were alone.

CHARLES. By gad! Do you know, it never occurred to me before! I say, do let me mop you up, my dear.

(CHARLES *takes out his beautiful clean handkerchief and applies it to* SUSAN'S *frock.*)

SUSAN. Oh, you are so nice and ordinary!

CHARLES. I say I wish you didn't think that, Susie. I'm not a bit ordinary underneath, you know.

SUSAN (*rapturously*). Oh, I'm sure you are . . . I love you to be . . . I don't want you ever to be anything that could surprise me.

CHARLES. I'll do my best. (*They gaze at each other.*)

ROBERT (*diplomatic and smiling*). I think I'd better take my drink into the garden.

SUSAN. Oh, no – there's no need to force things. (*So* ROBERT *takes his glass and sits down again.* SUSAN *settles herself demurely on the sofa and* CHARLES *perches besides her.*) You were saying, Charles?

PROSPER (*off stage from upstairs*). Susan!

SUSAN. There's Daddy, always interrupting my life. (*Shouting.*) What is it, Sebastian? (PROSPER *entering from down the stairs.*)

PROSPER. What is all that damn luggage doing on the back stairs? Who is arriving now? Joseph Stalin? Ah, no! (*His eyes fall on* CHARLES.) Brian Boru! Welcome to the Gare du Nord.

CHARLES. I say, it was terribly nice of you to invite me like this.

PROSPER (*crossing to the desk*). I invite you? Do you mean to tell me you were taken in by that piece of forgery?

SUSAN. Daddy!

PROSPER.The letter you received, sir, was written by my daughter. Bah! What of it! She has confessed all! Until I heard this news, I imagined myself the begetter of a harmless nincompoop. I now discover that I am the sire of one who combines in herself the unscrupulous brilliance of a Machiavelli, the unbending will of a Bismark, and the femine wiles of a Cleopatra, to say nothing of a first-class aptitude for forgery rivalling that of a Chatterton. I am naturally delighted. Lucrezia Borgia, kiss your father. You are to me a revelation.

SUSAN. Really, Sebastian . . . !

PROSPER. Kiss me. (*She kisses* PROSPER.)

ROBERT. You have been brushing up your English, haven't you, Sebastian?

CHARLES. I say, do you mean all that? (*To* SUSAN.) Did you forge that letter?

SUSAN. Yes, I did. I wanted you to come. What's forgery anyway?

CHARLES. I say!

PROSPER. Ah, you might well say! She wanted you to come so much that she must resort to crime. Look at her! Guilt is written in letters of fire upon her features. You see? These hands (*He holds* SUSAN'S *hands out*) – regard them please – they cannot dally with domesticity, bind up an aching brow, boil a potato ——

SUSAN. Daddy!

PROSPER. But they can forge! Oh yes. And they can clutch and grab and snatch at their prey. Charles. I am telling you, you are doomed.

CHARLES. I say, sir, am I?

PROSPER. Well, why the hell else are you here? To see me? No! Oh, Woman! To gaze as now, upon a man like you, so pure, so peaceful ——

SUSAN. Daddy; let go my hand!

PROSPER. And so pink; that brow (*he indicates it with the aid of* SUSAN'S *hand*) unclouded by one single thought – and all to be swallowed by this unrelenting morass of feminine purpose! Yes! You will watch your home, the stately home of your Cromwellian forebears, nattering with knick-knacks, tinkling with tea-parties, waving with napkins ——

SUSAN. Sebastian, no wonder I loathe you! Don't mind him, Charles. (CATHERINE *appears on the stairs.*)

PROSPER (*protecting himself from her*). I know her, Charles. She means to have you if she kills you in the process . . .

CHARLES. I say, you know – if I'd realised you'd invited me – if I'd known you cared – I'd never have slept in that car, I'd have . . .

SUSAN. Charles!

ROBERT. Did you sleep in a car?

CATHERINE (*still on the stairs – beginning to laugh*). Yes. He slept just behind the rowans, well within the ring. That's why he's here.

ROBERT (*rising – as they all look up*). Catherine!

SUSAN. Charles – that's our secret.

CATHERINE. Nobody has secrets today. (*She comes slowly down to face* CHARLES.) How do you do? So you're the man Susan was telling me about?

ROBERT (*rising, his glass in his hand*). My wife – Mr Lushington-

Carew.

CHARLES (*wide-eyed*). How do you do?

CATHERINE. Susan's description wasn't good at all. You're so different
. . . (*She smiles at him deliciously, then turns with gentle reproach
to* SUSAN.) Susan how could you have said all these extraordinary
. . .?

SUSAN (*hurriedly*). I went right down to the village to look for you,
Catherine. We met on the road and walked up here together. His
car broke down, you know.

CATHERINE (*still smiling at* CHARLES). Yes . . . You're welcome to
Bruenagally. (*There is a pause, while the others look startled*). Isn't
he Sebastian?

PROSPER. And so you are, madame. (*He bows, facing her.*)
         (*There is a pause.*)

CHARLES. Oh, I say . . . Oh!

SUSAN (*after a pause*). Where are my flowers gone? (*She moves
towards the table.*)

CATHERINE (*after a second's thought*). I had them thrown away.

SUSAN. And what the bloody hell did you do that for?

CATHERINE (*dryly*). I don't like to see things dying in water. (*To*
PROSPER): Do you, Sebastian? (*She says this with a slow, sweet
smile.*)

PROSPER (*after a pause*). When are we going to eat? Coming to the
garden, you others? (*He goes out.*)

SUSAN (*taking* CHARLES' *left hand and dragging him to the window*).
Come on, Charles?

CHARLES. What?

SUSAN. Come ON.

CHARLES (*still watching* CATHERINE). Oh! Yes – of course.

SUSAN (*catching his left arm*). Would you like a boat this afternoon?
Sebastian's not working today. We'll go and have tea on the
island, if you like. (CHARLES *and* SUSAN *go into the garden.*)

ROBERT (*leaving his glass on a table and crossing to* CATHERINE).
Catherine, what is the matter with you?

CATHERINE. Nothing.

ROBERT. I wish you'd tell me.

CATHERINE There's nothing to tell. (*She is leaning against the sofa
watching him.*)

ROBERT. How could you behave like that?

CATHERINE. How did I behave?

ROBERT. Rather atrociously, my dear. You made people uncomfortable.
Eve Sebastian.

CATHERINE (*with cool contempt*). Sebastian!

ROBERT. You behaved as though – well, as though you were the hostess, as though you – oh, you know what I mean. Honestly, darling, it was incredible. What made you do it? (CATHERINE *stares silently at him and says nothing.*) And what you said about dying in water – do you know about his wife's death? Yes, you did, because you told me Susan had told you.

CATHERINE (*after a pause*). Yes, I know.

ROBERT. Then it makes it unforgivable to have said what you did. He worshipped that wife of his and he worships Susan in his own way, too, and I can't stand by and see you ——

CATHERINE. Oh, I know all about Sebastian. All about him. He's a meddler.

ROBERT. What do you mean?

CATHERINE. He's a meddler. Meddling about with things he can't understand, with things he doesn't even —— (*Pause.*) Oh, never mind. Let him take care, that's all. Let him take care.

ROBERT. I can't think what's come over you. Catherine. I don't know you, I don't know you like this. (LEE *enters.*)

LEE. They're waiting for ye in the garden.

ROBERT. Thanks, Lee. (*He goes out.*)

LEE. They're waiting, Miss Catherine . . . (LEE *sees her face as she turns to him and stops dead.*) Who —— ?

CATHERINE. You know me don't you Lee? (*As she laughs, she slips past him.* LEE *looks after her in terror and makes the sign of the Cross, as the curtain falls.*)

# CURTAIN

# Scene II

*The same room, a few hours later. The afternoon sun dyes the room with a stormy ochre light.* LEE *is seated on the desk, his hands and chin reclining on a broom.* BAIRBRE *stands facing him, in an ecstacy of embarrassment and though we cannot all follow what they say, it is clear that the conversation is of an intimate and affectionate nature.*

BAIRBRE (*twisting the ends of her shawl between her fingers*). *Ara níl fhios a'm. Nél fhios a'm . . .*

LEE. *Déan machnamh air, a chailin. Seo, tabhair 'om póg anois. Póigín beag amháin.*

BAIRBRE. *Muise ní fhéadfainn.*

LEE. *Gabh i leith chugam. Gabh i leith!*

BAIRBRE. *Ní racha mé a dhiabhail!*

LEE. *Teara uait! Déan!* (BAIRBRE *comes slowly towards him. There is a pause.*) *Nois goire!* (*He beckons to her.*)

BAIRBRE. *Nach leor é seo?*

LEE. *Cupla céim eile. Ara déan!* (*She comes up to him and they kiss over the broom top, very demurely.*) (*In a hoarse whisper*): Ah, passion's a devil!

BAIRBRE. *Céard sin tá tú a rá?*

LEE. Never mind what I'm saying. (*He knocks over the broom and kisses her with enthusiasm.*)

BAIRBRE. *Sgaoil diom! Nach láidir drochmhúinte an sgafaire thu!* (*She runs below* LEE *and desk to garden window.* LEE *picks up the broom*): *Ora Laoi! tán cóluadar ag tiocht anois ón loch – tá Miss Sukey ar aghaidh 's i ag caoineachán.* (*She runs above* LEE *to the arch.* LEE *runs to her, catches her as she passes him, twists her deftly round and kisses her.*)

LEE. *Sguab leat amach so gcistinigh.*

BAIRBRE. *Déanfa sin.* (*She runs swiftly through the arch.*)

LEE (*following her*). *Fan leat nóiméad!*

BAIRBRE (*turning*). *Céard tá uait?*

125

(SUSAN *comes in from the garden. She carries a towel, a basket and a kettle, and is in obvious and snorting distress. The others do not see her.*)

LEE. *Seo!* (*He catches* BAIRBRE *in his arms up centre and repeats his practical demonstration of warm regard. She struggles a little.*)

SUSAN. Oh dear – oh dear – Lee!

BAIRBRE. *Muise sgaoil díom, a chladhaire! O! Miss Sukey!* (*She runs out to the kitchen.* LEE *turns sheepishly.*)

SUSAN (*sniffing*). Lee, how dare you! That nice refined girl, too, how dare you!

LEE. Now, now, Miss Sukey, 'tis all on the level. I'll marry her! I'll marry her!

SUSAN. So you say. (*Flinging the kettle and basket from her, she crosses to the sofa where, despairingly, she sits, and speaks through a cloud of tears and snuffles.*) I'm disgusted with you Lee, and with all your horrible sex, too. So there.

LEE. Ah, Miss Sukey, that's a desperate word for a young lady to use.

SUSAN. Well, I am. You're all the same. Now I know what unbridled licensury means. Two cases of unprecedented depravity in a single day, and I wish I were dead. Yes, and I mean it. (*She sniffs.*) Take your beastly broom and wallow somewhere else. If I've got to be an old maid, I'll be a sour one. I'll be a holy terror.

LEE (*crossing to* SUSAN *and perching on the arm of the sofa*). *Muise*, God be good to us, what ails you at all Miss Sukey. (*She sniffs.*) Whisper ails you *a stór*? Ah, come on now, you'll tell me all about it, 'tis the way you'll feel better.

SUSAN (*dolefully*). I would tell you if I hadn't proved you to be a deceiver like the rest with such a – wicked – lecherous – disposition.

LEE (*primly*). Ah, faith, you're wrong there, Miss – I got me vaccination marks and all.

SUSAN. I'm sure it is not Catherine's fault, really; I'm sure he started it all. Anyway, Catherine has got Robert, what could she want with Cathal Og?

LEE. Which?

SUSAN. Cathal Og. That's what he likes to be called. It's Irish for Lushington-Carew, didn't you know?

LEE (*after a pause*). Ah, they're making great improvements in the Irish these days all right. Is it how she have him coaxed away from yourself, Miss Sukey?

SUSAN. Well, it looks like it. Giggling and gurgling, the two silly fools, rowing round and round that blasted lake. I hope they get dizzy with it, that's all. I hope they both fall in and drown. Oh, isn't sex the limit, Lee?

LEE (*darkly*). Oh, 'tis fierce right enough, 'tis fierce.

SUSAN. Now, I'm in a temper . . . (*She blows her nose.*) And he was going to propose to me today. I know he was; you should have seen the way he held my hand.

LEE. When was that?

SUSAN. When he shook it. And what do you think. Lee? Can you keep a secret? (*She kneels up on the sofa.*)

LEE (*piously*). Every blessed word you say to me does be locked up in my bosom like a baggin of poitin.

SUSAN. Well, he'd been dining with the Lynch-Crossleys' last night and just as he was passing here about midnight, his car broke down and he thought of coming in to stay. But he didn't like to because he wasn't invited until lunch time and he thought Seebastian wouldn't like it, so he slept in the car all night and I put on a bath for him this morning and nobody knows a thing about it except me, and if you don't call that clandestine, what do you?

LEE. You're after taking the words out of my mouth.

SUSAN. And he said that he thought about me lots in the car and looked forward to a jolly good breakfast with me pouring out the coffee, he said. And now, he's all . . . sh! (*She crosses to the mantlepiece and dries her eyes.* LEE *rises and whisks across the room. He picks up the basket and kettle.* PROSPER'S *voice is heard outside.*)

PROSPER (*off stage*). Beyond this, of course, my knowledge does not go.

SUSAN. There's Sebastian and Robert – I don't want them to see me like this – take that basket away somewhere, I'm going to change . . . (*She goes up the stairs.*)

LEE. That's right, Miss, put on your best and wash your face and give her murder. Bloody murder! (LEE *takes the broom and basket and kettle and goes out to the kitchen, as* ROBERT, *followed by* PROSPER, *enters from the garden.*)

PROSPER. You want a drink?

ROBERT. No thanks. I'm too worried. That sounds silly doesn't it?

PROSPER. Not to me. Drink in a stomach of intelligence only intensifies an emotion, it does not change it. You are quite intelligent, Robert – it is an unpleasant surprise.

ROBERT. Why unpleasant?

PROSPER. Because it is so easy to explain his troubles away to a fool. I would like to say 'pah! There is nothing to worry about.' You see?

ROBERT. And you can't, can you?

PROSPER. No, not quite. There is something about her I don't quite like. You would call it atmosphere. I would call it the pupil of her eye ...

ROBERT. Oh?

PROSPER. Let us talk about something else.

ROBERT. Whenever anyone says that, there is always an awkward pause.

PROSPER. Pauses are seldom awkward. Conversations often are.

ROBERT. I often wonder how you can stick Connemara. To live in, I mean.

PROSPER. Do I live in it? I was in London last week: In a month's time I go once again to Africa. Besides, I love Connemara. Always I come back. Here I met my wife; Susan was born in this house; this is for me my home.

ROBERT. Yes, I can understand you loving the house.

PROSPER. In spite of Lucy's death, hein? (*He looks at the picture.*) If a place has bored you merely, you don't like it. If it has hurt you deeply enough, it grows to be a part of yourself. It is part of me, this house.

ROBERT. Yes. (*A pause as he moves about uneasily.* PROSPER *is ruminating.*) I wonder what she meant?

PROSPER. Who knows what she meant? What any woman means?

ROBERT. I'd wish you'd take me seriously for ten seconds. I'm worried.

PROSPER. And I'm worried about you, Robert. Anyone who takes life seriously for ten seconds is cause for concern.

ROBERT (*exasperated*). Sebastian!

PROSPER. All right, I'll give you eight seconds. What who meant about what?

ROBERT. Catherine. Today – when Thingumebob talked about sleeping in his car last night ... (PROSPER *does not reply.*) You heard her.

PROSPER. I didn't listen. I never listen to women, I look at them. What did she say?

ROBERT. She said, 'That was behind the rowans —— well within the ring. That's why he's here.'

(PROSPER *seems stunned by this.*)

PROSPER. She said that, did she?

ROBERT. She did. What did she mean? (*A pause.*) What have you got on your mind?

PROSPER (*shakes off the feeling . . . bantering but decisive*). Superstition.

ROBERT. Super . . . What superstition?

PROSPER. This house is supposed to be haunted, did you know that? It is built on a ring.

ROBERT. A ring?

PROSPER. A ring bounded by rowan trees. The ground within is supposed to be sacred to the Gentry, as these locals call them.

ROBERT. Fairies?

PROSPER. And other creatures of the underworld.

ROBERT. So that's what she meant . . . (*After a moment he asks with a deprecating little laugh.*) You say the place is haunted?

PROSPER. This house was built toward the end of the 18th century by the great grandfather of my wife. Yes, it is not all as old as it looks. This was the third attempt to build on this land.

ROBERT. What was wrong?

PROSPER. Both the earlier attempts had failed. The builders, the local workmen who knew, of course, the superstition of the ring, were frightened and the work was finally abandoned. Ivy grew over the walls. But this last time it went through. Richard Alexander Mallaroe, you see, was a sceptic. He was as scornful as you or I would be of the local belief that the ground on which he was building was a portion of a circle sacred to the ancient gods.

ROBERT. Sacred? How do you mean?

PROSPER. According to legend, the area stretching from the road behind the rowan trees to the far edge of the lake forms a circle which is sacred to the gods of the earth. (*He laughs and moves over to the fire.*) Gods and fairies! What could this contemporary of Voltaire, this Merchant Banker with his newly acquired fortune and his elegant house in Mountjoy Square – what could he have to do with these remnants of pagan beliefs? And so the disbeliever built this house: and here his newly married wife fell mysteriously ill and was believed to have lived with the people of the underworld: and after her return to normal health, the trees, which had been withered, flourished again. Sickness or death, you see, and the people believe it is the greedy earth-gods who are demanding human blood for their trees. And hence the invention of the Changeling. An emissary, one who takes the place of the human victim. And one, moreover, who feel rather in the position of a spy in an empty country.

ROBERT (*with a touch of impatience*). Very charming. But it doesn't explain Catherine, does it? Oh well, time will tell.

129

PROSPER (*watching him*). That is more true than you know.

ROBERT. How do you mean?

PROSPER. Just time. (*A pause.*)

ROBERT. I think I will have that drink after all.

PROSPER. Do. (ROBERT *goes over and pours himself a drink.*) Robert
. . . have you ever felt that things were unreal? (ROBERT *looks
up.*) That the colour of the sky, the sound of people's footsteps, of
your own voice, even of the words you are saying, were – beyond
your normal, your waking experience?

ROBERT. It is what I've been feeling all day. Ever since I woke. Even
in the sunshine there was something . . . (*He drinks.*)

PROSPER. Yes. Did you hear those men singing in the fields, this
morning?

ROBERT. I did. Why?

PROSPER. You say them?

ROBERT. No, I don't think I say them.

PROSPER. You didn't. They weren't there. Nobody has worked in
these fields for years and years.

ROBERT. What are you driving at?

PROSPER. I told you – Superstition and the Time Theory. (*The voices
of girls are heard laughing in the garden.*) Listen! (*The voices die
away. Only one of them is laughing now.*)

ROBERT (*looking out at the garden*). That's Catherine.

PROSPER. Yes, she's coming in. Robert let me speak to her alone.

ROBERT. What are you going to say to her?

(SUSAN *appears at the top of the stairs and slowly descends.*)

SUSAN. There! I've put on this. (*'This' is an old flowered georgette, a
little too large for her. Perhaps it was her mother's. At any rate it
looked well, probably, on someone else, long, long ago, and there is
a bouquet of flowers pinned to her shoulder.*) I've varnished my
nails. And I've used some of her scent, too, and if you like to tell
her you can, Robert. Smell! Isn't it lovely? (*She waves her hands
under his nostrils.*)

ROBERT (*trying to smile*). It's irresistible.

SUSAN (*with determination*). That's what it's meant to be. Are they
out there still?

ROBERT. Oh, I suppose so.

SUSAN. Just you wait and see. (*She sails, impressive and wounded,
towards the garden door.*)

PROSPER. Madame Pompadour!

SUSAN (*with hauteur*). Yes?

PROSPER. Tell Madame Dubarry I would like to see her, will you?

SUSAN (*coming down to her own level*). Madame Dubarry! Madame Cuckoo I call her. I'm sorry, Robert, but she has got you. Oh, I'll tell her you want her, Sebastian. Want her? Who doesn't – except me? (*She goes into the garden.*)

PROSPER. My poor Suzanne.

ROBERT. Sebastian . . .

PROSPER. You hop it, Robert.

ROBERT. But listen . . .

PROSPER. I won't listen. Hop it.

ROBERT. Oh, all right. (*He goes towards the garden.*)

PROSPER. No, not that way – out by the front door. Go for a nice long walk.

ROBERT (*obedient but grudging*). I wish I knew what you were going to say to her.

PROSPER. So do I.

ROBERT. I think I'll take a mac – it looks like rain.

PROSPER. Take what you like, but go. (ROBERT *goes through the archway.* PROSPER *gets out his watch. He puts it back into his pocket and then realises what is wrong.*) Twelve o' . . . H'm! (*He gets it out again and looks at it, then starts to wind it. Then he listens to it and shakes it. He listens again. Then he faces the big clock.*) Twelve o'clock . . . (CATHERINE *enters from the garden.*)

CATHERINE. What's the good of looking at that?

PROSPER (*turing slowly to look at her*). It amuses me.

CATHERINE. We agree at once. It amuses me, too.

PROSPER. Will you sit down?

CATHERINE. Thank you. (*She does so.*)

PROSPER. How are you feeling? Better?

CATHERINE. I haven't felt ill.

PROSPER. You were dizzy last night . . .

CATHERINE. Last night? Was I?

PROSPER. You nearly fainted.

CATHERINE. Really? Want to see my tongue? (*She puts it out to show him.*) Sharp, isn't it?

PROSPER. Put it in again, my dear, it will get cold. (*He offers her a cigarette.*) you will smoke?

CATHERINE. Smoke? No thanks. (*She is startled.*)

PROSPER. You never smoke?

CATHERINE (*watching him*). No.

PROSPER. Last night, I thought . . .

CATHERINE. I . . . wasn't myself last night.

PROSPER. Pardon me. Last night you were yourself. (*He sits right on*

131

*the sofa.*)

CATHERINE. Oh no, I wasn't . . . Sebastian! (*She goes over and sits by him, coiling up on the sofa by his side.*) You do like me to be here, don't you?

PROSPER. Yes. I like it very much. You are a most interesting young person.

CATHERINE. I like to be here too. I fit in here, don't I?

PROSPER. . . . Yes.

CATHERINE. You know, you must not think just because my tongue is sharp that I don't understand you. My eyes are sharp, too. I see many things . . . things you could never see yourself. How could you bother yourself about little things?

PROSPER. You are quite wrong about me. Little things annoy me excessively.

CATHERINE. But you don't do anything about them, do you? Poor little Susan. After all if it amuses her, why not? If her mother had lived . . .

PROSPER. If what amuses her?

CATHERINE. Oh, you can't blame her. What standards have you ever given her?

PROSPER. What are you driving at?

CATHERINE. Forging your name on letters to that silly young man. Throwing herself at him. Poor Susan! How could that type of healthy, happy young hypocrite ever bother about marrying her when he can get all he wants . . . (*She stops.*)

PROSPER. You should be careful what you are saying, my dear.

CATHERINE (*suavely, without moving*). How right you are. And it is probably all untrue, too. Just a sort of infantile boasting. But to see a servant like Lee drinking it all in . . .

PROSPER. Lee?

CATHERINE. Oh, she just said it to shock him, of course. Probably it is a sort of revenge for his stories about . . .

PROSPER. About what?

CATHERINE. No, it isn't fair. A man like that who has been with you for years. No. Past is past. When a woman is dead . . . Oh, it is all so wickedly spiteful. As if you could . . . you, loving her so much . . . as if you could have wished her to die.

PROSPER. They don't say that . . .?

CATHERINE (*gravely, looking straight at him*). Sebastian, you ought to leave this house. Why should you, a Frenchman, a celebrity, a man of the world, want to bury yourself for half of the year in a remote place among stupid people, people like Lee and Bairbre, and all those clods? Clods who spread lies about you.

PROSPER. Do they spread lies?

CATHERINE. Is is fair to Susan? Whatever the child has done, is it fair to let her grow up in a place where not only her reputation is questioned, but where stories are allowed to spread about her parents?

PROSPER. Why are you saying these things?

CATHERINE. Terrible stories. Terrible memories. (*There is a flash of lightening.*) I see that you are surprised at my talking to you like this.

PROSPER. Surprised? I am overwhelmed. (*He looks at her with abstract scientific interest.*) Do go on.

CATHERINE. Why do you cling to this place for your permanent home? Why must you always come back to it?

PROSPER. Am I to take it you do not approve of my living in this house?

CATHERINE. I can't see why you want to, that's all. I never could. None of us ever could.

PROSPER. What do you mean 'none of us'?

CATHERINE. Never mind that. Why do you cling so to this house?

PROSPER. Listen to me. When I heard you had married my nephew, Robert, and when yesterday for the first time I met you, I was charmed. I made you welcome to my house. My work is interrupted, but my Susan is pleased, so I am pleased too. Let us deal first with Susan. Why do you want to upset what might be a happy match for her?

(*There is a flash of lightening.*)

CATHERINE (*blandly but darkly*). Upset it? What do you mean?

PROSPER. Why tease a child by flirting with a young man who cannot possibly interest you? A young man with whom she is so happily in love. Why try to poison me even against servants? Why make your husband miserable? Look, before you have been in this house twenty-four hours ——

CATHERINE (*contemptuously*). Twenty-four hours!

(*A distant mutter of thunder is heard.*)

PROSPER. Yes, twenty-four hours. Excuse me, I want to shut the doors. I am not fond of thunderstorms. (*He closes the garden doors.*) You come to me with stories my servants are supposed to have told about me; why? You invent fantastic lies about the death of my wife; why? You question me about my living in the place I have chosen to live; why? What is all this balderdash about my leaving this house? Is it all some joke? (*She watches him. Her face is expressionless.*) What are you trying to do? Drive me away?

CATHERINE. I was speaking for your own good, Sebastian.

PROSPER. Really? That is very thoughtful of you.

CATHERINE. Oh, stay if you like, of course.

PROSPER. Thank you, I am going to stay.

CATHERINE (*coming up behind him*). In that case ——

PROSPER (*turning to look at her*). Yes?

CATHERINE. Nothing . . . I suppose the house will be Susan's when you're dead. If the lake doesn't claim her as it did Lucy.

PROSPER (*he is startled at this and at the thunder which comes a little nearer*). You know, I think you are the most preposterously cool customer I have ever met; If, from my point of view, you were not a lady, or I, from yours, were not a gentleman, I would probably kick you right out of what you apparently consider your own front door.

CATHERINE. Well, will it?

PROSPER. Will what?

CATHERINE. Will the house go to Susan?

PROSPER. What is all this about the house? What has it got to do with you? (*She stares at him in silence. Lightening illumines her face suddenly.*) Ah! I am sorry to speak like this but —— This farce has gone quite far enough. (*He rings the bell.*)

CATHERINE. Farce? I'm very much in earnest. Are you going to leave this house? (LEE *enters the room, his hands full of wild flowers.*)

PROSPER. H'm! Catherine, come over here for a moment, will you?

CATHERINE. No.

PROSPER. Why not?

CATHERINE. I know your tricks. You want to look at my eyes. Well, I want you to answer my question.

PROSPER. The answer is no.

LEE. Excuse me, sir, did you ring, sir?

PROSPER. Yes. Where is Miss Susan?

LEE. She's west by the lake looking for Mr Charles, sir. She'll be drowned in the rain, sir.

PROSPER. I wish people would keep away from the lake in these storms. (*He goes out through the archway.*)

CATHERINE (*after a pause*). What are you doing with those flowers?

LEE. Bairbre and me was plucking them when the rain came.

CATHERINE. Break live bodies into bits? Does that amuse you?

LEE. Maybe it do.

CATHERINE. And does it amuse Bairbre?

LEE. Maybe.

CATHERINE. What do the people here think of Bairbre, by the way? Do you know how anxious she is to marry you?

LEE. I don't understand you, Miss.

CATHERINE. Oh, I'm not blaming her. You know when a girl like that is left miserably alone . . .

LEE. Bairbre's not alone. She have her Mother and she have myself if she'll take me.

CATHERINE. Oh, then if her Mother doesn't know and you don't care, it's perfect, isn't it? She's a lucky little girl.

LEE. How's she lucky?

CATHERINE. I think it very noble of you to be willing to marry her in spite of . . . (*She breaks off and stands peering at him.*) You haven't heard. I shouldn't have spoken. Forget what I said. (*She shudders.*) Take those flowers away, please. (LEE *turns to go.*) What are you going to do with them?

LEE. Bairbre and me is going to make a wreath, Miss.

CATHERINE. For her?

LEE. No, for somebody else. (*She stares at him silently as he goes out. A shuddering sigh escapes her when she is left alone.* CHARLES *comes in from the garden in a mackintosh several sizes too large for him.*)

CATHERINE. Susan? Oh . . . I think she's in the summer house with Lee, probably.

CHARLES. Lee?

CATHERINE. Probably.

CHARLES. What's she doing with Lee? In the summer house?

CATHERINE (*smiling*). Curious question.

CHARLES. Well, I mean one doesn't usually whisk about in summer houses with a butler, does one? Storm like this, too.

CATHERINE. I think poor little Susan is superbly indifferent to the weather if she's accompanied. She'd whisk about anywhere with one.

CHARLES. Oh.

CATHERINE. It's not her fault. She's driven to it.

CHARLES. But she wanted me to go for a walk.

CATHERINE. Yes. And then you weren't available or she missed you or something and so . . . You know what I told you this afternoon. Poor child. She's young and impulsive and not overwhelmingly selective. And Sebastian has taught her that class distinction is as futile as morality. So what do you expect?

CHARLES. I can't believe that.

CATHERINE. Oh, it isn't that side of Susan's nature that frightens me. It's something else. Her mother's blood. That fatal, turgid . . .

CHARLES. But her mother was a most charming woman. Are you sure about what you says ——

CATHERINE. About her death? Oh! Women with that temperament are often charming in everything else. And their weakness is not their fault – they're simply in the grip of something stronger than they are and it ties life up in knots. That's all. And everyone who comes in contact gets involved. And their end is inevitable. If I knew you better ——

CHARLES. You said that in the boat today.

CATHERINE. Did I? . . . Oh, forget it all. Let's forget it, shall we? All this miserable business about her behaviour in America. Poor child. You'll find out soon enough if you marry her. And the you'll be able to deal with it. But do be very tender. With that strain in her, that may lead her and you – Heaven knows where. Help her. I'm afraid it'll be hard, but try, will you?

CHARLES. I wish I knew —— what to do.

CATHERINE. I could tell you —— all about it, but it would be unfair and cruel to her. Try to understand

SUSAN (*off stage*). Charles! Cathal Og! I'm drowning! Come and rescue me!

CHARLES (*going to the windows*). Where are you, Susie? Susie!

SUSAN (*off stage*). Summer house! Drowning!

CATHERINE. *Drowning:* Poor little Susan! (*She glances at Lucy's portrait.*) And how cruel of Sebastian to cut her out of that will. It's the sheerest . . .

PROSPER (*entering*). Hello! (*To* CHARLES): What are you doing here?

CHARLES. I wish I knew, sir.

PROSPER. Ah, it is you. I did not recognise you in my mackintosh.

SUSAN (*from the garden*). Charles!

PROSPER. Your fate cries out! Go away, Charles. (CHARLES *goes out into the garden.*) And what charming nothings have you been whispering in his ear?

CATHERINE (*sweetly*). I forget. Well, have you thought over our conversation?

PROSPER. It's not worth it. My answer is no.

CATHERINE. I see. (*A pause.*) Sebastian, do you remember what the people said here about Lucy Malloroe? (*She has crossed to the fire and is looking up at the picture.*) Poor Lucy Malloroe! Oh, she was so fascinating; wasn't she? Soft as a flower and wayward as a kitten. And always did things on the spur of the moment, didn't she? A picnic in the snow, a trip to Venice, a midnight boat on the lake. But one night she was drowned, wasn't she, and no one was there but yourself? (*She turns slowly and looks at him.*) And when you had dragged her poor little body to the shore, it was too late. So the coroner brought in a verdict of accidental death, didn't he? All most satisfactory. (PROSPER *sits down slowly at the desk.*) And then, as she had always wished, she was buried in the consecrated ground on the island between her father and her mother and only you were present at the ceremony. You and two others; a priest and a poet are dead, and who is their now to defend you against what people might say?

PROSPER. Defend?

CATHERINE. What a pity you and she had always been so aloof! Nobody ever knew what went on at Bruenagally. People thought you were happy together, but who knew? (*Lightning.*) Who could prove it was an accident – now?

PROSPER (*rising to his feet*). Go away from this house.

CATHERINE. Do you remember that French poet, Sebastian? He was your guest here at the time of the tragedy, do you remember? Tall, handsome Pierre Vernet, as opinionated and quite as attractive as yourself? Suppose you had been jealous on these long summer evenings? Suppose she had been unhappy? Either was possible, wasn't it?

PROSPER (*looking at* CATHERINE, *shaken and breathless*). What are you trying to do to me? How dare you speak of my wife like this?

CATHERINE. You and I know that her death was an accident. And your poet and your priest were the only ones who could have proved it for you – but they are dead, you see: as dead as Lucy is dead, and you are alone with Susan. (*Pause.*) You were the only witness at the inquest, weren't you? And now, if tongues begin to wag, what could you do? You'd be dragged through the mire of a macabre and mawkish scandal. You know the Connemara people: they have sharp tongues, but not bad ones. Yet if I were to start now . . . An elderly foreign crank with a taste for fairy tales and a reputation for being in league with the Devil . . . Oh! things would look lovely for you if I opened my mouth. Your innocence wouldn't save you from the mud. It wouldn't save Susan.

PROSPER (*he raises his head and stares into her eyes*). What do you want? Money?

CATHERINE. Money! No. I'll offer you money. I want Bruenagally. (PROSPER *walks to the fire.*) Robert would buy it from you. I could make him. I will make him. (*He shakes his head.*)

CATHERINE (*continues*). Well? Am I to have it? (LEE *enters and stands listening at the archway.*)

PROSPER. What do you want to do with it?

CATHERINE. Supposing I were to tell you I wanted the ivy to grow over the walls again, what would you say? (*A quiver of lightning illuminates her figure.*)

PROSPER. I would believe you. You want to destroy it, don't you?

CATHERINE. I'm going to destroy it. (*The thunder peals again.*) Whatever you do.

LEE (*suddenly*). Iarlais! (*He points his finger between her eyes and she turns to him.*) Iarlais!

CATHERINE (*whispering*). Get out of my sight. (LEE *shrinks back against the door, covering his eyes. She turns back to* PROSPER.) You have till tonight. It will be better for you if you do as I say. (*She smiles at him as she goes upstairs.* PROSPER *and* LEE *look after her. The thunder rolls into the distance and dies.*)

LEE. Why did you let her go? Why did you let her get away? Mr Sebastian, do you know not what she is?

PROSPER (*sitting in a chair and mopping his forehead*). Yes, I know. She is a very unfortunate lady.

LEE. Unfortunate. She's a flaming devil, that's what she is, spinning her wicked lies around the place like an old spider's web. 'Tis myself you should let deal with the like of that trash.

PROSPER. You?

LEE (*whispering hoarsely*). I know how to get rid of them —— The flowers and the salt and the ——

PROSPER. I thought you did not believe in this rubbish Lee?

LEE. Oh, whether I believe it or not, isn't it a desperate thing to have the likes of them getting into this place? Isn't it bad enough to have them scooting and skedaddling about the mountainy places, without putting their feet in a decent house? . . . Would you like a drink, sir?

PROSPER. I think, yes, I would.

LEE (*crossing to the drinks table.* There's a small *taosgán* left in the bottle, I think – ay, there is, thank God. (*He brings over a bottle and two small glasses*): Ah, 'tisn't yourself or your old books I'd know how to deal with that one. Didn't I know what was wrong when first I clapped an eye on her this morning? I seen that look in the face before.

PROSPER (*fixing him with his eyes*). Don't meddle in what you don't understand, Lee.

LEE. 'Tis too well I understand. (*He has poured out one glass and now holds up the empty one. Haltingly, he asks*): Would it be any harm, sir?

PROSPER (*taking the full glass*). I would like to see you, Lee, so drunk that you could mistake your grandmother for the Banshee.

LEE. Before God, sir. The way I am now 'twouldn't take me a thimble of porter to mistake yourself for holy St. Peter. God bless you, sir. (*He drinks.*)

PROSPER (*setting his glass down*). Well, the storm is over.

LEE (*going to the garden doors*). Ay, and the rain's over, too. Look, the sun's coming out again, thank God. I'll open the windows a touch. (*He opens the glass doors and stands sniffing the air.*) Aha! there's a grand wild smell in the air now, like young strawberry leaves. Oh, my, my. That one have me mesmorised. Begob, she's worse than the news on the wireless, isn't she? She is. You'd need a printed copy to folly her rightly.

PROSPER. If the radios of Europe and America were as lucid as this charming young lady, we should know more of the truth of this world and worry our heads about the next.

LEE (*moving forward a pace*). The next world? Surely to God they'll not allow the like of that trash in the next world, would they? (*He drinks again.*) Wait now! (*An idea strikes him.*) The next world! That's the only answer. (*He crosses to the desk, perches on it, and picks up the receiver.*)

PROSPER. What?

LEE. Why didn't I remember it before? Wasn't I the roaring damned idiot? Exchange! Exchange! Give me Lissbeg Three. (*The voices of* SUSAN *and* CHARLES *are heard in the garden.*) Lissbeg Three, do you hear me?

PROSPER. What are you doing? (CHARLES *and* SUSAN, *sharing a raincoat, enter from the garden.*)

SUSAN (*as she follows* CHARLES *through the garden door, shaking out the coat*). —— and how can we have them without rain? And you know you like water-lillies, Cathal. You did last summer, anyway.

CHARLES. I say, I've never been so drenched in my life. Do you mind awfully if I sit by the fire, sir. (*He sits on the sofa and begins to take off his shoes.*)

LEE. Hullo! Hullo there! Is anyone there!

PROSPER. Lee, what are you doing?

CHARLES (*as he removes shoes and warms his feet by fire*). Spot of phoning, isn't he?

PROSPER. I realise he is not milking a cow.

CHARLES. I say, Lee, which do you call it, *guthán or telefóna*?

139

LEE. We calls it a yoke, sir. Hullo there ! Give me Lissbeg Three!

SUSAN. Why are you ringing Lissbeg Three? That's Father Lohan's number. What do you want him for?

PROSPER. Father Lohan! I see . . .

LEE. Hullo! (*He looks at* PROSPER *silently and hangs up.*) 'Tis banjaxed.

CHARLES. I say!

PROSPER. Let me try it. (*He takes up the receiver.*) Allô! Allô! Exchange! Nobody there? Allô! (*He gives it up.*) No, it is dead. (*A pause.*)

PROSPER (*continues*). *Personne!* And now?

LEE (*going to the archway*). I'm going out to get him.

PROSPER. It is no use, Lee. You will not find him.

LEE. Why not?

PROSPER. Because . . . he . . . lives too far away. (*He crosses to the foot of the stairs.*)

LEE. Too far away! 'Tisn't a quarter of a mile.

SUSAN (*moving forward a few paces*). What's all this about, Sebastian?

PROSPER (*taking out his watch*). Never mind. Susan . . . (*To* LEE, *gravely and tonelessly.*) Do what you think best, Lee. (*He looks from the watch to the clock.*)

LEE. Yes, sir. (LEE *goes out.*)

(PROSPER *begins to mount the stairs.*)

CHARLES. I say, is anything wrong?

PROSPER (*looking at his watch again*). Time will tell. (*And he is gone.*)

SUSAN (*she sits by* CHARLES *on the sofa. After a pause*). Everything's sort of wrong today and it all began so beautifully. (*Another pause.*) What's the matter with Daddy? What's the matter with Lee? (CHARLES *does not reply.*) What's the matter with you?

CHARLES. Nothing . . . Actually.

SUSAN. Oh yes, there is, actually. You're duller than ever and not nearly so nice.

CHARLES (*weakly*). (*Protesting*): I say!

SUSAN. It's true. Sitting there like a Sunday night in the Kildare Street Club. I don't know what's wrong with you.

CHARLES. Oh, it's nothing. Really.

SUSAN (*after a pause*). Do you remember when you rescued me on my bike from being devoured by a herd of cows? You said I looked so small and frail that I ought to be taken care of.

CHARLES. Yes, I do, actually.

SUSAN. Well, I'm still small and frail.

CHARLES. Yes, I suppose you are . . . really. Ahem! I say, do let me dry your shoes with mine. (*He kneels and helps her off with her shoes.*)

SUSAN. Thanks. Don't you want to take care of me anymore. Cathal Og?

CHARLES. Yes. That's the damnable part of it.

SUSAN. What do you mean, damnable?

CHARLES. I mean, when I'm *with* you . . . you see . . .

SUSAN. Yes, Charles?

CHARLES. Well. I mean, when I'm with you I absolutely . . . I mean I simply . . . I mean I feel you're completely the sort of thing I sort of want. Oh I know I'm no good at expressing things sort of, but do you get me?

SUSAN. Of course, I get you, dearest Charles. We're both bad at guessing things. That's what's so perfect. We're both *non compos mentos.* I think it would be an ideal match. And I mean there's intellect on my side and social distinction on yours.

CHARLES. Side of what?

SUSAN. Blanket, of course.

CHARLES. Oh yes. But when I'm *not* with you ——

SUSAN. And though it doesn't seem to work with us it might come out in our children. You see, things like that often skip a generation, didn't you know?

CHARLES (*gazing at her*). Oh, yes. Like drink? . . . It's enthralling really, isn't it?

SUSAN. Oh *isn't* it? And we've such lots to talk about, too.

CHARLES. Yes. I wish it were easier to get it out, though.

SUSAN. Yes . . . you're the only person on the world who doesn't make me feel a fool. But ——

SUSAN. A fool! Why you'd be brilliant if you only could make up your mind.

CHARLES. No, there could never be anything brilliant about me, could there? I mean I think the only illusion I haven't got about myself is about my being brilliant, if you see what I mean?

SUSAN. Now I consider *that's* brilliant. I don't follow you I'll have to sleep on it, I think.

CHARLES. And I – I had made up my mind.

SUSAN. To ask me?

CHARLES. Yes, Susie. But you see ——

SUSAN. Then . . . (*With one of her flashes.*) What's Catherine been saying to you?

CHARLES. Catherine? Oh yes, well ——

SUSAN. I know. She's called forth the lower side of your nature.

141

CHARLES. Oh no. No, good heavens, no. I mean I don't think it'd make the slightest difference to me if she'd done that. But you see . . .

SUSAN. She said something . . . ?

CHARLES. It isn't exactly what she said. (*They look at each other through cooling airs.*)

SUSAN (*after a pause*). I think mine are dry. (*She goes sadly to the fire and begins to put on her shoes.*)

CHARLES. If anything, she sort of stuck up for you. She said she didn't believe . . .

SUSAN. Didn't believe what?

CHARLES. It's horribly difficult, Susie. It's sort of intangible. I don't believe it either. But . . .

SUSAN. What are you talking about?

CHARLES. No, she was terribly nice about you really – she said what hard lines it was that rumours should get about a . . . a charming girl like you and how . . . I mean what a pity it was that your father should believe them and cut you out of his will, and all that . . . (*He sticks hopelessly.*)

SUSAN. Go on.

CHARLES. And the tendencies you'd inherited that made you do these – oh, Susie, she swore she didn't believe a word of it, but I'd never heard these things before, you see and it —— (*He stares at her; his eyes drop.*)

SUSAN. You're afraid of me for some reason.

CHARLES. Well not ——

SUSAN. Yes, you are. You're afraid of me!

CHARLES. No. Not of you, I only ——

SUSAN. She's made you feel there's something wrong about me.

CHARLES (*his eyes wander about the room*). Not you exactly. It's about the whole . . .

SUSAN. And what's that you said about Sebastian cutting me out of the will?

CHARLES. She meant the house. Good thing, too, if it's true that it's always driven people to ——

SUSAN. To what?

CHARLES. Taking their lives into their own —— (CHARLES *pauses.*)

SUSAN. What do you mean?

CHARLES. I oughtn't to have repeated it.

SUSAN. But it's a lie! And you – you believed it.

CHARLES. Susie, I ——

SUSAN. I'm going up to my room.

CHARLES. Susie, let me explain. She said she ——

SUSAN. You and she seem to have done all the explaining. Lot of filthy lies. (*She runs away weeping.* CHARLES *from the foot of the stairs, watches her go.*)

CHARLES. Susie! (*He stands motionless.*) Lies. I hope to God . . . I mean . . .

HAMILTON (*appearing at the archway with bandaged ears*). Excuse me, sir, is the storm over?

CHARLES. What? Oh, yes.

HAMILTON. Beg pardon, sir?

CHARLES (*shouting*). Yes!

HAMILTON (*unwinding*). Well. I can't say I'm sorry. Bad omens, storms are. Excuse me, sir, have you seen my lady anywhere?

CHARLES. Mrs Mallaroe? No – no, I haven't.

HAMILTON. She's not in her room. Oh, look at you, sir.

CHARLES. What's the matter with me?

HAMILTON. Your clothes are positively steaming. Was you out in that storm, sir?

CHARLES. Yes. I think I'll go and change, actually (*He rises and moves round left of sofa to foot of stairs.*)

HAMILTON (*moving above right of desk*). I should, sir. Nasty primitive climate, isn't it? Just like the people. Primitive, that's what they are.

(ROBERT *enters up centre from right and crosses to centre. He wears a mackintosh.*)

HAMILTON (*to* ROBERT). Oh, Mr Robert!

ROBERT. Where's Professor Prosper?

HAMILTON. I'm afraid I don't know, sir.

(ROBERT, *crossing to fire, takes off his mackintosh and leaves it on chair below fire.*)

ROBERT. Seen Mrs Mallaroe? (*He turns to look at* HAMILTON.)

HAMILTON. I can't say I have, sir. And I can't say I have any desire to see her, sir! You'll pardon me, but since the first glimpse I had of her today – well! Lady into Fox, I call her.

ROBERT. I say, you do get through a lot of reading, don't you?

(LEE *rushes in through the garden door.*)

HAMILTON. What?

LEE. Where's himself? Where's Mr Sebastian?

ROBERT. I don't know. I thought you might. Hamilton, do you know where he is?

HAMILTON. I'm afraid I don't, sir. But from what I've gathered about the whereabouts and the whatnots of this establishment, he might be upstairs or downstairs or in my lady's chamber. (*She goes out through the archway.*)

ROBERT. What's wrong with you, Lee?

LEE. I don't know ... (*He moves towards* ROBERT.) ... I don't know what's wrong: But there's something wrong. Mr Robert, there's bad things going on in this place. I went cast a piece from the road to find Father Lohan ...

ROBERT. Father Lohan? What do you want him for?

LEE (*looking him steadily in the eyes*). I had need of him, sir. We all have need of him, everyone in this place, sir.

ROBERT. Well, go on.

LEE (*after a pause*). I couldn't get to his house.

ROBERT. Why not?

LEE. There was something stopped me. Mr Robert ... do you see that sun up there in the sky? 'Tis up there shining out over the mountains – am I right?

ROBERT. Of course, Lee. What on earth ... ?

LEE. When I got to the green ditch beyond the rowans – the edge of the ring we do call it here – the daylight stopped. (*He pauses, his face stony with fear.*) Mr Robert, I'm telling you the truth. You can come and see it for yourself. I'm telling you the truth, sir.

ROBERT. What do you mean, the daylight stopped?

LEE. It stopped as dead as though a candle was after being quenched with a blow of your fist. It stopped as if there was like it'd be a big black wall and it rising up out of thee ground. The place I was standing was in broad daylight and the birds were singing and the bees humming. But out there beyond the green ditch ... 'twas all pitch dark and I seen the moon, and it hanging up on the black sky like a lamp ... And when I tried to move I couldn't. I couldn't move a foot under me, sir. There was something there stopping me. Mr Robert ... I couldn't get to the priest's house.

ROBERT (*after a pause*). Come with me. (ROBERT *takes up his coat from the chair by the fire and goes out through the archway.* LEE *rises when* ROBERT *has gone, hesitates, and then rushes out after him.*)

(CATHERINE, *very beautifully dressed, comes slowly downstairs. With a subtle air of ownership, she surveys the room already aglow with the deep afternoon light of midsummer. She saunters towards the desk, takes up some papers, and finally, having chosen one, begins to read it.*)

CATHERINE (*reading*). 'Malicious ... Spiteful ... Malignant creatures of the underworld, whose purpose would appear to be to

144

replenish their own ebbing powers . . . certain trees sacred to the ancient gods, which unaccountably wither and whose recovery can only be assured by the infusion of human energies. There is, however, no single shred of evidence . . .' (*Her eyes grow murderous, her head goes up and she turns to her left to face the clock diagonally. Slowly, she tears the sheets of paper up into fragments, bursting into a frenzy of laughter and throwing the torn white shreds at the stolid face of the clock, she backs away, throwing up her arms as the curtain falls.*)

# ACT III

*It is the same room some hours later. The moon has risen again and the shadowy background of the big room is flooded with its light, but the lamps are lighted too and the fire is burning.*

*As the curtain rises,* LEE *is collecting ashtrays onto a silver tray which he carries.* PROSPER *and* ROBERT *enter from the dining room.* PROSPER *carries a small plate on which a slice of cake reposes. He eats the cake at intervals during the following scene.*

PROSPER. You have left some booze in the bottle. Ganymede?

LEE. I have, sir.

PROSPER. Then bring us the dancing maidens.

LEE. I will to be sure. Why not indeed, why not. (*And* LEE *goes out.*)

    (ROBERT *sits with a sigh.* PROSPER *looks at him, then pours two drinks. Pause.*)

PROSPER. Your silence, my dear Robert, is almost deafening.

ROBERT. I can't take it all in somehow. I can't get over what I saw with my own eyes. (PROSPER *hands* ROBERT *a drink.*) I thought it was Lee's fiery imagination, you see . . . drink . . . hysteria . . . anything you like. But I saw it. And I've seen her, too. And I suppose the whole thing's been . . . too much, that's all.

PROSPER. On this side of the road, the broad light of the day. And beyond, quite suddenly, black night, and the moon hangs on the sky. I wish you had told me before. I would like to have seen this non-existence of what we call time in this startling and visible form.

ROBERT. You only half believe me, don't you?

PROSPER. No, I fully believe you . . . All today, we in this house have been the prisoners of the hours. For us, somehow, somewhere, time has stopped. All my life, Robert, I have believed that this could happen; I never knew that it would happen to me. All my life, perhaps because of the accident of my name, I have dreamed of this link between my life and that of Shakespeare's hero.

ROBERT. Who?

PROSPER. Don't be alarmed: I do not mean Romeo. I mean that
magician who lived with his only daughter on an enchanted island.
You remember?

ROBERT. Yes! Why didn't you call her Miranda?

PROSPER. How could I know that we also were to find ourselves one
day on an island? An island, not of rocks and hills and woods set
in a perilous sea, but one that floated on the waters of time, a
sunlit island poised for a moment on the brows of eternal night.
(*He perches on the desk.*)
And what strange company has brought us here. This girl, your wife,
whose love for you has turned to sudden poison; what is she? Is
she what Lee believes? Or is she what I believe? This . . . how
does he say it? This . . .

> ' . . . . . . demi-puppet, that
> By moonshine does the green sour ringlets make
> Whereof the ewe not bites; and whose pastime
> Is to make midnight mushrooms, by whose aid –
> Weak monsters though ye be – I have bedimmed
> The noontide sun, called forth the mutinous winds
> And twixt the green sea and the azured vault
> Set roaring war . . .'

ROBERT (*after a pause*). 'Sweet roaring war . . .' That's what you've
done with your delvings into dangerous places.

PROSPER. ' . . . . . . But this rough magic
> I here abjure: and when I have requir'd
> Some heavenly music – which even now I do –
> To work mine end up on their senses that
> This airy charm is for, I'll break my staff,
> Bury it certain fathoms in the earth,
> And, deeper than did ever plummet sound,
> I'll drown my book.'

ROBERT (*after a pause*). But will you drown your book? Will you give
up this search for things you were never meant to find?

PROSPER. If God did not mean us to search, why are we here?

ROBERT (*rising to face the fire, and then turning sharply round to face*
PROSPER). But are we here?

PROSPER (*laughing*). Robert, what a wonderful question!

ROBERT. Oh, you can laugh!

PROSPER. (*He has gone over to the desk and is idly turning over his
papers*). What —— ? (*Missing something, he turns and discovers
on the floor the fragments of torn manuscript* CATHERINE *had*

147

*thrown there.*) Robert, you tell me to drown my book, do you? Look here! (*He holds them up to show him.*) All my notes of yesterday. Torn to pieces, you see!

ROBERT. Who did that?

PROSPER. Who do you think? (*He opens a drawer and lets the fragments fall into it.*) Hm! It doesn't matter, you know. They are not real . . . Oh, you'll see. Real things are all in the mind. Only matter is ephemeral, that is why it is the most inexplicable factor of our universe. Like those papers. (*He closes the drawer.*) Like this cake, you see? (*He bites a piece of the cake.*)

ROBERT. Do you mean that today —— the whole thing is a sort of communal dream? That it's not really —— that you and I are not —— you can't think that . . . (*His half-bantering tone dies; the smile leaves his face.*) If it is all a dream, how's it going to end?

PROSPER. It will end when her obsession ends. And ours, too, if you like. Mine anyway. This dread of her.

ROBERT. You feel it too?

PROSPER (*looking at him*). Of course, I feel it. Something cold and hostile . . . Ah well! You an I would be hostile if we felt ourselves surrounded by monsters.

ROBERT (*after a long look at him, rises and looks away*). I can't see . . .

PROSPER. She believes herself to be an immortal, Robert. To her we are monstrous and repellent. Yes. And if that obsession is ended – a shock – a slipping back into what we know as time ——

(HAMILTON *comes in through the archway.*)

HAMILTON. Can't find that James Joyce. I can't, and that's the end of it. Goodnight, gentlemen, I'm sure. (*She goes, after a brief glance round the room, upstairs.*)

PROSPER. There are moments when this communal dream you describe takes to itself a quality of nightmare, hein? Emma Hamilton! What part does she play in the comedy, I wonder?

ROBERT. Sebastian, what are you going to do about Catherine?

PROSPER. Whatever I do – or say – you must not be there, Robert. Her neurosis is not a dream. It is as real as that moon out there. It is just a trap into which we have fallen. (*He goes to the garden doors and throws crumbs from the cake he has been eating, out into the lawn,*) Dicky birds!

ROBERT. Calling the nightingales?

PROSPER. No nightingales in Connemara. (*Enter* CATHERINE *slowly down the stairs.*) Plenty of cuckoos. Lee believes she could be banished by a spell. I, on the other hand —— (*Looking up at the moon.*) I, think I shall walk for a little. I want to pit my thoughts against that moon. (*And he goes, his face turned to the moonlight.*)

CATHERINE. His thoughts against the moon! One outworn mechanism against another. (ROBERT *stares at her and says nothing.*) You're very silent. Have you been listening to Sebastian?

ROBERT. Yes, I have.

CATHERINE. Fatal. It's fatal to listen to people who meddle in things they don't understand.

ROBERT. I think he understands things amazingly.

CATHERINE. You think he understands me, don't you?

ROBERT. I don't know. I wish *I* understood you.

CATHERINE. Do you?

ROBERT. What's wrong with you, Catherine?

CATHERINE. Sebastian, for one thing.

ROBERT. Why have you turned against him?

CATHERINE. I haven't turned. I just think he oughtn't to be here, that's all.

ROBERT. Is that your reason for destroying his work?

CATHERINE. His work? . . . I'll destroy more than that. Unless he does what I've asked him to do.

ROBERT. Clear out of this house? (CATHERINE *nods her head slowly.*)

ROBERT (*continues*). I think you're mad, Catherine. Either I'm dreaming or you're mad.

CATHERINE. Oh? Then why not accept Sebastian's theory since you're so fond of listening to him? Believe that you *are* dreaming. Why not? That all this is unreal? One moment suspended in my mind and yours? One single moment between the ticking sound of a stupid wooden clock? Eternity instead of time? Does that help? Does it? (*He stares at her.*) You see, I know what he said to you. But whatever knowledge he may think he possesses doesn't alter life, our life – our earth – our war against invasion.

ROBERT. I can't understand you.

CATHERINE. We creep into your world between the ticked off seconds of your clocks like mice between the clocks of the floor. But once we're in your room, how may you get rid of us? Only by re-adjustment. You don't know the formula, you see. You didn't stop the clock. (*She comes close to* ROBERT). Give me this house, Robert. Say to Sebastian that you're willing to buy it. To buy it for Catherine. And give it back to me. Don't let me go away with a partial victory, Robert. I must go away in the end. You know that as well as I do.

ROBERT. Go away?

CATHERINE. Go back to those this circle in the earth belongs to. Being

149

with you here has made me ambitious. The flowering of the rowans – that's not enough any longer.

(*There is a pause, as* SUSAN *comes tearfully to the archway, looks at them for a moment, and goes quietly upstairs, sniffing dismally. They do not see her, but* CATHERINE *says*):

And everyone will be at peace if you do what I ask. And Susan will be safe. If you give me the house, she'll be safe.

(SUSAN *goes out through the upper archway on the stairs.*)

ROBERT. You believe all that. You really believe that you, yourself ——

CATHERINE. If one of the Mallaroes would give it up – in one brief second in his mind – the house would crumble. It would hurt nobody. As long as they remain Bruenagally will be in siege. It will always be unlucky to bring a bride through the doors of these walls. Always. Always. (*She begins to laugh softly.*)

ROBERT (*with a sort of dismayed impatience*). Oh, it's fantastic that you should think.

CATHERINE. You're not going to do it?

ROBERT. Make you a present of Sebastian's house? No.

CATHERINE. Then I must fight you as I fight the others. That's all, Robert. I thought you loved Catherine well enough to do this.

(*During these last speeches,* CHARLES *comes in. He hesitates hearing* CATHERINE'S *words, then comes forward.*)

CHARLES. I say, Mrs Mallaroe –

CATHERINE. Yes?

ROBERT. Excuse me, will you – I want to talk to Sebastian. Alone. (*He flings the last word at them both as he hurries out.*)

CATHERINE. I do hope you will excuse him. He's been dreadfully upset.

CHARLES. Has he? So have I, you know.

CATHERINE. I wonder is anybody really worth all this?

CHARLES. Do you mean – I mean – is he upset about her too?

CATHERINE. About Susan? Well, of course he is. Who wouldn't be who had any feeling for the child? Or for Sebastian either. Oh, it's no good. It's in the blood, my poor friend, it's in the blood, you see. (*She laughs as she says this, leaning towards him.*)

CHARLES. The awful part, is I'm sort of awfully fond of Susie.

CATHERINE (*softly*). I know.

CHARLES. And I find it frightfully hard to sort of believe, you know, all those ——

CATHERINE (*with bitter self-reproach*). I shouldn't have told you. No, no. I shouldn't. I don't think I shall ever learn one isn't thanked for that kind of friendliness.

CHARLES. Oh, I say, don't think I ——

CATHERINE. Because it was friendliness that made me do it. Friendliness to you both, you see. What a fool I am! As if you could think it was anything but the feeblest sort of interference ——

CHARLES. Oh no, honestly –

CATHERINE. Well, I should have thought that in your position. Yes. Yet, if someone had told me about Robert before I married him, I think –

CHARLES. Your husband?

CATHERINE. I think I'd have been grateful. (*She wipes her eyes for a second.*) Oh, do let's try to forget it all, shall we? It's the mere contact with people like these – the whole family – that's so unnerving. That odd, rather charming quality on the surface, and then deep down underneath it all this avid, relentless . . . (*She breaks off suddenly and begins to cry.*)

CHARLES. I say don't – oh really, please! I mean don't cry –

CATHERINE (*between sobs*). I hope you'll be able to cope with it, that's all. I hope Susan won't do to you what Robert's doing to me . . .

CHARLES. Catherine, don't. What is the trouble?

CATHERINE. Trouble! Look at me! (*She ceases crying and sits back very pale and shaken.*) Do I look to you a happy person? Do I? I have been married for less than a week. I thought at first I – no – I can't tell you. I couldn't tell anyone. But coming here, seeing where it all springs from – all that dark, hereditary . . .

CHARLES. Do you mean Mallaroe's unkind to you?

CATHERINE. Unkind? What a word! No – it's not unkindness. I could deal with that, I daresay. There's something – bad, Charles. You don't mind my calling you Charles, do you? It's something – in the mind. (*Her voice grows very grave, she repeats softly*): In the mind. There. I've said it. And I'm frightened. I feel so alone with them. I'm frightened of them. All of them. Oh, do forgive me. (*Her voice shakes; she nestles against his shoulder.*) I'm frightened. Frightened . . .

CHARLES (*uneasily*). There, there! You mustn't! There! (*And just as he kisses her,* SUSAN *appears; she stands staring at them as* CATHERINE, *with a certain graceful violence, disengages herself from his embrace, pushing his arms away.*)

CATHERINE (*apparently not seeing her, rises and turns to the fire*). Please don't let's have any more of this. The poor child loves you. You ought to remember that. I don't think anyone on earth has a right to ——

SUSAN. Has a right to what?

CATHERINE. Susan! Darling, what is it?

> (CHARLES *has risen and stands speechless with embarrassment, facing them both.*)

SUSAN (*to* CHARLES). Don't you want to know what it is? Charles?

CATHERINE (*with staggering simplicity and understanding*). I'll explain. Susan and I understand each other.

CHARLES. Yes, but I want to ——

CATHERINE. I think it'll be so much easier if you leave us alone for a little.

CHARLES. Do you want that, too, Susan?

SUSAN. I – yes, I suppose so.

CHARLES. All right. (*He goes unhappily into the garden.*)

> (*The two girls eye each other for a moment or two.*)

CATHERINE (*at last*). Well?

SUSAN. You said just now that we understand each other. Catherine, I wonder do you mean that?

CATHERINE. Of course I mean it. I hope it's true.

SUSAN. Catherine, why was he kissing you when I came in just now? Why?

CATHERINE. Why do you think men kiss women as a rule? Because they love them? No, you can put your mind at rest on that point. They kiss them because it's a habit, Susan.

SUSAN. Well, it's a very bad habit.

CATHERINE. All habits are bad. (*A pause.*)

SUSAN. Do you like hurting me, Catherine?

CATHERINE. I should hate to hurt you, my dear. And that's why I want to tell you something. Before you *get* hurt. So badly hurt that you'll never . . . oh, well.

SUSAN (*dully*). Go on.

CATHERINE. I wish for your own sake you'd try to forget this rather dingy young man.

SUSAN. Dingy? Is that why you let him kiss you?

CATHERINE (*smiling*). You are sweet, darling. So sweet, I can't bear to see you unhappy like this.

SUSAN. Well, he did kiss you. I saw him.

CATHERINE. I'm so glad you did see him. He's dingy and stupid and shallow – and so he kissed me. Because I'd been defending you –

SUSAN. Against him?

CATHERINE. Yes. He's so disloyal, Susan. And he's a liar. If you want to know the truth I got so furious with the things he said about you that I – well, I got upset. And then he tried to kiss me – to calm me down, I suppose. If I'd been as ineffably sweet as you, I'd have believed him. Oh no, darling. He's not worth your tears.

SUSAN. What sort of lies do you mean?

CATHERINE. Oh, about your mother. All that talk about suicide.

SUSAN. Why, he'd never invent a ——

CATHERINE. He'd hardly have to invent that, would he? No, probably he got it from Lee. It's common gossip.

SUSAN. Is it? That Lucy – oh, it can't be!

CATHERINE. Cheer up, Susan. People will invent fantastic things. Lies are the only means of escape from the world they live in. It's a pity Lee's such a liar.

SUSAN. I didn't know he was – oh, yes I did. At dinner tonight, I did.

CATHERINE. Oh?

SUSAN. Did you notice his hands at dinner?

CATHERINE. No.

SUSAN. They'd got bloodstains on them.

CATHERINE. What?

SUSAN. And when I asked him about them, he said something about killing a goat. (CATHERINE *rises slowly.*) Imagine killing a – what's the matter Catherine?

CATHERINE. Nothing.

SUSAN (*innocently*). You're not afraid of goat's blood, are you?

CATHERINE (*slowly turning her head towards her*). Of course I'm not – afraid . . . (*She walks away a little, then says in a bright, hard voice*): What do you think about Robert's buying the house, Susan?

SUSAN. What?

CATHERINE. We're buying Bruenagally. Didn't you know?

(*There is a second's pause.*)

SUSAN. I don't believe it.

CATHERINE. It won't make much difference to you, will it? Sebastian had no intention of leaving it to you, you know.

SUSAN. I don't care who he leaves it to. I don't care what happens to houses after people die – it's his house! It's our house! Why, Bruenagally's everything to Sebastian and me ——

CATHERINE. He must have changed his mind.

SUSAN. Oh, Catherine! (*She begins to weep.*)

CATHERINE. Poor little Susan. It's been a bad day for you, hasn't it? Your eyes opened about the world you're really living in. And all in a few hours. (SUSAN *weeps bitterly.*)

CATHERINE. Don't cry like that, my dear. You shouldn't give way so whole-heartedly to your emotions, Susan. That's what killed your mother, you know.

SUSAN (*looking up at her*). What?

CATHERINE. Men's lies. Husband's lies in particular, and their wives' incapacity of dealing with them. Look where it led her.

SUSAN (*helplessly*). You don't believe that. You said yourself it was lies.

CATHERINE. One gets used to denying things to the world in general. For appearances' sake. But *you* know it was true. Susan. Don't you.

SUSAN. No.

CATHERINE. It was a very kind and very simple way out. There are worse forms of death, aren't there?

SUSAN (*slowly*). I don't believe it.

CATHERINE. No? . . . You know what the country people thought, don't you?

SUSAN. About her being stolen?

CATHERINE. About —— evil things calling her away. Silly, wasn't it? Silly and rather horrible. That's where morbid fancies can lead the mind. How much more – complete – to know she went of her own free will.

SUSAN. Catherine!

CATHERINE. A very ordinary little grief. A very ordinary little ending to it all. So easy to understand, too. The stars go round just the same. The sun comes up in the morning whether one's there or not. Why live? If life has become empty, and soiled, and repellent? (*She has moved to* SUSAN *and now stands almost touching her.*) The lake is kind.

SUSAN. Don't. Don't come near ——

CATHERINE. You're not afraid, are you, of me? You, who can live in this house, facing a labyrinth of whispered lies and accusations and calumnies, are you afraid of me?

SUSAN. I don't know.

CATHERINE (*in a tone of deep sincerity*). You mustn't be afraid of the only person you can turn to. The only one. I'm your friend, my dear. I wish you could see that. Your presence embarrasses Sebastian badly. You know how anxious he was for your marriage with Charles. Rather painful, really. But you see, when these ugly little rumours reach a head, you'll be dreadfully in the way here, Susan. Of course, they're untrue. He wasn't directly responsible for your mother's death any more than you are responsible for inheriting so much from her.

SUSAN. What do you mean by that?

CATHERINE. I mean her unfittedness for life in a world that doesn't understand. A world that shrinks from everything you represent. Perhaps you're too young to realise how much the world does shrink from and loathe – all that.

SUSAN. All what? What do you mean?

CATHERINE. You know – you must have heard – about poor Lucy's mind? And that, you, yourself –

SUSAN. Catherine!

CATHERINE. When the world says that people are – ill, Susan, unfit, 'unbalanced' is their favourite word – there's only one answer. Get away from the world into another world. (*She laughs softly: her voice changes.*) If it weren't for Robert, I'd love to have you live with us. But you know what Robert is. It's not his fault. He's just been poisoned like all the rest.

SUSAN (*vaguely*). Robert?

CATHERINE. Yes. Oh, I know what it's like to feel alone. But you have got me. And you've got – how shall I say it? – you've got life, Susan. And day and night, and the moon and the lake. Those things don't mind if one is what the world calls sane or not. They're magnificently indifferent. Don't tell me you're afraid of the lake, what you call existence is unimportant, you know. People? A network of spawning activity, hostile or sycophantic or indifferent. What does it all matter whether one joins in the farce or is left outside in the cold – as you are left. Nature is oblivion, ultimately, and ultimately she's kind. Kinder than her children. If you pass through the lake, you can dance . . . Remember your mother. How comforted she was in the end. Out of all this muck and mire.

> (SUSAN, *with one small despairing cry, runs out into the garden.* CATHERINE *stands smiling gravely, watching her.* SEBASTIAN *calls through the archway.*)

PROSPER (*off stage*). Suzanne! Suzanne, where are you?

CATHERINE (*calling*). She's not here.

PROSPER (*entering*). Oh – where is she then?

CATHERINE. – I don't know.

PROSPER. Then who were you talking to just now?

CATHERINE. Was I talking? It must have been to myself.

PROSPER. That's a bad sign. I hope you gave yourself some good advice.

CATHERINE. Excellent. But I'm afraid I never take advice.

PROSPER. Even your own?

CATHERINE. Even my own. Well! Have you spoken to Robert about Bruenagally?

155

PROSPER. I have.

CATHERINE. Well, what does he say?

PROSPER. He thinks it is a fantastic idea.

CATHERINE. That's very interesting. What about you?

PROSPER. Well, what about me?

CATHERINE. You force me to say it, don't you? If I choose to speak –

PROSPER. You have spoken quite enough to and about everyone in the house. (*He gets out a cigarette case and a box of matches.*) Your charming little tongue, niece Catherine, has been like a viper pickled in vitriol.

CATHERINE (*carelessly*). What is vitriol, Sebastian?

PROSPER. Something that burns. (*Suddenly, he strikes a match close to her face. She screams and backs away.*)

CATHERINE. Take that thing away!

PROSPER. What's the matter with you?

CATHERINE. What are you doing? Trying to kill me?

PROSPER. You don't like me to smoke?

CATHERINE. I don't like fire – thrust into my face like that. What are you trying to do? (*Her voice has taken on a new queer tone of harsh authority.*)

PROSPER. Test you. That is all. Come over here, Catherine.

CATHERINE (*approaching slowly*). What are you trying to do?

PROSPER. You would not let me look at your eyes this afternoon, I want to look at them now. Will you let me? (*He puts out the cigarette.*)

CATHERINE (*with the sharp bravery of a cat facing a friendly but unfamiliar dog*). I'm not afraid of you.

PROSPER. There's no need to be.

CATHERINE. Don't you burn things again though ———— . Here are my eyes. (*She glares at him.*) Well, what do you see? The fires of hell?

PROSPER. I can see nothing.

CATHERINE. Of course you can see nothing.

PROSPER. You are too much in the shadow. (*He switches on the desk light as* LEE *enters unobserved by either* PROSPER *or* CATHERINE.) Oh! What an unhappy woman! All the troubles of twenty-four long years.

CATHERINE (*half-mocking, half in a dream*). Twenty-four years!

PROSPER. It seems longer, doesn't it? But it is not, you see. You have lived, Catherine, twenty-four years. Awful times you have had now and then, hein? And you have never told a living soul, have you? Not even Robert? Hein?

CATHERINE (*slowly*). Robert . . . ? Who is Robert?

156

PROSPER. Somebody who loves you.

CATHERINE. Robert? (*She begins to laugh softly.*)

PROSPER. Why are you so unhappy, Catherine?

CATHERINE (*unwillingly*). I don't want to be here. Not like this . . .
(*She makes a gesture as if to tear her dress off her. Her voice rises
like the wind.*) I don't want to cling to this borrowed thing like a
bat in the twilight, hanging to the barn roof. Hanging upside down
with black folded wings. I think your life is loathsome: foul
carrion crows feasting on dead meat and sticking severed flowers
in stagnant waters. Do you think I want your world? Do you think
I want to change it for my world? For thee woven dance and the
shine wind, and the flame of the stars? I don't covet your world. I
don't want to share it with you. I would destroy it all if I could. I
am bad only when I am with you: pious, joyless people of the sod.
Makers of rat-traps, spinners of evil! Building your festering
houses where our feet have danced, worshippers of metal, paying
lip-service to your tortured God! Leave me alone. You, who knew
three words of our language and dream you may argue us out of
existence: leave me alone! You can't send me away from
Bruenagally. You can't banish me from the fortress of the moon.

PROSPER. I don't want you to go. I want you to come back. Catherine!
I want you to come back. (*He speaks with measured
determination.*) And you can come back. You understand me?
You hear me? You can come back, if you chose.

CATHERINE. You are talking to that other, not to me. Why do you talk
to her? She can't hear you.

PROSPER. Where do you think she is? (*She stares at him in silence.*)
Where do you think, hein? (*A long pause.*) Answer me!

CATHERINE (*mockingly*). You'll see her again.

PROSPER. When?

CATHERINE. When thee rowan trees bloom.

PROSPER. Where is she now? Tell me. Where is she now?

CATHERINE. Under your feet in the hollow ground.

LEE (*calling through the door*). *A Bhairbre! A Bhairbre!*

PROSPER. Get out of this room, Lee.

LEE. I'll not go, sir.

PROSPER. Do as I tell you.

LEE. I'll not go while that thing is in the house. (*He points menacingly
at* CATHERINE.)

PROSPER. Lee!

LEE. *A Bhairbre adeirim! Tabhair an fleasg annseo chugam!*

BAIRBRE (*off stage*). *Tá sé agam!* (*She enters with a wreath of flowers.*)

157

CATHERINE (*turning violently to* BAIRBRE). *Is beag maitheas dhéanfas sé sin daoibh!*

PROSPER. You fool! Why did you make her look away from me?

LEE (*taking wreath from* BAIRBRE). You've a great tongue of the Irish, Miss Catherine. *Imigh leat, a Bhairbre.* (BAIRBRE *goes out through the archway.*)

CATHERINE. You fool! Your master was right, you're a fool. With your reeking hands. Goat's blood . . .

PROSPER. Go into the kitchen, Lee. And take that mumbo jumbo stuff with you. Leave this to me.

LEE. I beg your pardon, Mr Sebastian. I hope you'll forgive me. *Iarlais!* Listen to me. (CATHERINE *starts.*) Do you see these flowers? Fresh summer flowers they are and they wet with the rain and the storm. But the rain is red! Do you see that now. *Iarlais*? The rain is red, and there's snow sifting through the rain and it spilt down on the flowers like 'twould be fine white salt was in it, and the drops of rain is glistening like blood. Smell the flowers, *Iarlais*, and the salt, and the blood. Let me come near you. I'll not hurt a hair on your head.

CATHERINE (*smiling at him*). You can't come near me! (LEE *tries to move and fails,*) Drop the halter! Drop the halter! (*The wreath of flowers falls to the ground from* LEE'S *hands.* LEE *bends his head and falls to his knees and blesses himself.*)

PROSPER. I told you to keep out of this, Lee. Now, listen to me, Catherine. I want you to sit quietly down and answer my questions. Do you understand? There is nothing wrong, Catherine. Nothing that cannot be changed. Come over to me.

CATHERINE. So that you can pierce my eyes again with yours? So that you can get me off my guard? I know my weaknesses. What a pity, Sebastian, that you don't know yours.

LEE (*rising*). Go back to the rowans, *Iarlais.*

PROSPER. Catherine – when did you think you heard a voice calling?

CATHERINE. I heard no voice. It was I that called.

PROSPER. So you know that, do you? That's a very good start. It was your own voice calling.

CATHERINE. Catherine! Catherine!

PROSPER. Catherine, whom did you meet in the moonlight?

CATHERINE (*slowly, with effort*). Myself.

PROSPER. When you were a child, did you dream of moonlight? Of lonely places?

CATHERINE. What are dreams? We never dream.

PROSPER. What did Catherine dream about, do you think?

158

CATHERINE. About dancing.

PROSPER. With other people?

CATHERINE. With us. When we grew poor the rowans withered. The dancing stopped. When your wife died . . .

PROSPER. Yes?

CATHERINE. She was too guarded, you see. She slipped away because she had no wish to come. Not like Catherine who came to us in sleep. Nor Susan who comes in a little globe of despair.

PROSPER. Susan? How do you mean – Susan?

CATHERINE. Susan is on her way to us. Now.

LEE. *Iarlais!*

CATHERINE. Out there. At the edge of the water —— (*She breaks off.*)

PROSPER (*going to the window*). Susan! Susan!

CATHERINE. It's her own will. You can't stop a woman desiring what you call death. Can you?

PROSPER. Susan!

CATHERINE. You can't stir. That's what you classify as nightmare, isn't it? You can't move. Try.

PROSPER (*desperately*). Susan!

(SUSAN *comes to the door of the garden, a small, woebegone figure. For a second or so they stare silently at each other. Then she gives a little cry, and runs into his arms.*)

SUSAN. Oh, Sebastian! (*They cling together. There is nothing very much they can say.*)

PROSPER (*at last*). There. There, Susan.

SUSAN. Lucy never did that. You never made her unhappy enough to do that.

PROSPER. Look at me. You believe in your father, don't you?

SUSAN (*very beautifully*). Oh Yes . . . Sebastian, you're not going to sell Bruenagally, are you?

PROSPER. No. I never was going to sell it.

SUSAN. I'm so glad. There's only one thing about being miserable. You know the truth suddenly . . . and sometimes it isn't so bad. (*She hides her face in his coat.*)

PROSPER. So! You have found that out. *C'est bien.* Now, listen Lucy and I were always happy. Always. You can believe that. And now kiss me. (*She obeys him.*) *Tout sera bien. Tu verras.* And now go to your room and rest. You will not sleep at once. But rest. I trust you. *Compris?*

SUSAN. *Compris.* But I —— (*She looks fearfully at* CATHERINE, *who stands regarding her stonily.*)

159

PROSPER.You shall talk to Catherine when she is —— herself again. Run along.

SUSAN (*whispering*). I love you – more than anyone in the world, except Charles. (*She kisses him and runs away upstairs.*)

PROSPER (*with gentle irony, to* CATHERINE). Is your triber so poor that they must buy life through a child like that?

CATHERINE. Yes. As poor as that. But we shall go on living. Whoever you keep from us.

PROSPER (*fixing his eyes on her face*). Who do you really believe you are, poor disturbed soul?

CATHERINE (*slowly*). You think you know. Then why ask?

PROSPER. I do know. I want you to know as well.

CATHERINE (*slowly*). A human mind caught in the toils of an accident. Neurosis caused by a sense of guilt. The clock ticks, and then it is dislocated for a little, and through my mind time stops. And all the rest is my illusion casting its spell over you. But our earth will be fed again for all your talk. You've discovered what I am, you say. Then deal with me. Put me all the questions you wish. Probe my nerves; I haven't any nerves. Search my heart; it doesn't exist. Analyse my brain; there is no brain that you could ever gauge in this borrowed head that Lee would like to sever from its trunk. But my blood is pale, Lee – my blood is pale as quicksilver, not red like the blood of your slaughtered goat. Oh yes, I know what you've been up to. You and your clumsy murders. Ah, you are a pretty pair; you! (*She looks at* LEE) who have one inkling of the truth and use the methods of a child in arms, and you (*to* SEBASTIAN) blinding yourself with your own brilliance. And what does your brilliance reveal? It's like the moonlight, Sebastian, tricky and brief and deceptive, and it reveals what the moonlight reveals when it shines into this room; row upon row of classified opinions, disproved theories, printed lies.

PROSPER (*after a pause*). I know nothing, but I search.

CATHERINE. You search! Then why lay down the law? You and your neurasthenia! Lee and his incantations. Your conceptions of us and of our world are grotesque. We are neither non-existent figments of your inner disorders. Sebastian Prosper, nor long-nosed red-capped shoemakers. Bartley Patrick Lee. You (*to* PROSPER) deny me. You (*to* LEE) are afraid of me. Destroy me before I destroy you.

LEE (*lifting the wreath*). Take these flowers, *Iarlais*. (*He stops in his journey towards her.*)

PROSPER. Answer my question, Catherine.

160

CATHERINE. You've even forgotten the formula. Yet he had it all written out in a book. Who could banish the intruder? 'He who loved, and she who served.' Don't you remember even that?

(LEE *stands silently, the wreath drops from his hands onto the desk.*)

HAMILTON (*appearing on the stairs*). I remember —— I remember I left it on the desk. Silly of me forgetting it, wasn't it? Talk about Freud!

CATHERINE. Get out of this room! Get out!

HAMILTON. Whatever's the matter, Miss Catherine?

LEE. Stand back.

CATHERINE. Send that woman away! Send her away!

HAMILTON. Well, of all the ——

CATHERINE. Get out of my sight. (*She strikes* HAMILTON. HAMILTON *reels back a little, holding her hand to her face.*)

HAMILTON. That's enough! I give notice. I give notice, do you hear me? Nasty wicked temper. Where's that —— There! (*She snatches the wreath from the desk and throws it over* CATHERINE'S *head.*)

CATHERINE (*after a pause*). *Mo chéad mallacht ort!* (*She holds the wreath in her hands, but cannot get it off.*)

(ROBERT *comes in from the garden.*)

CATHERINE. You! You mouthing fool. You stand by and see them do this to me —— You! Who couldn't even find a chaste woman to be your bride. Catherine! What is your Catherine? A besotted drab with a score of lovers to her credit and you knew it, didn't you? She told you all about it, didn't she? You!

(*Suddenly,* ROBERT *strikes her across the face and rushes upstairs.* CATHERINE *wheels round once and then glares at the others, the wreath of flowers still dangling round her neck. She stumbles back a little and knocks against the clock. There is a whirring sound from the clock – then the lights go out.*)

(*As darkness falls, the sound of the whirring of the clock continues, and when the lights steal back,* HAMILTON *and* LEE *are alone in the room.*)

HAMILTON'S *voice.* Now you've done it.

LEE'S *voice.* 'Tis yourself has done it.

HAMILTON'S *voice.* Me? What have I done?

LEE'S *voice.* You've stopped the clock . . .

(*The moonlight and the red glow from the turf fire have crept back into the room. Nothing has changed since last night. Nothing, indeed, seems to have happened at all.*)

161

HAMILTON. No I haven't . . . (*The clock begins to strike twelve*,) There!

LEE. Then you've set it going again . . .

HAMILTON. When did all this happen before?

LEE. What?

HAMILTON. This! You and me and the clock. I said, 'now you've done it,' and you said 'no, it's you that done it,' and somebody else said ——

ROBERT (*off stage from upstairs*). Catherine! Catherine!

HAMILTON. I don't like this. I don't like this at all. (*She crosses and switches on some lights.*) Where's that book of mine – there! (*She takes up 'Ulysses' and bolts up the stairs, colliding with* PROSPER *who is coming down.*) Sorry, sir! Oh dear! Bad luck to cross on the stairs so they say . . . There I go again. There's something wrong. I knew I should never like Ireland. (*And she has gone.*)

PROSPER. Where is she?

LEE (*dazed*). She's gone back.

LEE. I – I don't rightly know, sir. I was taking a sup – 'tis St John's Eve, sir ——

PROSPER (*looking at him*). No – that was yesterday, or – (*He sneezes.*)

LEE. God bless you, sir.

PROSPER. I thought that damn thing had gone.

LEE. Look!

(CATHERINE *appears breathless and frightened at the garden door.*)

CATHERINE. What is it? What's wrong?

PROSPER. It's all right, my dear.

CATHERINE (*goes to* PROSPER). I don't know what I – where's Robert?

ROBERT (*coming down the stairs in a dressing-gown.*) Catherine!

CATHERINE. Robert! Oh Robert! (*They find each other somehow.*)

ROBERT. I was so frightened. I woke up suddenly and you were gone. And I'd been dreaming or – something. What's wrong? There's something ——

CATHERINE. I don't know. I've never done stupid things like that before. Oh, Robert.

ROBERT. Try to forget it, darling. You weren't yourself. (*She hides her face in his arms.*)

PROSPER. Robert! Not a word about that. She has forgotten already.

ROBERT (*blankly*). Forgotten? What? (PROSPER *looks at him closely, then makes an inarticulate grunt.*) What do you mean? (PROSPER *smiles.*)

CATHERINE. Walking in my sleep! I woke up under those rowan trees, Uncle Sebastian, I'm so sorry . . . (*She tries to laugh, then shades*

162

*her eyes with her hands for a moment.*) The moon was in my room. I don't usually do things like this, you know. (*She crosses to the fire and stares at her face in the mirror.*)

ROBERT. You went to the rowans – ?

PROSPER. Robert! Look! (*He has taken his papers out of the drawer of the desk.*) All my papers, you see? In perfect order. I told you there was never a shred of evidence.

ROBERT. Funny. I dreamt something about your papers being destroyed ——

PROSPER. Dreamt?

CATHERINE (*turning from the mirror*). What are you two talking about?

PROSPER. Nothing. Robert, take this baggage to bed.

CATHERINE (*going to him*). Goodnight . . . I'm afraid I've been a dreadful lot of trouble.

PROSPER (*relishing this*). Trouble? My dear, how could you think such a thing.

ROBERT. Come along, Eurydice.

CATHERINE. Why do you call me Eurydice?

ROBERT. I don't know, really.

PROSPER. Then don't try to explain. Never explain to a wife any of the names you call her.

SUSAN (*running down the stairs*). Catherine! Are you all right – ? I thought ——

CATHERINE. Hullo, Susan.

SUSAN. You —— (*She glances for a moment at Lucy's portrait and back at* CATHERINE.) Oh, Catherine! (*She is half-laughing, half-crying.*)

CATHERINE. Darling, what's wrong?

SUSAN. I don't know. I'm glad to see you back, that's all.

ROBERT (*leading* CATHERINE *up the stairs*). Come up to bed.

CATHERINE (*pausing for a second on the landing*). I feel so exhausted, as though I'd been dancing all night . . . (*She goes up the stairs with* ROBERT.)

SUSAN. Sebastian, what's up?

PROSPER. What do you mean, what's up?

SUSAN. Well, somethings up. Very far up. Did you hear what I said to Catherine? About being back? What did I mean?

PROSPER. Precisely what you said.

SUSAN. Then you know something that I – Cathal Og!

(*For in the middle of her half-remembering,* CHARLES LUSHINGTON-CAREW *enters rather sheepishly from the garden.*)

CHARLES. I say, *go mbeannuigh' Dia* . . . You know, God save all here! I'm most frightfully sorry, sir – I saw the light and I'd been dining with some people at –

SUSAN. Lynch-Crossleys.

CHARLES. Yes – that's right. Susie! My car broke down – Must have dropped off at the wheel or something – woke up with a stinker of a head, too.

PROSPER. Under the rowans, I suppose.

CHARLES. Yes. I say, sir, as I'm supposed to be lunching tomorrow, would it be terribly barging in – ?

PROSPER. If you stay the night? Of course you'll stay.

SUSAN (*radiant*). And you're not barging in, is he, Sebastian?

CHARLES. That's frightfully nice of you both. Rather a gruesome time to call, isn't it?

PROSPER. Oh, what is time?

CHARLES. Do you know, I've often wondered that myself. I say, Susie, you're looking very smart and grown-up.

SUSAN. Yes . . . (*They stare at each other.*)

PROSPER. Susan, take your guest to the dining room, the coal cellar, or where you will, I have work to finish.

SUSAN. Come into the dining room and have a night-cap, Charles. Lee, get a room ready. Pity you've just missed meeting Catherine.

CHARLES. Catherine . . . ? Now, that rings a bell.

PROSPER. I shall ring a bell if you don't go away.

SUSAN. Come on, Charles. (*She drags him to the archway.*)

CHARLES. Goodnight, sir, and thanks. Oh, *slán leat*, Lee!

(CHARLES *and* SUSAN *go out hand in hand.* LEE *stares at* PROSPER.)

PROSPER. It's all vanished, you see. A whole day lost in time. (*He rises and goes towards the picture over the fireplace.*) A whole day, detailed and crowded, slipped in between the strokes of the midnight clock. And why? What is the meaning of it all?

LEE. 'Tis a bad thing bringing a bride to Bruenagally. You knows that yourself, sir. (PROSPER *looks round from the picture.*) Ah well, maybe 'tis all right now. But if it is, 'twas the flowers and the salt and the blood that worked it.

PROSPER (*looking back at the picture*). Have it your own way. And now . . . Go to bed, Lee, I've some notes to make. (*He crosses to his desk and sits down.*)

LEE. Will I leave on the big lights?

PROSPER. No, the moonlight is good.

(LEE *switches out the main lights.*)

# THE MOUNTAINS LOOK DIFFERENT

## A Play in Three Acts

# CHARACTERS

MARTIN GREALISH, a farmer
TOM, his son
BARTLEY, a serving-man
MATTHEW CONROY, a miller
BAIRBRE, his niece
MAIRE, an old woman
BATTY WALLACE, her grandson
BRIDIN, a young girl
A PRIEST
NEIGHBOURS, A FIDDLER, AN ACCORDION PLAYER, CIVIC GUARDS

THE MOUNTAINS LOOK DIFFERENT was first produced at the Gaiety
Theatre, Dublin, on 25 October, 1948 with the following cast:

| | |
|---|---|
| MARTIN GREALISH | Denis Brennan |
| TOM GREALISH | Micheál macLiammóir |
| BARTLEY | Liam Gannon |
| MATTHEW CONROY | Seamus Healy |
| BAIRBRE | Sheila Burrell |
| MAIRE | Isobel Couser |
| BATTY WALLACE | John Battles |
| BRIDIN | Helena Hughes |
| A PRIEST | Godfrey Quigley |

The play was directed by Hilton Edwards in a setting designed by
Micheál macLiammóir.

The action of the play takes place on the farm of Martin Grealish in the West of Ireland on St John's Day and early the next morning, Midsummer's Day.

## ACT I

Outside the House  – Evening

## ACT II

Inside the House – That night

## ACT III

Outside the House – Next morning before dawn

# The Mountains Look Different

## ACT I

*The garden before the farm of* MARTIN GREALISH, *the corner of a gaunt stone house capped with a dark roof of thatch. A door with a window above it stands half-open; a pot of geraniums is in the window at the side of the door; a loose stone wall with gate in it runs from the house to meet a barricade of rocks and stones. Rocks and stones rise savagely out of the earth beyond the wall, they crouch and loom alternately in the sunshine with patches of heath and fern and shallow pools of water between them. Far away, in the golden light of the evening, are the peaks of bare mountains.*

*It is a desolate place. A wooden bench stands in the garden, and there are a few bushes of fuchsia whose blooms show crimson among the leaves, but there are no trees. The sky is loaded with lurid summer clouds, girdled with light. Some long spades, a ploughshare, a cart-wheel painted orange-red, and a scythe lean against the wall, and over all broods sunshine and silence.*

*No one is visible. A melancholy sound of fluting is heard, and after a moment or two* BATTY WALLACE *rambles on in his naked feet into the yard, a tin whistle to his lips. He is a gawkish, hatless creature of about twenty, his tousled hair falls over two vacant and staring eyes; his face is unshaven and he wears a loose suit of bawneens – the greyish-white home-spun flannels of the west. He advances uncertainly, still playing his tune, to the windows of the house, then he takes the whistle from his lips to let the silence take possession once more, and peers foolishly through the panes, then he turns and wanders in the direction of the stables.*

*Presently* MATTHEW CONROY, *an elderly countryman wearing his best clothes, a rough grey suit, stiff collar, and bowler hat, appears at the gate and stares up at the house. A dog is barking, then is silent.*

CONROY. Is anyone there? *(The dog begins to bark again.)* Ah! stop your big mouth! Is anyone there?
   *(The dog is silent. No one answers.* CONROY *comes in through the gate.)*

171

CONROY. Is anyone within? God save us 'tis like a tomb. Hullo there! Hullo!

> (*Bartley, a young man of twenty or so, appears from the yard on the far side of the house. He wears patched trousers, heavy boots, a collarless flannel shirt, and a waistcoat into whose armholes bawneen sleeves have been stitched. He peers at the newcomer in the vaguely puzzled way of a man unused to strange faces.*)

BARTLEY. 'Morra!

CONROY. 'Morra, young fellow. Is anyone in the house at all?

BARTLEY. Himself.

CONROY. Mr Grealish is it?

BARTLEY. That's right.

CONROY. Will you tell him I'm here, so?

BARTLEY. I will, why wouldn't I. Who are you?

CONROY. Matthew Conroy.

BARTLEY. Conroy.

CONROY. Out of Rossbeg.

BARTLEY. That's a long way. Is it to come walking it you did?

CONROY. I came car.

BARTLEY. Right enough. (*He walks to the gate.*) I thought I heard a – Oh! does the yoke belong to yourself?

CONROY. It does.

BARTLEY (*admiringly*). Now! She's a great little one isn't she? Would she go fast?

CONTROY. She would. Will you tell himself I'm here?

BARTLEY. Mr Connolly, ha?

CONROY. Conroy.

BARTLEY. There's a power of Connollys around this place. Ah! they're not much. Not much at all. That's a great little yoke, mind you, would do a journey on roads the like of these roads. My soul, she'd plough the rocks. (*Unwillingly he tears himself from the contemplation of the car and turns to the house.*)

GREALISH (*appearing at the door where he stands for a moment in silence*). Well?

BARTLEY. This man wants to see you. He have a motor outside.

GREALISH. Hold your whist, you. (*To Conroy.*) What is it?

CONROY. I'm wanting to see yourself, Mr Grealish. Grealish, that's right isn't it?

GREALISH. 'Tis.

> (*He watches* CONROY *narrowly.* GREALISH *is a tall powerfully built man of about sixty, shrewd, suspicious, and humourless.*

*His manner is taciturn. He has the air of a man who wields a certain authority in the narrow world in which he lives and who would be lost if for a moment he stepped outside it. As he speaks the dog begins to bark again – the barking ends in a long whine.)*

CONROY. That's a big brute of a dog you have there.

GREALISH. I've three.

CONROY. 'Tis about your son I want to talk to you.

GREALISH. Tom?

CONROY. That's the man.

GREALISH. Well?

CONROY. Did you know he was married?

GREALISH. I did. Bad luck to him.

CONROY. Your son got hold of a fine girl let me tell you.

GREALISH. Could be. Would you be the father?

CONROY. Her father and mother is both dead, God rest them. I'm her uncle out of Rossbeg.

GREALISH. Is that so now?

CONROY. Matt Conroy.

GREALISH. I thought the name was Joyce.

CONROY. I'm her mother's brother.

GREALISH. (*The sound of the tin whistle is heard at some distance.* GREALISH *pricks up his ears. Then he turns to* BARTLEY.) Is it that close to your head your two ears are growing they have no hearing left in them at all? What is it ails you Bartley to be standing there putting the two eyes through us like we were a circus? Let you leg it out of that back to the cows.

BARTLEY. Yes Sir. (*He is about to return to the yard.*)

GREALISH (*shouting after him*). And don't let the mare loose. (*He stares at* CONROY *with a faint hostility.*) Will you come into the house?

CONROY. I'd as lief stay here. 'Tis a fine evening thanks be to God.

GREALISH. 'Tis. (*They eye each other and cough. The tin whistle stops dead, and Batty is heard whimpering.*)

CONROY. This is a nice bit of a place you have up here, and the mountains all round you.

GREALISH. Devil a bit in it but stones and water.

CONROY. Ay! 'tis lonesome. Lonesome.

   (*He looks over at the mountains, then sits down on the bench.*)

GREALISH. Rossbeg you're from, ha?

CONROY. 'Tis. (*He begins to fill his pipe.*)

GREALISH. Conroy . . . Is it yourself owns the mill there?

CONROY. Ay!

GREALISH. Bedad it's what I'm thinking, your niece had a right to bring a dowry to my son.

CONROY. Her father had nothing.

GREALISH. And her mother died young, ha?

CONROY. She did.

GREALISH. Bairbre Joyce, ha? (*He leans against the wall.*)

CONROY. My niece is a good girl, Mr Grealish. A very nice smart bit of a girl altogether.

GREALISH. How do you know that?

CONROY. Why wouldn't I know it?

GREALISH. And she beyond in London thirteen years?

CONROY. And what if she was?

GREALISH. Thirteen years is a long time, Matthew Conroy, long time and a bad time. And London's a big place and a bad place.

CONROY. Sure no place is all bad, Mr Grealish.

GREALISH. Some places is. London's bad. I was in it, I know.

CONROY. Many was in it and they found good there as well as bad.

GREALISH. It done bad to me. There's no sense now discussing it. Let you go on about your niece.

CONROY. I've a letter from her here in my pocket.

CONROY. Wait now – Where's this it is – wait – Ah! here it is. Wait now –

(*He opens the letter, puts on his glasses and begins to read with laborious clarity and no sense of punctuation at all.*)

'Dear Uncle Matty'. There you see? 'Tis from herself – 'Dear Uncle Matty ——'

GREALISH. Oh! She's very loving, all right.

CONROY. Mmm! 'Dear Uncle Matty, By the time you get this letter I will be on my way back home. Well Uncle, I have great news for you altogether . . . I have just got myself married to a very nice steady fellow . . .'

GREALISH. Steady is it? Shy must know little about him.

CONROY (*after a glance of subdued indignation*). . . . 'nice steady fellow Tom Grealish is his name, an Irish chap and a great Catholic . . .'

GREALISH (*sardonically*). Go on.

CONROY. '. . . I know you will be charmed to hear this: well, Uncle Matty, I am giving up my job . . .'

GREALISH (*joylessly*). Why wouldn't she?

CONROY. '. . . giving up my job. Working in a hotel would wear you out and I am tired of it all. I am wanting to have a great rest.' You

174

see, she has lines drew out under that . . . 'a great rest. Tom's father has a farm at Clochrua . . .'

GREALISH. And there's more lines drew out under that I suppose ha?

CONROY. There is not then '. . . farm at Clochura, that is only twenty-five English miles out of Rossbeg. Tom says his father is a stern sort of a man . . .' (*He glances up at Grealish.*)

GREALISH. Don't stop.

CONROY. '. . . I feel ashamed I have no money nor nothing at all I can bring Tom only myself. Well, God knows I will do all I can to get on with Tom's father. Please God I'll see you soon at home. We'd a right to be in Ireland on Thursday 20th. Hoping your health is great as this leaves me at the present. Your loving: Bairbre Grealish.'

GREALISH. Bairbre Grealish.

CONROY (*folding up the letter*). Well, Mr Grealish, that's what has me driving over to you here.

GREALISH. Thursday 20th, ha! That was yesterday.

CONROY. They'd be in Dublin yesterday. They'd a right to be home this night.

GREALISH. Three fine daughters I had, Matthew Conroy, and two of them praying nuns in Galway and the other married, a cross-eyed terror with a brood of screeching brats beyond in Boston. Five strapping sons I had, one of them a holy priest bent down on his two knees at the butt-end of Hong Kong and three belted peelers and they steering the traffic of America. And the sole survivor of that crew, Tomas, ha? to go lepping over to London for to get himself laced up with a strange one, a wife his father never laid an eye on no more than if she was a raging devil out of hell, and nothing with her . . . devil a red penny, do you hear me? And myself, is the stern father should be sitting at home by the fire as mild as a robin and giving all I have to the two of them . . . Ah no, Matt Conroy, no. Devil a penny will my son get from me, nor the wife he brings with him. They'll be lucky indeed to be welcomed itself.

CONROY. Ah, Mr Grealish the young chaps, the young chaps! They're tired of having a match arranged for them the way it was for the likes of us in the olden time.

GREALISH (*scornfully*). Young chaps! A big soft stammering slob, thirty and three years he have put from him. And two good matches I made for him myself, and he walks out of them. No good enough for him, ha? And away with him to London then for to get himself spliced with an old doll maybe would scare the crows and she sitting by the fire beyond when the night is dark sipping her tea and scratching her back, and she pining for the life of the city and the farm rotting away to the devil around her ha?

CONROY. That's not Bairbre Joyce.

GREALISH. How do you know? You that never laid an eye on her for thirteen years?

CONROY. I did then. I seen her a year ago in London.

GREALISH. Is that so? (*He fills his pipe carefully.*)

CONROY. Sixteen years old she was and she leaving home – Ah man, she was great looking. Swanky clothes and two blushes on her cheeks; as bright as a candle she was.

GREALISH. Hm!

CONROY. So I —— I brought a little present for her, something to wear like. (*He takes a small flat box wrapped in brown paper from his pocket.*) Maybe if I don't see her tonight you'd hand it over to her? (*He hands* GREALISH *the box.*)

GREALISH (*takes the box for a moment in his hands then suddenly gives it back*). You'd a right to give her that yourself.

CONROY. And I'm . . . I'm leaving her the mill at Rossbeg when I die. I've nobody else. No children you see. We'd only one child. A girl too. She died. So that's why . . .

> (*He falls silent for a moment, twisting the cardboard box in his hands.*)

GREALISH. Well?

CONROY. And I'd like to settle something on her now. 'Twon't be very much.

GREALISH (*after a pause*). You might as well come into the house. 'Tis St John's Eve too. We'll wet the bargain.

CONROY. Be good to her, Mr Grealish. She's a good girl.

GREALISH. We'll see. Come in. (*He goes to the door.*)

> (BARTLEY *comes in from the yeard.*)

BARTLEY. Master! Master! They're coming!

GREALISH. What?

BARTLEY. They're coming west along the road, sir. Over from the bus at the cross they're coming and they legging it along sir, and they having bundles in their arms. Master Tom and a strange one along with him, sir, they're coming this way.

> (*He dashes through the gate and out of sight.*)

GREALISH (*looking after him*). If 'twas the King of Spain was in it you wouldn't lep higher, you big gawm.

CONROY (*at the gate*). There they are!

GREALISH. Are you certain?

176

CONROY. 'Tis Bairbre anyway. There's a bonefire behind her. (*Exitedly.*) God, you'd think 'twas for herself they were lighting it. 'Tis a mile away behind her on the mountain and you'd say she was walking out of the heart of it. My soul, they're a great pair!

(*The dogs begin to bark.*)

Are them dogs on the leash?

GREALISH. They are under lock.

CONROY. Thank God for that. Will we go meet them?

GREALISH (*uneasily*). I've a . . . No, I've a couple of things to do . . . I'll see you within.

CONROY. Wait a minute! (*But* GREALISH *is gone closing the door in Conroy's face.*) Queer sort of welcome. (*He returns to the gate.*) Bairbre! Bairbre!

(*The dogs bark furiously; then are silent.*

BAIRBRE *enters through the gate followed closely by* TOM GREALISH; BARTLEY *brings up the rear.* TOM, *as his father has suggested with more truth than flattery, is a broad-shouldered young man, fleshy and muscular at once with a suggestion of great physical strength and of an immense and disarming simplicity. He is dressed in his best suit, the blue serge so well loved by the country people, a fancy shirt and tie, and a brand new cap. He carries a couple of cheap suitcases but has obviously given the bulk of his belongings over to Bartley who is heavily laden with bags, brown paper bundle, two bulky packages covered with newspaper and a mackintosh.*

BAIRBRE *herself carries only a travelling coat and a handbag, having also, we can gather, given over her burdens to the care of Bartley. Her black clothes, although quiet and in reasonably good taste, give the curious impression that they are deliberately designed and worn in order to reduce to a minimum the violent flamboyance of their wearer; and small insuppressible details betray the inner turbulence and love of finery that have been hers for many years. She wears white gloves. The handbag she carries is large and tawdry, a bunch of many-coloured artificial flowers flaunts itself on her breast, her lips are a little too scarlet. She looks, in spite of her gay and citified appearance, weary and exhausted, but her face lights up when she sees* CONROY *standing at the gate. Her voice, when she speaks is deep, powerful and husky, her accent a queer rough maxum-gathering affair whose roots are deep in the west of Ireland but whose surface is coloured with the brazen languor of Soho.*)

BAIRBRE. Uncle Matty!

CONROY. Well now!

BAIRBRE. Uncle Matty! Imagine you – well! This is himself. Tom, this is my Uncle Matt. This is my husband.

CONROY. How are you?

TOM (*grinning*). I'm very pleased to meet you.

BAIRBRE. Yes.

> (*They smile nervously at one another.*)

TOM (*to* BARTLEY). Bring them old things inside. Where's himself?

BARTLEY. He's within.

TOM. How's the mare?

BARTLEY. She's great.

> (*But his eyes are fixed on* BAIRBRE *and it is plain he finds her quite as great as the mare.*)

TOM. Be off with yourself. And bring them things with you.

BARTLEY (*to the world at large*). Bedad she's a marvel isn't she? A marvel! My God! She's as good as a circus.

> (*He staggers under his lead into the house.*)

TOM. Cheek of that fellow!

BAIRBRE. Uncle Matty! You're looking fine.

CONROY. You're not too bad yourself. But where's them roses in your cheeks?

BAIRBRE. Ah? (*She laughs, a little nervously.*)

TOM. Ay! begod – you're terrible pallid since we left London. Are you alright?

BAIRBRE (*hastily*). I am of course. (*To* CONROY.) When did you come over?

CONROY. Tonight. I'll have to get back. Do you know what I believe?

BAIRBRE. What?

CONROY. I believe them cheeks was all . . .

BAIRBRE (*shortly*). I was ill since then. Tom, where's your father?

TOM. Musha, I was wondering. Come into the house till we find him.

BAIRBRE. Oh no.

CONROY. Why not?

TOM. He'll be expecting you.

BAIRBRE. Let him welcome me so.

CONROY. There's the country girl still. London didn't change you at all.

BAIRBRE. London? Ha! (*She looks out at the mountains.*) 'Tis nice here, isn't it! Listen!

> (*They are all silent.*)

CONROY. What?

BAIRBRE. Quiet as the grave, eh! Not a sound . . . What are they lighting them fires for?

TOM. Sure, wasn't I telling you. 'Tis St John's Eve.

BAIRBRE. I'd forgotten that. (*To* CONROY.) Seeing them mountains makes me feel like I was a kid still. They're the wrong way round from this place. (*She laughs.*) They look different somehow.

CONROY. You're south of Rossbeg here.

TOM. I'm going to look for my father. What the devil's keeping him?
 (*He goes into the house.*)

BAIRBRE. Don't be long . . .

CONROY. A very nice young fellow.

BAIRBRE. He's alright. (*She takes off her gloves slowly.*) My clothes is all wrong. I'll change my dress tonight.
 (*She pulls off her hat and rumples up her hair.*)
Imagine me coming to live in a place like this.

CONROY. You'll find it lonesome.

BAIRBRE. Not with him . . . Uncle Matty . . .

CONROY. Hm?

BAIRBRE. What way is his father?

CONROY. Ah! He's the way Tom told you.

BAIRBRE. Yes. I don't care.

CONROY. What made the two of you come back?

BAIRBRE. I wanted to.

CONROY. And himself?

BAIRBRE. Things isn't too good in London at all.

CONROY. But you'd a fine job?

BAIRBRE. I had of course.

CONROY. Running a hotel must be great. You'd see a power of life and merriment I'm thinking.

BAIRBRE. Yes.

CONROY. Why would you never let me see the place when I was beyond?

BAIRBRE. Ach! 'Twouldn't interest you.

CONROY. They gave you fine wages, ha?

BAIRBRE. Not too bad . . . I was on commission like, see? Times 'twould be good, and times like . . .

CONROY. And you gave it all up for himself, ha?

BAIRBRE. What? Oh yes. I didn't want . . . Tom didn't want me, like, to go on you see. Not now we're married.

CONROY. How long did you know him?

BAIRBRE. Two months, and nine days. I've each day counted. We're married now three days. (*She examines the ring on her finger.*) Nice, isn't it?

179

CONROY (*examining it*). Great style . . . Whisper, Bairbre. What made you . . .

BAIRBRE (*with sudden exasperation*). Listen to me, if you're going to ask me more questions, will you lay off it? Lay off it, see?

CONROY. I wasn't . . .

BAIRBRE. I don't want to talk about London, nor my job, nor Tom's job nor anything. I'm tired, see? I want a rest. I don't want to have to think about nothing for a bit. Nothing at all. Nothing at all . . . I'm sorry.

CONROY. 'Tis alright, girl.

BAIRBRE. I'm sorry, Uncle Matty. Here, give us a fag, will you? Oh no, maybe not.

CONROY. I don't smoke them. Just the old pipe.

BAIRBRE. I got some in my bag. Will it be alright?

CONROY. Sure, why not?

BAIRBRE. I didn't know. (*She produces a cigarette and lights it.*)

(BARTLEY *comes out of the house and stands near the door watching her.*)

CONROY. All the girls smoke nowadays.

BAIRBRE. Even in this place, ha?

BARTLEY. Ah sure, they're walking chimneys around here. God forgive them. Trapesing around in their naked feet and a fag sticking out of their gob, 'tis outlandish.

BAIRBRE (*after a brief glance at* BARTLEY.) What does he do on the farm?

BARTLEY. Sure I do everything. Bit of ploughing, milking the cows, cleaning up the place. It do rise desperate dirty. Would there be any chance at all for a chap like myself beyond in London do you think?

CONROY. Sure, what'd there be for the likes of you? Sweeping up the gold off the streets, is it?

BARTLEY (*with gloomy ambition*). I'd always a notion I'd make a great detective.

BAIRBRE. A split, ha?

BARTLEY. A which?

BAIRBRE (*absently scornful*). A split. A Flat. A Nosey Parker. Yes, you'd be great at that, wouldn't you?

BARTLEY. Do you not like detectives?

BAIRBRE. Me? Oh, I'm nuts about them. Why wouldn't I be? (*She blows a cloud of smoke out of her mouth and laughs.*)

CONROY. What'd my niece know about the likes of them trish-trash?

BARTLEY. 'Tis what I'm thinking she looks as if she might know all sorts.

BAIRBRE (*stepping ominously towards him*). What's that you said? You be careful of that slit in your mug or maybe you'd get another, see. (*She stops suddenly, then says nervously.*) You've a power of talk, young fellow. Don't mind him, Uncle Matty.

BARTLEY. I didn't mean no harm.

(*He goes off to the stables. Resentful and muttering.*)

CONROY. What ails you, girl?

BAIRBRE. Ah nothing. I hope I'm not going to have trouble with that lad. Oh, where's Tom? Why doesn't his father come to see me?

CONROY. Would you not come inside?

BAIRBRE. I'll not put a foot through that door till I'm invited.

CONROY. Ah, now.

BAIRBRE (*she regards the house mornfully*). I'm telling you . . . It's a nice house. Looks dark though. I'll get the walls painted up a bit. I'll make a home here. Where there's nobody knows nothing about anything.

CONROY. What's that?

BAIRBRE. Just the mountains. And the breezes blowing. And backwardy people. (*She looks at* CONROY *as though hardly seeing him.*) I'm going to like that.

CONROY. Ach, I suppose we're very backward.

BAIRBRE. Maybe 'tis the best way to be.

CONROY. How did you get on with the people in London?

BAIRBRE. They're alright. The girls is alright, some of them.

CONROY. I wonder now what made you choose Tom Grealish? You must have had a power of fellows to choose from.

BAIRBRE. Fellows? Yes . . . (*She blows the smoke through her nostrils.*)

CONROY. I'm glad you're going to settle down.

BAIRBRE (*staring about her*). Yes. I'm going to settle down.

CONROY. Life can be very nice when two people is happy together.

BAIRBRE. Yes. (*She stubs out her cigarette and smiles at him.*) Tom and me's going to be anyway.

CONROY. That's good. (*He looks at his watch.*) Whisper, Bairbre, I'll have to be getting along home.

BAIRBRE. Ah no!

CONROY. I brought you a present. (*He hands her the box.*) There. 'Tisn't much at all.

BAIRBRE. Uncle Matty! (*She tears off the wrappings.*) What is it? Oh!
(*She holds it up so that it falls loosely over her hands . . . It is a vividly coloured handkerchief of printed silk. She regards it in silence for a moment.*)

181

It's grand.

(*Suddenly she bursts into tears, holding the scarf to her face.*)

CONROY. Bairbre! What ails you, girleen?

BAIRBRE. I don't know. I don't know, honest to God I don't. It's lovely. Thanks. No, don't touch me . . . don't start slopping over me or I'll start all over again. (*She arranges the scarf round her neck.*) I'm sort of tired, see – it's that journey – and the change and everything – don't you mind me. And don't say nothing to Tom about me turning on the taps I mean – sure you won't? (*She fishes out a compact from her bag.*) Look what you done to me. Good job I don't do my lashes no more, isn't it?

CONROY. What are you talking about?

BAIRBRE. No, I said 'twas a foolish thing to be crying about nothing. (*She inspects herself in the mirror. She returns the compact to her bag. Then straightens herself up, and says:*) There! How do I look?

CONROY. Very, very nice altogether.

BAIRBRE. Looks quiet, I mean? Not too la-di-da, no?

CONROY. 'Tis perfection.

TOM (*emerging rather sheepishly from the house*). Himself isn't too well. He's lying on his bed for a bit. He'll be out to you later, he says.

BAIRBRE. Oh? What's wrong with him? (*Her voice is cold with disappointment.*)

TOM. What's wrong with you? Is it crying you were?

CONROY. Ah, not at all.

BAIRBRE. What'd make me cry? Look at the grand present I got from Uncle Matt. How do you like it?

TOM. 'Tis smashing. Smashing, mind you.

BAIRBRE. I hope your father will think so too.

TOM (*dismally*). Ay, I hope to God he will.

CONROY. I'll be hitting to road.

TOM. Won't you step inside for a drink? There's lashings within for the neighbours. A big barrel of porter.

BAIRBRE. Ah, do.

CONROY. No, thank you kindly.

TOM. A ball o' malt, ha?

(CONROY *shakes his head.*)

Or we've a sup of mountain dew.

CONROY. I'm on the wagon.

TOM. Ah, that's too bad.

BAIRBRE. Mountain dew! 'Tis a long time since I heard of that.

CONROY. No, I'm off. (*He goes to the gate.*) My soul, will you look at them bonfires? There's one, two, three – five of them blazing away like the devil.

TOM. Ah, 'tis foolishness.

(*They all stare round beyond the gate.*)

CONROY. Well, goodbye, young fellow. Be good to her now.

TOM (*grinning*). To be sure, to be sure.

CONROY. Let you be a good wife to him. There's a power of bad ones in the world.

BAIRBRE. I'm going to try.

CONROY. That's my little girl. (*He kisses her.*) I'll be over on Monday, young fellow. I want a talk with your father – Goodbye now.

TOM. Good luck.

(CONROY *goes off followed by* BAIRBRE *and* TOM.)

TOM'S VOICE. There she is now! 'Tis a nice jewel of a car, mind you.

CONROY'S VOICE. Bedad, 'tis old she's getting. Ten years I have her now. She runs very sweet.

BARTLEY (*coming from the stables, a broom and a pail in his hands, muttering*). 'Careful of that slit in your mug,' says she, 'or I'll cut your throat,' says she, 'I'll slit your throat from ear to ear,' if ever you heard the like of that from the mouth of a tinker's bitch. 'Slit in your mug,' says she . . .

(*The sound of the car starting away is heard, and the voices of* CONROY, BAIRBRE *and* TOM *saying 'Goodbye'.*)

BARTLEY. Oh, the yoke!

(*He runs through the gate. The car retreats. The sunshine deepens into a reddish glow.* BARTLEY *returns followed by* TOM *and* BAIRBRE *who carries her new scarf in her hand. We can surmise she has been using it to wave her uncle farewell.*)

TOM (*to* BARTLEY). Let you get back to the house and tell your master we're waiting.

BARTLEY. In God's name why would ye not come in?

TOM. Go on now. Be off with you!

(BARTLEY, *muttering something about a slit in his mug, disappears.*)

Why would you not come in for pity's sake?

BAIRBRE. I'll wait. TOM. Aren't I enough to welcome you?

BAIRBRE (*shakes her head somberly, then speaks in order to change the subject*). I like it here anyway. 'Tis a great change from London, isn't it?

TOM. Ay. (*He sits on the bench and holds his arms out to her.*) Come here, will you?

BAIRBRE. I want to look at the mountains.

TOM. Come here whan I tell you.

(*She looks round, at first with a show of slightly haughty surprise, then she smiles and comes to sit beside him.*)

TOM. Bairbre?

BAIRBRE. Hm?

TOM. Tom and Bairbre. Bairbre and Tom. God forgive you, you've me clean cracked. Do you know what?

BAIRBRE. Have I?

TOM. Sentimental. Do you know what I mean?

BAIRBRE. I do.

TOM (*wondering if it is all real*). Let's have a look at the ring. (*She gives him her hand.*) God, I'd be ashamed of my life.

BAIRBRE. Why?

TOM. When I think 'twas your money that bought it.

BAIRBRE. Listen, you're not to think about it. Do you hear me? Never no more. Never let me hear a word about it.

TOM. Sure I can't help tinking. (*He leans his head on her shoulder.*)

BAIRBRE. Well, don't. Tom, Don't. Don't worry your head about things like that.

TOM. I'll have to be worrying soon.

BAIRBRE. You'll pay me back. And then I'll buy —— I'll buy ——

TOM. What'll you buy?

BAIRBRE. Things for the house. I'd like to see things nice. We'll see what's wanting. It'll be fine to have a home. Makes you feel life's important. Maybe it isn't, but it's a good thing to feel. (*She sighs.*) Give us a light, will you?

(*She puts a cigarette between her lips. He produces a box of matches.*)

TOM. My fags is within in my coat. Will you give me one?

BAIRBRE. This is the last one. We'll share it.

TOM (*giving her the match box*). Like we did the first one. The first one of all. Do you remember?

BAIRBRE. Why do you not light it for me?

(TOM *takes the box and obeys her.*)

God help you, you're as rough as a dog. Maybe that's why I like you. (*She lights her cigarette and blows out the match.*) There.

(*She hands him the cigarette.*)

TOM. Standing there in the rain under that arch by the pub. Remember? What's this the name was?

BAIRBRE. The Garden of Eden.

TOM. That's a queer thing, isn't it?

BAIRBRE. Why?

TOM. Such a name!

BAIRBRE. 'The Garden of Eden'! And the rain pouring down!

TOM. And all them coloured lights dazzling your eyes up from the gutter.

BAIRBRE. There was a barrel-organ playing in Greek Street.

TOM. You asked me for a light. As bold as brass.

BAIRBRE. And then I said: 'Aren't you smoking too' didn't I?

TOM. And I'd no fags left.

BAIRBRE. And 'twas too late to buy any more.

TOM. And we shared the old fag.

BAIRBRE. You can share it now.

(*He hands her the cigarette. She smokes in silence for a little.*)

TOM. Do you know what come into my mind and we drinking tea in that Italian place?

BAIRBRE. What?

TOM. I thought you might be one of them bad ones.

BAIRBRE. Did you now? (*She continues to smoke.*)

TOM. I did. God forgive me.

BAIRBRE. What made you think a thing like that?

TOM. You looked too nice to be good.

(BAIRBRE *begins to laugh helplessly. Then she leans her head on his shoulder.*)

BAIRBRE. I do love you, Tom. I love you so much.

TOM (*cheerfully*). Sure of course you do. Why wouldn't you?

(*He takes her cigarette from her and puffs complacently.*)

BAIRBRE. What made you change your mind about me?

TOM. Being a bad one, is it?

BAIRBRE. Yes.

TOM. Sure wouldn't a bad one have axed me up to her place on the spot and axed me for money and all class?

BAIRBRE. Would she?

TOM. Oh yes indeed. Oh, she would certainly! 'Twas three weeks before you'd allow me to come to your little room. Do you remember that?

BAIRBRE. I do.

TOM. Three weeks, and I meeting you every single evening, rain, hail or moonshire, and the two of us drinking tea in every shop and shelter we'd find.

BAIRBRE. 'Twas nice.

TOM. 'Twas, mind you.

BAIRBRE. I wish we could meet all over again.

TOM. And when you'd let me in at last we'd sit on the two chairs every night and you'd wet the tea, no more about it. That wasn't like no bad one, was it?

BAIRBRE. No.

TOM. The picture of the little lad and he making bubbles on the wall. And the yellow cushions on the chairs. Remember? Ach, you looked like a painted devil would coax a saint, and you were as starchy as a nun. You're like my father would shut down his two eyes and roar out a couple of prayers and he only to hear the name of wickedness and it breathed out in a whisper wouldn't stir a rib of hair on your head.

BAIRBRE. Your father's a good man, so?

TOM. Good is it musha, he's a holy saint out of heaven and as cranky as a gander. And he as innocent as a baby. Same way as yourself. You wouldn't know nothing about the devilment does be going on in a place like London. Sure my God how would you?

BAIRBRE (*rising restlessly*). How would I?

TOM. The devil knows what them flighty ones be up to. Coaxing country chaps and the like. Roaring, rampaging, gambling, gallivanting, screeching and swearing, drinking champagne and porter, lepping around when the nights is warm, and they stripping off their clothes and . . . Oh my God.

BAIRBRE. Isn't it a great deal you seem to know about the likes of them?

TOM. There's bad ones in the world and there's good.

(TOM *rises and goes to her, standing behind and putting his arms about her. Dusk is falling.*)

You're one of the good ones. The strong ones.

BAIRBRE (*not looking at him*). Always believe that. Always.

TOM. Times I do be thinking 'tis too good you are altogether . . . Bairbre?

BAIRBRE. What is it?

TOM. There's a little speckle on your arm no bigger nor a graneen of tea. What is it?

BAIRBRE. A burn I got from a lighted sod and I a girl. 'Tis what they say 'tis lucky.

TOM. 'Tis nice. 'Tis the shape of a little star . . . Bairbre?

BAIRBRE. Yes?

TOM. When will you?

(*She does not answer.*)

When?

BAIRBRE (*whispering*). I don't know. Maybe tonight.

TOM. Maybe. Maybe . . . Ach, I could understand it before. But we're married now.

BAIRBRE. Three days.

TOM. Three days and three nights. You love me, don't you?

BAIRBRE. Isn't it well you can ask me that?

TOM. And you know I love you.

BAIRBRE. I do.

TOM. Then when are you going to prove it to me?

BAIRBRE (*still staring away over the mountains*). If you could only believe it from me I'm proving it to you now.

TOM. How are you proving it?

BAIRBRE. Are you thinking I don't want what you want? Just as badly as you? You're wrong. When I'd see you in a crowd, 'tis like seeing a light in a dark place. When you'd put the two hands on me, 'tis like two fires burning me. Ach, I wanted you alright. Only I couldn't. Not at first. I wanted something else. I'm still wanting it. Now that we're here – maybe. In this clean place. And the two of us knowing 'twasn't only that we wanted. Yes, here, maybe, maybe I could. (*She turns and faces him.*)

TOM (wide-eyed). 'Tisn't a sin you know. When two people's married.

BAIRBRE. A sin? (*She begins to laugh again.*) Oh Tom!

TOM. What are you laughing at?

> (BAIRBRE *continues to laugh wildly, carressingly, stroking his hair and his ears as if he were a child.*)

> (*Very gravely he says*) Are you laughing at sin?

BAIRBRE. No . . .

TOM. Times I don't understand you at all. As shy as a plover, as meek as a nun, yet all the while . . .

BAIRBRE (*softly*). Well?

TOM. I don't know . . .

BAIRBRE. Kiss me.

> (*He kisses her.*)

> It's getting dark.

TOM (*raising his head*). See the blush of them old fires? Wait now. (*He leaves her and looks over the wall.*) Oh be cripes! . . .

BAIRBRE. What's wrong?

TOM. I'd be afeared of my life the flames'd spread the way they did five years back. Oh, by all the saints will you look at them idiots. (*He shouts to someone on the hillside.*) Hora! Hora! 'Mhicilin! Fainic a gcuirfea an ait tri theine! Ta na stablai ro – chongarach do na lasrachai' – an amhlaidh is mian leat muid losga nar mbeatha, a phkeidhee?*

---

*For translation of these and other Irish phrases in the play see Appendix.

A MAN'S VOICE (*far away*). Beag a' Baol! Beag a' Baol!

(*Some boy's voice laughs on the mountain side.*)

BAIRBRE. 'Tis queer hearing Irish again. I thought I'd forgotten it.

TOM. Bedad, 'tis more than Irish them lads'll hear out of me. Fan'
orraibh nomead! (*He makes for the gate.*) Fan' orraibh!

BAIRBRE. I'll go along with you ——

TOM. No, this is my job. Wait here a minute. I'll be back. Hora!

(*He goes out through the gate.*)

In ainm an diauail ceard ta ar siul agaibh annsin?

(BAIRBRE *stands looking towards the bonfires, then turns and
begins to walk up and down. The noise of laughter and dispute
dies away. A faint sound of singing is heard in the distance.
Some mountainy men are chanting a country song.*)

BAIRBRE. 'Tis nice. 'Tis nice . . .

(*She returns to the gate and leans over the wall. Then she goes
to the bench where her bag is lying and looks for a cigarette.
There are none left.*)

Damn!

(*She puts the bag back and turns once more to the gate when a
thought strikes her. She returns to the bag and takes out a flask
which she considers.*)

No! (*Reluctantly and with an effort she replaces the flask and goes
back to the wall.*)

(*She leans over the wall, watching the flickering of the bonfires
and listening to the song: as the last notes die away* MARTIN
GREALISH *comes out of the house. He stands at the door
silently looking around the garden. His eyes fall on* BAIRBRE.
*He regards her for a few seconds: she does not see him for her
back is towards him. He takes out a pipe and very deliberately
fills it. Then he produces a match. Before he strikes it she calls
over the hillside.*)

BAIRBRE. Tom! Tom!

(GREALISH *starts. He comes forward a little.*)

GREALISH. Who are you calling?

(BAIRBRE *turns from the wall and looks at him.*)

BAIRBRE. Good evening.

GREALISH. What's that you said?

BAIRBRE. I said good evening, Mr Grealish.

GREALISH. Who are you?

BAIRBRE. I'm Bairbre, Mr Grealish. You're Tom's father, aren't you?

(*He stares at her without a word.*)

BAIRBRE. I hope I'll be a good wife to your son, Mr Grealish . . . Is

188

there anything wrong?

GREALISH. I thought I —— How long were you beyond?

BAIRBRE. Where?

GREALISH. In London; how long were you there?

BAIRBRE. Thirteen years.

GREALISH. Thirteen!

BAIRBRE. It's nice to be in the country again.

GREALISH. It's a lonesome stony sort of a place you've come to.

BAIRBRE. I don't mind that, it's a good thing to be lonesome sometimes.

(*The pipe drops from* GREALISH's *hand.*)

BAIRBRE. You've dropped your pipe.

(*They both stoop to pick it up,* GREALISH's *hand comes into contact with* BAIRBRE's, *after a second she pulls her hand away.*)

GREALISH. There's a pain in my head tonight, like t'would be an old tune, maybe I'm wrong. Wait! 'Tis rising dark. Maybe . . . (*He comes close and stares into her face.*) No. I was right.

(BAIRBRE *stands motionless, staring at him.*)

Go out of this place.

BAIRBRE. Why do you say that?

GREALISH. Go on. Get out. You'll not stay here. Not if you've married my son a hundred times. You'll not stay here, I'm telling you.

BAIRBRE. What right have you to . . .

GREALISH. Right? I'll show you what right.

BAIRBRE. What? What?

GREALISH. It is the same.

BAIRBRE. I don't know what you mean.

GREALISH. Look at me. Do you remember my face?

BAIRBRE. No.

GREALISH. Are you telling the truth?

BAIRBRE. I never seen you before. Never.

GREALISH (*after a pause, during which he does not take his eyes off her*). Maybe 'tis better so.

BAIRBRE. Ehat's wrong? What have I done?

GREALISH. You know better what you done than anyone.

BAIRBRE. I do not know. How would I?

GREALISH. You're after marrying my son aren't you? You want to be living in my house.

BAIRBRE. Amn't I telling you I'll make him a good wife?

GREALISH. A good wife! Look at you!

BAIRBRE (*with an effort at defiance*). Well?

189

GREALISH. My son's a fool. But he's clean. As clean as his shirt.

BAIRBRE. I know that.

GREALISH. He don't know you. Do you want me to tell him?

BAIRBRE (*after a pause, in a half-whisper*). Who are you? (*He does not answer.*) Why do you want to send me out of this place before I put a step into it? Why? (*With sudden fury.*) Tell me!

> (GREALISH *begins to laugh softly. Then the laughter dies and his face goes cold.*)

GREALISH. You're after forgetting me. Well so much the better. I'll welcome you tonight. 'Tis the only thing we can do, isn't it? (*He begins to laugh again.*) But tomorrow you'll go. (*He stoops and picks up his pipe. Regretfully.*) Or I may have to tell my son. You see. Just to put him on his guard, like.

> (BAIRBRE *looks at him in terror.* TOM *comes through the gate.*)

TOM. 'Tis alright now . . . Hullo!

BAIRBRE. Hullo!

TOM (*coming to her side*). Well, father. This is herself.

GREALISH (*lighting his pipe, his eyes off* BAIRBRE). Ay.

TOM (*beaming*). This is my da, Bairbre.

BAIRBRE. I know.

> (*A pause.*)

TOM. Well, are ye not going to shake hands?

BAIRBRE. We're after meeting.

GREALISH. We were having a chat and you above on the mountain-side.

TOM. That's great.

GREALISH (*moving to the door*). Come inside the house, my son's wife.

BAIRBRE. Thank you kindly.

TOM (*holding out his hand*). Come along.

GREALISH. And welcome to you – this night.

> (BAIRBRE *looks at him silently.* TOM *takes her hand and half drags her over the threshold.* GREALISH *hesitates for a moment, then squares his shoulders and follows then in as*

# THE CURTAIN FALLS

# ACT II

*Inside the house, about two hours later.*

*It is a wide irregular kitchen whose many angles and corners are lost in a network of shadows and whose air is one of a worn and specious simplicity. The usual wide country hearth, the usual stone floor and rag mats; a dresser with speckled delph, a wooden settle, a ladder leading to a sleeping loft, sugán chairs, china dogs; a collection of farming implements and fishing-tackle is piled against the wall and there are three pictures, two of the Holy Family and one of the leaders of the Easter Rising of 1916. In the window there is the pot of geraniums we observed in the first act from the exterior of the house, and between it and the door a lamp backed with a tin reflector is nailed to the whitewashed wall. Another door leads off an inner room, and at the upper side of the hearth there is a passage that leads, we must suppose, to a rude sort of scullery, for it is from here that* BARTLEY *now emerges and comes over to the table.*

GREALISH, BAIRBRE *and* TOM *sit at a table covered with a white cloth and the remains of an evening meal.* BAIRBRE *is drinking tea in silence,* GREALISH *has a glass of whisky before him and a bottle; the two men are smoking.* BARTLEY *begins to collect some things from the table.*

TOM. Sure I could have had my pick of any of them. Am I right, Bairbre? Ha?

> (BAIRBRE *forces a smile, nods, and sips her tea.*)

TOM. Beautiful big lumps of girls walking the streets in droves they were and devil a man to be seen half the time.

BARTLEY (*enviously*). Oh merciful hour!

> (*He carries some dishes awkwardly to the dresser, then goes into the scullery.*)

TOM. There was one lassie, an old Scotch one, living in a place called the Harrow Road, oh great style man! She was made to get me.

GREALISH. Ah God give you a pair of eyes to see your big ugly mug.

TOM. Maybe you don't believe me, ha? You don't know nothing about London nor the big world. I'm telling you. Weren't you only in it one time for ten days or the like?

GREALISH. 'Twas enough then.

191

TOM. And that was nine years back, the time there was a power of monied chaps sweating and swanking around the place, and tall shiny hats on them – finer lads than yourself maybe was an old fellow would be too wore out to enjoy himself right.

GREALISH. Is that so now? (*Ironically.*)

TOM. Ach, you always put on me and I staying forever in this place since the time I was a lad dragging stones for you and minding cows for you and you making me think there was no good in me at all.

GREALISH. Well, aren't you the great little bragger?

TOM. I'm as big as yourself. I'm a married man now, (*he winks elaborately at* BAIRBRE) and I after seeking my fortune in the big world.

GREALISH. And what class of a fortune did you find?

TOM. Herself. Now! And I got a couple of nice cushy jobs too . . . like (*his voice slackens.*)

GREALISH (*with relentless indifference*). Like what?

TOM. Sure I could have joined the British Army if I'd wanted.

GREALISH. Musha, God help the British if they were driven to take in the like of you.

(BARTLEY *returns with a bucket of water and a basin.*)

BAIRBRE. Where do you wash them things?

BARTLEY. Here.

BAIRBRE. I'll help you.

BARTLEY. You'll spoil your grand dress.

BAIRBRE. I'll change it. (*She goes towards the parlour door.*) Isn't this the way to our room?

TOM. 'Tis. Through the parlour. Don't be long!

BAIRBRE (*opening the door*). Ah yes.

(*She goes out.*)

GREALISH. Well, you didn't marry a talkative woman.

TOM. Ah, she's shy. Times she do have a power of talk.

BARTLEY. Bedad she do. That one have a tongue would blister you.

TOM. Hold your whist, you.

BARTLEY. Oh, that's true. 'Twas to ask her I did did she know many people beyond in London and she gives a screech and a lep like a devil out of hell and says she, 'I'll cut your throat' says she, 'if you axe me the likes of that,' says she. 'By this and by that,' says she, 'I'll slit your ugly gobbet,' says she. 'I'll plaster you,' says she . . .

TOM. She said no such thing.

BARTLEY. Faith she did then, and 'tis what I'm thinking she'd do it too, and myself to be unawares, before I'd have a Hail Mary out

192

of my mouth, God save us, she's a holy terror.

GREALISH. Let you hold your whist and clear out of that before I'd lay you out on the floor with my fist.

BARTLEY (*crestfallen*). Yes, sir. (*He backs away fearfully.*) What about the washing up?

GREALISH. Herself can do it. 'Tis a woman's work.

> (*A sound of distant cheering is heard from outside. They all look up.*)

BARTLEY. That's the people still dancing at the bonfires.

TOM (*impatiently*). Bonfires! . . . (*His mind goes back to the question in hand.*) Herself isn't used to the likes of them jobs.

GREALISH. Never you mind what jobs she's used to. (*To* BARTLEY.) Go along out of that.

> (BARTLEY *lingers.*)

Well, what are you waiting for?

BARTLEY. May I bring the heifers west 'til I walk them?

TOM. Ah, such foolishness.

GREALISH. Who are you to say what's foolish? My heifers was always walked through the fines on this night of the year and 'tis well you know it.

TOM. Them old piseogs. Devil a bit of good ever I seen coming out of the like. My God, no wonder people think we're backwardy.

GREALISH. 'Tis yourself'll go backwardy down on the flags if I hear another word out of you. (*He pours himself a drink.*)

BARTLEY. I'll bring the heifers, so, will I?

GREALISH. You will. I'll be over later. Drive them out careful now.

BARTLEY. Yes, sir.

> (*He runs out.*)

TOM. Driving cattle through a bonfire for good luck, sure God help us if we've nothing better to do nor that.

GREALISH (*with violence*). Will you leave your tongue off old ways and good practices or God forgive me, I'll give you a clout in the jaw. 'Tisn't yourself or your fine *new* ways will bring any luck on this house at all. I'm master here. Don't you be forgetting it.

TOM. 'Tis time you quit then, I'm thinking.

GREALISH (*rising*) How dare you? How dare you?

TOM (*subdued but still alive*). Im not a child no longer. I'm a married man.

GREALISH. A married man. Ay and begod 'tis a grand sort of a married wife you're after bringing to me through the door this night.

TOM. Bringing to you, is it? That's a good story.

(*The cheering is heard again.* GREALISH, *his glass to his lips, looks gloweringly at his son and says nothing.*)

'Twasn't for to please yourself I brought her – you nor nobody else.

(BAIRBRE *enters in a plain dark dress and stands looking at them. They do not notice her.*)

GREALISH. Nor you didn't please me with her neither. A strange one with nothing for a dowry but a couple of promises from her old uncle would pour honey in your ears and then slip out of the place unbeknown, ha? A useless looking lassie out of London, God save us, and she decked out like a streeling peacock.

TOM. Let you not be chatting talk about her at all. Is it yourself, that couldn't get no woman to look at you for your broody temper and your nettly tongue, and you a widow-man with a power of riches and a score of acres.

(GREALISH *begins to chuckle with sinister relish.*)

Well, 'tis true and you'd no right to be annoying me.

(BAIRBRE *comes forward and pours the water into the basin from the bucket. Then she brings the basin to the fire and heats the water with some from the kettle.*)

When did you come in?

BAIRBRE. A while back.

(TOM *glances at his father, who rises.*)

GREALISH. I'm going to the bonfire.

(*He drains his glass and goes out through the archway, somewhat unsteadily. A door is heard to open, then it is slammed to.*)

TOM (*after a pause*). Were you long at the door?

BAIRBRE. I heard some of it.

TOM. Ah, don't worry.

(*She does not answer but busies herself washing the dishes.*)

Don't worry your head about my Da. He does be a very cross old fellow. Too holy he is altogether I'm thinking.

BAIRBRE. Maybe.

TOM. Well, don't mind him.

BAIRBRE. Uncle Matty will keep his word, Tom.

TOM. About your fortune is it? Aren't you fortune enough for me the way you are, God bless you. You to be standing there before me without a penny and you in your naked pelt this minute, 'twould be enough for me. Now!

BAIRBRE (*amused*). You're not asking much, are you? Where's the young lad?

194

TOM. Is it Bartley? Ah, he went hopping off to the fires, bringing down the heifers for good luck, God bless us and save us.

BAIRBRE. They used to do that when I was a girl.

TOM. You're a girl yet . . . What's worrying you?

BAIRBRE (*she looks at him, then down at the dishes she is washing*). I can't tell you.

TOM. I don't like to see you washing dishes.

BAIRBRE. I like it.

TOM. Is it my Da's worrying you?

BAIRBRE. I'm going to tell you. Your Da says he seen me some place before.

TOM. Well, maybe he have.

BAIRBRE. He says he knew me.

TOM. Well, maybe he did.

BAIRBRE. He didn't. I never seen him.

TOM (*suddenly strikes his fist on his knee*). O begob he's at that game, is he?

BAIRBRE. What do you mean?

TOM (*gravely*). O bedad I'm afraid he have no love for you.

BAIRBRE. Go on, what do you mean?

TOM. One time before – 'twas about five years ago in the summer time like this – a stranger comes, a Dublin fellow, poking around the place he was with a little notebook in his hands and he striving for to learn Irish, do you see. Ah, the Dublin people is a bit cracked, you know, 'tis how they like to try to talk the Irish like and be reading it out of books and that class of thing.

BAIRBRE. Yes.

TOM. Well, this lad had my Da driven clean out of his mind in an hour with his 'what do you call this?' and 'What's the name for that?' and 'Did you ever hear tell of Finn Mac Cool?', and my father gives him one big black look and says he, 'Look at me,' he says, 'Take a good look,' says he, 'do you not remember my face?' says he. 'I do not,' says my man. 'Well faith I remember you,' says my father, 'and begob,' says he, ''tis a bad memory I have of you,' says he. 'And let you sweep away with yourself out of this,' says he, 'before I have the law down on you for what you done to me,' says he, 'in the time that's past.'

BAIRBRE. And he – he never seen him?

TOM. Ah never in his life. Sure, weren't he joking about it after? 'Twas the way he let on to know him, you see, to get rid of him like . . . (*A sudden thought strikes him.*) Oh bedad I hope he don't think ——

195

BAIRBRE. What?

TOM. I hope he don't think to get yourself out of the house that way? By frightening you?

BAIRBRE (*relief and hope showing in her face like a light*). Well, we'll try not to let him, will we?

TOM (*with burly self-confidence*). Is it try?

BAIRBRE (*beginning to laugh*). Oh Tom, thank God I told you! Thank God I told you! Now I'll get on with the things.

TOM (*dubiously*). Do you want me to help you? Like the Yankee chap done in that picture we seen in London?

BAIRBRE. Sure you'd break them. Sit down and smoke.

TOM. What about a sup, ha? (*His eyes are on his father's whisky bottle.*)

BAIRBRE. What?

TOM. A sup? (*He raises the bottle and looks at it.*)There's a power of good whisky left in that. He have porter as well for the neighbours will be flocking in again the night is done. Come on now.

BAIRBRE. Ah no.

TOM. Musha, why not? Just to celebrate, ha?

BAIRBRE. Ah no, I don't want to. (*Nervously she finishes wiping the last plate and starts to arrange the things in a pile.*)

TOM (*the bottle in his hand, taking two glasses from the dresser*). I never seen you with a drink in your hand since first I knew you.

(BAIRBRE *gives him a curious glance, half-sad, half-mocking.*)
Come on now. 'Tis good stuff. (*He pours out two glasses.*)

BAIRBRE (*smiling*). Well, just for tonight maybe.

TOM. Water?

BAIRBRE. No.

TOM (*surprised*) Oho! You're the hard one. (*He pours water into his own glass from a jug on the dresser and hands her the other.*) Now!

BAIRBRE (*regarding it as one might regard a wild cat one would like to have tamed*). Well here's —— (*She stops.*)

TOM. Here's to us.

(*They drink a little.*)

BAIRBRE. A-ah! (*She sighs, closing her eyes for a moment.*)

TOM. Great, ha?

BAIRBRE. Yes.

TOM. You're after changing your dress.

BAIRBRE. Do you like it.

TOM. I do, mind you. But 'tis terrible drab looking. You've the appearance of a country girl.

BAIRBRE. I am a country girl.

TOM. Indeed you're not then. You're a real swank, aren't you?

BAIRBRE (*delighted with this*). Am I?

TOM. You are, of course. Even in that. Is it me marry a country girl? With the big bosom and the big legs and the smell of the cows off her? You smell like a beautiful shop. What are you laughing for?

BAIRBRE. Because I'm happy. God, that's great news you're after giving me.

TOM. About you smelling so sweet?

TOM. 'Tis the way you're not used to it, praise be to God.

BAIRBRE. 'Tis of course . . . Though do you know, Tom, before I met you, I'd . . . I'd have an odd glass. Now and again like.

TOM. Would you now?

BAIRBRE. I would . . . Times I'd be lonesome. Or when I'd meet a few friends.

TOM. You told me you didn't know nobody in London?

BAIRBRE. Ach! They weren't much use to me. But in the hotel I was working in of course there'd be times there'd be an odd party or the like. (*She sips.*)

TOM. Who'd give the party?

BAIRBRE. Och! Gentlemen like and their lady friends. (*With sudden harsh gaiety.*) Hey, you're not working. What's wrong with you, Lofty? Here's to what we like whether it's good for us or not. (*She clinks her glass against his and crooks her arm through his arm.*) That's the way, ha?

TOM (*astonished but pleased*). What's on you?

(*They both drink.*)

BAIRBRE. Whew! That's strong . . . You know what I'm going to do here? (*Her arm still linked in his she begins to gesticulate, holding her half-filled glass in her hand.*) Do you know, sweetheart? I'm going to hang curtains on that window. Curtains, see? With big bright colours all over them. That's when we get some money. Then I'll have a tablecloth on the table, see maybe the same stuff as the curtains like so it'll all be matching. Oh, the matching's very important. Couple of cushions splashed around. And I'll have pots of flowers. I always wanted flowers. In the country nobody bothers about flowers. We'll have lashings of them – everywhere – everywhere – yellow flag-flowers, wild roses, cowslips, appleblossom, Och! you'll see. 'Twill be a bower, like – A lovely bower. Look! – (*She breaks from him.*) Here and here, the whole place swimming in them, big branches of flowers and fine green leaves on them. Flowers every place, and the bees coming in through the door and they looking for their share of honey in the

197

summertime. (*She begins to laugh, then swallows the rest of her drink, then looks at him gravely.*)

TOM. God, I never seen you like this before.

BAIRBRE (*subdued*). No. Now you know you'd better never give me no drink. One small sup and away I'd go, sure I'm hopeless . . . It don't suit me. It don't suit me . . . (*Half to herself.*) Never no more. I hate it – lousy muck – I hate it, do you hear me? (*She sets down the glass.*) Ach, Tom, we're going to make a fine place here, we're going to have a grand life from this out, you and me. I'll coax your father. Some way I'll make him like me. I'll make the place so he'll not know it. I'll get Uncle Matty to do something for us. I'm sure he've a power of money. I'll make your father like me. I'll make him.

TOM. Ach, that's the girl.

BAIRBRE. I'll have a talk with him, will I? Maybe if I could have a little talk with him, just the two of us alone like, do you think would he ever come round?

TOM. Musha, why wouldn't he? Though he's a hard man to coax I'm telling you.

BAIRBRE (*gaily*). I'll find a way, never fear.

TOM. When I was a little lad after my mother died, God rest her, he used to be waking me up in the morning with a skelp of a wet towel and it tied in knots like a ship's rope. He would! He'd turn down the sheets on the bed in the loft beyond and give me a larrap on the bare backside, God forgive him. Oh yes! 'Here's one for the Stallion and one for the Mare,' he'd say. ''Tis morning time,' he'd say. 'One for the Stallion and one for the Mare.'

BAIRBRE. 'One for the Stallion and one for the Mare?' (*She stands very still.*) What did he mean by that?

TOM. Sure God knows. I used to think 'twas the way he was a touched cracked. Of course he's not a strong man at all, you know. Times he do be gasping like an old sheep and he only after walking a mile or so out of this to Gort-na-gopple or when he'd be rubbing down the old mare he have itself.

BAIRBRE (*to herself*). 'One for the Stallion, one for the Mare.'

TOM. Why do you keep saying that?

BAIRBRE. I don't know.

　　　(*A burst of cheering goes up from the mountain outside, very faintly, a door is opened and closed.*)

TOM. There's himself coming in. I'll slip out to the bonfire – 'twill give you a chance . . .

BAIRBRE. No, wait!

TOM. Whisht! I'll go out the other way. (*He goes to the parlour door.*) Put honey on the top of your tongue!

> (*He goes out, closing the door quietly.*
>
> BAIRBRE *stares after him, then nervously tidies away the glasses and the whisky bottle on the dresser.* GREALISH *enters, looks around the room, comes to* BAIRBRE *silently and takes the bottle from her.*)

GREALISH. Where's my son?

BAIRBRE. He went out to the bonfire ——

GREALISH. 'Twasn't to go with his father he could of course. (*He holds the bottle up to the light.*) Somebody's after having their share out of this.

BAIRBRE. Tom asked me would I have a drink with him.

GREALISH (*dryly*). And you wouldn't find it in your heart to go again him, of course?

BAIRBRE. I took a glass.

GREALISH. The first one ever you took, I suppose.

BAIRBRE (*after a moment's pause*). I don't drink. Not as a rule.

GREALISH. Is that so? Well, you'll break your rule this night and you'll have one with myself.

BAIRBRE (*reflecting*) I don't mind, Mr Grealish.

GREALISH (*regarding what is left in the bottle he pours it all out in one glass*). There's not enough in this for two. Easy now, I've better stuff nor that.

> (BAIRBRE *watches him with nervous fascination as he takes a bottle from under the dresser.*)

This is the real stuff, Bairbre Grealish. Sit down now. (*She obeys him.*) We'll drink a small sup together. (*Breathing heavily he sits down to face her, the table between them, and pours out two glasses.*) There.

BAIRBRE. Thank you. It looks like water.

GREALISH. It may look like water, but you'll find it hasn't the taste of water. Did you ever before taste the mountain dew?

BAIRBRE. I don't think I did.

GREALISH. You don't think you did? 'Tis a bad memory you have. Well here's to yourself in the time to come.

BAIRBRE. Thank you.

> (*They drink.*)

GREALISH. Drink it all.

BAIRBRE (*forcing a smile*). 'Tis strong.

GREALISH. 'Tis good.

(*They drain their glasses, then put them down together.* GREALISH *lifts the bottle and pours himself another.*)

GREALISH. Here's to you tomorrow. (*He starts to pour the stuff into her glass.*)

BAIRBRE. Oh no.

GREALISH. You must drink to your journey tomorrow.

BAIRBRE. Why – Why do you want me to go away tomorrow?

GREALISH. Drink up.

    (*They drink.*)

BAIRBRE. Why do you want me to go away tomorrow?

GREALISH (*staring at her*). Because you're no fit wife for my son.

BAIRBRE. If 'tis the fortune ——

GREALISH. If you've seven hundred fortunes and they piled up to the clouds of heaven you're no fit wife for my son.

BAIRBRE (*unable to meet his eyes*). You've no right to say that to me.

GREALISH (*after a pause*). Isn't a queer thing now, you and me to be drinking together again?

BAIRBRE. Again?

GREALISH. Only there was a crowd of fellows inside in the room with us now, and they leaning over a bar and one leg cocked up on the grand shiny rail, and an old music box, maybe, and it braying out music like an ass in the rain only for a penny you'd push in a brassy slit, and yourself and myself sitting there and our backs to the wall, soldiers, niggers, boxers, sailors, the devil knows what elbowing their way for a drink, and the two of us with the hands gripped, wringing the fingers, breaking the knuckles, breathing out smoke in each other's mouths . . .

BAIRBRE (*hitting the table*). Stop it! (*She walks to the fireplace, her back to him.*) It isn't true. I don't believe it. I don't believe it. (*She turns on him.*) I never seen you in your life before. Never. You can't frighten me letting on you know all about me. 'Tis myself knows all about you. That't what's wrong. Trying to frighten people away that'd ever come near you or your old bit of a farm. Och, I know all. Tom told me about you and the way you wouldn't have the decency to welcome nobody in it. Try your old talk about pubs and niggers on someone else. I don't remember nothing about it.

GREALISH. Amn't I after telling you your memory's bad?

BAIRBRE (*with a new spout of violence*). What are you driving at anyway? That you met me some place before, is it? Well, supposing you did, what about it? I met a score of people I wouldn't remember.

GREALISH. Ay and more than a score I'm thinking.

BAIRBRE. What are you driving at?

GREALISH. Come here and sit down.

BAIRBRE. No.

GREALISH. You'd better.

BAIRBRE. Ah look – Look, Mr Grealish – I'm after marrying your son. I want to be a good wife to him – I want to live happy and peaceful in the house here – I'll make it grand – I'll work all day and all night – you'll see what I'll make the place. I know you don't want me here – why would you and you a widow man is used to having the place to yourself – but I'll do my best. I'll make a good home. I know I can. I know it.

GREALISH (*looks at her in silence and pushes Bairbre's half-filled glass towards her*). You're not taking your drink at all.

BAIRBRE. I don't want to drink.

GREALISH. Just to please myself. (*His tone is dangerously conciliatory.*)

    (BAIRBRE *hesitates and then drinks.*)

BAIRBRE (*trying to smile*). There.

GREALISH. That's better.

    (*He pours out two more glasses. They are both getting drunk.*)

BAIRBRE. I'll work hard to please you ——

GREALISH. Is that so now?

BAIRBRE. Ay.

    (*They both drink a little.*)

GREALISH. Let's have a look at your arm, will you?

BAIRBRE. Why?

GREALISH. Roll up the sleeve, will you?

    (BAIRBRE *begins to roll up her sleeve.*)

No, the other one.

    (*She looks at him and then obeys.* GREALISH *takes her arm in his hand and examines it. Then he looks at her silently.*)

BAIRBRE (*rolling down her sleeve*). If you think you met me before, Mr Grealish, I can't remember it. Can you not try to forget it?

GREALISH. Why would I? (*He raises his glass.*) Come on.

    (*They clink glasses; his face is smiling, hers is very grave.*)

One for the Stallion and one for the Mare, ha?

BAIRBRE. No! (*She sets the glass down and rises, turning brusquely away from him and walking over to the wall by the picture of The Leaders of 1916.*)

GREALISH. Do you remember that picture hanging over your bed in your little room? The yellow blind drew down again the light, and the rain streaming down through the fog without, and the traffic roaring? God forgive me, I've a fierce long memory.

(*The sound of cheering is heard again to rise from the mountain, then it dies away.*)

BAIRBRE (*turns to say something and changes her mind*). Why didn't I know?

GREALISH (*with ferocious contempt*). How would the likes of you know anything? How would the likes of you remember one man from another? Wasn't I only one poor amadan in a thousand, ha? Just one among a thousand other poor idiots?

BAIRBRE (*hardening instinctively*). Ay. Maybe that's all you were.

GREALISH. Nine years ago. The one shame of my life.

BAIRBRE. Oh? What are you going to do?

GREALISH. The one shame of my life, I'm telling you. Devil a thing. You're clearing out, that's all.

BAIRBRE. I'm not clearing out without a fight. You think you know all about me, because you met me once, and I suppose 'tis the way you paid me my price or I'd have remembered you well enough from the start this night. Oh yes, I'm not pleading to be no better nor what I was. I was a whore, see, like a million others. Yes. You know that. I was hungry, I was thirsty, I was sober, I was drunk, I had friends, I had enemies, I was in rows and fights, I was in pubs and jails. I done everything. Everything.

GREALISH (*after a pause*). How did you come to live a life like that? A decent Irish girl you were once, ha?

BAIRBRE. Aren't Irish girls the same as others?

GREALISH. They got their religion.

BAIRBRE. I lost mine. It's happened before. I was sixteen when I went to London because the life was dull at home. Dull! My God! And I didn't know how to do nothing, see? I lost five places because I was too damn ignorant to keep them. I never even knew why I lost them. All I knew was I didn't like loneliness. I didn't like the cold nor the dark. I didn't like drudgery. Respectable people does be great slave drivers, Mr Grealish. When I found there was nothing but work I couldn't do or starvation, or letting them know I was a failure at home, I turned to bad people. Bad people is good company, you know. Fellows like yourself, Mr Grealish, Irish or English, Jewmen or Greeks, young men or old men always ready with a drink and a laugh, fellows up from the country maybe, or over from Ireland, and they lepping for a chance to live the life they wouldn't dare live at home. For one night, ha? And they filling your two ears with whisper-talk, and they plastering kisses on your lips the same time they'd be giving you false names for fear you'd blow on them and you to be meeting them again. God! Don't I know all about them?

GREALISH. Would you wonder at it? 'Tis ones like yourself is the shame of the world.

BAIRBRE. A woman can't sell nothing without there's a call for it, don't you believe it.

GREALISH. Are you standing there making a defence for yourself. You should be ashamed to open your mouth.

BAIRBRE. Well I'm not, not to the likes of you, nor I'm not making no defence, I'm telling you something. When I met Tom, he was different. Ah, he was no better maybe, but he was ignorant, see? He didn't recognize me, do you get that now? He didn't get my number.

(GREALISH *makes as if to speak but she silences him with a gesture.*)

No, you're going to listen to this. He didn't see no paint nor smell no drink off me. (*She covers her face for a second with her hand and then continues.*) We started knocking around together. I began to tell him lies. And all that time I never even let him kiss me.

GREALISH. A likely story.

BAIRBRE (*violently*). I don't give a damn whether you believe me or not . . . Yes, I do care, for if you believe me maybe you'll . . . Well, I went to a priest one night, see? I wanted to get back something I'd lost. And I told him everything. And he helped me too. He tried to help me. He told me to do – what I done.

GREALISH. A priest told you to marry a decent man?

BAIRBRE. Yes.

GREALISH. If he'd known that you and that man's father ——

BAIRBRE. Ah! . . .

GREALISH. What do you think he'd say? (*Takes a gulp from his glass, watching her.*)

BAIRBRE. Och, I don't know . . . I don't know!

GREALISH. Think that over. (*His voice sinks to a low whisper.*) When you're laying in my son's arms in the one bed, think it over.

BAIRBRE. I married your son three days ago and I never lain in his arms yet. Never. Let you ask him.

GREALISH. And you expect me to believe that, do you? (*He begins to laugh hoarsely.*) Oh Merciful God!

(*His laughter seemd to choke him. He coughs and splutters and chokes then, finally, pours himself a fresh drink and grows very grave. He looks up at her with cold hatred.*)

What brought you back to this place?

BAIRBRE. I'd no money left.

GREALISH. And he was after spending all of his on you, I suppose?

BAIRBRE (*involuntarily*). All of his, is it?

GREALISH. What's the truth about them jobs of his?

BAIRBRE (*evasively*). I don't know.

GREALISH. You'd best be telling me.

BAIRBRE. He'd bad luck.

GREALISH. I knew it. So my fine London bucko was sponging on yourself all the time, was he?

BAIRBRE. He was not.

GREALISH. Liar!

BAIRBRE. I'm no liar.

GREALISH. You're lying now. Sponging on you he was, and you earning your filthy wages. Let's look at that ring! (*He rises and goes close to her.*)

BAIRBRE. No!

GREALISH. 'Twas yourself bought that, ha?

BAIRBRE (*she bows her head for a moment*). Supposing I did?

GREALISH. How was it your money gave out?

BAIRBRE. I couldn't go on. I told him I'd lost my job. So I had . . .

(*They are close to each other now.* GREALISH *is holding her hands in his. There is a pause. Presently she says in a whisper:*) Let me go. Let me go! You filthy —— (*She wrenches herself free.*)

GREALISH. You'll go alright. You know that already. (*He returns to his seat by the table and sits there rubbing the back of his fist against his ribs and breathing heavily.*)

BAIRBRE (*coming to the table*). Mr Grealish, will you give me a chance? For God's sake? I'll be a good wife to him – I'll go to the priest here and I'll get his advice – we'll go together, you and me – I'll obey him too, I'll take his advice, I'll do what he tells me – whatever it is. Only don't make me go away from Tom. You'll not do that, I know you'll not do it. Look, look, if 'tis the fortune you're thinking about I'll write to Uncle Matty – I'll write him this night. He have money, – didn't he promise yourself he'd do something for me. I've got to be with Tom. I've got to. I've got to. I couldn't live no longer without him. I wouldn't. What'd I do? Where'd I go? Where'd I go?

GREALISH. You'd go back where you came from.

BAIRBRE. Where I came from. (*She thinks for a moment.*) Did you ever go walking through London and it late at night? And you alone? No, you never did. If you did itself 'twouldn't be the same for the likes of you. You're a man. Go there as a woman. Alone. And you waiting for a glance before you'd get your supper, and you wiping the slobbering rain-drops off the mirror in the bag to see are you fresh enough meat for to be bought. When the streets is full 'tis no so bad. (*Bitterly.*) Busy nights is not so bad, don't you think it. There's noise and you get to like noise after a time, because it's not so cruel as the silence. There's lights and there's drinks, and who the hell cares anyway. But when 'tis late and your chances is gone maybe – God! what chances – you listen for footsteps and you say 'Goodnight' and they passes you by or they stops and laughs, belching and bargaining over you, same as if you was a heifer at a fair. Oh no. I'll not go back to that. Not for nobody in the world.

GREALISH. And what's to stop you getting honest work?

BAIRBRE. Honest work, is it? The likes of me was destroyed for honest work from the first night I was paid to play at love. Is it the likes of me to be scrubbing and scouring, keeping myself sober and straight and respectable, rising alone in the black dawn and sleeping alone when the night comes down, for what? For what? There's only one thing on the ridge of the world can save a woman who has lived the life I'm after living and that's a man, see? One man. Nothing else. I've found that man. And if I can't keep him 'twould be better for me to die. Oh much better. (*Slowly.*) No. 'Twould be better for me to die.

   (*A pause.*)

GREALISH. Sit down there.

BAIRBRE (*whispering*). Yes. (*She obeys him.*)

GREALISH (*after a pause in which he knocks out his pipe slowly on the heal of his boot*). This is a lonesome place, Bairbre Grealish. 'Tis lonesome and 'tis cold. 'Tis the great wonder to myself you'd want to be staying in it at all.

BAIRBRE. 'Twouldn't be lonesome for me.

GREALISH. Twelve years it is now I'm a widow-man, and I barely three score. But you see I made a vow I'd never marry.

BAIRBRE. Why?

GREALISH. I'd reasons. (*He raises his glass and looks at her over the rim.*) So you want to stay here, do you?

   (BAIRBRE *does not answer.*)

Maybe we might think out a way. (*He drinks and sets down the glass.*)

   (BAIRBRE *stares at him. Slowly he turns his head to look at her again.*)

205

You never belonged to my son. How long do you think that's to go on?

BAIRBRE. I don't know.

GREALISH. 'Tis a strange world. (*He drains his glass. His voice thickens.*) And 'tis terrible full of sin. Times I do be wondering is it too hard we are, the one again the other.

(*She sits intently, listening.*)

I don't like to be talking in this place at all. I'd often a notion my son would be listening at the door there . . . 'Twould be the pity of the world he to hear the things the likes of you and me would have to say to each other . . . (*A pause.*) There's many a fine thing I could be doing for you only you to understand me. 'Tis fine hours we could be passing together, yourself and myself when the nights is dark, and my son abroad at his work. In case you're still wanting to stay in this place I've no wish to open my mouth about you. But you'll make up your mind before morning. (*He passes behind her chair.*) 'Tis myself is taking the risk, God help me. What's one sin more or less to the likes of you?

BAIRBRE (*turning her head slowly to look at him*). You deserve to die for that.

GREALISH. You've the hasty tongue. Think it over . . . Let you think it over this night and tell me your mind.

BAIRBRE. I —— (*She thinks rapidly.*) Alright.

(GREALISH, *gazing at her through his haze of poitin, begins to laugh again, softly.* TOM *appears at the door, radiant, a lighted sod in his hand.*)

TOM. Begod them heifers trampled the ashes like heroes! Here! Take the sod from me! 'Twill bring you luck, girl.

GREALISH. Take the sod from his hands, woman of the house!

(*Pause.*)

TOM. Did you hear what he said?

(BAIRBRE *comes slowly forward and takes the sod from* TOM's *hands.*)

BAIRBRE. That was the way I was burned and I a young girl searching for luck in the fire. (*She puts the sod on the fire.*)

TOM (*follows her to the hearth. Whispering to her*). How did you get on together?

GREALISH. Let you not be whispering to yourselves, the two of ye. We got on fine, and we're going to get on better. We're going to get on grand. I'm telling you, grand!

(TOM *is delighted at this and joins in his father's laughter.*)

TOM (*To* BAIRBRE *as he helps her to rise from her knees*). Now what

206

did I tell you? Begod, she'd coax a badger!

(*There is a knock on the door and it is at once pushed open by* BRIDIN RONAN, *a young girl, dressed in a red petticoat and bodice and a heavy black shawl. She carries a big cabbage-leaf in her hands which contains a pile of strawberries.*)

BRIDIN. Good evening to ye all!

TOM. Is that yourself Bridin Choil Ronain?

BRIDIN. 'Tis. Bartley Patch is after telling me ye were home, and I'd nothing at all, so here's a couple of fresh strawberries for you, Tom Grealish's wife, and my hundred blessing with them!

BAIRBRE. Oh thank you. Thank you kindly. (*She takes the strawberries.*)

BRIDIN. Oh dear me, you're beautiful, God bless you, you're as shiny as a posy.

BAIRBRE. Thank you.

BRIDIN. Eat them, ma'am, they're sweet as sugar. (*To* TOM) God strengthen you, mister, aren't you the lucky man! (*She shakes hands with him.*)

(*There is another knock at the door and* MAIRE, *an old woman in black appears accompanied by* BATTY WALLACE.)

MAIRE (*as she bears down on the bride*) God save all here!

(GREALISH *mutters something unintelligible.* TOM *and* BAIBRE *return the salutation.*)

TOM.
BAIRBRE.} Good evening to you!

MAIRE (*continuing*). Musha, there she stands, God bless her, as pure as the snow. Batty, draw near!

(*The young man, who carries a basket, approaches, dumbly smiling.*)

Let you draw over now, Batty, – ah, he's deaf as a post, Lord save him – 'til you show the brace of ducks.

(*During the following speeches the kitchen fills slowly with neighbours.* BARTLEY *appears with* TWO YOUNG MEN *of his own age in their best suits, one of them carrying a melodeon, the other a fiddle. A very* OLD MAN *in a bawneen leaning on a stick, and* THREE COUNTRY WOMEN *in red, enveloped in their shawls. The rear is brought up by* TWO CIVIL GUARDS. *All the guests carry gifts excepting the* GUARDS *who add nothing to the scene but the imposing solidity of their presence and the clouds of smoke that issue from their cigarettes.*)

BAIRBRE. Now isn't that very good of you?

(*The neighbours press round* BAIRBRE *smiling and saying:*

*'God bless you, ma'am.'*)

MAIRE. Ducks, girleen, a young duck do be very sweet eating out and out. Oh Lord bless us and save us, you haven't the appearance of strength on you at all. (*With gloomy relish.*) Oh my soul, I hope it isn't to fade away on you she will, Tom Grealish, and she bearing the first child you'd give her, the way me daughter done when Batty here come into the world. Do you remember that, Mairtin? Do you remember, neighbours? And there he stands, this minute, God bless him – give them old ducks here to me, Batty – and him a gamey young hero would clatter the brains out of judge or jury would dare to say a word against his granny, and the poor mother he never laid eyes on and she stretched out under the green sods and myself roaring prayers after her.

TOM. Ah you're a great lad surely, Batty.

(BATTY *beams and grunts, his head moving slowly from side to side.* TOM *turns to the gathering crowd.*)

God save ye all!

NEIGHBOURS. Good luck to you, Tom Grealish!

God bless you, Mr Grealish!

Here's a bag of meal for you, ma'am, and my hundred thousand blessings with it.

TOM. Will we go west in the parlour? There's a power of drink within.

GREALISH (*grimly*). 'Tis only porter then. There'll be no fear of the hard drop for the likes of them. (*He turns away and lights his pipe.*)

NEIGHBOURS. Good luck to you!

Ah, he's the hard man. There's porter within.

God bless ye both!

Long life to you, ma'am.

Are you going within, Cole Yank?

BAIRBRE. Thank ye – thank ye all!

BRIDIN. The ashes is red yet on the mountain, my feet was near blistered.

MAIRE (*her voice rising imperturably through the others as they file into the parlour*). Oh, isn't it a glorious thing a lone woman to have a man around the place the way he could be putting in a word for her or be striking a blow for her, and she not able to make a stir for herself with the dint of the weakness does be on all female women, God help us! Batty, move west, 'tis inside the parlour we're going, och I suppose 'tis the way you'll want to be drinking a sup to cheer her, and she turning her face on the hard bitter road of married life. Oh my God, when I think of the olden

208

times when myself was a young girl was led blushing like the rose by the big hairy lad – that was your grandfather, God bless him, – that's stretched beyond in the relic these twenty years now and he dead and buried decent, no more about him, but myself crying tears down for him morning, noon and night.

BARTLEY (*to* BRIDIN). Come on with myself, will you?

BRIDIN. I will.

(*They run out.*)

MAIRE (*ushering* BATTY *and the rest of the crowd towards the parlour door*). Oh 'tis Batty will be able to give the great dance – wait now, I'll leave the ducks down here . . . (*she does so*) – the great dance altogether and he praising the beauty of the bride. Tune up, Cole, Johnny the Boat? till you see the shower of steps. Dance, you devil, dance.

(*The* FIDDLER *plays and* BATTY *dances grotesquely. A cheer goes up.*)

NEIGHBOURS. Ora Batty my love you are! Hesn't he the great little feet, God bless him? Oh, he's a terror. Long life to you, Batty Wallace! My love this night! God, he'd tame the thrushes. You'd a right to be proud of him Maire Jack, God bless you. My soul, he'd dance to Heaven.

GREALISH. Ah, let you dance within.

TOM (*to* BAIRBRE). Are you coming?

BAIRBRE. I am.

(*They go into the parlour.*)

MAIRE. There she goes, the Lord strengthen her!

(BAIRBRE *passes her with* TOM.)

God save her, I don't think she've long to live at all.

(*She goes with* BATTY *and the remainder of the party.*

GREALISH, *left alone, walks up and down for a moment, lost in thought – he is befuddled with drink, but his brain is working. A burst of laughter from the parlour causes him to turn his head in that direction. He closes the door, shutting out the noise. He pours himself a last drink, draining the bottle, then blows out the lamp on the wall, and crosses unsteadily to the fireplace where he relights his pipe from one of the candles on the mantelpiece. Then sits by the fire smoking, his glass in his hand, lost in thought. The parlour door opens slowly and* BATTY WALLACE *comes in. He stands staring vacantly in front of him, a smile on his face.*)

GREALISH (*glancing up*). What has you standing there?

(BATTY *grins.*)

What are you doing there, you big slobbering clown?

(BATTY *comes forward, still grinning, and making faint unintelligible noises with his lips.*)

Get out of my sight! Do you hear me? Get out in the yard!

(*He rises and goes threateningly towards him.* BATTY's *smile dies away, he grunts fearfully and begins to back towards the outer door.*)

And don't be letting the mare out again. Don't let me catch you creeping about them stables the way I did last Martin's Day or by all the saints I'll give you a belting you'll remember till you'll go under the sod. Do you understand that now? I want no sweating slobs to be hanging about this place. Go along out of this before I stretch you with my fist. Go along.

BATTY. Ah!

(BATTY *backs out through the door into the garden.* GREALISH *closes both doors and goes back to the fire. The* FIDDLER *begins to play 'County Mayo' and a* MAN'S VOICE *sings the song. There is a sound of applause and of boots striking against the stone floor.*

TOM *comes out of the parlour accompanied by a shaft of yellow light and the noise of conversation. He closes the door.*)

TOM. What has you sitting in here without the lamp?

GREALISH. Ach! Them and their ceilis.

TOM. They're thinking it queer you not to be within with the company.

GREALISH. I want a word with herself.

TOM. Is it Bairbre?

GREALISH. Who else?

TOM (*pleased at this*). Musha, why not? (*He turns to go back, a thought strikes at him and he pauses.*) What do you think of Bairbre?

GREALISH. I don't know.

TOM. Isn't she very different from the big, clumsy ones does be filling up the houses around this place?

GREALISH. Maybe she is.

TOM. She's a great girl, let me tell you.

GREALISH. Will you do what I'm after bidding you.

TOM. I will . . . What do you want to say to her?

(GREALISH *turns his head slowly and looks at his son.*)

I will . . . (*He goes back to the parlour, closing the door behind him on the laughter within.*)

(GREALISH *rises, knocks out the ashes from his pipe, takes a lantern from the corner of the kitchen and examines the wick.*

BAIRBRE *comes in from the parlour.*)

BAIRBRE. Tom told me you wanted me.

GREALISH. Close the door.

(BAIRBRE *stares at him.*)

Go on.

(BAIRBRE *obeys him.*)

BAIRBRE. What do you want?

GREALISH. I want to see yourself.

BAIRBRE. What for?

(*A pause. He stares at her.*)

GREALISH. That son of mine is no better nor a fool. And fools do have long ears. Didn't I tell you I'd no wish to be talking in this place?

(BAIRBRE *does not answer.*)

You know the stable where I keeps the black mare? 'Tis a short piece only beyond the back of the yard. 'Tis a good quiet place and a strong bolt on the doors without and within. I'll see you there. 'Twill be quiet. (*He lights the lantern with a spill from the fire.*)

BAIRBRE (*presently she speaks*). I've my mind made up. Mr Grealish. I'm going to speak to Tom.

(*Song stops – applause.* GREALISH *raises his head and regards her. The fiddle begins on a slip-jig in the next room; the gay, childish, monotonous notes floating incongruously through the closed door.*)

The two of us will go out of this tomorrow. Together.

GREALISH. And where do you think you'll go to?

BAIRBRE. I've three pounds and a few shillings left. We'll go out of this together.

GREALISH. You'll find it hard to give him the reason of your going.

BAIRBRE. I'll tell him you don't want me. I'll tell him I'd never be happy in this place.

GREALISH. Let you do that; let you make a move to get my son to go out off with you. I'll tell him what I know.

BAIRBRE. You'll never do that . . . You'd be afraid to tell him about yourself.

GREALISH. There'd be no need. (*With drunken insinuation.*) Would you wish to tell him that side of the story?

(BAIRBRE *stands motionless for a second, then suddenly flares out:*)

BAIRBRE. Get out! Get out of my sight!

GREALISH. Sh! (*He comes close and puts his hand over her mouth.*) Do your raving in the stable. The black mare have no tongue but her

211

own. (*Whispering.*) Are you going to stay quiet? (BAIRBRE *nods.*) (*He takes his hand away.*)

BAIRBRE. I'll stay quiet.

GREALISH. I'll see you below. Don't be long.

BAIRBRE (*her face expressionless*). I'll follow you.

(*He goes out softly through the yard, taking the lantern with him.* BAIRBRE *stands for a moment, considering. The music of the slip-jig continues. She puts her hands to her throat as if she were unable to breathe. She feels the scarf round her neck. Her hands drop to her side then, but her face does not change. She turns slowly and goes out the way that* GREALISH *went —— The noise of the slip-jig and the cries of the dancers grow louder as the*

# CURTAIN FALLS

# ACT III

*Outside the house, two hours later. It is still dark, and the light in the kitchen window still burns.*

*As the* curtain rises, *the fiddle is heard playing a reel, and there is the noise of footsteps dancing in the house. As the sound dies away and the applause breaks out, a horse's hoofs are heard galloping far away. The hoofs come nearer to the house, pause, and then gallop into the distance.*

BRIDIN *comes out of the house, her shawl falling about her shoulders. She is followed by* BARTLEY *who is a little drunk.*

BRIDIN. Listen! There! Did you not hear it?

BARTLEY. I did not.

BRIDIN. Listen!

> (*They are silent, their ears cocked for the sound. But the horse is far away.*)

BARTLEY. There's nothing.

BRIDIN. I heard it right enough. And the dogs was barking too.

BARTLEY. 'Tis the music sets them off.

BRIDIN. I'm certain sure I heard a horse and it galloping.

BARTLEY. 'Tis that old speckledy horse out of Flaherty's you heard maybe. He do always be breaking loose.

BRIDIN. 'Tis cold isn't it?

BARTLEY. The dew's falling.

BRIDIN. 'Tis blue as water.

BARTLEY. What's blue?

BRIDIN. The air. You'd think 'twas under the sea we were.

BARTLEY (*sitting down heavily*). Ay.

BRIDIN. Let's go back to the house. Will we?

BARTLEY. Ah, stay for a minute, will you?

BRIDIN. Will we?

BARTLEY. Sit down here with me.

BRIDIN (*sitting down*). 'Tis nicer like now we're all in the kitchen. 'Tis more natural like in the kitchen. 'Tis a beautiful party. I suppose 'tis now they'll be carrying on till morning?

BARTLEY. Ay.

213

BRIDIN. I got two sweet cakes and a glass of porter. 'Tis a fright.

BARTLEY. What's a fright?

BRIDIN. Porter. Fierce bitter it do be.

BARTLEY. If you was a man 'tis the bitterness would please you.

BRIDIN. Do you tell me that? It must be a very queer thing to be a man – Ha?

BARTLEY (*gloomily*). It is, mind you.

BRIDIN. Oh, I'm sure 'tis fierce.

BARTLEY. Ah, responsibilities! Responsibilities!

BRIDIN. What's that you're saying?

BARTLEY. Responsibilities.

BRIDIN. Oh yes.

BARTLEY (*after a brief glance at her*). Ah, what's the sense in talking to you?

BRIDIN (*brightly*). There's no sense in doing anything is there?

BARTLEY (*after a pause*). What happened that poor amadan?

BRIDIN. Batty Wallace is it?

BARTLEY. Ay.

BRIDIN. I don't know. He went away.

BARTLEY. That grandmother of his didn't put no pass on it.

BRIDIN. Ah, she wouldn't mind him whatever he'd do. He do be lepping the hills like a lamb, God help him, and he a lonesome hawk wouldn't do no harm to nobody. Why won't she mind him?
    (*He puts his arms round her.*)
Ah, don't put your arm round me, I don't like it.

BARTLEY. You do like it.

BRIDIN. Too young I am to be married.

BARTLEY. I didn't axe to marry me.

BRIDIN. No, but you're thinking about it? Aren't you?

BARTLEY. How do you know?

BRIDIN. Sure, what else'd make you put your arm around me?

BARTLEY (*removing his arm*). Ah, you've great notions, haven't you?

BRIDIN. Why wouldn't I have? Haven't my father three score pounds in store for me?

BARTLEY. Have he?

BRIDIN. The way I'll be able to take my choice. (*She smiles at him, very demurely.*) You've a blue face on you. 'Tis the morning's whitening on the sky. 'Tis queer the appearance do be on everything early in the morning isn't it? And 'tis silent. Listen! (*She puts her finger to her lips, whispering.*) Do you hear that?

BARTLEY. What?

BRIDIN. Sh!

*(The dog begins to bark.* BAIRBRE *comes to the gate from the direction of the stables. She seems drunk, she is staggering a little, her scarf is in her hands.)*

BAIRBRE *(to the dog, in a low whisper).* Shut up! Sh!

BARTLEY. Sh! Don't move.

*(He and* BRIDIN *crouch down by the wall.* BAIRBRE *slips in through the gate, not seeing them.* TOM *appears at the door.)*

TOM. Ara, what ails them dogs? Will you hold your . . .

*(He sees* BAIRBRE *who starts and then draws near him.)*

Where were you all this time, Bairbre?

BAIRBRE. I took a turn that's all – I wanted the air.

TOM. Where's himself, do you know?

BAIRBRE. No. Did he not go up to his bed?

TOM. He must have.

BAIRBRE. Let's go in will we? 'Tis cold. *(He takes her in his arms.)*

TOM. Ay, they're all asking for you.

*(They go in together, his arm round her shoulders. They close the door. A drunken shout arises from the house.)*

BRIDIN *(after a pause).* She's lovely isn't she?

BARTLEY. Sh!

BRIDIN. I said she's lovely isn't she?

BARTLEY. 'Tis unknown to me what way she is.

BRIDIN. Ara, she have beautiful things. I slipped inside in the room and they dancing the hornpipe, and there were all sorts scattered out on the bed and on the little table that's in it, rakes for her hair and they all shining colours, and silky stockings and leather gloves and the smell of raspberry blossoms off them, and powder for her face mind you, and little brusheens like on sticks for to clean her mouth.

BARTLEY. My soul, she'd want them.

BRIDIN. Do you not like her?

BARTLEY. I do not.

BRIDIN. I likes her then. But I'd feel sorry for her, mind you.

*(A pause.* BATTY WALLACE *runs to the gate unseen by* BRIDIN *and* BARTLEY, *looks up at the house, and silently runs off in a different direction.)*

BARTLEY. What's on you?

*(*BRIDIN *is sniffing the air.)*

What is it?

BRIDIN. I thought them bonfires was quenched.

BARTLEY. Yes. *(He sniffs.)* Wait. *(He runs to the gate and looks round the mountain. A red light flickers dully from the stables.)* My soul, 'tis on fire! Come on with you!

(*They both rush out in the direction of the light. The galloping of horses' hoofs is heard again, circling round the hills. A* WOMAN'S VOICE *begins to sing "Jimmy Stor".* BAIRBRE *comes out of the house and walks slowly across the garden. Her face is expressionless. She comes to the rocks at the side of the garden and stretches out her hand to steady herself on the stones. The song continues.* BARTLEY'S VOICE *is heard in the distance.*)

BARTLEY. Fire! Fire! The stable's on fire! Help! Bridin, go west to the well! Fire! My master's dead! My master's burned! Fire! (*He comes rushing through the gate.*) Mister Tom! Mister Tom! Neighbours!

(*He rushes into the house without seeing* BAIRBRE.)

The stable's on fire! My master's dead! The black mare is gone and the door was closed! My master's dead! He's dead!

(*The song stops. The* GUARDS *and* BARTLEY *appear, followed by the* NEIGHBOURS. BRIDIN *runs through the gate.*)

BRIDIN. Bartley! Bartley!

TOM. Out of my way. (*He comes out of the house.*)

NEIGHBOURS. Merciful God! A spark from the bonfires! Bring out a blanket! Bring out a blanket! Oh, my God! What's that you're saying! He's dead! He's burned! God have mercy on him!

MAIRE. Batty! Batty! Where are you? Where did you go, son? Where did you go? Batty! Batty!

NEIGHBOURS. Maybe 'twas himself! No, 'twas a spark from the bonfires.

(*They all rush out of the gate. Their voices rise to a shout at the sight of the flames, then die down.* BATTY *comes from behind the house and stares in the direction of the light. It flickers and dies down.* BAIRBRE *stands motionless. A moan of dismay goes up from the crowd, then there is silence.* BAIRBRE *goes on her knees and begins to mutter something, half sobbing, her face hidden in her hands. Presently we hear what she is saying.*)

BAIRBRE. Mother of God . . .

TOM'S VOICE (*far away*). Give me them boards. Here! Take his feet. Take his feet.

BAIRBRE. Holy Mary, Mother of God. (*The voices of women.*) Och! Ochon!

TOM'S VOICE. Let ye stay behind. (*The voices of women, drawing nearer.*) Oh! Oh! Oh! Cover his face.

A WOMAN'S VOICE. Take my shawl.

BAIRBRE. Pray for us sinners now and in the hour of our death.

216

(*She covers her face in her hands. Silence. The people appear:* TOM *and* ANOTHER MAN *are bearing the body of* GREALISH *on a couple of boards; it is covered with a woman's shawl. They carry it into the house.*)

MAIRE. Batty! Batty!

(*She puts her arm about him and leads him into the house after the others.*)

Where were you, little son? Where did you go from me? Oh, lift him soft. Say a prayer. Say a prayer.

(*The house is silent.* BAIRBRE *half staggers to the door.* BARTLEY *comes out and sees her.* BAIRBRE *stands very still.*)

BARTLEY. Why are you not within, down on your two knees?

BAIRBRE. Where are you going?

BARTLEY. For the priest.

BAIRBRE. Ay. For the priest.

(BARTLEY *goes to the gate.*)

What happened?

BARTLEY. He was drunk. The thatch fell on him and it burning. And the straw was blazing inside.

BAIRBRE. He's dead?

BARTLEY. He's breathing yet.

(*He rushes away.*)

BAIRBRE (*she looks after him wildly, then back at the house. Then she looks up at the sky*). No! He's dead. He must be dead. Make him die. Make him die. Please. Don't let him live. If he lives he'll . . .

(*She is silent, sinking to her knees again. The house is silent too. Slowly then a* WOMAN'S VOICE *rises in a wailing lamentation.*)

THE WOMAN. Ta se imithe uainn! Ta se imithe uainn.

OTHER WOMEN'S VOICES. Ochón. Ochón. Ochón go deo.

THE WOMAN. Bron ar an mbás! Bron ar an mbás!

OTHER WOMEN'S VOICES. Ullagón! Ullagón! Ochon go deo.

(BAIRBRE *listens, raises her eyes and blesses herself. She falls to the ground and covers her head with her hands.*)

THE WOMEN'S VOICES. Ullagón go deo! Och. Ochon!

(BRIDIN *comes out of the house, her shawl about her head, weeping. She stands at the door for a few moments, then sees* BAIRBRE *and comes forward to her.*)

BRIDIN. Mrs Grealish.

BAIRBRE. What is it?

BRIDIN. 'Tis a bad story, isn't it?

BAIRBRE. Ay.

BRIDIN. I couldn't stay . . . It brings the tears out of me. Are you not going within?

BAIRBRE. What would I be doing within?

BRIDIN. You'd say a prayer.

BAIRBRE. Come and sit here.

(BRIDIN *sits on the ground beside her.*)

You're young, aren't you.

BRIDIN. I am.

BAIRBRE. Too young you are to be crying over a dead man.

BRIDIN. I can't help crying when I sees dead people.

BAIRBRE. You'd a right not to be looking on death. 'Tis a poor ugly thing for the living to look at.

BRIDIN. But isn't it death is waiting for us all? and 'tis what my mother says, it may be a better thing nor life.

BAIRBRE. Better than life? Oh yes! Better than life.

BRIDIN. And yet I can't help crying.

BAIRBRE. You're very young. Look at me.

(*She and* BRIDIN *look at each other.*)

Don't be crying. Maybe you'll make a good life for yourself.

BRIDIN. Maybe.

THE WOMEN'S VOICES. Ochon! Ochon go deo!

BAIRBRE. I'd a right to be in the house and I down on my knees saying prayers by the side of the man I'm after marrying. And I can't go.

BRIDIN. Why can't you go?

BAIRBRE (*she looks at Bridin*). Never do nothing you'll be ashamed of. Oh, there's a foolish thing to say. And the worst of all is to be doing the same thing over and over 'till it don't have any meaning no longer. When you get to that you're finished, see? Because you can't find no sense nor meaning in anything at all. Not in killing itself. You're finished. You can go through life in a glass case and be proud you're so safe and so clean, or you can step out bold and be spattered with mud. One way's as bad as another.

BRIDIN. I don't understand you.

BAIRBRE. It doesn't matter. (*She shivers.*)

BRIDIN. You're cold. I'll lend you my shawl.

BAIRBRE. Oh no.

BRIDIN. I'm going within.

(*She fastens the shawl over* BAIRBRE'*s head.*)

BAIRBRE. Thank you.

BRIDIN. There.

BAIRBRE. Ay, go back to the house and say your prayers. Make your keening for the dead like a woman would get her share of silver for prayers and lamentations. But don't shed no real tears. (*She hangs her head down.*)

BRIDIN. His face is all covered up. His hands is burned.

BAIRBRE (*raising her eyes in terror*). Go inside!

>(BRIDIN *looks at* BAIRBRE, *rises, and goes back into the house.* BARTLEY *comes through the gate with* A PRIEST.)

BARTLEY. This way, father. Please God you'll be in time.

>(*The keening rises again from the house.* BARTLEY *and the* PRIEST *look at each other and go silently in through the door.* BAIRBRE *rises and begins to pace to and fro. Suddenly* TOM *appears on the threshold. Seeing her he closes the door and comes to her.*)

BAIRBRE. Tom.

>(*He stares at her without speaking. His breathing is rapid.*)

Tom, what is it? What is it? What's wrong with you? Tom!

TOM. My father ——

BAIRBRE. Oh Tom.

>(*She puts her arms about him. He stands rigidly, not returning her embrace.*)

TOM. My father was alive when they brought him within. He was trying ——

BAIRBRE. Yes?

TOM. Trying to speak he was.

>(BAIRBRE *looks at him without answering.*)

TOM. I put my ear to his mouth. 'Twas barely I could hear him.

BAIRBRE. What did you hear?

TOM. You know well what I heard.

BAIRBRE. What do you mean?

TOM. 'Tisn't true is it? 'Tisn't true. He was lying. The last words he said was lies. Black lies . . . Go on. Tell me they was lies.

BAIRBRE. What did he say?

>(*They stand gazing at each other. Her hands drop to her sides.*)

TOM. He said you murdered him. 'She murdered me,' he said, 'that – harlot of yours.' (*She does not speak.*) Why? (*He takes her roughly by the shoulders.*) What is it I'm looking? Tell me?

BAIRBRE (*dully*). Did he say 'murdered'.

TOM. They're whispering inside 'twas Batty Wallace maybe burned the stable. My father was hard on him. Would he do the like of that to be even with my father? Or did the wind blow a spark from the fires on the mountain? . . . Why is there black marks on my father's throat? Nobody else seen them marks, but I seen them. I seen them.

219

(*She is silent.*)

Tell me 'twas that poor dumb fool done it. Tell me that and I'll believe you. In God's name ——

BAIRBRE. Quiet! (*She puts her hand over his mouth.*) It's all true. What your father said. It's all true. Now you know. I'm not lying to you no more.

(*He flings her hand away. She turns from him and walks away.*)

TOM (*after a pause*). I don't believe it. (*He sits down and stares dully in front of him.*) I don't believe it.

BAIRBRE. Well, it's true. Every word.

(*A pause. She takes a long breath and looks at him, then turns her head away and speaks as if she were speaking to herself.*)

BAIRBRE. I don't know why I'm telling you this . . . I did it, the way he'd never be able to tell you. And now – I'm going to tell you myself. Yes. (*She walks up and down for a moment.*) Your father did know me. That was true too. He met me in London years ago. Once, that's all. And he paid me my price. No, don't say nothing. I didn't remember him at first. Then after that I did. And I asked him not to tell you. And then he offered – for to make a bargain with me.

TOM. No.

BAIRBRE. I wouldn't keep the bargain. I went to the stable the way he asked me. I tried to argue with him. But all the while I knew what I was going to do. He quenched the lantern. We were in the dark. He tried to force me, I did it. I did it. With this. (*She puts her hand to her throat where the handkerchief is knotted.*) Uncle Matty gave me this. I thought he was dead. I thought I'd killed him. I didn't even do that right.

(*She begins to laugh, bitterly, then recovers herself and looks at him. He stares up at her, then slowly rises to his feet.*)

When I opened the door to get out the mare galloped away. I was afraid. I brought a sod from the fires and burned the thatch . . .

TOM. You killed my father.

BAIRBRE. Well – Are you going to give me up?

TOM. Give you up?

BAIRBRE. To the police I mean?

TOM (*nodding slowly*). The police. Yes.

(*He turns towards the house.* BAIRBRE *makes no move. He stops.*)

I don't know what I'll do. (*He looks at her.*) If you was a bad one, why would you never –

BAIRBRE. I loved you . . .

220

TOM. You was bad and my father was bad. As bad as any filthy – all my life, and I thinking . . . (*And her face quivers. She says nothing.*) Oh my God, if all the holy priests of the four quarters of the globe had told me that and they bent down on their knees before me, I'd not have believed them. If the angels of God were to have come down out of the sky, and they with the truth written white as lightning on their mouths I'd not have believed them.

BAIRBRE. Don't.

TOM. Selling yourself! And you taking their filthy money, and you lying to me up to my teeth day in day out for all these weeks and months.

BAIRBRE. Never after the first day I met you. Never once. I swear that. If I die this minute I swear that's true.

TOM. But you went on lying to me.

BAIRBRE. I loved you. I wanted you never to know. (*She looks at him and breaks off.*) I'd have died of the shame. I loved you.

TOM (*suddenly coming to her, his arms about her*). We'll go away. (*She shakes her head.*) Ay, we'll go away. No matter where.

BAIRBRE. Go away? How can we go away?

TOM. They don't suspect nothing. If they finds anything at all there's nothing to be proved, is there? 'Twas nothing but an accident. We'll go away.

BAIRBRE. We can't. No more than the stones could go.

TOM. 'Tis almost morning. We'll go away. I don't care what you done. (*They cling together.*) I don't care. I don't care.

BAIRBRE. You'd never be sure of me no more, I see that plain enough now. If you was to see me talking to anyone or I was late coming into the house and the night falling. You'd think, you'd wonder.

TOM. I wouldn't, I wouldn't.

BAIRBRE. Ay, you would! I'd never stand it. T'wouldn't work Tom, when you're after seeing dirt on a face you'd remember it always. All the time. Oh I thought I could be different because after I met yourself I look different in my own eyes. But it was only in my eyes – like the mountains. See? The mountains look different from this place in my eyes. But all the while they're the same aren't they? You can't change them, you can't change anything. Let me go. Please.

TOM. Never. I'll never let you go.

BAIRBRE. Oh Tom.

(*One of the* CIVIC GUARDS *and* ANOTHER MAN, *their coats over their arms, their shirts unbuttoned, come through the gate from the direction of the stables. They pause on their way to the*

221

*house.*)

GUARD. The fire is quenched, Tom.

TOM. Thank you. We're coming in now.

GUARD. Ay. There's a power to be done.

(*He and his companion go into the house.*)

TOM (*after a moment's pause*). Let you slip in the back way. We'll get a handful of things together. There'll be a bus at the cross at nine. If we stay they may commence talking. We'll walk as far as we can.

BAIRBRE. If we get as far as the cross itself we'll be lucky I'm thinking . . . The cross. (*She stops short, puzzled by her own thought.*)

TOM. We'll be together.

BAIRBRE (*her eyes kindling*). Do you mean that? Do you mean it?

TOM. I do.

BAIRBRE. Then we'll risk it.

TOM. Come one.

(THE PRIEST *comes out of the house.*)

PRIEST. Tom Grealish.

TOM (*turning*). Yes, father.

(*They shake hands.* BAIRBRE *pulls the shawl over her head.*)

This is my wife, father.

PRIEST. This is a sad night for you I'm afraid, Mrs Grealish.

(BAIRBRE *does not speak but nods.*)

Your father met a terrible death. 'Tis my sorrow I could not have been with him before. (*Looking at them both.*) You have my heart's sympathy.

BAIRBRE (*almost inaudibly*). Thank you, father.

PRIEST. All the way from London you came, I hear, ha?

BAIRBRE. Yes.

PRIEST. This must seem a lonely place to you. A lonely place, and a wild one, I suppose, for a person that's used to a great city. 'Twas a poor welcome you got. But you'll find great peace among the mountains here, with the help of God.

BAIRBRE (*raising her eyes to look at him*). Do you think will I?

PRIEST (*after a pause, puzzled and serious*). You've known a lot of sorrow, Mrs Grealish, I can see that. If I can help you at any time at all let you come to visit me.

BAIRBRE. Thank you.

PRIEST (*to Tom*). There'll be a deal of things to settle. You may need my help. The farm is yours now, isn't it? It belongs to the two of ye. Let ye do well with it as your father would have wished.

TOM. Yes.

222

PRIEST. You were a good son to him . . . I think, mind you, the two of you should be inside in the house.

TOM. My – my wife was very upset like, father.

PRIEST. Of course, of course. But let the two of ye go in now when you feel you have the strength and say a prayer for his soul. And I'd like to see yourself, Tom – I'd like to see both of ye – at my house after six o'clock mass, if that'll suit ye.

TOM. Yes, father.

PRIEST. Your father was a stern man. But in many ways he was a fine one. (*Gently.*) Let ye go in now and say a prayer for him. Remember, he's very close to you both now – closer may be than he was and he alive. (*He looks round at the sky.*) 'Tis lightening. (*He looks from one to the other.*) Well, God bless ye both.

(*He goes out through the gate.*

BAIRBRE *stands staring in front of her.* TOM *makes as though to embrace her. Very gently she pushes him away.*)

TOM. What is it?

BAIRBRE. I'm not going away with you, Tom.

TOM. What?

BAIRBRE. You heard what he said? I can't go away with you.

TOM. But you told me you ——

BAIRBRE. I've changed my mind.

TOM. You'll go with me if I have to drag you.

BAIRBRE. The farm is yours. Make it a good farm. I'm only after bringing poison to it.

TOM. Listen ——

BAIRBRE. The priest is after saying your father was close to us, closer than he was and he alive. He was right.

TOM. What do you mean?

BAIRBRE. Your father would stand between us till the hour of our death. Ay! and beyond it, maybe.

TOM (*he takes her in his arms*). I'm not afraid.

BAIRBRE. We're not going to live like that. I'm only sad for one thing. I never belonged to you the way you wanted. Goodbye, Tom.

TOM. Bairbre!

BAIRBRE (*wildly*). Let me go! (*She wrenches herself free.*)

TOM. Where are you going?

BAIRBRE. I'm going to give myself up.

TOM. No!

BAIRBRE. There's nothing else for me to do. I'll not go back to the hell I'm after living in for thirteen years. Nor I'll not walk out of this with yourself and a dead man between us. Nor I'll not creep away through the back door by killing myself neither. On no!

TOM. Listen to me, Bairbre. Listen.

BAIRBRE. I wish God would help me to do it, I wish something would help me!

(*A long wail goes up inside the house.* A WOMAN'S VOICE. *It is followed by a murmur of other voices, low and menacing.* BARTLEY *appears at the door.*)

BARTLEY. Tom! Tom! There's black marks on his throat! Your father – he was murdered! There's marks on his throat! 'Tis what they're saying Batty Wallace killed him! Tom, come inside – come inside! They're after accusing Batty – They're after arresting him!

(*The voices grow louder.*)

BAIRBRE (*suddenly, in a loud voice*). Neighbours! Neighbours!

TOM. Wait!

BAIRBRE (*thrusting* BARTLEY *aside and standing on the threshold*). Neighbours! Men and women, come out of the house! Come out! Come out!

(*The* VOICES *die away.* BAIRBRE *backs into the garden as the people come out of the door and stand in a half circle near the wall of the house, staring at her in amazement. Among them is* BATTY, *whose arms are held by the* GUARDS.)

Listen to me! Listen, all of you. Listen! That lad you have there has done nothing. Nothing no more than any one of yourselves. No, let me speak!

(*A pause. They all look at* BATTY. MAIRE *goes on her knees sobbing. The crowd turn their eyes slowly on* BAIRBRE.)

Neighbours! Men and women! I killed the man that's within! I strangled him with this scarf.

(*She pulls the scarf from her neck and holds it out.*)

(*The people, with a low murmur, back away from her a pace.*)

BAIRBRE. And I burned the stables with a lighting sod from the fire on the mountain.

(*She falls to her knees, the shawl about her head, the scarf in her hands.*

*The* GUARDS *move forward to arrest her. The first rays of the morning sun fall on her.* BATTY WALLACE, *sitting on the stone fence starts to play his tune again as* BAIRBRE *turns and walks slowly out of the yard, followed by the* GUARDS.)

# THE CURTAIN FALLS

# THE LIAR

*A Duologue with Choral Interjections,*
*Translated from the Original Irish of*
*Micheál macLiammóir*

# CHARACTERS

A Young Woman
A Middle-Aged Woman
An Older Woman
A Young Man
A Middle-Aged Man
An Older Man
Nonie
A Mother
A German Lady
Martin

The play was firest produced at the Gate Theatre, Dublin, On 7 October, 1969 as part of the Dublin Theatre Festival, with the following cast:

| | |
|---|---|
| A YOUNG WOMAN | Biddy White-Lennon |
| A MIDDLE-AGED WOMAN | Máire O'Hanlon |
| AN OLDER WOMAN | Joan Stynes |
| A YOUNG MAN | Rober Carlile |
| A MIDDLE-AGED MAN | Séamas Healy |
| AN OLDER MAN | John MacDarby |
| NONIE | Máire Ní Ghráinne |
| A MOTHER | Eileen Crow |
| A GERMAN LADY | Mary Cannon |
| MARTIN | Patrick Bedford |

The play was directed by Hilton Edwards and the Setting was by Robert Heade.

The scene is set on the Mailboat and in a café in the West of Ireland.

*Night. A long bench on board the Irish Mail. At one end of the bench three men sit together: in the middle there is an empty space. At the bench's other end sit three women. Men and women alike are working people in travelling clothes, the best they have. Little bags lie at their feet and on their knees. One young man has only a parcel done up in paper. The travellers vary in type and even, it may be, in certain details of dress, yet their faces are mask-like in expression. At the two opposite extremities of the bench sit a man and a woman, both of them in their late sixties, then a man and a woman of about forty-five, then a very young man and a girl of perhaps twenty-one. They sit for a moment without speaking.*

*Faint music over. Then there is a rattling of cans and of chains: A seagull screams: a fog horn blows.*

MEN & WOMEN.   Soon she'll be leaving the harbour,
                     We're all on board
WOMEN.           And we'll be staring back at water
MEN.              growing wilder
WOMEN.                    dimmer,
MEN.                           darker
MIDDLE WOMAN.  Under the last Wicklow star.

WOMEN.           Homesick already for neighbours
YOUNG WOMAN.  and shops
MIDDLE WOMAN  for the
                     kettle on the fire
                     the lacy
                     windows in the teapot twilight.

*(The* MOTHER *appears. She stands irresolute listening.)*

OLDER WOMAN.  The children growing tall,
YOUNG WOMAN.                  the hats
                     in the hall,
MIDDLE WOMAN.         and then
                     the holy water over the hair-tidy
                     and the door safe-closing on the dead of night.

(*The* MOTHER *moves to join the group, but changes her mind and passes them.*)

YOUNGER MAN.   I'll sing a song in the bar; maybe some lonely chap.
Will stand me a pint or a girl tell me her name.
I'm great company, my God, I'm irresistible.

MIDDLE MAN.   Wedged in like cattle, drinking porter
Or standing on the deck till we'd see Welsh hills
Rising up out of the waves like a litter of pigs under the sea-sick dawn.
Ah, the long black buckling train, the curly broken sandwich, the
Cup of rocking tea and in London the devil knows what.
I'm worried.

OLDER MAN.   Ach, I was there before I'm used to it all
And my days are half spent and I don't care no more.
Working in London, sallow streets without end
All full of shops and jobs and pubs: there is no end.
No end to what I'll do:
Maybe I'll pull through.

OLDER WOMAN.   Oh, will my sister be there to meet me? Getting old
I'd never have come at all if nobody's there at the station.
Wherever it is and myself turning round like a feathery weathercock
Fool in a wheel of strange faces
Oh my, oh my.

MIDDLE WOMAN.   I'll say a prayer, I know what I'll do, I'll say three Hail Marys.
I'll make a Novena, I'll pray to St Anthony
Go down on my knees, I'll rejoin the sodality, I'll
Kneel down to wash my face, I'll rise up every morning
I'll offer up Masses I'll batter my way
I'll never lose my faith, never, never.
England or no England I'll never slip nor slide
My two sons in the Legion of Mary and a private word every night with Bernadette.

228

Oh there's no one like the Man Above, I know
   what I'll do
I'll open the heavens, I'll have a cup of tea.

YOUNG WOMAN. I'll be rich I'll be gorgeous, it'd be easy for me,
I'll begin it all quiet, I'll smile my way through
I'll wear velvet jeans and sell roasted chestnuts in
   the
Long glittery streets and my dreams will come true
Through my smile, my bright teeth in the fog-
   shiny dusk

YOUNG MAN. (*To* YOUNG WOMAN.) Going to London?

YOUNG WOMAN. Where do you think? (*To* MIDDLE WOMAN.) Bloody
eedjut. (*to HIM*) But you must be saying some
things I mean, reely, where else would I be
going?

YOUNG MAN. It might have been Birmingham. Or Liverpool.

YOUNG WOMAN. Birmingham is it?

WOMEN. Liverpool?

ALL THREE WOMEN. God!

MEN & WOMEN. London, London, London.

YOUNG WOMAN. London. That's the place. (*As he sidles along to sit
beside her.*) Is that your luggage?

YOUNG MAN. It is.

YOUNG WOMAN. Keep to your own side of the bench, so.

YOUNG MAN. (*As he obeys.*)
She'll be sick and sorry one day
When I've got money and when I can pay
Shirts and socks and pigskin bags
Lashins of tips, expensive fags
A Cadillac car as big as a lorry
That's the day she'll be sick and sorry . . .
I'll give London three months honest to God and
   then
I'll be a burglar. I always wanted to be a burglar.

YOUNG WOMAN. That's the class you'd have to beware of.

229

Thanks be to God I know my onions.

MIDDLE WOMAN. Go to a hostel.

YOUNG MAN.  Let yourself in as slick as a whippet,
Combination. Safe. Right left turn and slip it
Open as stiff as a monk at his prayers
Diamonds and dough and the cops on the stairs.
Bang! Bang! Pow! Pow!

(*As he says the last two words he holds two imaginary revolvers.*)

MIDDLE MAN.  Will you dry up for God's sake.

OLDER MAN.  We're all trying to think.

(*Now* NONIE *joins the group. She sits next to the* YOUNG MAN *who is staring in front of him, his elbows on his knees, hands drooping.*)

NONIE.  (*To* YOUNG WOMAN.) Is this right for second class?

YOUNG WOMAN.  Sure.

NONIE. Thanks. (*She fingers her bag and stares about.*) If I could roar crying I'd feel better so I would. How will it be when he looks at me in a new shiny room and himself and his mother all grandeur and style? I'll be prostrated with the journey. I'll never hold up my head. Oh won't I though. I'm as good as they are any day. Only he wanted me he'd never send the fare-money. A strong cup of tea till I wash the two eyes, my two sparkling eyes he said it, my Tokyo nose, my Hiking Girl lips and a couple of Hail Marys, my good 9/11d scarf on my unfortunate head, oh God, oh God! What'll I do? (*She sobs suddenly.*)

OLDER MAN. Take no notice.

MIDDLE MAN. Leaving home.

OLDER MAN. They're all the same.

MIDDLE MAN. Take no notice.

OLDER MAN. Don't cry, sure it'll be all right.

MIDDLE MAN. Put in a word to St Christopher. Ach, God! I was forgetting. He's after going west now same as Philomena. All the same now he's grand for a journey.

(*The ship heaves: They all lurch with its movement.*)

OLDER MAN. Merciful God, isn't it fierce?

(*The ship heaves again.* NONIE *is propelled for a moment*

*against the* YOUNG MAN *who rouses himself from his dream and looks at her, smiling. She smiles back nervously: her smile dies like a candle-flame blown out.*)

YOUNG MAN. Hello there. (*His grin broadens.*)

NONIE. Hello. (*She shifts away and sits near* THE YOUNG WOMAN.) Excuse me.

YOUNG WOMAN. That's OK (*She regards* NONIE *briefly and looks away.*) She'll never get anywheres. Never. She'll be a nursemaid. Oh yes. Other people's kids. Up and down the bay window terraces and the two chizzlers pulling at the string bag and the young one bawling out his lungs in a wet pram: 'Want to go home to mammy!' Aha! And meself lepping and screeching with the laughter. Oh give us this day our nightly champagne. Oh yes. Why not? When I'd feel the devilment rising up in my bosom I might do worse than be drinking champagne. I might do a great deal worse.

YOUNG MAN. What's the good of that for crying out loud? 'Get out of your bed', says he, 'when the bad thoughts comes into your head and do a couple of rounds of shadow boxing.' Yerra, for God's sake, shadow boxing!

MIDDLE WOMAN. Father Mulally, I said to him then straight out plain I said 'The Doctor', I said, 'told me I was to have no more children.' And he telling me my husband should have more control over himself. 'You don't know Joseph Aloysius,' I said, 'or his passionate nature.' 'Then put him in another room' says he. 'There isn't another room, Father.' 'Then put him at the other end of the bed.' Now really. I'd love that cup of tea, God, I'd love it.

(*The* MOTHER *who has been watching now overcomes shyness and joins them. She comes walking unsteadily with the ship's motion. She is a comfortable person from the West of Ireland. She surveys the seat and its occupants.*)

MOTHER. Would there be a small space here?

NONE. Oh yes. (*She moves closer to the* YOUNG WOMAN.)

MOTHER. (*Sitting down between* NONIE *and the* YOUNG MAN *and gazing in front of her.*) Without I'd get seasick I wouldn't care. All the same wasn't it bad enough in the train bumping east with me out of Galway and all the lonesomeness, the miles and miles nothing but stones and blackbirds thinking back there all the time. I'm lonesome for the water and the houses, the small fields and the thorn bushes. Oh will I see it again? The Long Walk and William Street, Shop Street, Buttermilk Lane, Spanish Arch and the devil knows where, up and down by Lynskey's, west by the sea or home by Taylor's Hill. Oh my my my, and only the clock tick tock on the wall tick tock drive you mad and only for that . . . Ah and the room where the boys used to be sleeping, all of them in America now, might as well be dead and buried. Martin, the last of them now in London oh dear me oh what'll it be like at all, you see he's a good boy and a good boy after all and he sent me the fare yes the ticket, the ticket, wait now I remember. I do not remember. I don't I don't.

NONIE. Did you lose something?

MOTHER. Thanks be to God. (*She produces the ticket and laughs.*) Oh my! My son sent me that.

NONIE (*producing her ticket with no difficulty at all.*) My husband sent me that.

MOTHER. Some men are not so bad you see.

NONIE. No indeed. (*She turns away.*) Men? Lying, boasting, bragging, teasing, drinking, swearing, snoring, squeezing. Love him, leave him. Never believe him. No! never believe him, never! (*She turns to the* MOTHER.) Not so bad at all. My husband's very considerate.

OLDER WOMAN. Considerate considering all things I've no doubt. No doubt at all. Ah but life is very sad isn't that right Aunt Moley I said. God help my Aunt Moley living in a world of her own. How's me mother? says she and herself 89, how's me mother? says she. Dead I says. Ah no! she says. Mammie dead? Dead and buried this 42 years I said Oh God rest her says Aunt Moley, poor Mammie and how's your brother Jack? Dead says I. Ah no sure Jack couldn't be dead sure he's only a boy. Dead says I. And how's his poor suffering wife? Dead says I. Ah no! sure they're all dead Maudie she says only you and me. And I'm not Maudie says I! Sure I'm sitting with you here Patricia's my name and I'm not dead but Maudie is. Maudie is what? she says. Dead.

OLDER MAN. Dead as a doornail.

OLDER WOMAN. Oh God be good to us says she sure everybody's dead. Not everybody says I. Not at all says I, there's your own eleven sons and daughters, Moley. All alive and kicking. Sons and daughters? she said. Sure I was never married was I? You were so I said to John Slattery I said – John Slattery Moley said ah you're pulling me leg Maudie sure I never would 'a' married John Slattery. I hated the sight of him. Oh isn't old age a fright and me all alone on the station at Euston maybe. Like as if I was dead meself. Dead.

OLDER MAN. Dead as a doornail. Ah God rest poor old Jemmy he wasn't the worst no not the worst blind drunk elephants every

Saturday night telling his poor wife he was kept at the office no not the worst.

MIDDLE WOMAN. Not the worst poor Bridie but oh merciful hour me cousin Monica always unkind to me poor mother. Lord be good to her: always unkind to me mother and wasn't the same Monica knocked off of her bicycle in the heel of the hunt on the Dublin Road be a passing lorry. Killed dead on the spot and not a priest nor a brother near her. And although of course we're taught that God's mercy is infinite still you never know.

MIDDLE MAN. You never know what'll be in store for you. London how are you, and living with me London relations, roaring the hearts out of themselves over the noise of the telly ah things are changing and why did I tell them I was out in Easter Week who fears to speak well I do for one. No blotting it out what's the use of telling lies if you can't prove them. A-ah!

YOUNG WOMAN. Lies. Lies. Lies Pack of liars and drunken bowsies all of them. I'm as good as any of that crowd any day. Common as ditchwater, what about a factory oh Janey the rules and regulations clocking you in and the noise, God, clatter the brains out of you be freer selling chestnuts who knows some rich fella come along a bag of chestnuts miss and what about a bit of dinner with me did anyone ever tell you you'd a gorgeous pair of eyes take a pair of sparkling oh I'll get on fine Nanette of the Niteries read all about me in the News of the World, never know your luck. (*Flings out hands: says to* MIDDLE WOMAN.) Sorry!

MIDDLE WOMAN. That's all right.

YOUNG WOMAN. Begging your parsnips Auntie Freezebottom. Thinks she's someone!

YOUNG MAN. Thinking they're someone everyone thinking they're someone these days but bedad I'll show them all some day. Ah 'twas always in me inside of myself burning twisting scorching shouting like thunder to be let out. If I can keep clear of the young ones be cripes they's ruin your career wouldn't they still it's a long time since I gave meself a crick in the neck looking back after them and the skirts blowing up along the Mall oh get out for shadow boxing. Yerra, 'tis all nonsense. Oh my God why didn't I choose Dublin wouldn't it be nearer two excursions a week Thursday and Sunday but London's more chances for any class of devil's work, if the straight and narrow have no chance for me 'twill be Highwayman Harry or Seamus Feeney Money or your life ha ha hands up or your life's not your own no time for thinking no time for consideration.

NONIE. Ah yes, he's full of it.

MOTHER. What's this you were talking about?

NONIE. Consideration. My husband. He's full of it.

MOTHER. Ah God forgive me, my thoughts were astray. What's this you said?

NONIE. I was saying my husband is very considerate.

MOTHER. You're very young to have a husband.

NONIE. Yes.

MOTHER. Is it the way you're going to join him?

NONIE. (*Nodding.*) In London.

MOTHER. Is he in work there?

NONIE. He is. A nice home . . . he says.

MOTHER. My son have a beautiful home . . . he says. And a beautiful wife . . . he says.

NONIE. Oh?

MOTHER. I'm in holy dread of meeting that one.

NONIE. Why, isn't she a nice girl?

MOTHER. Nice? Oh she's as raving beauty and she have a title. Now.

NONIE. A title?

MOTHER. I didn't meet her yet. All the dukes and lords in Dublin was there at the wedding. Oh the presents from the gentry: silky sheets in a silver ring, dishes and toast-racks and they bursting out lashing and glittery over the tables like herrings you'd see in a net and the moon rising, lashings of red ale, porter and whiskey in swinging buckets of cracked ice, a blessing from His Holiness in a gold frame and a cluster of shells in the corners and sugary cake as big as the Claddagh. Oh, by all accounts, I'm telling you.

NONIE. I wish I'd 'a' had a wedding like that.

MOTHER. (*Primly ecstatic.*) Money and rank doesn't always bring joy. Oh no. She's a martyr to her nerves.

NONIE. Your daughter-in-law?

MOTHER. Nerves. A martyr. Any person the least ways common or rough, any little spickle-speckle of dirt or disorder, anything wouldn't be fine as a fair, she'd let a small little screech out of her like a young lark would glimpse a hawk and she'd go off in a class of a coma. Would you believe that?

NONIE. I would.

MOTHER. I wouldn't then. Times I do be wondering.

NONIE. Grand ones does often be that way. My own mother-in-law does be that way inclined.

MOTHER. Now.

NONIE. Oh yes. A title and all. Fifty-two dresses, a dress for each week of the year and she'll sit in the parlour playing Canasta with the best in the world and she pouring the tea out of a golden pot. She'd cock up the snout at anyone wasn't as grand as herself. He'd never let me meet her at all.

MOTHER. What did he want to marry you for so?

NONIE. I don't know. (*She turns from the* MOTHER.) Yes. It hurts me at first but then when he'd look at me and his two eyes dark as night falling over Capel Street, our little room there deep as a shadow under the bird's wing of the roof and his kisses like bees on my eyes and my throat, oh what did I care how grand he had been in his boyhood, the Lords of the West and his mother and father, and all the fine life he had left to go searching away through the world for the bravest adventure. A war-time commando he was, a parachutist, a journalist in the Argentine, a soldier in the Foreign Legion, a naval cadet that went sailing the seas, and home with him then to strike a blow for the Border. What are you laughing at?

MOTHER. You reminded me of someone.

NONIE. Till he fell in love with myself. Oh can I forget him coming in that day to the cafe, a packet of Shannons please . . . now what on earth put it into his head to do it that way.

> (*The cafe:* MARTIN *comes in, arrives at counter and, after some furtive glances about him, produces a penny and raps it urgently against the till: he says in a strong German accent with overtones from Hollywood*)

MARTIN. Is somebody not there?

NONIE. (*Appearing, wiping her hands on a towel.*) I'm sorry, I was washing up. The other girl's off. Did you want something?

MARTIN. (*As their eyes meet he becomes more German than ever.*) Twenty cigarette. Shannon, isn't it?

NONIE. Twenty Shannons? Oh yes.

MARTIN. Sank you. And have you perhaps . . Ach! I do not know how you say in English . . . paper isn't it?

NONIE. Paper? What class of paper?

MARTIN. The news. To read. In German we call this –

GERMAN LADY. (*At table.*) Nachrichten. So! Sie sind Deutscher?

MARTIN. (*Glaring suspiciously and with horror at her, turns his back on her, pulls his hat down and his coat collar up and says to* NONIE.) Have that dame pay her check and beat it if you love me, lady.

GERMAN LADY. Verrückt! Amerikanor. (*Slapping bill down on counter.*) Now! Please.

NONIE. Merciful hour. (*To* GERMAN LADY *she says, pulling herself together.*) Thank you . . . Wait till I see now . . . That'll be two and ten pence ha'penny.

GERMAN LADY. (*Fumbling with her bag.*) Ach! Ja . . . my change . . . Danke. (*Looking at Martin.*) He is, I think, quite mad, this man. (*Goes off.*)

NONIE. (*As she absentmindedly deals with till and money.*) Thank you very much. (*She turns to* MARTIN.) Are you a film star or what?

MARTIN. Well . . . I've stood in a couple of times for Gregory Peck, you know . . . And I went down Niagara Falls once, doubling for Tarzan of the Apes . . . Can't remember the guy's name for the moment: kind of a squarehead name . . . but I reckon nobody would say I was a star (*he regards her, says suddenly.*) Gee! What made you think I was a star?

NONIE. Oh I don't know. You could be one, couldn't you?

MARTIN. Could I? . . . Say! I figure I could. I figure I am, in a way . . . (*He glances over his shoulder nervously and says.*) Ah . . . Mademoiselle, you 'ave forgot-en per'aps my cigarette . . . Ah a-ha!

NONIE. Who are you now? Maurice Chevalier?

MARTIN. (*Back to what he imagines is California.*) Sh! That guy over there's watching me . . Can't you see he's watching me?

NONIE. What guy? Where?

MARTIN. (*Abruptly he is in Earl's Court.*) Arty sort of chappy with a beard . . . actually, and corduroy bags . . . Look at him! . . . Sort of creeping out of the door, sort of. Don't care for the look in his eyes.

NONIE. But he has his back to you.

MARTIN. (*Close as can be to the Spanish Arch.*) Ah there's some lads and you'd think they'd eyes in the back of their spines, so you would.

NONIE. Merciful hour! Your Shannons.

MARTIN. (*As she turns he shakes his head clear of the spell: a dog coming out of the water.*) Ah yes.

NONIE. (*Turning back, there cigarettes in her hand.*) Now sir.

MARTIN. Now . . . sir . . . aha! You see the truth is (*and he gives another furtive glance over his shoulder.*) I'm in trouble.

NONIE. Is it the trouble you're really in? Or the trouble you think you're in?

MARTIN. (*Eyeing her uneasily.*) Uncanny aren't you?

NONIE. What class of trouble?

MARTIN. What do you mean 'class'?

236

NONIE. Why do you say 'class' that way?

MARTIN. (*Rather Earl's Court again with, it may be, a dash of Trinity, even of Oxford.*) I was thinking of my people . . . all those ghastly, boring, boiled-shirted, bloated b . . . Ah well. Particularly of my mother. She's so –

NONIE. Do you not like your mother?

MARTIN. Oh it's not a question of like. She's so . . . Oh you know, the old home, the family tradition, the stifling everlasting last of the Mohicans, kind hearts and coronets . . . oh you wouldn't understand. That's why I had to break away, you see. Absolute clean break. Away from huntin' shooting and what have you. I was suffocated. When I think of mother sitting there, sort of enthroned in oak panelling with orchids and golden teapots on the table and those baronial bores waiting to play Canasta . . . Look here. I haven't paid for the cigarettes. (*He produces some coins.*) What about seeing you tonight?

NONIE. What for?

MARTIN. What's your name?

NONIE. Nonie.

MARTIN. Nonie. (*He laughs shortly, meditatively.*) We might drive or dine or something . . . What about a cup of tea? I mean *now* . . .?

NONIE. You're very strange. You're like a lot of different people all mixed up.

MARTIN. But I am a lot of people all mixed up. (*USA*) Just crazy – no, that's kind of corny. No. But I do want to tell you how it began. (*Suddenly he becomes himself.*) It all began with a mirror and my mother swinging me round her by the two wrists. Up I flew like a swallow round and round and my heels higher than my head and the two of us roaring with the laughter. (*Suddenly he is a West End star.*) It was absolutely hilarious if I may say so, and darling, imagine! Me two feet – (*He coughs in a refined self-deprecating manner.*) My tiny feet – aah!! I was about five I suppose – they came into collision or what have you with a mirror, I mean a looking glass. It flew apart, me mother let a screech out of her and 'twas near she came to letting me fall. The splinters flew round the room like falling stars and there was a bit of my face in all the seven splinters: seven is it or seventeen or seven hundred, or like the seven hundred years of bitter oppression (*French.*) And oh lala! you can imagine 'ow I 'ave felt, mademoiselle!

NONIE. A bit of your face in each bit of glass? Sure how could that be?

MARTIN. (*West End again.*) Well there *was* in every single fragment. And I thought sort of Who am I? What am I? Darling, can't you

237

see what I mean, sort of? (*USA*) Gee Whiz! I said to myself: Why be one lonesome little guy when I might be seven or seventeen or seven hundred? (*He is now Maurice Chevalier again.*) Et voila! From that day, mademoiselle, I 'ave, so many personalities . . . (*USA returns*) So I figured I ought to see a head-shrinker.

NONIE. What's that?

MARTIN. Oh don't you know? A psychiatrist. Well, it's a sort of subsidised confessor. But much more explanatory. So I went around to one and this guy made me lie right down there on a sofa and tell him the most scary dreams and all the evilest thought about my childhood. (*He is back in the English shires.*) Of course, Mother was absolutely *furious*. She said if Lord Rosmuc ever heard one *word* –

NONIE. Who is Lord Rosmuc?

MARTIN. My uncle. Mummy's eldest brother. Actually. Crashing bore. I'm his heir.

NONIE. His which?

MARTIN. His . . . oh, you know. (*Suddenly once more and much more definitely himself, he says.*) Look; I can't pretend to you.

NONIE. Oh I think you can.

MARTIN. No. Not to you. I'd have to tell the truth to you.

NONIE (*wide-eyed and still as stone.*) Would you?

MARTIN. I would. Some day I would –

NONIE. When?

MARTIN. I don't know . . . (*In a puzzled voice.*) I don't know really you know, why I carry on like this. I wish I did know. I'm at it all my life: ever since I can remember. And sometimes I wouldn't be certain myself what was true and what wasn't. 'Tis a kind of – ach! I don't know – I mean I think that what I told you about the mirror was a fact, and I think that . . . *could* I see you again? 'Twouldn't be maybe to drive or dine because I've not much money at all at the moment . . . (*English shires again.*) Fact is, my boring uncle . . . *there* I go again! And I don'want to: to you. But I do want to talk to you and you to talk to me. I've a feeling that you'd make everything real . . . and simple . . . and clear to me: oh much clearer than the psychiatrist. You know, the lad made me lie down on a sofa and tell him my dreams.

NONIE. Was he real? The psych-elist?

MARTIN. The psychiatrist? Oh yes. We-ell, he . . . (*He regards her dubiously for a moment, then, still in his own voice.*) I *would* like that cup of tea.

NONIE (*in a dazed dream.*) I'm sorry sir, 'll get it for you. (*She goes.*)

238

MARTIN (*to himself.*) What could a psychiatrist do for me that that one couldn't do? Ah . . . 'twould take her a long while maybe. But she'd teach me more in the heel of the hunt than any . . . than any . . . than any . . . She'd know it all in the end. Know it all. Nonie! Where are you? Where's that cup of tea?

(*His voice is drowned by the blast of a ship's horn. We are back on board.*)

NONIE. And he looked at me then and he stayed for a cup of tea and myself slopping it all in the saucer with dint of my trembling fingers. It was love, was it yes it was it was, and his fingers were trembling too, and then every day the cigarettes and tea but we never drove nor we never dined, but there were the Commandos and the Argentine and the Boys on the Border . . . Oh was it all true and did it all happen or which of his stories are true and which are the lies? (*She looks at the* MOTHER.) I don't know what he wanted to marry me for. I was only a waitress in a little café.

MOTHER. I that a fact?

YOUNG MAN. We're after leaving the harbour, we're all on board.

YOUNG WOMAN. And we're all staring back at water growing wider, dimmer, darker, thanks be to God, and the darker the better.

MIDDLE MAN. Homesick already for neighbours and pubs and old friends.

MIDDLE WOMAN. The holy water over the hair-tidy, the Angelus ringing at six and at six.

OLDER MAN. Under the last bright star.

OLDER WOMAN. Grandchildren taller, the prams in the hall. And myself in the way. No, better put up with my sister in London.

MEN & WOMEN. God help us London Town.

NONIE. That's all I was. A waitress in a little café. The Friendly its name was.

MOTHER. Is that a fact? The Friendly. Ah 'tis a nice friendly sort of a name. Same as the matches, you know.

NONIE. And his mother stopped all his money on the head of him marrying myself.

MOTHER. There's a misfortune. And she with a title.

NONIE. A Countess she is. Countess Cathleen Concannon.

MOTHER. Cathy Concannon?

NONIE. Countess Cathleen Concannon.

MOTHER. Oh my God.

NONIE. What is it?

MOTHER. Aren't men the rip-roaring liars?

NONIE. What ails you?

MOTHER. Whisper . . . Is your name Nonie?

NONIE. How did you know that?

MOTHER. Nonie Nolan, ha?

NONIE. That's what it was before I married Martin.

MOTHER. The Honourable Nonie . . . The Honourable Nonie de Nolan . . . to marry my son Martin again the will of her family. Martin. That's him. Oh that's the best one yet. And he was always the same. 'Twas in the blood someway. And d'you know what I'm going to tell you? I always knew the lies was in him from the first. I suspected it when he was a babby and I feeding him, sitting at the window watching the gulls flying round over the Barnas road and then one day I knew it for sure, long before he knew it himself. He would have been about four or five and there I was one day swinging him round by the two wrists for he always loved to go swinging ever after the Circus coming in west from Loughrea, and the two little bits of feet he had under him broke the mirror. Ah the woe day! The splinters of glass were flying this way and that and I'd a queer notion his face was in every splinter and it with a different look on it like 'twould be seven, ay or seventeen faces maybe. Oh my my! And he no more nor four and a half and he tricking and sporting and letting on he was riding a hobby-horse. But I thought with the changes of his face and the words and the laughter and the cries that came flowing out of his mouth: 'You're a play-actor! Nothing but an old play-actor. Ah isn't it you will go travelling the world letting on to be what you're not!'

NONIE. He saw the faces in the splinters too. He told me so.

MOTHER. How could he? Sure they weren't there. 'Twas only a notion of my own.

NONIE. Did you tell him so?

MOTHER. Never. That I can remember . . . No . . . Isn't life very strange? Isn't my son very strange? With his lies and his dreams? Grandeur and romance from the day the mirror broke and after that he'd go creeping out in his little shirt out over the Long Wall, later on by the Claddagh and east to the Square, spinning his tales to the boys in the doorways, telling his lies to the travelling tinkers. 'Twas off an old wireless he got his first notion, out of any old yoke of a gramophone playing any bit of an old book he'd be studying. Oh daughter, my daughter, 'tis you and myself will have the fine life with him from this day out, and all London to be listening to him and our two selves only to be knowing the truth. 'Tis we'll have the hold on him, the bold sailor from the rocking seas.

NONIE. The merchant prince from the cities of the south.

MOTHER. The bandolero from the deserts of America.

NONIE. The parachutist out of the clouds of heaven.

MOTHER. Him that was never in no army nor no navy in his life no more than the man in the moon: him that never done nothing only to be coming out like an echoing jackdaw with any class of a sound he'd hear. Or is it a parrot I mean? Oh – and wait till you hear this from me: didn't he get his fare to Dublin out of me, and didn't they give him a job there as as sort of an attendant, and usher, that's what he called it, in some palatial big sort of a cinema, and there he'd be strutting up and down day after day, strutting and swanking and he gathering up one notion after another and one grandeur after another. Oh yes, James Cagney, Maurice Chevalier, David Niven, the devil knows who he'd let on he was. Round the World in Eighty Days and how are you! Ah, but he always sent home the odd postal order. God help him. He's a good son.

NONIE. His mother!

MOTHER. Who else?

NONIE. And I was afraid to meet you.

MOTHER. I was afraid to meet yourself.

NONIE. With your grand golden teapot.

MOTHER. With your cake as big as the Claddagh.

NONIE. My blessing from the Pope, my golden frame and the shells in the corner.

MOTHER. My fifty-two dresses, my titled canasta. Ah well. He gave me a great picture of you, me poor girl.

NONIE. And me of you. But why – ?

MOTHER. Whey did he do it?

NONIE. Why is he going to break it? Ah! He knew we'd meet of course, in the heel of the hunt.

MOTHER. He invited us both.

NONIE. Yes. I know why.

MOTHER. Maybe. He can always have his lies. London will be big enough for them. Yourself and myself –

NONIE. We're his truth. He couldn't keep us apart.

MOTHER. I've a couple of snaps of him when he was a little lad. (*She rummages in her bag.*)

NONIE. Have you?

MOTHER. Look.

MEN & WOMEN. The city's smoking cauldron waits under the dawn,

241

And call in both lover and beloved
To where the mother, already enthroned,
Knowing all truth, drowsily smiles
And puts a welcome before her new child.

# PRELUDE IN KAZBEK STREET

# CHARACTERS

SERGE KOVALEVSKY
JEAN-LOUIS
MRS BATY
ANDY
MADAME GONZALES
FRANCISCO GONZALES
WILLIAM VANDAMM
ROBERT MARSHALL

The play was first produced at the Gate Theatre, Dublin, on 9 October 1973 as part of the Dublin Theatre Festival, with the following cast:

| | |
|---|---|
| SERGE KOVALEVSKY | Christopher Cazenove |
| JEAN-LOUIS | Gerard McSorley |
| MRS BATY | Nora O'Mahony |
| ANDY | Patrick McLarnon |
| MADAME GONZALES | Helena Carroll |
| FRANCISCO GONZALES | Micheál macLiammóir |
| WILLIAM VANDAMM | Philip O'Brien |
| ROBERT MARSHALL | Aidan Grennell |

The play was directed by Hilton Edwards and the setting was by Robert Heade after a design by Molly McEwen.

The action of the play takes place in Serge Kovalevsky's apartment in the Avenue des Liles, Paris, during several seasons of the Gonzales Ballet.

*Prelude:*   AUTUMN from the SEASONS by Glazunov

# ACT I

SCENE I:   An evening in May

*Interlude:*   THAMAR, Symphonic Poem by Balakirev

SCENE II:   The same, six weeks later – An evening in July

# ACT II

SCENE I:   Six months later – A morning in January

*Interlude:*   CARNAVAL, by Schumann

SCENE II:   Two months later, 27 March

245

# ACT I

## Scene I

SCENE: *An apartment in an hotel on the Avenue des Lilas, Paris. We are in the sitting room of what is clearly a suite of rooms which includes, although these remain unseen, bedrooms, bathrooms, a kitchen and spacious entrance hall. The effect is of the luxuriously impersonal comfort of a good French hotel with a leaning towards the taste of the 'belle époque', for there are piles of cushions on sofas and chairs and these, as well as the semi-circular tower-like window that looks down on to the street below, are elaborately carved and sometimes heavily draped. So too is the archway that separates us from the entrance hall. The only visible sign of occupation when the curtain rises is the furniture which includes a low table standing in front of the sofa and covered with coffee things; a silver pot, cups, glasses and various liqueur bottles.*

*Although we can see nobody at the moment, we can hear most plainly, two male voices engaged in violent altercation. It is obvious that one of them, older and deeper than the other, belongs to a Frenchman. The other voice, although the row is conducted in French, was obviously not born to that language, though he is very fluent and occasionally idiomatic. We may as well call the owners of the voices by their names, though the Frenchman, at the present moment so audible, remains invisible throughout the play.*

SERGE. Bon, bon, bon, alors! J'en ai assez. Et tu partiras tout de suite si vraiment tu sais ce que tu dis. Maintenant! Maintenant! M'entends-tu?

JEAN-LOUIS. Oui, je sais exactement ce que je dis, mon petit Serge. Je sais toujours ce que je dis. C'est là peut-être mon drame. Je ——

SERGE. Ton drame à toi? Ha! C'est drôle, ca!

JEAN-LOUIS. Mais, c'est vrai! Et je non peux plus! Je non peux plus toi, Serge.

SERGE. Ça vent dire que tu vas me plaquer? Hein?

JEAN-LOUIS. Plaquer? Ah non, mon pauvre Serge, je ne te plaque pas.

247

C'est toi qui me jette dehors.

> (*At this moment, as* SERGE *is heard to give a shot of raucous laughter,* MRS BATY, *a small dauntless cockney in a black dress and satin apron and a dark red cardigan appears. She listens intently and murmurs 'Ts, ts, ts. At it again' and beckons to somebody off stage.*)

MRS BATY. Andy! Ssh! (*She beckons again and is joined by a young man wearing black trousers and tie, a white shirt and white coat.*)

JEAN-LOUIS. Oui ah oui, tu peux rire. Mais treize fois pendant la dernière semaine tu màs dis (*shouting in imitation of* SERGE) 'Va t'en! Va t'en!' Je n'attendrai pas la quatorzième fois – cela porterait malheur ——

SERGE. Eh bien je répète. Va t'en, espèce de sale tête de cochon! (JEAN-LOUIS *gives a lengthy national mirthless chuckle as* MRS BATY *interjects.*)

MRS BATY. Oo-er, fancy Mr Serge calling him a dirty pig's head!

SERGE (*shouting*). Tu me fais vomir.

MRS BATY. Says he makes him sick: so does me. (JEAN-LOUIS' *voice is heard giving the national chortle.*)

ANDY. Oh merciful hour!

MRS BATY. Shocking, isn't it? Shocking. There's only one word for it, it's shocking.

ANDY. Ssh!

SERGE. Tu me fais vomir!

JEAN-LOUIS. Voila. Il faut mieux que nous nous séparions. C'est logique!

SERGE. Logique! Logique! Logique! Ah merde!

JEAN-LOUIS. Ah! Merci!

MRS BATY (*to* ANDY). Just as well you can't understand French.

SERGE. So get the Hell out of here! Get out before I kill you. (*There is the sound of a blow.*)

ANDY. Aha, now the fun's beginning. Desperate.

MRS BATY. Ssh!

JEAN-LOUIS. Eh mon petit, doucement, doucement. Je suis plus grand et plus fort que toi, tu sais! (*Another blow and a shout from:*)

SERGE (*shouting in English*). Oh get out. And take your lousy luggage with you! (*There is the sound of bag after bag and suitcase after suitcase being flung downstairs during which operation* ANDY *and* MRS BATY *react with suitable jerks of their bodies and casting up of their eyes.*)

> (*There is a moment of silence.*)

MRS BATY. It's the ALL Clear, dux.

ANDY. Thanks be to God!

(*A last suitcase, heavier than all the rest, is flung violently downstairs. Then a door bangs, which causes the biggest display of all between the domestic pair on the stage.*)

(*There is silence again for a moment.*)

MRS BATY. I thought Air Raids was a thing of the past. Oh well, come on, we'd better get back to my kitchen. Kitchenette I should say. Thank heavens he's not dancing tonight.

ANDY. If he ever dances again, God help him.

MRS BATY (*all in one breath*). Don't be soppy dear of course he'll dance again he's a very big star and don't you forget it you dress him at the theatre you ought to know. (*She takes a long breath and resumes*) Stars can't afford to let their private upsets let the show down. I'd like to see this Paris season without him, or any other Ballet season anywhere else come to that. Anyway, he'll get over this. This isn't the first time there's been a blow up between these two, as you know.

(ANDY *begins to collect the remains of the coffee things, muttering to himself as he does so.*)

ANDY. Oh be the hokey, isn't French fellows the fright? Gay Paree, how are you? Sure you might as well be living in the zoo.

(*Unsteadily* SERGE *enters from the hallway. He is a slightly built young man between 25 and 30: at the moment he is deathly pale, his hair on end, and the collar of his evening shirt – for he wears no tie and no jacket – open at the neck. Ruefully he is rubbing his shoulder as if in pain. With a single ejaculation of 'Swine!' he rushes blindly into the door that leads presumably to the bedrooms.* ANDY *and* MRS BATY *watch his exit with apprehension.*)

MRS BATY. Poor soul! I hate seeing him like that. Good job if it *is* the end, if you ask me. That Jean-Louis wasn't the companion for him, with his la-di-da ways and his lady friends all over the place any time he got half a chance. But what's going to do without him, poor old dear? Oh well . . . (*She is gone.*)

(ANDY *resumes collecting of coffee things, the cups, coffee pot, liqueurs etc.* SERGE *comes in from the bedroom with a handkerchief and a bottle of Eau de Cologne: he is dabbing his cheek and chin.*)

SERGE. Bloody Swine.

(ANDY *ceases his activities with the coffee things.*)

ANDY. Did you say something Mr Serguy?

SERGE (*brokenly*). Yes I did: I said Bloody Swine.

ANDY. Yes sir.

SERGE. Oh not you, Andy. Only get those things cleared away, will you?

ANDY. I will of course, why not?

SERGE. And you'd better . . . better do out Mr Jean-Louis' bedroom, you and Mrs Baty. He – he won't be staying here any longer.

ANDY. Oh, is Mr Jean-Louis going away, sir?

SERGE. He's gone away. As you know perfectly well.

ANDY. Sure how would I know?

SERGE. Nothing wrong with your hearing, as far as I know.

ANDY. That I may drop dead if I heard a thing at all except the two of you passing remarks . . . Anyway, wasn't it all in French? God bless you, Mr Serguy. Cheerio sir. (*He carries the tray out.*)

SERGE (*to himself*). Cheerio! Oh my God! (*He picks up a hand-mirror from the table and regards himself, feeling with his right hand his forehead and chin and gazing intently into his eyes.*) *That's going to be a nice bruise tomorrow. Well, he'll have a few worse ones: let him explain those away to his dreary friends – Ach! . . . But what am I going to do without . . .? Ah! (He takes up the telephone and talks, we assume, to the concierge.*) Allô allô, Madame. Passez-moi Elysées 6445 s'il vous plait . . . Oui . . . Merci . . . Allo! Madame Gonzalez s'il vous . . . Maggie! Darling what a bit of luck! Look Maggie, I'm in trouble . . . Yes, again! No, this time it's serious . . . No, don't be a difficult woman, now there's a good girl. Look, are you free? . . . Going to the theatre? So was I . . . Darling, I know I'm not dancing tonight, that's why I was going . . . yes, with him . . . but we're not going any longer . . . but look it's only about a quarter to seven . . . Five to is it? Well, spare me a few minutes if you can will you? . . . Well of course I sound upset. Because I am . . . well could Paco pick you up here? . . . Bless you: you . . . now don't spoil it all by saying that: I do *not* make a habit of weeping on shoulders. Not even yours . . . Right: tell Paco and hop into a taxi and come along to me! . . . What? (*He gives a sudden peal of laughter.*) My God, I'm laughing! I thought I'd never never . . . no, it shows how much you've cheered me up already, you see! Bless you, darling. A tout à l'heure. (*Bangs down the receiver and covers his face with his hands and rocks up and down for a moment. Enter* MRS BATY. SERGE *seems not to notice her but continues to rock to and fro on the sofa. Then, with a sudden violence, he twists himself round and, lying on his back, observes* MRS BATY *looking at him with a certain sympathy.*)

SERGE (*with an effort*). Hullo Ruby.

MRS BATY. No you smile it away dear, that's what you've got to do. Smile it all away. He'll probably be back again before you can say knife.

SERGE. What are you talking about?

MRS BATY. I'm talking about Monsieur. Monsieur Jean-Louis. I'm only prognosticating dear. It wouldn't surprise me in the least if he came waltzing back here tonight. It wouldn't really. Oh! and I've got an instinct about things: runs in my family you know. Oh yes, my aunt Doll – my mother's sister she was, and she became a fortune teller. She was known as Madame Zara. Oh she was a knockout, and so could I have been if I hadn't gone into the theatre business – and I met Marcel Baty my hubby who was an electrician to the Gonzalez Ballet when I joined the wardrobe during their London season. A Froggie too: well, why not, I mean, the Froggies are all right if you know how to handle them *which* I do. I might have taken up fortune telling here, only for the language difficulty. Well I mean I can jabber away in a manner of speaking, but, I mean it's never the same as your own tongue, is it? But I've still got the instinct you know. 'All is dark, all is dark . . .' And I'm telling you Monsieur Jean-Louis will be back here with you sooner or later.

SERGE. No he won't. He won't come back.

MRS BATY. Well if he doesn't you can say good riddance. He didn't appreciate you. Oh he was ever so proud of you being a big star and him being your great pal and all that, but I mean as a human bean! (SERGE *gulps*). He *didn't* dear. Come on, cheer up, Mr Serge. It isn't like the Irish, you know, not to look on the bright side. Funny I always forget you're Irish. Come on; let me make you a nice cup of tea, or perhaps you'd like a nice whiskey and sodar or something . . . and get into your black tie like a good boy and go off to the ballet.

SERGE. And sit there all alone, I suppose?

MRS BATY. You? All alone? I'd like to see it. No, you go along with Madam Gonzalez and that hubby of hers. He *is* your impresario after all, and you're all good pals. Why don't you go along with them? (ANDY *is heard whistling in the kitchen as the door bell rings.*)

SERGE. Because I don't want to. (*Shouting*) Shut up *please*, Andy! And open the door will you? (ANDY *crosses to the exit. To* MRS BATY:) And I wish you'd shut up too darling, much as I love you. But Madame Gonzalez will be here in a few minutes.

MRS BATY. What are *you* poking your nose in for, Andy Kee-oh? (*For*

251

ANDY *has appeared from the entrance hall and stands silent for a moment.*)

ANDY (*at* MRS BATY). The name is Keogh.

MRS BATY. Well, that's what I said, isn't it? Kee-oh. (ANDY *goes out muttering.*) Him and his brogue . . . Here wait a moment. I've got a psychic feeling coming on. (*A buzzer sounds.*) All is dark, all is dark. And what have we here? I see a stranger, a fair-haired gentleman with a jolly good heart for you . . .

ANDY (*re-entering from the kitchen*). Excuse me a minute: amn't I after hearing the buzzer? Excuse me! (*He darts from the room.*)

MRS BATY. There: what did ti tell you? I wouldn't be a bit surprised . . . (*There is a moment of tension.*)

ANDY (*appearing at entrance*). Madame Gonzally is coming up sir.

MRS BATY. There you are you see! What did I tell you?

ANDY. She's not a stranger and she's not a gentleman, she's a lady.

MRS BATY. Well, what's the difference?

    (ANDY *makes for the kitchen as* MAGGIE GONZALEZ *appears, small, radiant, and beautifully dressed.*)

SERGE. Maggie! (*He moves towards her, and they embrace fervently.*)

MAGGIE. I must love you very much, you bird of all-omen. I was just halfway through a laight and delicious repaust when you rang.

SERGE. You're terribly sweet.

MAGGIE (*in her own voice*). No dear: terribly possibly, but not terribly sweet. Savoury if you insist. How's life, Ruby?

MRS BATY. Could be worse dear. It could be worse, I daresay. Oh well, I must be off. I'll be late if I'm not careful. Luckily everything's ready for DON QUIXOTE and those Spanish divertissmongs. And TAMAR doesn't go up till nine fifteen. Excuse me both. (*She fixes her hat at the glass.*)

MAGGIE. Who's Ta – Oh! of course! The revival of TAMAR.

MRS BATY. Tamar, Queen of Georgia.

SERGE. Not the Marching into Georgia one. The one in the Caucasus. She was historical, what's more.

MRS BATY. Not the sort of historical we used to have at my school in Pimlico. No! Sort of Henry the Eighth and Jack the Ripper in female form I'd call her. She used to waylay gentlemen going over the Kazbek Pass – nice subject for a ballet I must say – yes, waylaid gentlemen, lured them into her bedroom for you can guess what, then did them in, and started waving out of the window for the next gentleman. Nothing but a kleptomaniac, if you ask me. Oh well, Toodle-oo! (*She goes.*)

MAGGIE (*looking after her*). She doesn't *really* mean klepto, does she?

Still, she's much too well-informed to be a wardrobe mistress.

SERGE. That's why I get her to take care of me here as well. And she loves coming round to me here: God knows why. (*Listlessly.*) Want a drink, darling? (*He sits down.*)

MAGGIE. No thanks. Now tell me. What's the trouble, Serge?

SERGE. Jean-Louis of course.

MAGGIE. Yes, I know that. But what's happened? You look like the morning after the thousand and one nights before. He hasn't been beating you up, has he?

SERGE. Oh he got back as good as he gave. But it's so disgusting, that sort of thing. Anyway, he's gone.

MAGGIE. For good?

SERGE. Oh yes.

MAGGIE (*after staring at him for a moment in silence.*) Serge, you'll be raging with me, but I think perhaps it's a good thing. (*An involuntary movement from* SERGE *which she overrides.*) No, listen to me for a moment. You old baby. You spoiled, misunderstood, *self-pitying* baby. Jean-Louis was never the man for you Serge. Never. You'd hardly a taste in common. And God knows he knew it, and so did you in your heart. Oh he was fond of you in his own way. But it was his own way from such a long way off, you see. All there really was between you was founded from his side simply on admiration for you as an artist – no, not even that – no, for you as a famous person. You were important. Even the people of his own world – smart, successful, commercial Paris, for God's sake, the *grande bourgeoisie* and their wives – even they raved about you from season to season. To say nothing of the really great world here, and you know what a crashing snob he was at heart. And through you he met the lot of them. And because of you they accepted him and invited him everywhere. You fell for him, you silly *bostún*, and of course he was flattered and thrilled: he reacted and you thought it was going to be permanent. And, God give you sense, you let him know it! Lunacy! Then of course it began to wear thin and now he's gone.

SERGE. Yes, he's gone.

MAGGIE. And you're frightened of being alone, and stewing in self-pity, which is not the most attractive emotion dear. Now, lecture over, ahem, ahem! So you can give me a drink.

SERGE. What do you want?

MAGGIE. I'll have a nip of cognac – just a nip, dear, to keep out the cold. Just a teeny weeny double brandy. (*He pours a brandy for her.*) Ah! But I'm deeply sorry for you, my darling. Thanks. Now

253

you talk.

SERGE. That's a cue for silence, if ever there was one.

MAGGIE. Well, I'll give you a lead. Aren't you taking anything? (*He shakes his head.*) Why are you so frightened of your own company? I think you're marvellous company. So does everybody. Even when you're in the depths. *Sláinte.* Why?

SERGE. '*Sláinte . . .*' Oh that takes me back so many years.

MAGGIE (*thoughtfully.*) Yes, years and years – Dublin. Ha-ha! Serge, how long have you and I known each other?

SERGE. I was ten . . . I'm twenty-seven now . . . that makes seventeen.

MAGGIE (*laughing suddenly*). Ha! I'll never forget my first sight of you coming into Madame Alvarini's in O'Connell Street that day clinging to your mother's hand and I (*suddenly very refined and superior.*) Ai was already a sweet second year girl of course: Ai knew all about the business. (*Suddenly herself.*) And, as soon as I looked at you, I thought 'There's a dancer.'

SERGE. Madame Alvarini . . . her real name was Bolger. Remember?

MAGGIE (*in deepest Dublinese.*) Chrissie Bolger, that's right. Don't interrupt. I thought 'There's a dancer.' And that was before you'd done a single step. It was the way you walked and the way you moved your head. I ——

SERGE. I must have been a little horror.

MAGGIE. You still are, darling. No, you're not, you're very sweet.

SERGE. Sweet I may be but I'm still a little horror. A little horrified horror . . . Listen, this is something I've never told even you before.

MAGGIE. Oh my God, what am I in for now?

SERGE. Don't worry, it's not medical. But it may be psychiatric . . . Maggie, do you think I'm going pots?

MAGGIE. No dear: I think you've *gone* pots. I think the century's gone. I think we've all gone.

SERGE. No, I don't quite mean like that. It's this. Your talking of me as a child in Dublin reminded me, because it all began then – no, long before then – and it's this. A feeling that everything – not only animate things, people and animals and so on, but everything – was alive. Not even only trees and flowers and living things but everything: clothes, books, pens, and toothbrushes . . . everything. (*He stops.*)

MAGGIE. Go on.

SERGE. And I never could bear the thought even of them being alone.

MAGGIE. Ah!

SERGE. I'm not a tidy person by nature, but if I saw a shoe in one corner and its fellow in another for example, I'd have to put them together so they could talk and be friendly. And If I'd said carelessly to someone 'I can't bear that tie, or that shirt, or whatever it was' I'd have to whisper to it afterwards 'Take no notice, you're gorgeous really, and everyone admires you', so their feelings wouldn't be hurt.

MAGGIE. Darling. But you *are* a little crackers.

SERGE. Yes . . . And lately I'm obsessed by the thought of death.

MAGGIE. At your age?

SERGE. Yes at my age. Not only my death but theirs. All those inanimate things. 'He's wearing me out, he's wearing me out' a shaving bush would say. 'I can't last much longer.' And I'd try to comfort it. And that used to get on – what's his name? – Jean-Louis' nerves. 'Mais, c'est idiot, mon petit.' he'd say. 'T'es fou!' Perhaps he was right. Perhaps I am mad.

MAGGIE. I thought you'd never told anybody? Not even me?

SERGE. He used to catch me talking to them.

MAGGIE. Darling, it's all from the same thing: it's all that fear of loneliness. It's ingrained in you.

SERGE. Yes. I know. It's a disease.

MAGGIE. But there's no need for you to work yourself up about it all. Go on talking to your toothbrush as long as you like. It doesn't hurt anyone, and perhaps the toothbrush enjoys it. And think of all the wonderful things, Serge, not the sad crazy ones. Our life's chock-a-block with them, you *amadán*. You're a great dancer – not just a good one: a great one – and now the world knows it. Not only our old Dublin, but London, Paris, New York, Berlin, Vienna . . . 'one of the most spectacular male dancers since Nijinski' . . . and they didn't mean the racehorse either . . . you ought to be a very happy young man, Serge.

SERGE. I know. And I'm utterly miserable.

MAGGIE. I realise that. Now, tell me the truth: it isn't all because of Jean-Louis is it? You had a Freudian blackout about his name just now – you almost forgot it so he can't have meant everything in life to you – so isn't your misery partly because of the world's attitude to your sort of person?

SERGE. I wonder? Yes, I think it is, probably.

MAGGIE. Of course the law's barbarous. Made by half-wits and approved of by half-wits. The Anglo-Saxon law anyway. But it's not like that in France or any civilised European country. And it's changed in England now, too.

SERGE. Oh it isn't that worries me. Never did. It isn't the law, it's the laughter.

MAGGIE. Mm! People always laugh at what they can't understand. They think your sort of person unnatural, you see.

SERGE. Unnatural? Tell me what, in what we call civilised life, is *natural*? Are supermarkets natural? Or central heating? Or wearing clothes? Or watching television?

MAGGIE. No, but some of them – I don't say all, I say some of them – are charming.

SERGE. So are lots of other things. What have people got against my sort?

MAGGIE. You don't produce.

SERGE. We don't breed, you mean. The others do. But rats and snakes breed too, and microbes and lice and God knows what. That's natural for tigers to eat monkeys and antelopes and humans: that's natural, but it's not very charming is it?

MAGGIE. Especially for the monkeys and the ante-what did you say?

SERGE. Antelopes, dear. And as for not producing, we do produce. Some of us anyway. We produce, not children, I know – but some of us produce works of art and science, and ——

MAGGIE. You're thinking of Leonardo.

SERGE. Oh and Plato and Socrates and Michael Angelo and Shakespeare and a few others.

MAGGIE. Shakespeare had children.

SERGE. So did Oscar Wilde, come to that. The only one person in the whole hierarchy of famous men and women that everybody knows about because there was a scandal and an imprisonment they could lick their lips over. All the others of the same persuasion the world shuts its eyes to or flatly denies the facts. (*In a shocked voice.*) 'You are surely not suggesting that Shakespeare . . . '

MAGGIE. Even poor Sappho. (In an even more shocked voice.) 'It is by no means proved that Sappho was anything but a healthy, normal woman.' So she probably was, poor cow, but she *did* write a lot of enthusiastic notes about those lady friends, didn't she?

SERGE. But so many of them were lucky – the people we've talked about I mean – they could love and be loved by either sex. And have children too. I often wish I could. Or do I? With life as it is today? No, the world's obscene giggling: the world's turning the whole thing into Tart for Tart's sake, that makes me miserable too.

MAGGIE. But that side does exist among your sort, Serge.

SERGE. Indeed, I'm afraid it does. Don't I know it? But it's not the

256

only side. Any more than brothels or the whores of Piccadilly or the Place de l'Etoile are the only side of heterosexual love. If my sort of person is represented in a book or a movie as high or low camp, something that's both comic and contemptible, people will lap it up: if it's pornographic, it's acceptable permissiveness: but if it's given one shred of dignity or reality, God help us!

MAGGIE. Now don't get your rag out, Serge. I'm with you. You're preaching to the converted. So cheer up. Come on! (*She claps her hands and slaps him on both cheeks.*)

SERGE. Don't I've had enough of that for one evening, Maggie.

MAGGIE. You didn't come to blows, did you?

SERGE. In the end we did, yes. That was my fault. I hit him first.

MAGGIE. That's not like you.

SERGE. What *is* like me? What's wrong with me?

MAGGIE. You know. And I know. It isn't your fault.

SERGE. Oh I don't mean that. I mean this panic-stricken inability to be alone . . . Yet I love being alone . . . when I want to be. For hours together sometimes. But there must be somebody I go home to. Or somebody who comes home to me. I can't breathe without that, I can't work, I can't rest, I can't sleep . . .

MAGGIE. I know. I'd be the same I think if I hadn't married Paco. Do you know how I fell in love with him? No idea who he was. Just a stranger (*she warbles.*) I'd no idea he was the famous Francisco Romero Gonzalez of the Gonzalez Ballet. He pursued me for months but in the end I got him. Aha!

SERGE. You're so lucky, Maggie. You always were. I think you were born under a lucky star.

MAGGIE. Virgo the Virgin dear, and I defy you to deny it. For weeks before I got my wicked way and he proposed marriage we could only say four words to each other. He hardly spoke any English except 'yes' and 'No' and 'Blast your eyes' and his French was almost as limited as mine. But I was equal to it, dear. I hadn't been a member of the Gaelic League for nothing. I took lessons in Spanish four times a week, and before you could say 'Knife' I was saying 'Sí, si!' I could also say 'Caramba' and 'Casamiento?' which means Marriage. So I peeped at him one day – like this – and said 'Casamiento? Sei, sí!' three times and he said 'Sí, sí, sí' three times as well. So there we were.

SERGE. And everybody thought ——

MAGGIE. I know what everybody thought. That I married him because I wanted star parts in the Gonzalez Ballet.

SERGE. Well you disproved that soon enough by stopping your

dancing before the wedding bells had even begun to ring. It's the only think I could never forgive you for, Maggie.

MAGGIE. What's that? Never forgive me for getting out of that touring kip I was in?

SERGE. No: for giving up dancing. You're a born dancer.

MAGGIE. I'm not.

SERGE. You are.

MAGGIE. Darling Serge, if I was ——

SERGE. Grammar, dear. *Were*, not was.

MAGGIE. Ah to hell with you. Right: if I were – repeat: *If* Ai *were* – I wouldn't have given it up, would I? But I wasn't you see. The height of my classic career was when I danced the fourth of the four swanlets – cygnets, what do you call them? – in *Swan Lake*. (*She gives a rapid and grotesque sketch of the opening movement in 'Swan Lake' to her own hummed accompaniment.*) '*Pom*-dum-dum-*dum-dum-diddle-um-dum*: Pom . . .' etc. down '*De-de-oh-poo-POO!*' That was about my highest mark. And quite right too. No, Serge, no. God never meant me for a ballerina.

SERGE. Why bring God into it?

MAGGIE. Why? Because it all comes from God of course, you silly ass. When you find out what He wants you to do, you do it if you've any sense.

SERGE. Yes, I know that's true. But how do you find out what He wants you to do?

MAGGIE. Well *you* found it out, didn't you?

SERGE. What He wanted me to *do* perhaps. But what does He want me to *be*?

MAGGIE. Ah, that you have to find out yourself. By continually asking Him, perhaps. You know: 'Now come on, dear God! Help me to be what You want me to be! Come on, God, do Your stuff.'

SERGE. Yes . . . do you know Maggie, both you and I are religious in a way. Isn't it awful?

MAGGIE. Isn't it ghastly? But there it is darling, and there's no blotting it out. And do you know what I might have *ought* to have been, if you follow my English?

SERGE. A happily married woman, you lucky bitch.

MAGGIE. Yes dear. And possibly – I say just possibly – A Comic. A low one I think. (*She goes through a swift and mad routine in silence: she is faintly reminiscent for a moment of Chaplin.*) Or possibly – I say just possibly – a rather broadminded police lady. (*She directs traffic with terrifying skill for a moment, then answers an imaginary questioner or two.*) Ladies' convenience? Of course:

258

just round the corner on the left. That's right! . . . Oh it's the gents' you want? Forgive me: your hair-do rather confused me for a moment . . . Ah! Look! I've made you laugh! (*Suddenly he buries his face and sits miserably huddled in a corner of the sofa.*) Ah Serge! Serge darling! Forget my fooling. Let yourself go: tell me everything.

SERGE (*sniffing into a handkerchief*). Forgive me. I am sorry, really. But it's hell, this continued belief that I've found the right person to share – to share life with me – and then finding I haven't, I haven't, I haven't, I never have. They're all the same, these so-called friends that last for four or five months and then bounce off in a storm of abuse and insults. They're killing me . . . oh, I feel so ashamed, Maggie.

MAGGIE. Not with me. Surely! You know I know everything about you.

SERGE. Of course I do. No, not ashamed of that side of me. Ashamed of this – this awful terror of being lost. Lost. The moment I step off the stage. And I'll never – (*he stops.*)

MAGGIE. Never find the right companion?

SERGE (*nods and murmurs*). Mm. I don't think I ever shall, you see.

MAGGIE (*they sit in silence for a moment*). Tell me what sort of person – what sort of man – *would* be right for you?

SERGE. Oh, I don't know really. Well, normally he'd have to be normal, if you see what I mean. I mean he'd have to be habitually normal. And it's hopeless because the habitually normal man, if he's the right kind of normal man, is married. At least once in his life.

MAGGIE. Well, go on.

SERGE. And if his wife is living and if they're not separated it would either mean that he was deceiving her, which would be hateful . . .

MAGGIE. Yes, I agree there.

SERGE. Or that he caused her pain, you see. Which would be more hateful still.

MAGGIE. You think it better to be deceived than hurt?

SERGE. Oh, I suppose I do. But they're both horrible. And I couldn't bear to be the cause.

MAGGIE. Of suffering?

SERGE. Or of tactful diplomatic deception. No, Mag.

MAGGIE. Now stop it Serge, or I shall burst into several tears and gallop away in all directions.

SERGE. Sorry!

MAGGIE. Are you looking for an artist?

SERGE. An artist? No, I don't think so . . . but somebody deeply interested in the arts . . . Someone who understood them, someone who could tell me things I know nothing about. All these Jean-Louis' are killing me – killing me.

(ANDY *is heard shrilly whistling 'I'm dancing with tears in my eyes' from the direction of the kitchen*).

ANDY'S VOICE (*off*). Ah the Tuneful Twenties, sir. Sorry sir.

MAGGIE. You did believe you loved Jean-Louis. Until about six weeks ago.

SERGE. Yes . . . I suppose so. Yes, it's true. How is it you know everything? Everything: Always?

MAGGIE. I don't know everything always, my lamb. But I do know you. And I saw it was wearing thin.

SERGE. Not only on my side.

MAGGIE. Oh I didn't notice his side. Or really understand it either. I never saw him clearly. I just saw a typical French businessman: all the French virtues and all the French vices. He was intelligent, sharp as a knife, superficially a little over-cultivated, charming manners – that's the good side – he was also sensual, greedy, over-pernickety, over critical, irascible, a little too mad about women ——

SERGE. Yes.

MAGGIE. Typical! Comic, isn't it, how nearly everyone typical of his or her nation is fundamentally commonplace? Ever noticed that? No artist is you see. Especially the great ones. I bet you anything you like that Michael Angelo wasn't a typical Italian, or Shakespeare a typical Englishman.

SERGE. Or Nijinsky a typical Pole? Or Karsávina ——

MAGGIE. Karsávina! Wasn't she the original Tamar?

SERGE. Of course she was. Fantastic, I believe. And we were to have gone to see it tonight. Jean-Louis I mean . . . we were supposed to have gone together.

MAGGIE. Come with Paco and me. Come on! You're half-ready as it is: all you've got to do is add a black tie and your dinner jacket. Do!

SERGE (*relapsing into gloom once more*). I couldn't. I couldn't. I'd only be thinking ——

MAGGIE. Cheer up. Shake yourself to bits and come along. Paco will be here (*she looks at her watch*) in five minutes or so.

SERGE. Darling, thanks so much. But I couldn't.

MAGGIE. You couldn't. Anyway you feel you couldn't and that's good enough for the moment. But your *reason* for feeling you couldn't isn't quite complete you know. You think it's because of Jean-Louis. Well it's not. It's largely because of Tamar.

SERGE. What on earth are you talking about?

MAGGIE. Now God forgive me, darling Serge, but it strikes me forcibly who you really are.

SERGE. Inquisitive of me, but I'd love to know. So tell me.

MAGGIE. You, Serge Krasovsky, originally known and still registered on your Irish passport as John Joseph Cassidy, you must know who you are. Don't you? Or do you?

SERGE. I don't think so.

MAGGIE. Then I'll tell you. You are Tamar. That's who you are.

SERGE. Oh don't be ——

MAGGIE. Don't interrupt dear, or I shan't explain. You are Tamar, my lad, the man-trap of Kazbek. You've even got a tower window, although I don't suppose you lie on jewelled cushions waving a rose red scarf at them. You don't need to. The wonder to me is why this Avenue des Lilas is not called Kazbek Street. Like Tamar, Queen of Georgia, you – or Fate – lure these unlikely people into your life ——

SERGE. Now that's unfair. Why do you say that?

MAGGIE. Because I believe it to be true. Look Serge . . . You need a life companion and that life companion has to be a man. I understand that completely. What's more – and you can laugh this one off if you want to – I pray every night of my life that you may find him. I do. The fact that your nature demands such a man doesn't shock me, or anything like it. That the person you're looking for must be what is known as a normal man is your tragedy. And I understand that too. One of your own sort might just as well be a woman. Of course I understand: but it's his tragedy as well as yours. Because the normal man, though he may experiment because of a temporary infatuation or merely for amusement's sake, can't last out for very long. Or if he can he's the rarest animal in the world. He may exist somewhere: I hope to God for your sake that he does. But Serge – you told me twice if not three times tonight that these friends of yours were killing you.

SERGE. So they are. Well?

MAGGIE. Well they're not, you see. The boot's on the other foot. Oh I know Tamar didn't want a companion for life: she wanted a new thrill in the shape of any unfortunate bastard who happened to be journeying past her tower on the Pass of Kazbek. And when she'd had her way with them she bumped them off. Didn't she? Well, so do you.

SERGE. I think you're being horrible.

MAGGIE. Oh I know you work more slowly than Tamar did. *You really* want love, affection, intelligent companionship; not mere sensation like that poor nympho in her tower. But you keep on mistaking your man, and when you discover your mistake you slowly – I think unconsciously – begin to destroy him. (SERGE *opens his mouth to speak, but she gets in first.*) You meet these friends of yours and of course they're dazzled by you at first, flattered by a famous artist who is also a grand companion, lots of fun generous and attractive, and before they know where they are they're caught. They're living with you, basking in the reflection of your triumphs, sometimes battening on you – Well – then you find out what they are really like and *you* kill *them*!

SERGE. Go on. You're most encouraging.

MAGGIE. No, don't be annoyed with me.

SERGE. I'm not. Because I know in my heart that you're my only real friend. I wonder why you're not a man?

MAGGIE. I wouldn't be your type if I was, dear. And you certainly wouldn't be mine.

SERGE (*in mock indignation*). How dare you?

MAGGIE. Well, you wouldn't. If we could have an affair it would be a hopeless flop. Oh no. I like the type you like. Large and strong and preferably rather silent. Like my Paco. Can you imagine a silent Spaniard? Andaluz too. It's a contradiction in terms. Besides, he thinks I'm the cat's whiskers. Which of course I am.

SERGE. Yes, you are. I adore you. But I'm sorry you think I'm like Tamar.

MAGGIE. Only the *killing* part, darling. You're not the cheap promiscuous sort like so many of your tribe, God help them, sure what else can they do? But you want your companion and you won't rest till you find him, and mark my words, darling, before you can say 'knife', that rose-red scarf will be fluttering away at the window of your tower . . . (*She glides voluptuously to the tower-like window that occupies a corner of the room and gazes down into the street, waving an imaginary scarf, chanting in operatic fashion*) 'Come up, come up, my super Prince! Come up and be mine till I murder you!' (*Looking back into the room*) No luck, dear: a car has drawn up but it's not the Prince, it's only Paco.

SERGE (*going to the looking glass*). Oh splendid. Maggie, my bruise isn't showing yet, is it?

MAGGIE. Not so you'd notice.

SERGE. I'll tell Paco I bumped into the lift.

MAGGIE. As if he'd believe you! He's known you *and* Jean-Louis for ages. Don't you remember, it was he who introduced him to you?

SERGE. Yes it was. On Friday the thirteenth of – what month was it?

MAGGIE. January, wasn't it?

SERGE. That's it. Friday the thirteenth of January: just before the opening of the Monte Carlo season. And now ——

MAGGIE. It's Saturday the thirteenth of May. *Saturday*, dear, not Friday, so cheer up.

SERGE. It's the thirteenth just the same. (*A bell is heard.*) There's Paco! (*Andy rushes across the stage to the entrance door:* SERGE *rises and regards the expected bruise on his chin.* MAGGIE, *gazing at herself in a compact, says casually*)

MAGGIE. Take my tip, my darling, and don't go blurting out anything about this row to Paco. He doesn't understand rows unless they begin in Spanish and end in peals of laughter.

ANDY (*at the entrance*). Senyer Don Frasisky Ramérry Gonsally. There I got it right that time. (GONZALES *enters: he is a man of about fifty with a certain portly grace and immaculate tails and white tie.*)

SERGE (*shaking hands*). Don Baco, welcome! I mean Bienvenu – I man Bienvenido ——

MAGGIE. Go on now, say Céad míle fáilte and be done with it.

PACO. Gracias! Habla ya divinante español, no?

MAGGIE. He says you speak Spanish gorgeous.

PACO. Claro! Corazón! (*He takes* MAGGIE *in his arms and kisses her tenderly*) Pero dónde está el amigo?

MAGGIE. He wants to know where is old Nobody's Child? (To Paco) Jean-Louis? Oh . . . Jean-Louis? Oh . . . Jean-Louis se fué ——

PACO (*puzzled*). Se fué? Porqué?

MAGGIE. Se fué . . . visitar su madre, que está enferma.

PACO. Ay, la pobre! Pero que tiene?

MAGGIE (*without blinking an eyelid*). Paperas.

PACO. Paperas. Ay Madre! Pero es muy contagioso, lo sabes?

MAGGIE. Oh sí. (*To* SERGE *out of the corner of her mouth*) I'm after telling him your fellow's old one is laid up with mumps.

SERGE. Well really, Maggie.

MAGGIE (*with an enormous wink at* GONZALES). No te apures Paco: no es verdad.

PACO. (*with satisfaction*). A-ah! (*He shakes hands with* SERGE *enthusiastically and slaps him on both cheeks*) Me alegre – I am content – for *you*, ha? Serge!

263

SERGE (*to Maggie*). What have you been saying to him?

MAGGIE. Nothing dear – nothing at all. I'll explain later. Now get on your tie and come on with us. It's getting late.

PACO. Qué está diciendo, Ma-ggi?

MAGGIE. Nothing: I mean Nada! Nada! Come on Serge. (*To* PACO) Yo quiero que venga con nosotros.

PACO. Sí, como no? Poor supuesto! (*He beams encouragingly at* SERGE *and slaps him on both cheeks.*) Ya vendrás, no?

SERGE. I'm getting tired of this slapping business. What does he say?

MAGGIE. He says Yes why not? But of course!

SERGE. But of course what?

MAGGIE. Of course you're coming with us he says. Didn't you, darling? (*To* GONZALES)

PACO. Ha?

MAGGIE. Lo dije – oh it doesn't matter. Come on Serge darling: get your things on or we'll be late and you'll miss your round of applause as we sail into our box. (*She picks up an enormous fan and makes a superb imaginary entrance, bowing and blowing kisses to all sides.*)

SERGE. Please forgive me both of you – I can't. (*He presses the bell push: we can hear it ringing. Then, to* PACO) Paco, I'm so sorry: I can't. No puedo. No quiero.

PACO. You don' *want*. Ah! (*Hand on heart*) I am sorry. Pero ya te entiendo. I understan' you. Yes. Bloody fine English, ha?

SERGE. Splendid. Wish I could speak Spanish like that. (ANDY *comes in.*)

PACO. You espeak goodly Espanish – Yes! (*to* MAGGIE) Vamos, Pues vamos, alma mía.

ANDY. You rang for me Mr Serguy?

SERGE. Yes. Monsieur and Madam Gonzalez are going.

ANDY. And are you not going with them sir?

SERGE. No.

MAGGIE. You're looking blooming, Andy.

ANDY. Same to yourself, God bless you Madam.

MAGGIE. I told you Paco would guess. He's a wicked old wizard. Bueno: vamos, brujo. And cheer up my darling Serge! (*She kisses* SERGE.)

PACO. Holá Brujo she call to me! One bitch!

MAGGIE. Not bitch! Witch: male tense, I mean gender. Come! on! (*To* SERGE) I'll ring you tomorrow, Serge. And keep that rose-red scarf waving: Bless you, baby!

PACO. Bebby Bebby! Díos mío what a language – a (*to* ANDY.)

264

Thanka ——

ANDY. This way sir. Madam.

> (*And they are gone. Left alone,* SERGE *wanders round the room for a moment, then disappears to the bedroom. Almost at once the telephone starts to ring.* SERGE *comes hurrying back, a dinner jacket slung over his shoulders like a cloak: he is fastening a black tie. Hearing the bell he stops with a jerk, then crosses to the telephone, stops again then turns his back, throws his jacket on the sofa, and finishes his tie at the looking glass: then he puts on his jacket, gazing menacingly at the telephone as he does so.*)

SERGE (*muttering*). Let him ring. I bloody well won't answer him.

ANDY (*coming in from the hall*). The phone sir: will I answer it?

SERGE. No. Let them ring. (*They listen.* SERGE, *after a moment of reflection, lifts the receiver and listens*) Jean-Louis? Non. Non, non et non . . . (*He hangs up and sits staring in front of him*).

ANDY. Ah now, I suppose that's the end of that fella.

# CURTAIN

# Scene II

SCENE: It is six weeks later. SERGE *is in a black dinner jacket and tie and is listlessly looking through a book.* ANDY *enters from the kitchen and, after hovering about at the drinks table among the glasses and bottles, gives an excellent imitation of a racking cough. This he repeats until Serge looks up and says:*

SERGE. My God, if that cough's real you should take something for it, Andy. If it's not, you should go into drama and find a part of someone in a sanitorium.

ANDY. Yes, Mr Serguy. I was trying to attract your attention.

SERGE. Splendid: you've done it. Well, what do you want?

ANDY. 'Tisn't meself wants anything sir, I was just wondering would you be going out?

SERGE. No. I don't feel like going out.

ANDY. I think you're kidding yourself sir. Except for the theatre you didn't put a foot outside the door for a month. You're not dancing tonight and if you're going out, what are you all dressed up for?

SERGE. What? Oh I don't know.

ANDY. Well if you're not going out you should relax, so you should. Could I do anything for you? Would you like a nice rub-down with Eau-de-Cologne like I do do for you after the ballet?

SERGE (*smiling*). No thanks.

ANDY. Mr Serguy, if you don't want anything more and as 'tis me night off would it be OK now if *I* was to go out a bit earlier like?

SERGE. Of course, Andy.

ANDY. The way it is, there's a picture on the Boulevards Italians in English and I'm lepping to see it, so I am. Everything else barring two films is all in French, sir. Ah the French people is marvellous people in some ways: they're making great strides in *their* language, no doubt about it.

SERGE. Yes: most nations are. (*The doorbell rings.*)

ANDY. I'll open it sir. And may I go out then?

SERGE. Yes of course. Have a good time, Andy.

ANDY. Thank you sir. I'll be in sharp in the morning sir.

(*He disappears through the archway at the back.* SERGE, *standing at the writing-desk, starts to look at some letters: his back is to the archway. After a moment a tall man, wearing an overcoat and carrying a small suitcase, appears at the archway accompanied by a silently protesting* ANDY. *The stranger – his finger to his lips – makes very softly, the sound that spelt 'Ssh' and gently propels poor Andy away. Then,* ANDY *having discreetly withdrawn,* MR WILLIAM Z. VANDAMM, *having placed his suitcase on the floor with his overcoat flung over it, advances stealthily on tiptoe towards* SERGE *and playfully puts both hands over* SERGE'S *eyes.*)

VANDAMM. Guess who it is, Howard!

SERGE (*pulling the other's hands away and turning to face him.*) What the hell?

VANDAMM (*backing away in confusion*). Gosh!

SERGE. Who are you?

VANDAMM. Gee, I'm sorry. I truly am. I'm sorry I . . . I thought ——

SERGE (*coldly*). Well?

VANDAMM. I thought you were Howard – I mean I thought you were Howard . . . Howard Erikson-Skinner. Old friend of mine, you see – I mean – I always stayed here when I came over to Paris – with him and his wife Marie – I mean I'm totally confused. I'm so sorry! I'm so sorry! But this apartment *is* 14 Bis, isn't it?

SERGE. Yes it is.

VANDAMM. Hell, I don't know. Seems I've made a big mistake all the same. I was wondering . . . why they never answered my letter from New York . . .

SERGE. It doesn't matter. Won't you sit down?

VANDAMM. Why . . . well, thanks. Thanks a lot. (*He sits down opposite* SERGE.) You're very kind. But I don't know – I feel so silly . . . it's kind of embarrassing . . . (*He and* SERGE *are half-laughing: he half-nervously,* SERGE *with mild amusement.*)

SERGE. Don't bother your head about it.

VANDAMM. They must have floated off to their place on the Riviera: St Paul de Vence – Howard and Marie Erikson-Skinner I mean. I guess I'll find me a room at the Louvre for tonight and call them from there.

SERGE. The Louvre?

VANDAMM. Oh not the Art Gallery. I mean the Hôtel; du Louvre . . . you know. Right there close by the Comédie Française.

SERGE. Oh yes, of course.

VANDAMM. And may I repeat my apologies for crashing in on you like

267

this and thinking you were somebody else?

SERGE. Oh forget it, forget it! Tell me, would you like a drink or anything?

VANDAMM. Why I'd love a drink, if it's not putting you out.

SERGE. Oh things like drink don't put me out.

VANDAMM. Seems to me that nothing at all could put you out (*he laughs a little nervously.*)

SERGE. Ah you don't know me. (SERGE *has risen and crossed to the wine cabinet.*)

VANDAMM (*staring at him*). No. I guess not ... All the same ...

SERGE. Whisky? Gin? Brandy?

VANDAMM. Oh not brandy, thanks so much. I haven't dined yet ... (*He is still staring at the other.*) I was wondering ...

SERGE. Vodka?

VANDAMM. Wonderful.

SERGE. What do you like with it? Tonic? Dubonnet? Cinzano? (*which he pronounces à la française.*)

VANDAMM. Straight, I think. Or on the rocks. I can't get along with those French things.

SERGE (*pouring out two drinks*). Ah, you prefer your vodka *à la russe*?

VANDAMM. À la Rousse? Oh yes, Russian style. Well, vodka is kind of Russian isn't it?

SERGE (*gravely*). We are led to believe so.

VANDAMM (*scrutinising first his glass and then* SERGE: *very thoughtfully*). Russian ... Oh well, here's how – (*they both drink a little:* VANDAMM *suddenly jerks his glass from his lips.*) Say! Russian: that has just made me think. Excuse me, but am I mistaken?

SERGE. Oh surely not twice in such rapid succession?

VANDAMM. No, I mean seriously, no kidding . . . aren't you the dancer?

SERGE. Oh yes, I dance a bit you know.

VANDAMM. You most certainly do. My God! You're Serge Kovalesky.

SERGE. Yes.

VANDAMM. Well I'll be . . . Did you ever in all your life hear anything so goddam crazy as that ? It's a – oh I don't know – it's something I never in all my born days dreamed would ever happen to me. Why I mean I've been your greatest fan in the world. No, that's silly again because you have such millions of the greatest in the world and they're all your greatest fans. (*He drinks:* SERGE *is watching him with pleasure and amusement.*) No, I will frankly admit that is another piece of sheer stupidity, of utter and complete absurdity on my part, but you'll have to forgive me and it's not just the drink. (*He takes another gulp.*) It's just that I am plain overcome. I mean, since that first night I saw you – three years ago was the first time in *The Golden God* – (*he drinks.*)

SERGE. Oh yes.

VANDAMM. And then . . . you danced as the Prince in *The Firebird*.

SERGE. No, I'm afraid not. I never danced in *Firebird*.

VANDAMM. Oh! . . . (*A short pause.*) Are you sure?

SERGE. Dead certain. Yes. (*But he is smiling.*)

VANDAMM. Oh my God! Another mistake. What must you think of me? What must you ——

SERGE (*laughing.*) It's a perfectly natural mistake. I might easily have danced in it.

VANDAMM. But you didn't, Goddammit, you didn't! you didn't! Oh I'm such a . . . I'm so dumb . . . But you *did* dance *Dark Magic* didn't you?

SERGE. Oh most decidedly.

VANDAMM. Right at last! Ah, goodee, goodee! And on that same night as *Dark Magic* didn't you dance in something about a rose? Spectre or something?

SERGE. *Spectre de la Rose.* Yes, that's right.

VANDAMM. Well, well. Ever since then I've seen you in twenty-two different ballets. Gee, that makes me feel like a . . . would it be terrible if I – may I have another drink?

SERGE (*smiling*). Of course. Help yourself.

VANDAMM. Gee, thanks. I'm behaving so badly . . . It's plain silly . . . (*He stretches out his hand and lifts the bottle, gravely surveys it and puts it down.*) No, No, I'm not going to touch one more drop. Because if I did I'd be sillier still. (*They laugh together.*) No sir. No: I want to tell you as a sober and I hope normally reasonable man – after all, Goddammit, I'm over here in Paris on a Sabbatical you know, doing a thesis on French scientific development in the Twentieth century so I'm not altogether the stupid gushing jerk I must appear to you – I want to tell you how grateful I am not merely for the enormous pleasure your dancing has given me in more than three years now, but for this . . . this stupid mistake of mine that's turned into this wonderful chance.

SERGE (*enquiringly*). Chance?

VANDAMM. Why, of meeting you like this. Personally meeting you. Actually talking to you. I can't make it out . . .

SERGE. Then don't try. Things one succeeds in making out turn into disappointments sometimes.

VANDAMM. Oho! You seem to be a bit of a philosopher too as well as being a first-rate – oh, more than that, a great – artist. You're a remarkable guy, and you don't know the kick it gives me to get to know you like this: look! Say, when I've fixed up at my hotel, would you care to have a little dinner with me somewhere tonight? Any place you'd like to go. I'd call you from the Louvre and get into a tuxedo and fix a time and place – I mean I take it you're not dancing tonight?

SERGE (*laughing*). No: if I were, I assure you I wouldn't be talking to you here, would I?

VANDAMM. No . . . no I guess not . . . you'd be getting all ready in your dressing-room and I'd never have met you at all. So it's lucky for me.

SERGE (*politely*). For me too.

VANDAMM. I'm glad. Then you will dine with me? I've just got to make up somehow for bursting in on you like this and making so many blunders. So where would you like ——

SERGE. A thousand thanks. But I'm afraid I can't tonight.

VANDAMM. You cant'? Oh my, you're dated somewhere else I suppose.

SERGE. No I don't think so.

VANDAMM. Oh! I figured as you were wearing a black tie ——

SERGE. Oh, the black tie is because I'm in mourning.

VANDAMM. Why, but ——

SERGE. Don't let that worry you. It's for nobody important. Just myself. Remember the woman in the Tchehov play? (*With a slight Russian accent.*) 'I am in mourning for my life. I am unhappy.'

VANDAMM. Gee, you're funny.

SERGE. Yes I'm beginning to think I am. I don't feel funny. Not a bit.

VANDAMM (*sitting down in amazement*). You astonish me. I mean I can't imagine a guy like you feeling any way but on top of the world.

SERGE. Don't you believe it. Look – before you go – will you have a little one for the road? (*He pours him a drink.*)

VANDAMM. Why, thanks a lot. Yes, I think I will. If you'll let me meet you again sometime. How about lunch tomorrow? Thanks. (*He takes the glass from Serge.*)

SERGE (*pours a drink for himself*). I'm afraid I'm rehearsing until three. I'm dancing tomorrow night.

VANDAMM. You are? Why, that's wonderful! I'll be there, if I can get a seat. And if I can't, I'll just stand. What'll you be dancing?

SERGE. *Golden God* and *Symphony in Black.*

VANDAMM. Wonderful. I never saw that one.

SERGE (*with a touch of irony*). Not the Prince in *Firebird.*

VANDAMM. Gosh, I'm such a silly blundering jackass.

SERGE. No: I was being malicious. I'm sorry.

VANDAMM. I don't think that was malicious. Kind of quick, maybe. (*He grins.*) Look, will you be free after the show tomorrow?

SERGE. Well – yes, I've just remembered . . . Yes, I suppose I will be.

VANDAMM. Well, may I come round to fetch you and give you supper somewhere?

SERGE (*slowly*). Yes, I think so. Ask for me at the entrée des artistes.

VANDAMM. The entrée . . . oh yes, the stage entrance, hm?

SERGE. Yes. I'll leave a message. Sláinte!

VANDAMM. How's that?

SERGE. That's the Irish for Here's How!

VANDAMM. Irish? Why of course: you're not Russian – of course you're not – you're Irish! So here's – what word did you say?

SERGE. Sláinte!

VANDAMM. Slann-cha! Did I get it right?

SERGE (*as he drinks*). A-ha.

VANDAMM (*having drink*). I still can't believe it. Drinking a slann-cha with you, of all people in the world . . . why it's crazy! (*He rises, glass in hand.*) Here's to tomorrow! It's crazy (*He drinks.*) It's crazy!

SERGE (*soothingly*). I know. You mean it's crazy.

VANDAMM. Well so it is. Goodnight – and thanks again! (*They shake hands, the glasses, naturally enough, now in their left hands.*) It's crazy! And yet it all seems so easy and natural somehow.

SERGE. Easy and natural! . . . Yes, I do hope so. (*They drink again, draining their glasses as the curtain falls.*)

# ACT II

## Scene I

*The scene is the same, six months later. It is a fine morning in January, and the sunshine without reveals the remains of a certain chaos within, with which* MRS BATY *and* ANDY *have been valiantly coping.* ANDY *stands holding an already heaped-up tray, to which* MRS BATY *is adding as many bottles and glasses as it will bear.*

MRS BATY. There now, that looks a bit more like it. Ts, ts, ts! Never saw such a mess since last week's party. Never. (*She has planted the last bottle on the only available space on the tray while speaking.*)

ANDY (*with a delicate irony*). You're sure now you wouldn't like to tie the sofa round me waist and let me fly away?

MRS BATY. Carry those things out and look smart about it too. And shift those chairs round to their proper places. (*She proceeds to do this herself as* ANDY *carries the laden try to the kitchen.*)

ANDY (*as he goes*). Ah, yez'll have me dead between the lot of you. I'm only telling you (*he is gone.*)

MRS BATY. Shift them round I tell you. (*Singing as she moves the chairs herself.*)

> 'Oh shift round a little bit further
> Shift a little bit further round!
> What you seem to think is a sorter
> Curiosity out in the water
> That's my missus and she'll be here in half a jiff,
> So shift a little bit further further further
> round the cliff!'

Shocking! (*Re-enter* ANDY.)

ANDY. Look what I'm after finding in the kitchen. (*He holds up a lady's shoe.*)

MRS BATY. What? Here, let's have a look. (*She takes it from him.*) I know who that belongs to. That belongs to that Pepita Sanchiss, that Spanish floozy.

ANDY. Floozy? Go 'way owa that, she's not a floozy. Or if she is itself, she's a gorgeous one.

MRS BATY. Gorgeous is as gorgeous does, dear. Throwing her shoes about and traipsing home on one of her bare feet, I presume. Oh well, that's what she's accustomed to more than likely. She and her Rapsodies espagnols and that scowl on her face all the time. (*She makes a fearful contortion of eyes and lips.*) Flamenco or whatever they call them, all bent knees and bad temper: got sick of it. Here take that into the kitchen. (*As* ANDY *carries the slippers away, shouting after him.*) And bring me a bucket, for these ashes . . . cigarette ends everywhere! Spanish!!

ANDY (*returning with the bucket*). Well 'tis my opinion you hates all the Spanish crowd, fellas and girls all the same.

MRS BATY. Oh no I don't. Mr Gonzales now, he's a very nice gentleman for a Dago, though he talks so funny. And Rosario Mendiss: she's not so bad. And Mr Valera ——

ANDY (*awestruck*). Is it Dev you mean?

MRS BATY. Don't be soppy dear: Antonio Valera of course, that Pepita's partner, poor man. Very nice manners he's got. Speaks a bit of English too. And he can dance classic well too: not like most of that crowd . . . There! That's about all. Was the whole company here last night? Looks to me as if the Tout Paree had been here when we came in first. What a first night!

ANDY. Did you ever see so many calls for himself in your life? Twenty-six curtains he got. And they all roaring out his name!

MRS BATY. Oh he's a marvellous dance, there's no denying that. *Hommage á Nijinsky*: well I mean it's an homage to Mr Sere as well as to a poor dead Russian. Homage – that means honour in *case* you don't know.

ANDY. God! I thought I'd never get him into his tights at all for the Rose Ballet ——

MRS BATY. *Specter de la Rose* to you.

ANDY. Sure I know that. He was shaking with the fright. And then he sails out on the stage like there wasn't a worry in the world on him.

MRS BATY. *And* that last exit! Sailing out of the window like a beautiful mauve-coloured bird: you would have sworn he was on a wire. Here, hold that pail closer.

ANDY. Well, he wasn't.

MRS BATY (*as she empties the ashtrays and wipes them*). Of course he wasn't, you ignorant great . . . he's a dancer, not a puppet or a trick cyclist.

ANDY. What's a puppet?

MRS BATY. You know what you want is somebody who'd teach you a few words in English apart from God bless us and One for the Road and Up the Republic. A puppet, dux, is a sort of doll that can't move without somebody else pulling its wire.

ANDY. God bless us! (*He gazes at her, awestruck.*)

MRS BATY. And Mr Vandamm from the USA is, so to speak a case in point. Not that I don't like Mr Vandamm. I do. He's very generous and considering he's an American he's very gentlemanly. But he seems to be absolutely incapable of making a move without a suggestion from Mr Serge.

ANDY. Ah that's true enough, God knows.

MRS BATY. Mind you, he's sitting very pretty since he came to stay here. Lap of luxury as you might say. Did he put in an appearance yet?

ANDY. He did but he didn't want any breakfast. Just a glass of orange juice and away with him a few minutes before yourself came in (*he carries away the bucket.*)

MRS BATY. Living like a lord. And he'll be back before lunch I have no doubt wanting coffee or cocktails or both. I don't know what they'd do without me I'm sure. Wardrobe mistress at the theatre and lady help here – nobody but a genius or a lunatic like me would ever do it, dear.

ANDY. Ah you're always saying that. Oh! I forgot to tell you – they'll all be having their lunch together.

MRS BATY. All? Did you say all?

ANDY. Ah no, only the two gents and Mr and Mrs Gonsally.

MRS BATY. In a restaurant I sincerely hope?

ANDY. Of course, where else?

MRS BATY. Wouldn't surprise me if they wanted it on the roof. (*A bell rings twice.*) There that's Mr Serge for his coffee, I suppose. Get a move on young Andy ——

ANDY. OK. (*He makes for the kitchen*).

MRS BATY (*shouting after him*). And I've got the morning papers here for him – don't forget to bring them into him. All opened up for him at the theatre page, God knows nothing much else seems to interest him . . . Oh there you are, good morning to you I'm sure Mr Serge. (*For* SERGE *has appeared at the entrance to the bedrooms. He is clad in pyjamas and a dressing gown and is rubbing his hands and face with the aid of a bottle of Eau-de-Cologne.*)

SERGE. Hullo Ruby! Did I hear you say you had the papers for me?

MRS BATY. Yes: they're all here. All open at ——

SERGE. All right the. Let's know the worst.

MRS BATY (*handing him a pile of opened Paris daily papers*). There won't be any worst. Like to take a bet? What a first night! What a triumph! Never heard such applause since Madame Cellas sang Normer at the Opera.

SERGE (*eagerly scanning a paper*). Yes, I must have had friends in front, mustn't I?

MRS BATY. Oh you are a scream dear, you really are. Anyway you're honest about reading your notices. I can't stand the type that pretends they don't read their notices. (*Affecting a very lofty accent and manner.*) Newspaper notices, may deah? Nevah glance at them! Pulling their own legs if you ask me. Excuse me if I finish my polishing, won't you? (*She continues her labours with the duster.*)

SERGE (*throwing the paper away*). Well that one's all right anyway. Good for all of us.

MRS BATY (*looking over his shoulder as she passes*). There, that one's open at the page. I had a look at it myself: looks like a rave to me. Oh and there's been a terrible to-do in the Chamber of Deputies dear ——

SERGE. Oh that! Yes, this one's good too.

ANDY (*entering with a coffee tray*). Ah you're up already. Good morning sir!

SERGE. Morning, Andy. (*He continues to read: he is now opening the third paper, reading a headline.*) 'Bravo Kovalevsky' Well that's all right. (*Opens another.*) Where the hell – ah! 'Serve Kovalevsky et Olga Prokovska en toute leur splendeur . . . la grace incomparable de Kovalevsky' – that's all right!

ANDY. Will I bring this to your bed now?

MRS BATY. No: put it down here. (ANDY *puts the tray on a small table and draws it towards* SERGE: MRS BATY *hands him a glass of fruit juice: he takes it mechanically, saying nothing and continues to read.*) There now. I'll pour it out for you. (*She pours coffee and milk.*) Have a nice roll dear? (*A pause:* ANDY *and* MRS BATY *regard the dancer and his paper in silence.*)

SERGE. My God!

ANDY. What ails him?

MRS BATY. Shut up!

SERGE. Blithering old dodderer!

ANDY. Anything wrong sir?

MRS BATY. Hop it!

ANDY. Hop it yourself. Why would I hop it?

MRS BATY. Well, keep your trap shut then. (*There is another pause*

275

*during which* SERGE *breathes noisily through his nose.*)

ANDY. Ach, I might as well fix up his room, so. (*He disappears in the direction of the bedroom.*)

SERGE (*reading*). 'Artists admirable, sans doute, mais le comparer au plus grand danseur du siècle, peut-être de –' 'to compare him to the greatest dancer of the century, perhaps of all time, is, to us who saw Nijinsky himself, not only embarrassing . . . it is pathetic . . . more than once I had to look away.'

MRS BATY. Oh the cheek of it! What's his rotten name?

SERGE. Durand, Jean-Pierre Durand . . . What does his name matter? He's not important.

MRS BATY. I should hope not indeed. You'd do much better not to read them, dear. And don't forget you've got that interview at twelve.

SERGE (*in horror*). Oh my God, oh no! Ruby! Why did nobody remind me? Who's it with?

MRS BATY. Well, I'm reminding you now, aren't I? And what did you want to get rid of that secretary for, that nice Miss Baker?

SERGE. Miss Baker? Oh yes dear, Baker! She didn't know French well enough for one thing. (*He resumes reading.*) 'En l'Apres Midi d'un Faune . . .' 'In the Ballet of the Faun he brought an unpardonable note of crudity, a lack of that spiritual ecstasy underlying physical desire which made Nijinsky's interpretation so exquisite . . .' (VANDAMM *enters bearing a sumptuous bouquet.*)

VANDAMM. Why you're up already! That's fine. Look Serge, I saw these and I couldn't resist them.

SERGE. Look at what this bastard says about me here!

VANDAMM. Say, what's wrong? You ought to be on top of the world after last night.

MRS BATY. Well he's not, Mr Van. Not by any means he's not. He's had a bird in some rotten three-halfpenny rag and it's depressed him. Oo! Look at these lovely posies, Mr Serge. Oo! Aren't you going to say Thanks a million to your kind friend?

SERGE (in a deliberately mechanical voice like an idiot child reciting). Oh, thanks, thanks a million, dear Uncle Billy for booful booful flowers. (*As himself, in a towering rage.*) But have you seen this? Have you cast your eyes over this prose-poem about me? Have you?

VANDAMM. What's wrong, Serge?

MRS BATY (*always tactful*). I'll go and put these in water. They are super, Mr Bill, they really are, and he'll appreciate them when he comes to himself. (*She is gone.*)

SERGE. 'To us who saw Nijinsky himself . . .' It's enough to make me hate the name of Nijinsky ——

VANDAMM. Look Serge, there's no need to carry on like this: you'll only drive yourself crazy. What does it matter what the papers say? Think of last night – think of the sale at the box office – I called in this morning: they're milling around like ants: it's terrific.

SERGE. Oh I know all that. I know. You don't understand, Bill.

VANDAMM. Don't I? Well, maybe I don't. But I certainly was impressed last night. I felt so proud of you. You just don't know.

SERGE. Now it's my turn to say 'Well, maybe I don't know. Maybe I don't understand' But I do, Bill, I do, you see. That's the tragedy.

VANDAMM. Tragedy?

SERGE. Yes, the tragedy. It isn't just the fact of getting a bad notice. It's coming face to face with what one believes is a lack of understanding plainly set out in print. And that may impress thousands of readers so that they are prejudiced and blinded before they see one. Maybe it's all true: maybe I am as lousy as that notice says.

VANDAMM. But Serge, honey, *is* it as bad as all that?

SERGE. Listen to this . . . 'In the Ballet of the Faun he brought an unpardonable note of crude passion, a total lack of that spiritual ecstasy illuminating physical desire which made Nijinsky's interpretation so supreme.'

VANDAMM. But who among your enormous public is going to be put off by that?

SERGE. Oh dam my enormous public. What about the effect on me? No, Bill, you don't understand. You love dancing . . . you love what you see. You love the *result*, you love the glitter and glamour of it all.

VANDAMM. Well what else could I love about it?

SERGE. Oh I'm not blaming you. Only a fool would blame a man like you for not totally understanding the process of the *making* of a work he enjoys.

VANDAMM. I don't quite get you Serge.

SERGE. But that's what I'm saying. You don't quite get me. In fact you don't get me at all. Look: put it this way. I have a car, haven't I?

VANDAMM. You certainly do have a car. And she's super.

SERGE. Yes, well, I also have a chauffeur and either you or he drives. I enjoy being driven about in it because it's comfortable and I like looking out of the windows.

VANDAMM. Ah! . . . But what exactly does that ——?

SERGE. But I can't drive the car myself: I haven't a notion of how it

277

works or how it was made, and the whole meaning of its mechanism is for me a mystery I'm not even interested enough to try to solve. Isn't that true?

VANDAMM (*smiling*). It certainly is. Remember when I tried to teach you to drive? Gosh! I never could have believed that anyone of your brilliance could be so totally dumb about anything.

SERGE. Well there you are, you see.

VANDAMM. And when I attempted to explain things in the simplest way you just yawned right in my face.

SERGE. Well, you'd be exactly the same if I attempted to explain how our minds work when ——

VANDAMM. Oh but Serge, damn it all, you can't compare a sheer miracle of super mechanical creativity to – well, how do I put it? to show business?

SERGE (*in a moment of wild despairing amusement*). Oh – ha ha ha ha!

VANDAMM. What are you smiling at, honey?

SERGE. I don't know. Just the smile of despair I suppose.

VANDAMM. Are you mad at me?

SERGE. What? No, I don't thik so. No. But I am feeling ominous, somehow. Ominous, Bill.

VANDAMM. And it's not only on account of one stupid critique, *is* it? Be honest now . . .?

SERGE. Not entirely. Though I feel it's yet another sort of gulf between us.

VANDAMM. You mean I really don't understand you? I figured ——

SERGE. We don't really understand each other. I don't think it's my fault. And I know it isn't yours.

(*There is a pause. They look at each other. Then* VANDAMM *says slowly.*)

VANDAMM. It is, you know.

SERGE. It is what?

VANDAMM. My fault. Basically.

SERGE. What's on you mind, Bill?

VANDAMM. I feel guilty. That's all. About you. See?

SERGE (*after a pause*). About me? Yes I was wondering.

VANDAMM. You were? How long?

SERGE. About a week I think.

VANDAMM. You're uncanny.

SERGE. Why do you say that?

VANDAMM. Serge, I don't know how to tell you this. But I've got to tell you. For the last week – no, it's ten days now – I've been living a lie with you.

SERGE. I thought so.

VANDAMM. I told you you were uncanny. Well now I'm going to tell you something else.

SERGE. It's about that girl you used to know in America, isn't it? The lady doctor?

VANDAMM. My gosh, you've done it again! In the old times they'd have burnt you at the stake as a sorcerer. OK you're right: it's about Susan. The one I told you about. She's turned up again.

SERGE. In Paris?

VANDAMM. Yes.

SERGE. You told me it was all over.

VANDAMM. So it was. And that was why ——

SERGE. It made things possible with me.

VANDAMM. I guess so. Are you made at me?

SERGE. No. I think it was inevitable.

VANDAMM. I am crazy about you. You know that. I *still* am.

SERGE. But you're in love with her. You *still* are.

VANDAMM. Are you mad at me?

SERGE. Dear Bill, if you ask me that again, the temptation to go mad may prove irresistible.

VANDAMM. I feel such an ornery, mean, low-down son of a ——

SERGE. Did you leave your horse in the hall?

VANDAMM. Did I leave my *what* in the hall?

SERGE. Your bucking bronco? You're talking like a Western

VANDAMM. Oh Serge, be serious. Please!

SERGE. I'm perfectly serious. I should be miserable if I thought I could ever be more serious than I am at this moment.

VANDAMM. Gee, you're hard to understand.

SERGE. I know. And I'm sorry. But you've go to go back to – what's her name? – Susan.

VANDAMM. You mean you want me to?

SERGE. Now Bill: make an effort to take that burning eagerness out of your voice.

VANDAMM. You make me feel so ——

SERGE. I'm not going to bitch things up. You go straight back to Susan. And marry her.

VANDAMM. I don't think I could leave you now. I don't think I could. I'd hate not to see you again.

SERGE. Can't we be friends still. Just ordinary friends I mean?

VANDAMM. I don't know that I could face that. I . . . anyway, Susan – (*He stops confusedly.*)

SERGE. Well?

VANDAMM. Susan would never – I mean I don't think she'd ever stand for that.

SERGE. But aren't husbands allowed to have ordinary friends? Surely they are?

VANDAMM. Maybe, but Susan knows – I mean I've told Susan everything. About you and me, I mean.

SERGE (*after a motionless pause*). That was very adventurous of you, Bill.

VANDAMM. I don't see why. After all, she's a doctor. She's quite aware of – things. And she's read the Kinsey Report. And Freud, and all that. And I figured she'd understand . . .

SERGE. Well?

VANDAMM. Well, she just didn't. She broke right down; it was ghastly. She cried and cried: she nearly went into hysterics.

SERGE. Take her to a – no; marry her first, and then – take her to a psychiatrist.

VANDAMM. She *is* a psychiatrist, Goddamit.

SERGE. I see. So what does she suggest? (*But he is laughing.*)

VANDAMM. She wants me to promise her faithfully that I'll never see you again.

SERGE. Ah, how wonderful women are! What realists! What technicians! All sweet psychiatrist reason until the man they want appears and then all tears and relentlessness.

VANDAMM (*full of self-reproach*). They're no worse than we are I guess.

SERGE. Your guesses are not invariably correct, Bill.

VANDAMM. Well, let's say they're no worse than I am – I mean I can be reasonable most of the time, but give me a couple of drinks and a girl I can let my eyes linger over, and I go crazy. Can't help myself.

SERGE. Yes, I noticed that last night with Maggie.

VANDAMM. You did?

SERGE. Of course I did. And if I'd been a woman I would have had hysterics. On the spot.

VANDAMM. You would?

SERGE (in Americanese). Oh, I certainly would. I'd have said, 'Say, what are you trying to do to me, Baby?'

VANDAMM. You're such an extraordinary guy.

SERGE. You've discovered that, have you?

VANDAMM. Yes. You're always surprising me, always coming out with such unexpected . . . anyhow, Maggie wouldn't have anything to do with me.

SERGE. I noticed that too. And you're never going to see me again.

VANDAMM. I don't know what to do. I mean about you and Susan. Which of you . . .? I mean I can check a bill of quantities. I can analyse a critical path, and explain the process of a complex computerised system. They have their complexities but they're simple if you see what I mean, compared to ——

SERGE. Compared to your own reactions to Susan or me . . .?

VANDAMM. And my own behaviour in your own home –

SERGE. I haven't got a home. Except the theatre.

VANDAMM. No, well . . . your apartment then.

SERGE. Oh, you're thinking of Maggie last night. But I understand that; she's very attractive.

VANDAMM. But it wasn't only Maggie, Serge. It was Pepita too.

SERGE. Pepita Sanchez?

VANDAMM. Aha. I carried on with her like crazy, and she couldn't say a word I could understand, only rolled her eyes and shouted a lot of Spanish. And she bit my arm too, and then she threw her shoe at me and made a getaway down the stairs. Oh I – I – I was disgraceful. But I can't help it. I just can't help it when I see an attractive –

SERGE. You'll be all right when you've got a woman of your own. You'll be all right.

VANDAMM. Do you believe that?

SERGE. I intend to believe it. And I'm more convinced than ever, Bill, about what you ought to do.

VANDAMM. And what is it?

SERGE. You ought to go back to Susan. And you ought to marry her. And then you ought to take her to a psychiatrist.

VANDAMM. And not see any more of you?

SERGE. You might arrange alternate visits.

VANDAMM (*shocked*). You mean see Susie and you alternatively?

SERGE. No. See Susie and the psychiatrist alternately.

VANDAMM. Well, if you're not the most extraordinary guy.

SERGE (*gentle, but amused and sad*). You did a remark on that before, you know.

VANDAMM. Well, it's true.

SERGE. When things are awkward between people who are fond of each other truth is the only refuge. So we'll say goodbye. As good friends.

VANDAMM (*barely audible*). I didn't say anything about all this before your opening night was through. That was why I. . . .

SERGE. Thanks Bill: that was sweet of you. My opening night . . .

(*Suddenly remembering* the Durand notice.) My God, what a night! And what a morning after! First there's this foul nonsense about me in Veritable, and then you and your psychiatric Susie!

VANDAMM. Hey, Serge honey, don't ——

SERGE. What a day! What a life! 'Pour nous qui avons vu Nijinsky –' Where the hell is it? (*He picks up the paper. At this moment the front door bell rings. Totally unconscious of any sound* SERGE *reads in a shaking voice.*) '. . . For us who saw Nijinsky himself' Well if he *did* see Nijinsky he must be too bloody old by now to get himself into his seat in the theatre let alone be capable of writing about it. (ANDY *crosses to archway.*) Philippe Durand! Doddering, cock-eyed old cretin! Silly blithering bloody b . . . bastard!

ANDY (*pausing in his journey*). God forgive you, sir! (*He goes to the door.*)

SERGE. There! Burn the lot of them! Tell somebody to light the fire with the whole bloody lot.

ANDY (*at the entrance*). Madame Romera Gonsally!

SERGE. Light the bloody fire with them!

> (MAGGIE, *blooming and beautifully dressed, appears just as* SERGE, *having torn and rolled the newspaper into a football, hurls it across the room in her direction.* MAGGIE *neatly catches the football regardless of the bouquet she is carrying.*)

MAGGIE. Oh well held sir! . . . What's biting *you*, my angel? Hullo Bill!

VANDAMM (*abashed at the sight of her*). Why hello! . . . Seems he's had a bad notice, Maggie.

MAGGIE. One, one only, out of nine raves. Read all the others and pull yourself together, Serge.

SERGE (*lying flat on sofa.*) I'm not aware that I'm falling asunder.

MAGGIE. Well you are. Now don't behave like a spoilt baby: it makes Bill and me feel so elderly. And look, I've brought you these. Lilies for purity, sweetheart, and aoh! so sort of deliciously funereal. (*She places them with over-elaborate reverence on his chest.*)

SERGE. A million thanks darling. (*He pulls her down to him and kisses her.*) But saying they're funereal in that camp voice doesn't make the remark less true. Come and sit down. (*He pulls her towards him.*)

MAGGIE. Aaah! Don't make me squash them! (*She sits on the sofa's end where his feet are: he flexes his knees and sits beside her, holding the flowers and smelling them.*)

SERGE. They're divine! But they do smell sort of mystical and final somehow – don't they?

MAGGIE (*looking from one man to the other*). Hey, what's up between you two? You haven't been quarrelling, have you?

SERGE. No, we haven't quarrelled. (*There is an uneasy pause.*)

VANDAMM (*awkwardly*). I'm kind of worried and ashamed of myself about last night, Maggie – if I may still call you Maggie?

MAGGIE. You can call me Bernadette what's-her-name if you like, dear.

SERGE. Ha! (*A guffaw.*)

MAGGIE. Well Bernadette is my second name after all. Could you believe it? But why are you ashamed of yourself about last night? You introduced no modern improvements.

VANDAMM. No, but . . . Well I feel now I made myself a nuisance to you . . . the fact is I was not myself . . . I'd taken a lot of liquor . . .

MAGGIE. Are you implying that your passionate protestations were not from the heart but from the bottle? Oh fie, for shame, Mr Vandamm.

SERGE (*rising*). Don't be ridiculous, Mag. And thanks again for the flowers. I'll get Ruby to put them into water. (*He carries the flowers to the kitchen.*)

MAGGIE (*crossing to a chair and sitting down*). What's wrong with him?

VANDAMM. I don't know. It's the bad notice, I guess.

MAGGIE. The what? That one by old Durand in Verité? But nobody takes Durand seriously.

VANDAMM. Ssh!

SERGE (*re-entering*). I've got to shave and bathe and get dressed. Please excuse me. Will you? (*He goes out to the bedroom.*)

MAGGIE. Don't be too long, darling. (*To* VANDAMM.) I wish you'd tell me what's really wrong. I hate people who won't tell me what's wrong with other people.

VANDAMM. He's all upset, and so am I, Maggie.

MAGGIE. Darling, I can see that. I'm not totally blind yet, even if I do have to wear spectacles when I do my thought reading.

VANDAMM. Do you do thought reading?

MAGGIE. Frequently, now come here and sit down. (*He sits on sofa. She takes her spectacles from her bag and sits beside him.*) Now! Look me in de vites of mine eyes, mein Billie! (*He looks at her.*) Aha! I knew it. And it's nothing to do with old Durand's notice either. It's about you and Serge. Isn't it now?

VANDAMM. He wants —— (*a pause.*)

283

MAGGIE (*holding the spectacles in her two hands*). Well go on. He wants you both to part. Doesn't he?

VANDAMM. Looks like that.

MAGGIE. And you don't want it too. Only you're not wholehearted about it. Any more than he is really. Am I right?

VANDAMM. I'm not sure about that.

MAGGIE. Well I am. Wait a minute. (*She replaces the spectacles on her nose and twists his face towards her.*) Look at me: Look at me, you Big God knows what. (*She peers into his eyes.*) Oh I say! What do I see here, as Ruby says when she can see nothing at all. Oh! There's a woman here: oh, and she's a one, she's a one I'm telling you!

VANDAMM. A woman?

MAGGIE. And she means to marry you. Ah yes she does. What is more she almost undoubtedly will. And what a time you'll have with her!

VANDAMM. Gee, you're uncanny. You're more uncanny than Serge.

MAGGIE. I'm right about the lady, aren't I?

VANDAMM. I suppose you are . . . Serge wants me to marry her.

MAGGIE. Serge wants ——? She's determined to, you mean, and Serge doesn't want to stand in the way.

VANDAMM. Well that's one way of looking at it, I suppose. And I figure that all in all it may be the wisest thing to do.

MAGGIE. The wisest thing! So you're going to leave a great artist and a great friend like Serge all alone even though you know he dreads being alone. You'll go scooting off to her though you don't love her any more – probably not as much – as you love him.

VANDAMM. Love him? Maggie ——

MAGGIE. *Now* what is it?

VANDAMM. Love him? Why Maggie, of course, he's a wonderful friend, but ——

MAGGIE. Well?

VANDAMM. A perfectly wonderful friend, but Goddammit, Maggie, he's not a woman.

MAGGIE. That at least is clear.

VANDAMM. But when you talk about loving, I mean are you suggesting there's anything unnatural between us?

MAGGIE. From my point of view, no. From yours apparently, yes.

VANDAMM. For Heaven's sakes, what are you suggesting.

MAGGIE. That you're lovers as well as friends. Don't be a fool Bill. And don't play the hypocrite with me. It doesn't suit you.

VANDAMM (*rising and walking up and down*). Oh, my God!

MAGGIE. And don't get in a panic. Look Bill I know Serge and I love

284

him: Oh not as you do. (*A snort from Vandamm makes her add*) – no, please listen for a minute – I love him more than anybody in the world except Paco, my husband. But I love Serge *only* as a friend: without passion, without sensual desire, without jealousy, without romance, if you like. And I understand him. I understand his horror of loneliness. I understand his need for a companion who'll be lover as well as friend, his incapacity of feeling any sensual attraction to a woman however much he may like her, however much he may admire her beauty or her charm. It's tragic for him, but I can see nothing unnatural about him – good God, it's nature herself who created him that way – so where's the unnaturalness, if you follow my English? And I can only see the tragic part of it because of the world's attitude towards him and his tribe.

VANDAMM. You shock me, Maggie.

MAGGIE. And you shock me, Bill, so we're quits. And you shock me because you take the same attitude as that world that condemns him, and all the while you're taking an advantage you're ashamed to admit.

VANDAMM (*stopping in his stride to and fro, and speaking in a measured, menacing voice.*) So you think I'm that way, do you? I'll soon show you! (*He pulls her to her feet, takes her roughly in his arms and covers her face and neck with kisses.*)

MAGGIE (*treating it as a joke, but coldly struggling as well she might, for* VANDAMM *is a large man and seems more than able for the job he has undertaken*). Don't be such a jackass Bill – hey! Help! Help! – Unhand me, Mr Vandamm, unhand me immediately.

VANDAMM (*muttering*). I want you, I want you.

MAGGIE. Well, you can't have me: Aah! Stop it you big animal! (*She suddenly remembers Dublin*) or be the hokey as sure as there's a – Aah! – God in Heaven – I – yaah! – I'll bloody well choke you! (*By this time the struggle had developed into a fantastic dance, chiefly directed by* MAGGIE, *though her seducer thinks that all is due to him. She prances to and fro, escaping from his arms by what seems to be the method of Jujitsu. As he catches her for the last time, she pushes him reeling away crying.*) Stop it you fool, stop it, stop . . .

MRS BATY (*coming in from kitchen*). Anything gone wrong Madam?

MAGGIE. Yes, Mr Vandamm has . . . Heavens! what a clumsy dancer you'd make, Bill! I was just showing him a few simple little steps, Ruby, and he . . . he trod on my foot —— (*A bell rings suddenly.*)

VANDAMM. That's Serge's bell. Excuse me. (*He vanishes into the*

285

*bedroom.*)

MAGGIE (*holding her throat*). Oh my God!

MRS BATY. Foot hurting you, dear?

MAGGIE. Not nearly as much as my throat. I had to shout at him to prove my point.

MRS BATY. Well you seem to have proved it all right. He's proper upset, you can see that.

MAGGIE. He's not the only one. And it's not about his dancing.

MRS BATY. As if I thought it was: you don't think I didn't take that with a pound and a half of salt did you? He's upset about Mr Serge, that's what he is. And so are you.

MAGGIE. Oh may be. (*She gazes at herself in a compact with melancholy eyes.*)

MRS BATY. And so am I madam. I'm downright upset. Oh, madam dear, I've got a hunch those two are coming to a finish again. Mr Serge I mean and ——

MAGGIE. So have I, Ruby. Poor old Serge.

MRS BATY. Poor old Serge you may well say. Poor old dear. I don't know what's going to happen to him if those two part as you might say. And there's been no row, you – happy as sandboys they were –

VANDAMM (*coming in from the bedroom*). It's you he wants Andy. (*For* ANDY *has come in from the kitchen unseen by* MRS BATY *who starts.*)

MRS BATY. Oh you gave me a turn, Mr Nosy Parker.

ANDY. Always the harsh word, always the bitter glance. Thanks be to God I can afford t'ignore you.

SERGE'S VOICE. Andy?

ANDY. Coming sir, coming! (*He goes.*)

VANDAMM. I'm sorry Maggie. Honest. I'm real sorry . . .

MAGGIE (*in deepest Chicago*). Forget it, baby, forget it. (*As herself.*) Have you made it up with Serge?

VANDAMM. We haven't had a row.

MAGGIE. Well go and have one and then make it up forever. (*The phone bell rings as he exits.*) It's all right. I'll take it.

MRS BATY. Now what's up I wonder?

MAGGIE. Allô allô! Oui? . . . Ah Paco. Si soy you Maggi. Que dice? No! No! Impossible!

MRS BATY. I got that one all right. Quite like French really, isn't it?

MAGGIE (*holding up a hand for silence*). Ay! Y no estará capaz de bailar esta noche?

MRS BATY. Like French gone up the pole in a manner of speaking.

Hop it Andy. (*For* ANDY *has appeared from the bedroom agog with excitement.*)

ANDY. All he wanted was his new tie. God forgive him, he's terrible helpless.

MAGGIE (*at telephone*). No! Pués vendremos al teatro. Sí. En seguida.

ANDY. Which side won, Miss?

MRS BATY. Which side won? I suppose you think this is a football match on the telly, you ——

ANDY. Well sure there is a match today. Dublin v. Wexford.

MAGGIE. Sí. Tan Pronto que posible. (*She hangs up.*)

MRS BATY. What is it dear?

MAGGIE. It's a pretty kettle of fish, that's what it is. (*She sits staring gloomily in front of her.*)

SERGE (*as he emerges from the bedroom door with* VANDAMM *who wears an expression of utter misery.*) And cheer up, Bill. Cheer up, dear Bill. I think you're going to be very happy.

VANDAMM. Oh Serge, I feel such a ——

SERGE. Ssh!

VANDAMM. I'll be back this afternoon for my things. And maybe ——

SERGE. No, I'll not be here. I have said Goodbye, Bill, and God bless you.

VANDAMM. I – Goodbye! (*He goes.*)

MRS BATY. And what's gone wrong with him?

SERGE. Nothing. It doesn't matter. He'll tell you himself later. What I want to know is what's gone wrong with all of you? Maggie, what is it?

MAGGIE. Trouble at the show, that's all. We'll have to go to the theatre, Serge. It seems Pepita Sanchez won't be able to dance tonight. She lost a shoe somehow last night, flew away from here without it and couldn't get a taxi, and walked home – nearly three kilometres – in her stockinged feet in the pouring rain, one stockinged foot anyway. And she's twisted her ankle badly. And she's down with a violent chill and the doctor is fearing pneumonia if she stirs from her bed. Anyway, she can hardly walk let alone dance. And that's the situation.

ANDY. Merciful hour! Ah, the shoe!

MRS BATY. Do shut up dear, there's a good boy. (ANDY *runs into the kitchen muttering.*)

MAGGIE. And all her big Flamenco numbers are tonight, of course. And as you know she was to have danced Colombine in Carnaval with Serge. Her night in fact.

SERGE (*suddenly clapping his hands.*) Thank God! Something real to worry about!

MAGGIE. What do you mean? Something real?

MRS BATY. Pewmonia, dear, Pewmonia's real enough. Unless you're a Christian Science of course. Then there's nothing real at all except Mary Baker Eddy.

SERGE. Now God forgive me! Because Pepita is a very good and charming girl (*Mrs* BATY *snorts*) – whatever Ruby thinks – and I'm desperately sorry about her being ill. But she's saved my life. I've got to work: we've all got to work, now.

MAGGIE. All hands to the pumps! What are you talking about?

SERGE. Tonight, of course, Carnaval won't suffer: Olga can dance Colombine, we've rehearsed it together twenty-nine times already, and she's going to do it next week anyway, and she was raging about Pepita getting it for the premiere. It's the Spanish half of the programme that could go to hell. And so . . . (*A pause.*)

MAGGIE. Well, come on . . . Come on! (*For there is another pause.*)

MRS BATY. All is dark: all is dark . . . Got it! I know! He means Tamar.

SERGE. Point killer! Yes, Tamar, of course: Tamar was going on on Wednesday in any case. We'll rehearse all afternoon. Morales will take Olga and me and the girls in Carnaval in the rehearsal room: Washinsky and Valera can take Tamar on the stage – Nina is perfect already – let's fly down to the theatre and consult Paco. We'll have to get his approval.

MAGGIE. Of course. But you oughtn't to be working all day with Carnaval tonight and the Rose as well. You'll be worn out.

SERGE. Who cares? I want to be worn out.

MAGGIE. I believe you'd pop in Scherezade and the Sleeping Princess as make-weight if they wanted you to.

SERGE. Andy why not? Tell me that! Oh Mag, there's life in the air again. It's like springtime. (ANDY *enters with a slipper in his hand.*)

ANDY. Have a look at this now! This is the one I found in the kitchen this morning.

SERGE. Hand it over! (*He takes it.*) Oh Bill! My poor drunken prudish amorous Bill! You've put her life in danger and maybe you've saved mine. (*He gives the slipper back to* ANDY.) Keep it carefully, Andy. I'll bring it back to Miss Sanchez.

MRS BATY. Kitchen's the best place for it. And for her too, if you ask me. Not that I don't pity her for catching pewmonia, if she has caught pewmonia: leading men on and then throwing her shoes at them. Whenever something goes wrong with a girl it's always the girl's own fault, that's what I always say.

MAGGIE. Do you always say that, Ruby? You should never repeat yourself, dear. Men don't like it.

MRS BATY. Ho! Don't think much of their opinions. Here, if we're doing Tamar tonight I'll have to be off. That scarf she waves out of the window has been missing since the dress rehearsal last Friday, as I happen to know. (*She disappears to the kitchen.*)

MAGGIE. Ah, the rose-red scarf.

SERGE. Don't!

MAGGIE. Why not darling?

SERGE. Brings back memories of that day ages ago when you compared me to the vampire of Kazbek.

MAGGIE. I'm sorry.

MRS BATY (*re-appearing as she pulls on a short fur jacket and fixes her hat at the mirror*). Excuse me, dears. Just want to see me titfer's all right. There! Don't I look sweet?

MAGGIE. Divine as always, Ruby.

SERGE. The toast of Paris. Andy Ruby! On your way out, tell Pierre to bring the car to the door. We're coming to the theatre at once. Good luck, Ruby!

MRS BATY. Same to you, Mr Serge, and God knows you don't need my good luck wishes in the theatre. I wish I could say the same for your private life. Oh well, toodle-oo both! (*She is gone.*)

SERGE (*in imitation of* MRS BATY). Toodle-oo: toodle-oo – toodle-OO . . .' (*he works out a Harlequin movement with both arms and feet to the air of the opening bars of Schumann's 'Carnaval'. He is sitting on a chair.*)

MAGGIE (*conducting an imaginary orchestra as she continues to hum on the same words*).Toodle-oo de do Doo Doodle-oo Too Toodle-oo Do Doodle-oo!

SERGE (*leaping up*). God! Why must the curtain come down? Ever? Why?

MAGGIE. Some day perhaps it never will! Too Toodle-oo Too Doo!

SERGE. Come on! (*They almost dance out of the door, still singing.*) Too Toodle-oo Too Too! (*which is taken up by the orchestra playing the opening of Schumann's 'Carnaval' as the curtain falls.*)

# CURTAIN

# Scene II

*It is about 2.30 in the afternoon: a March day.* SERGE *is alone at the window, gazing into the street. Presently he rises and comes to the desk, takes out a diary and begins to write.*

SERGE. March – 27th is it? Yes . . . End of *Homage à Nijinsky* season in Paris tonight. Triumph for all. Madrid next . . . three weeks' season at the Apollo. Travel to Rio de Janeiro . . . when? . . . Ruby!

ANDY (*entering from kitchen*). Yes sir!

SERGE. I never knew your name was Ruby.

ANDY. No it's not sir, thanks be to God. She's out, sir. Did you want something, Mr Serge?

SERGE. I want to know the date when we'll be flying to Rio. Would you know it, I wonder?

ANDY. I would of course. We flies out of Madrid.

SERGE. Madrid is a city, not a date, you ass.

ANDY. So it is, you're perfectly right. But isn't it a date as well? I often heard you say 'twas a lovely date for the Ballet?

SERGE. Yes, but what date in the year?

ANDY. Oh. Oh my God! You'd want a calendar for that sir. And we goes by some place in Africa sir. Dacky or Dackary or something.

SERGE. Dakar. Yes I know. But what day in the month, what month in the year?

ANDY. Wait now, I has a little calendar some place. (*He runs into the kitchen. Serge continues to write.*)

SERGE. I'm going to count the days for Madrid and Rio when I can find the dates . . . Been alone now for two months and am getting used to it as one gets used to toothache. Paris intolerable except for the theatre . . . (*The doorbell rings*).

SERGE (*shouting*). See who that is Andy. There's a good man.

ANDY. Can't find me calendar anyplace, Mr Serguy: wasn't that the bell ringing?

SERGE. No, it was a pipe-band: go and open the door, you big loony. (*Andy darts to the door and admits Maggie.*)

290

ANDY. Ah welcome miss, good evening, lovely fresh day thank God.

MAGGIE. Yes isn't it divine Andy? There you are my love (*to* SERGE.) Don't think I'm just dropping in: I did warn you yesterday and I'll soon be making an exit and there's a bottle of what everyone loves except me who finds it gives me hiccups. (*She presents him with a bottle.*)

SERGE. Champagne! Oh Maggie, thanks.

MAGGIE (*taking a compact from her bag as she sits down*). That's what you get for being so good. (*Regarding her face in the compact, she gives a piercing scream*) My God! What a face! (*Singing.*) Is it I? Is it I? Mirror, Mirror tell me truly!

SERGE. Yes, and her name was Maggie too. Maggie and Mephistopheles and Faust: don't worry my angel, you look marvellous.

MAGGIE. Oh much as usual, I suppose. Plain but oh so wholesome. (*She puts the compact away.*) Now Serge, you *are* going to see this Marshall man today, aren't you?

SERGE. What Marshall man?

MAGGIE. Haven't you got it down? The ballet and opera man – the critic – Robert Marshall. I thought you'd started keeping a diary? Haven't you got your appointments in it? You'll never be a Mr Samuel Pepys, darling, will you?

SERGE. I only put down important things. And I want to find out the date for when we leave for South America.

MAGGIE. Open Madrid April the 3rd. Fly to Rio via Dakar April the 27th. Open Rio 7th May. You ought to have me as secretary and forget that frog-faced Mademoiselle What's-this-her-name-is.

SERGE (*rushing to the diary*). Let me get that down – Leave Madrid for Rio April the 27th. Open Rio – what date did you say?

MAGGIE. May the 7th. Now what about today?

SERGE (*triumphantly*). March 27th! Aha! (*Speaks as he writes.*) Maggie called at three and brought me champagne.

MAGGIE. And what about Robert Marshall at 3.30 p.m.?

SERGE. Never heard of him.

MAGGIE. Well you ought to have heard of him. He's very distinguished. He wrote raves about you in London last June and he's been trying to contact you here God knows how many times.

SERGE. Oh . . . yes . . . he was the man who put the Homage to Nijinsky into our heads, wasn't he?

MAGGIE. Into my Paco's head. Yes. You never met him, did you?

SERGE. I can't remember.

MAGGIE. Oh you'd remember if you had. I met him once. He made a

291

television interview with six of us to go with the Nutcracker Suite. He and his wife: me dear! Such glamour you never saw! She made us all feel like crossing sweepers. They're both sweet. I think you'll like them.

SERGE. I don't seem to like anyone very much these days. Except you and Paco and Nina. What a dancer! What a partner!

MAGGIE. Well, it's Petrouchka tomorrow night, so you'll be happy.

SERGE. Yes. The last night of the season . . . God forgive me, do you know I'll be glad to get away from Paris for a bit.

MAGGIE. I thought you adored Paris.

SERGE. So I do. You know I do.

MAGGIE. Well?

SERGE. It's this room perhaps. This flat. Too many memories. Too many ——

MAGGIE. – Ah my poor old Serge.

SERGE. Oh you needn't pity me. I do all that myself.

MAGGIE. Yes, I've accused you of that. More than once, I know. But now . . . I wasn't going to say this but now I'm going to. And your interviewer will be here in a few minutes, so I'll be brief. (*She assumes a business-like air.*)

SERGE. Well go on. Be it.

MAGGIE. It's this. I want to tell you how much I admire you.

SERGE (*incredulously*). What?

MAGGIE. I do. For sticking it out so well.

SERGE. Oh that!

MAGGIE. No, let me say it. You've faced the worst fear of your life and you're living with it now for nearly two months. And you've only shown it in one way.

SERGE. Have I?

MAGGIE. And I don't mean in your life off-stage. Even with me you never moan about it or even discuss it. But ——

SERGE. Don't say it shows in my work?

MAGGIE. Well, it does. But only here and there. Only at certain moments.

SERGE. But that's unforgivable.

MAGGIE. I tell you it's only at certain moments. Only in certain parts – in Carnaval, for example.

SERGE. Harlequin in Carnaval? Yes, I was afraid of that.

MAGGIE. At the first performance you were marvellous. Even I was taken by storm. And that was the night of the very day you sent Bill Vandamm away. And you'd been rehearsing and you'd had all those upsets about Pepita.

SERGE. She's much better, by the way, thank God. She'll be back on Monday.

MAGGIE. I know that. Don't interrupt me dear. But since that night . . . Anything in the gay and happy and comical mood . . . A shadow seems to follow you. It's there all the time.

SERGE. A shadow?

MAGGIE. And it's because you're alone. And you're not meant to be alone. (*The telephone rings: they stare at it.*) I'll answer it. (*She takes up the phone and says.*) Alló, allô! Oui . . .? Oh, it's you! How are you? I don't know: hold on a minute. (*Her hand over the receiver.*) It's Bill.

SERGE. Give it to me. (*He takes the phone*) Bill! . . . No . . . Haven't you married Susan yet? . . . Well, marry her. And don't call me again until you do . . . No . . . I said NO. (*The last 'No' is a shout: he slams down the receiver.*)

MAGGIE. Oh, you're hopeless. (ANDY *emerges from the kitchen*).

ANDY. What did I do wrong this time Mr Serguy?

SERGE. Nothing, Andy. You did nothing wrong.

ANDY. 'No, no, no' says he. My God! I thought the house was after falling down. Will I put out the drinks for the newspaper man sir?

MAGGIE (*for* SERGE *has relapsed into silence.*) Yes, do Andy. (ANDY *proceeds to the task.*)

SERGE. That's the third time in two days he's rung. Today is the first time I answered him.

MAGGIE. He wants to come back to you.

SERGE. Well he's not going to. One should never use a bellows to a fire that's gone dead.

MAGGIE. What a problem child you are.

SERGE. Yes. Because my life – outside the theatre – isn't a life at all. It's nothing but a prelude to something that never happens. Oh well! there's always you to bully me, darling. I wonder will you always be there?

MAGGIE. As long as there's a breath in me poor body. You need never wave a scarf out of the window for me.

SERGE. Bless you.

MAGGIE. What are you doing tonight?

SERGE. I hadn't thought. I don't think I can sit through Swan Lake again.

MAGGIE. Nor do I. Nor does Paco. He wants a night free. So why don't we all dine together somewhere?

SERGE. I'd love to.

MAGGIE. Good. We'll call for you. Eight o'clock? Nine?

SERGE. Oh I think nine. (*There is a loud knock on the door.*) Come in.

MRS BATY (*appearing*). I thought I'd give a little tap in case there was an private conversation going on. Good afternoon both.

MAGGIE. ⎫ Good afternoon Ruby.
SERGE. ⎰ Hullo Ruby.

MRS BATY. Excuse me being out if there was anything you wanted Mr Serge, but I was looking for some extra material at the Printemps, and you can guess what it's like in those big shops in this day and age: you could wait to be served till Doomsday. If you know what I mean by Doomsday.

MAGGIE. Yes I think we know.

MRS BATY. Thought you might not have it in the RC Church, as you're not supposed to read your Bible. Not supposed to blow your noses in the RC Church, as far as I can make out. Wouldn't suit me.

SERGE. Well we have heard of Doomsday.

MRS BATY (*darkly*). Well that's just as well because it's coming closer every day. And it's all in the Book dear. Oh yes. Every sign of the coming of the end of the world. And it's all in the Good Book. Oh yes. (*In loud impressive tones.*) *Summer shall be as Winter.* Well, look at last summer. I spent my holidays with my sister Doris in Clacton-on-Sea: three solid weeks of perishing cold. *Night shall be as day.* Well, look at Piccadilly Circus. Look at the Champs Elysees. Anyone could read a book at midnight there if they wanted to, which judging from their faces they wouldn't want to.

MAGGIE. Ruby, you're terrifying.

MRS BATY. *Man and woman shall be unrecognisable from the one from the other.* Well look at my daughter. Well you can't look at her because she's in Hammersmith, but if you could you'd see the point. Worn trousers since she was fifteen and that's twelve years ago now: drinks mild and bitter, smokes a pipe and swears like a navvy. She's all right though: I mean she got married last year.

MAGGIE. And who's the lucky man?

MRS BATY. The bridegroom? Oh you ought to see him dear. Hair down to his waist and a lovely silver earring. He's nice though.

MAGGIE. He sounds divine.

MRS BATY. I wouldn't go as far as that. But he makes lovely pastry. Light as a feather. So you see, Doomsday is nigh. (*The doorbell is heard.*)

SERGE. So is my interviewer man.

MRS BATY. I'd better make myself scarce. You won't want me hanging about. (*She turns towards the kitchen and is bumped into by*

ANDY, *who rushes in.*) Clumsy!

ANDY. I'll go open it, sir.

MRS BATY (*as she goes out*). That's right: make yourself useful. (*She is gone.*)

SERGE. Do Andy. (TO MAGGIE.) That's him.

MAGGIE. I'll be off.

SERGE. No, wait just a few minutes.

MAGGIE. Anything to oblige.

ANDY (*at entrance*). Mr Ronnie Marsaple.

MAGGIE (*aside to* SERGE). The name's really Robert Marshall. But what's in a name?

(ROBERT MARSHALL *enters. He is a tall Englishman with hair that is greying at the sides, and keen intelligent eyes: the only remarkable feature in an otherwise pleasant but unremarkable face. He is conventionally dressed, and wears an overcoat and gloves, the right one of which he takes off as he advances towards* SERGE, *his hand extended*).

MARSHALL. How do you do?

SERGE (*shaking hands*). How do you do?

MARSHALL. I must apologise for being late: I got hopelessly held up, and I did try to ring you but couldn't get through – you know what the Paris telephones can be like in a temperamental mood. (*He sees Maggie.*) Oh, I beg your pardon – I didn't –

SERGE. Maggie, Mr Marshall: Madame Gonzalez.

MARSHALL. Enchanté, Madame. (*He bows over her hand.*)

MAGGIE. Thanks. So am I. But I speak English – not perfectly perhaps, but much better than French.

MARSHALL (*laughing*). Of course! I should have remembered that Francisco Gonzalez had married an Irish wife.

SERGE. Yes he did. Wouldn't you like to take off your coat?

MARSHALL. Thanks so much. (*As he takes off his coat, which* SERGE *hands to* ANDY).

SERGE. Hang that in the hall, Andy.

ANDY. Yes sir. (*He takes the coat away.*)

MARSHALL. But – excuse me – haven't I met you somewhere before? About five years ago, was it?

MAGGIE. Yes, that was me. One of the six from Nutcracker Suite in your ballet series on BBC. What a memory you have!

MARSHALL. Not difficult to remember you. So you're the Irish wife. But you had a Russian name – Marya –

MAGGIE. Marya Petrovna, that's right. And I put on a Russian accent just to camp things up because you terrified me out of my normal

295

speech.

MARSHALL. Oh, I'm sorry. Because I enjoyed that interview more than any of the others. So it was you?

MAGGIE (*after a glace at* SERGE). Well you see it was the fashion when I was a ballet student for dancers to be Russian.

MARSHALL. So you're really an Irish dancer like Mr Kovalevsky. (*He looks at* SERGE.)

SERGE (*smiling*). And Anton Dolin.

MAGGIE. Yes, but not what we understand as an Irish dancer in Ireland. You know, taddle-umps to doodle oodle do do do! (*She executes a morsel of slip-jig.*) Ah me lovely medals! Yes, Maggie Kelly – that was my real name – that would have been fine for the 'Walls of Limerick' but not for – you know.

SERGE. So she became Marya Petrovna.

MARSHALL (*laughing again*). I see.

MAGGIE. I must be going: you want to interview Serge, not me. But by the way, how is your beautiful wife? (*There is a pause.*)

MARSHALL. My wife died last year . . . in California. We were – I mean I was – doing some interview work in Hollywood.

MAGGIE. Oh. I'm so sorry.

ANDY (*re-appearing*). Is there anything at all I can do for you any more, Mr Serguy?

SERGE. No thanks, Andy.

ANDY. Thank you sir. God bless ye all. (*He disappears.*)

MARSHALL (*amused*). From Ireland too, I gather?

MAGGIE. From Ballyjamesduff, I think you told me, Serge?

SERGE. Don't be an ass, Maggie.

MAGGIE. Can't help it. Now I'm really off too. (*She looks from one man to the other.*) Good luck for the interview. Goodbye Mr Marshall.

MARSHALL. Goodbye, Madame Gonzalez. I hope we may meet again.

MAGGIE. Thanks. So do I. (*To* SERGE.) Goodbye, darling. Paco and I'll call for you at about a quarter to nine.

SERGE. Won't you have a drink or anything before you go?

MAGGIE. No thanks. I'm going to my dressmaker's, and that should only be done after prayer and fasting. Goodbye! (*And, as* SERGE *sees her to the exit, she says*) Darling, I don't by any chance see that rose-red scarf a-flutter, do I?

SERGE. What do you –? Oh! Until tonight, Mag. (*She has gone.*) She's quite wonderful, isn't she? One of the really brilliant spots in my life. Do sit down, won't you?

MARSHALL. Thanks. (*He does so.*) Yes, she is quite wonderful. Quality like quicksilver. She's very fond of you, isn't she?

SERGE. No fonder than I am of her.

MARSHALL. Pity she's married, Or is it?

SERGE. I don't think. She's radiantly happy. And so is Gonzalez.

MARSHALL. There's a remarkable man. I'm hoping to get in touch with him before you leave for Madrid. About an idea I hope may amuse him. I'm anxious to do some work with his ballet. Do you think that will be possible?

SERGE. You?

MARSHALL (*laughing*). Oh don't be alarmed. Not as a dancer. As a writer on dancing: an observer from close quarters. At my own expense. How do you think he'd take it?

SERGE. Might be delighted. Why not? Only you might find it difficult. You see his English is very elementary, and his French . . . well, his French is limited too, though not so much. But of course you've met him already.

MARSHALL. Yes, and I do speak Spanish: limited but reasonable.

SERGE. Ah then that'll be all right . . . Tell me, Mr Marshall, are these interviews you're doing . . . (*He pauses.*)

MARSHALL. You're the first on my list you know.

SERGE. Am I? I'm flattered.

MARSHALL. You were going to ask me –?

SERGE. Yes. I wanted to know: are these interviews for our London paper? I suppose — are they confined to ballet and ballet people?

MARSHALL. No. They're confined – I suppose that's the best word though it's a very large confine – to acting, dancing, singing.

SERGE. Opera singing?

MARSHALL. Opera, chiefly, yes. Ballet, drama, opera.

SERGE. In that order?

MARSHALL. In a way, I suppose. From my own preference point of view, yes.

SERGE. Interesting.

MARSHALL. Oh?

SERGE. To me, yes. Because, although ballet is my own art, I always think of it in a way as being the third of the three: if you see what I mean. I mean I think 'Oh, he's a great tragedian', or, 'Oh, she's a great soprano.' As for me . . . well, I'm a dancer. That's all.

MARSHALL. Do you really feel that? Oh, that'll have to go in. Not only in the newspaper interview, but in my book.

SERGE. Oh, you're going to write a book?

MARSHALL. You see, as I'm utterly unable to dance or act or sing, the only think left for me is to write about the people who can.

SERGE. I envy you. I'd love to write. But I can't. I can't do anything much it seems to me. I can't write or paint or understand politics or even drive a car.

MARSHALL. But you can dance.

SERGE. And that's about all.

MARSHALL. Isn't it enough?

SERGE. I don't know really. While I'm doing it it seems enough. It seems the greatest thing in my life –

MARSHALL. Well you can be sure that it's *among* the greatest. Among all the arts, dancing is the oldest.

SERGE. Is it?

MARSHALL. Of course. Have you never heard that 'Dancing stands at the source of all the arts that express themselves first in the human person'?

SERGE (*enthralled and pleased*) I'd never heard of that. It's very encouraging. I'd love to believe it.

MARSHALL. And have you ever heard that 'If we are indifferent to the art of dancing we have failed to understand, not merely the supreme manifestation of physical life, but also the supreme symbol of spiritual life'?

SERGE. My God, you are an amazing man.

MARSHALL. Oh, that's not me. It's Havelock Ellis.

SERGE. Who?

MARSHALL. Havelock Ellis. Ah, he was no fool. He was merely underrated.

SERGE. I suppose he must have been. I never heard of him.

MARSHALL. Ever heard of Lucian?

SERGE. I don't think so. I told you: I'm just a dancer. And a very ignorant one.

MARSHALL. Ah, but you can do the job that the other fellows can only talk about.

SERGE. But I want to learn so much. I'd love to know about things. I mean the sort of things you seem to know about. What did Lucian – it is Lucian, isn't it – what did he say?

MARSHALL. Dancing, Lucian said, is as old as love.

SERGE (*soberly.*) Oh. (*There is a pause.*)

MARSHALL. Has that cast a gloom?

SERGE. What? Oh – no – no. I don't think so.

MARSHALL. Outside your work . . . I take it you don't consider yourself a lucky person, do you?

SERGE. This isn't part of the interview, is it?

MARSHALL. Good God, no. Please forgive me – I'd no intention –

SERGE. It's all right. As long as it's not for the newspaper I mean you're quite right. I'm not a particularly lucky or happy person at the moment. And, strangely enough, I don't mind your asking me – well, what you did ask me – I don't mind a bit.

MARSHALL. I'm glad. Thank you.

SERGE. Because I feel somehow as if I knew you. Do you always have that effect on the people you interview?

MARSHALL. I don't think so, no. But you're very different.

SERGE. Am I?

MARSHALL. You know you are.

SERGE (*laconically*). Oh.

MARSHALL. I'm going to be quite frank with you.

SERGE (*instinctively backing into his shell*). I wonder are you right to be?

MARSHALL. I'm the sort of man who never before has wished to know the artists he most admires. Especially the dancers.

SERGE. I think you're right there. Dancers as individuals are disappointing as a rule. Except to other dancers perhaps.

MARSHALL. That's possibly true. But for years and years I've wanted to know you. And I've always funked it.

SERGE. And I'd never – forgive me if I sound rude – I'd never even heard of you.

MARSHALL (*laughing*). You see I was right. You are exceptional.

SERGE. Until today when Maggie – Madame Gonzalez – told me how famous you are. But I – (*He stops dead.*)

MARSHALL. Oh I'm not famous. Just well known in television circles. That's not fame – success, if you like.

SERGE. Success? Oh, to me it means simply applause, flowers, rave notices in the press, autographs, money . . . I suppose I'm horribly ungrateful. So many people envy me. God! If they only understood how empty that leaves . . .

MARSHALL. I know.

SERGE. Of course there's always the work itself. The discipline. And at the moment of dancing it's as though all the lamps of the world were alight. But when the curtains come down, what was all the fuss about? Nobody really answers . . . Oh I know that sounds ——

MARSHALL. I'm answering.

SERGE (*looking straight at him*). Yes, I can believe that. But you see I ——

MARSHALL. What were you going to say?

SERGE. (*with deliberation*). That I don't want to form any new – any new –

299

MARSHALL. You've suffered a good deal. Isn't that true?

SERGE. Put it that way if you like Anyway . . . (*He laughs.*) like Garbo, 'I want to be alone'.

MARSHALL. You're not the sort of person who ought to be alone.

SERGE. Yes I am . . . Anyway there's no time in my life for – well for new relationships. There are two new ballets for the Nijinsky sequence in preparation and next week we leave for Madrid.

MARSHALL. And after that for South America. I've always wanted to see South America.

SERGE (*after regarding him speechlessly for a moment.*) Really?

MARSHALL. Yes, really. So if Don Francisco approves of my idea . . . *You* can always tell me to hop it if I bore you.

SERGE. You're incredible.

MARSHALL. So are you.

SERGE. Look here. What about our interview?

MARSHALL. Oh yes. The interview. (*As he speaks he produces notebook and pencil.*)

SERGE. Would you like a drink before we begin? I'm not dancing tonight –

MARSHALL. Oh, I know that.

SERGE. So I can join you . . . Gin? Dubonnet? Vodka? (*He goes to the drinks table.*) My God! There's Maggie's champagne.

MARSHALL. I think champagne would be perfect.

SERGE. How does one open these bloody things?

MARSHALL. I'll open it for you, if I may.

SERGE. From what I gather, you'll insist whether you *may* or not.

MARSHALL (*he handles the bottle with practised hands*). Yes. With or without success. (*The cork pops.*)

SERGE. Success! I couldn't do that if I tried all night.

MARSHALL. You shouldn't need to try very hard about anything on earth.

SERGE. – Or in the heavens? (MARSHALL *hands him a glass.*)

MARSHALL. – Or in the heavens. (*They raise their glasses.*)

SERGE. To your book!

MARSHALL. To our book. (SERGE *shakes his head.*)

SERGE. Sláinte!

MARSHALL. Happiness!

SERGE. Happiness? Who knows?

MARSHALL. Want to bet? (*They drink.*)

# FINAL CURTAIN

# MICHEÁL mac LIAMMÓIR

## ON
## PLAYS AND PLAYERS

# Diarmuid and Gráinne

It was all very dim and soulful and my own words sounded drugged and high-falutin in my ears. A love scene was in progress: the daughter of the High King of Ireland was making shameful advances to Torin Thatcher who in his turn was struggling manfully with what I felt he must have regarded as a long, dull part. I became terror-stricken as I watched the progress of my play. Was this really what I had written, this monotonous and dopey elaboration of an old tragic tale, this tasteful compromise between Maeterlinck and the Love Songs of Connacht? It must be the players' fault. No, no, it was not; they were slow perhaps, and dull, their voices were wrong, some of them lacked variety and passion, but it wasn't that that made me bored and wretched, it was myself. 'You silly, meandering, imitative, impotent, yearning, cow-eyed fool', I muttered; and I began to take an interest for a while in my neighbours and their comments to each other during the intervals: 'Beautiful, isn't it really . . . so melancholy dear, the true Celtic melancholy. Do you remember *The Immortal Hour?* Yes. Ah, but then Miss Ffrangcon-Davies; so wonderful. This is very like it, don't you think so, dear? Of course I love this sort of thing. My grandmother was partly Irish you see.'

I turned my eyes and ears to the stage again. It was amusing for a while to hear the Anglo-Irish of my translation on these trans-channel lips, to hear Diarmuid addressed as 'Jahmidd' and the daughter of the King as 'Grone-yah'; but one soon wearied of these exotic pleasures and I was depressed by the end of the evening, not by the production but by my own soul. I could see that my Celtic twilight had died where it had been born, in a reactionary exile among the buses and clattering paving-stones between Soho and the Marble Arch, a worn-out garment from the last generation but one; and that if I was to write again all must come from myself, not from my elders and betters, who in their turn had been embittered by the babel of Fleet Street and by bad news from home.

And so after a brief speech, made self-conscious by my desire to be rid of it all, I left them, after excusing myself from a charming invitation to a party; and when an old friend from Paris asked me in the Café Royal what had brought me to London I said, 'To see the

302

old year out,' and five minutes later was congratulating myself on my unconscious symbolism.

*All for Hecuba*

# Where Stars Walk

This is my first play in the English language.

I had written a lengthy tragedy on legendary themes as well as two short comedies in Irish, and my Gate Theatre partner, Hilton Edwards, had filled my head with ambitions to write a new legend play about Midhir and Etáin. We talked of this for years in a series of long and increasingly vague conversations, for both of us, I think, realised that the day of mythical romanticism was at its lowest ebb in the theatre – not that it was dead, for fashions in art do not pass out of existence any more than the moon, or the tide, or the needles of the clock – and gradually I began to forget my immortal lovers and to become more interested in the daily life of Dublin that laughed and whispered and cracked its derisive whips through the hours of my work in the theatre; and a little while after that a friend told me of a red-headed servant girl who had come into his house, and how his wife had found her walking in her sleep in the midst of imaginary scenery and persons of great splendour.

My friend, his thoughts full of Freud and of Jung, had his own theories about it all, but I, in the middle of his talk, found myself remembering Etáin wandering in sleep through the corridors of Tara and dreaming of the immortal country she had forgotten, and presently, one event leading to another, I decided – again at my partner's suggestion – to combine it all in a species of modern comedy that might amuse the Dublin audience and leave me with enough of the unseen world partially to satisfy an incurable craving.

*Programme note to 1957 revival*

# The Mountains Look Different

*The Mountains Look Different* is constructed in the main from a Greek model: that is to say it is concerned with the lives of three people, a wife, a husband, and a father, who are thrown into conflict brought about by certain events that have passed before the rise of the curtain. Over these three characters the fates hang, and their story is worked out within the limits of the unities of time and place, the action being more or less continuous.

The subsidiary characters follow the Greek custom of contributing, each one, his share to the building of the tragedy: the farmhand Bartley, for example, is the Messenger who bears the tidings of events; the uncle of the Woman brings the gift which plays a significant part in the development of the action; the Neighbours form the Chorus of witnesses, and so on.

The crime, too, is committed beyond the view of the audience, though its result, as was the custom in Greece, is seen by them; the play opens and closes before the door of the house of fate, and the victim makes formal confession of her sins before the people, the Chorus, as Oedipus and Orestes proclaimed their misdeeds before the people of Thebes and of Athens.

The play is a morality in the sense that, like the plays of Greece, it tells of sin and its atonement, and I wrote it in this way because I wished to experiment with a modern theme in an approximation to a classic form.

Whether I have done my work with understanding or not is for an audience to judge; and it is because there has been some controversy and much misunderstanding over this two hours' traffic of the stage that I offer this brief outline of a method of writing, fully conscious that it is an unusual thing to do but with the hope that it may help towards an enjoyment of certain qualities, both old and new, that I believe it to possess.

A play is not necessarily good or bad because its structure is planned on classic lines; but whether a woman's appearance please our individual taste or not, it may be of interest to learn that the gown she is wearing follows in its essence a design of ancient tradition and is not a garment borrowed from some wholesale manufacturer with whose productions so many eyes, unschooled in all but their immediate surroundings, have become familiar.

*Handwritten manuscript in possession of Northwestern University, Evanston, Illinois*

\*     \*     \*

17th August 1950:  . . . My play *The Mountains Look Different* is being tried out in German at Innsbruck and entitled *Feuer* by the translator, Mimi Zoff, who tells me: reception Magnificent, a phrase leading inevitably to the modifying and familiar statement that Press Opinions are Mixed, some of the describing it as Masterly and others as Crude and Brutal (fancy, me!): the latter school of thought having a great deal of dirt to throw at the audience who are bitterly reported as having 'seemed to delight in this sort of thing'. . . However, my own original (though private) opinion that it was a perfectly gorgeous play and that Tolstoi's *Powers of Darkness* had better look out having by this time evaporated, I am less easily transported to Heaven or Hell by what anybody thinks or prints on the subject than I would have been seven years ago when I wrote it.

*Each Actor On His Ass*

# A Slipper for the Moon

I began to dream of a play that still sleeps at the back of my head which would trace the lives and adventures of a group of players who like ourselves would travel from town to town and from one country to another. All over the world I thought they could be led, yet never would they leave the theatre; their eyes and ears for ever bounded by proscenium and borders and light-battens, their minds travelling no further than the dusty brick walls at the edge of the stage. 'How easy to produce!' I said, for all could be effected with no scenery or properties; flats would be piled against the walls, and hanging ropes and dangling sandbags cast strange shadows on the faces. *The Sleeping Beauty* should be the theme; the palace where everyone lay in a profound slumber, heedless of weeds and brambles thickening to a forest outside the windows: the symbol of the sterile, haunted limitless dimensions of our world. It should open with a rehearsal, the rehearsal of a pantomime perhaps, giving a rational explanation for the lack of a conventional set; in the first act a quarrel was in process, the orchestra on strike, the autumn rain was beating on the roof, the players dissatisfied, the leading actor in tears . . . and they would move from rehearsal to café, from railway station to ship's cabin, from Dublin to Cairo, yet never for one second would they move from the stage . . . the theatre, like the engulfing night, claiming them for ever, its tentacles about their necks. 'Look,' the heroine would say, 'that is the sky; it grows dark; the stars, my beloved, are coming out'; yet she would point to hanging rope and dangling sandbag and she would know as she pointed, and the audience would know, that for her there was no escape, until she was weakened by a kiss, and the kiss would be given by the leading actor and she would murmur: 'Not now, not yet; look! The curtain is going up!' and as she pointed into space the last curtain would fall.

*All for Hecuba*

# The Theatre

The Theatre to my mind is the most incalculable thing in the world, for it offers no tangible guide, outside its simplest forms, the Musical or the Circus, as to what is desired or expected. This all of us who have ever worked in it have known since time began, but it continues to astonish.

*Each Actor On His Ass*

# Acting

To be an actor demands a curious and complete surrender of the self and of many personal claims, and I reflected how all art is a wrestling match with life, and how acting more than any other art is a demonstration of rebellion against the mundanity of everyday existence. Far from being a copyist of life's surface tricks or a facile repeater of traditional antics, the actor should live with such delicacy, with such intensity, that he brings manner and style to all the unimportant trifles of gesture and speech, so that the eating of a fruit, the folding of a letter, the raising of the arm, the donning of a cap, all become in his hands images of significance, profound mirrors of character. To act is to live for a moment with an intenser life, to pass bodily into the sphere of sorrows and of joys greater than our own, to thrust the shoddy surface of what we call real life upwards to a transforming radiance; and while the painter must see and the poet and musician hear with passion before they hurry to canvas or to paper and ink, the actor must note all down with calmness and precision and must then give to the single moment everything he possesses, soul and voice and body, the inner and the outer selves. He works with himself as surely as a philosopher does with his brain, or a prostitute with her body . . .

*All for Hecuba*

\*     \*     \*

Actors are sometimes asked: 'How do you feel when you are acting? I have heard your voice break and seen sometimes the tears run down you cheeks: do you really believe at such moments that you see your father's ghost, or you friend's body hacked to pieces by his enemies, or find yourself old and unwelcome in your daughter's house?'

The questions are never, I think, answered, because not even the

306

most analytical actor can find an answer that is wholly true. The acting process is too intricate a series of phenomena to be explained by a formula. Is it perhaps comparable to that twilight in the mind which in dream knows its body to be asleep in bed and yet endures all the terrors and pleasures and sorrows of life that for the moment is its only reality?

One thing is certain: 'Acting is believing'. The actor, more than any other worker, has need of the gift of faith in what his reason knows to be the trickiest image of truth, or how can he become, even for one moment, somebody else?

\*     \*     \*

The actor must be in harmony with himself or he shatters the confidence of his audience; that is why, to him, any profound self-analysis may prove fatal. No honest man, looking into the mirror of his own soul, could be his own best friend.

\*     \*     \*

It is so much easier to close a book without offence, even in the middle of a chapter, than to leave one's seat in the theatre in the middle of a play. That is why the actor is often insufferably thin-skinned, and why, when the stage-actor retires exclusively to the studio and the screen, he ceases to belong to the tribe. He has passed into the sphere of those to whom the breath of living communion has been turned into a conversation on the telephone.

*Theatre in Ireland*

# Studying a Part

*3rd March, 1956:* Hard work on rehearsal for *Seagull* all day in Ballet room behind the stage, and am delighted to find Trigorin is easy to learn. Not, necessarily, to play. There are two things that make a part easy or difficult to study. First: the actor's faith, not only in the character or in the story, but in the author. Second: the author, who, in order to win the actor's faith, must possess, as well as dramatic skill, sense of the theatre and all the essentials that are plain to us, either a beautiful and personal music (Shakespeare, Yeats, Wilde), or he must be so pure and whole, so simple, so close to truth, that all the while his thought is made clear (Ibsen, Shaw, Tchehov). It may be that Tchehov in his own Russian has also the beautiful and personal music: one cannot judge this from a translation of a language one doesn't know. It is certain he has clarity, purity of soul, and overwhelming sense of truth. So near he comes, powerfully and tenderly probing and revealing the secrets of the human race; the actor has only to *follow him closely* and then to listen to the pulsing of his own heart.

How great he was. What love is mingled with the admiration one feels for him.

*Each Actor On His Ass*

# Œdipus

*28th March, 1956:* Last night the first performance of *Œdipus* and *Man of Destiny*: did not see the second as I was half-dead with terror over the first, but heard that Eithne and Paddy Bedford played well.

I am never happy or at my best on a first night, especially in tragedy. Those moments when one feels the sense of power – the chief reward of the tragic actor – are too rare and too fleeting and are prone to destruction at the hands of the senses: a feeling of loss, of strain, of a *fruitless searching*. I think I succeeded in the long speech – where Œdipus tells the story of the murder of Laius to Jocasta, but a strange idea went stalking through my mind: the stifling and terrible sensation of truth and of guilt and of the terror of destiny seemed to force me to play it all as if I were a child crushed to his knees by fear. Looking back at it now I feel I was too conscious of the secret – that my wife was my mother – which is unknown to Œdipus at the moment of his telling the tale of the murder. Yet to me it seems that somewhere in the dark places of the unconscious he *is* aware of it all, when everything relating to his normal life is forgotten for a moment, or for another moment when his hand is on her breast, or it may be for whole hours together in the shadows of his mind when he lies in sleep at her side. Yet how to express this without confusing the audience and oneself as well I have not discovered. I am convinced that a *part of the imagination of man* is aware of much more about the mysteries of his destiny than has yet been determined, and that the actor must reveal this partial wisdom and share it with his listeners is clear to me, or his acting becomes a false thing lacking both spirit and blood.

*Each Actor On His Ass*

308

# Audience

*9th May, 1956: Œdipus* tonight: audience so entirely silent and receptive that it was easy to give them all we had. The theatre is very like a game of tennis, except that the mysterious people on the far side of the net appear to be unconscious of the fact that they are playing too.

*Each Actor on His Ass*

\*       \*       \*

But we were learning all the time, chiefly the lessons of the stage and a little – too little, as I think now – of the temper of the Dublin public, who like every public in the world is capricious and unaccountable, and who, unlike most others, is neither wholly provincial nor wholly metropolitan in its reaction. It is essentially Irish in its demand for the satisfaction of a sensitive and voluptuous ear, in its patient attention to the telling of a story, in its quiet response to the charm of a personality, and its almost total indifference to the pleasures of the eye, of the falling of light upon a beautiful object, of the high notes of two vivid colours in the austerity of a neutral setting of the peaked and angular grouping in a massed pattern of movement. It is metropolitan in its rapid and merciless seeing through a maze of pretty trappings and carefully rehearsed effects to the ill-formed bones, not so much of a bad play but of a poor story; in its readiness to experiment in a new and unknown work; in its instinct for personality and its adherence to integrity in acting. It is provincial in its unfailing worship of hackneyed situations, of garish, time-worn Irish jokes, of blindness to visual subtlety and shabbiness alike, above all in its lack of ability to discriminate, not between the first and third rate, but between the second and the tenth. In this, of course, it has been given little help by the newspapers, for very often the journalist who reports, let us say, on McCormick's distinguished performances at the Abbey will use precisely the same mildly glowing *clichés* for a description of some well-meaning bungle of the same part in a town-hall production by a suburban amateur group; and no sort of guidance can be looked for from a press at once so indifferent and so prejudiced.

*All for Hecuba*

# Critics

But the wicked things were often good to us, however misguided they may have been, and of course we flew, as all actors after a new production will fly, to read our notices, and were for some time elated or enraged by what we saw. I felt then as I feel to this day that a brilliant school of criticism could have worked wonders for the Irish stage, but that to create this one of two methods would be necessary. Either the existing critic would have to write in a far greater intimacy and understanding with author and producer, actor and designer, during the hours of creation, a witness if not a contributor to the labour of production; or else he would have to be a genuine stranger to all these activities, still more to the men and women who shared in them. In this case one would have to ship one's critics over from some outer world, never to allow them the slightest intercourse with the personalities of the theatre or with the intrigues therein, and to replace them with a fresh batch as soon as that familiarity with the intimacies of our situations, inevitable in so small a community, began to set in. In this way only would an unhampered view of our work be possible in a city on whose stages we are all seen to often and in too many different plays, and among whose walls coteries and factions are as numerous and as ardent as in a public school.

*All for Hecuba*

\*     \*     \*

Paul Carroll's *Shadow and Substance* tonight. Not, I fear, very well done. Found I couldn't be too hard on them: their endeavour and sincerity quite apparent. No people who are trying to do anything *at all* should meet with mere discouragement in this land of ruin and weed. One must tell them the truth but one should, in the manner of a tactful dentist with his wheel, go gently. Every illusion one takes from the searcher must be replaced by an image of the truth, if indeed one can find it oneself. This country teems with aesthetic misfortune, with talented individuals incapable of an hour of work, with conceited jackanapes who imagine they are artists because they think they'd like to be, with pompous incompetent critics who fatuously praise or indiscriminately rend . . .

*Each Actor On His Ass*

# BIBLIOGRAPHICAL CHECKLIST

Compiled by John Barrett and Frances-Jane French

**Plays**

*Oidhche Bhealtaine* (May Eve), Government Publications Office, Dublin, 1932.

*Lulu*, Government Publications Office, Dublin, 1933.

*Diarmuid agus Gráinne*, Government Publications Office, Dublin, 1935.

*Ill Met by Moonlight*, James Duffy, Dublin, 1954.

*Where Stars Walk*, Progress House, Dublin, 1962.

**Prose**

Oidcheanna Sidhe . . . Fairy Nights, Talbot Press, Dublin, 1922.

*Lá agus Oidhche* (Day and Night), C. S. Fallon, Dublin, 1929.

*All for Hecuba*: An Irish Theatrical Autobiography, Methuen, London, 1946, 2nd edition, Progress House, Dublin, 1961.

*Theatre in Ireland: Drámaíocht in Eirinn*, Department of External Affairs, Dublin, 1950.

*Ceo Meala La Seaca* (A Honeyed Mist on a Frosty Day), Collection of Autobiographical Essays, Sáirséal agus Dill, Dublin, 1952.

*Put Money in Thy Purse*: The Filming of Orson Welles' *Othello* Methuen, London, 1952.

*Aisteoirí faoi dhá Sholas* (Actors between Spotlights), Sáirséal agus Dill, Dublin, 1956.

*Each Actor on His Ass*, Routledge & Kegan Paul, London, 1961.

*An Oscar of No Importance . . . being an account of the author's adventures with this one-man show*, Heinemann, London, 1968.

(with Eavan Boland), *W. B. Yeats*, Thames & Hudson, London, 1971, and Viking, New York, 1972.

*Enter a Goldfish*: Memoirs of an Irish Actor, Young and Old, Thames & Hudson, London, 1977.

**Poetry**

*Bláth agus Taibhse* (Flower and Ghost), Sáirséal agus Dill, Dublin, 1964.

**Works in Collaboration**

(with Eavan Boland), *W. B. Yeats and his World*, Thames & Hudson, London, 1971.

**Contributions to Books**

'Problem Plays', in *The Irish Theatre – Lectures delivered during the Abbey Theatre Festival, Dublin, August 1938*, edited by Lennox Robinson, Macmillan, London, 1939.

'Introduction' to *J. M. Synge's Plays, Poems and Prose*, Dent, London, 1964. (Everyman's Library, No. 968).

'Introduction' to *Ireland*, (Photographs) by Edwin Smith, Thames & Hudson, London, 1966.

**Contributions to Periodicals**

'Transference: a story', *Dublin Magazine*, August 1925, Vol. 111. pp. 9–14.

'Transference: a story', *Dublin Magazine*, Oct–Dec 1926, New Series, Vol. 1, No. 4, pp. 39–44.

'Swaggering Caravan' (Extracts from the unpublished memoirs of Micháel mac Liammóir), *The Bell*, Dublin, Jan. 1943, Vol. V. No. 4, pp. 253–265; continued in Feb. 1943, Vol. V. No. 5, pp. 347–355; continued in April 1943, Vol VI, No. 1, pp. 33–42; continued in June 1943, Vol. VI, No. 3. pp. 193–203; continued in Jan. 1944, Vol. VII, No. 4, pp. 293–303; continued in March 1944, Vol. VII, No. 6, pp. 487–495.

'Some Talented Women', *The Bell*, Dublin, May 1944, Vol. VIII, No. 2, pp. 117–127.

'Hamlet' (Text of talk given on BBC Third Programme, 1964), *University Review*, Dublin, Summer, 1966, Vol. I, No. 5, pp. 37–42.

**Translations**

*Diarmuid's Lament* (Words translated from the Gaelic by Micháel mac Liammóir, with music composed by John F. Larchet). Piggot and Co., Dublin, 1937.

*Each Actor on his Ass* (Memoirs, translated from the Irish by the Author), Routledge and Kegan Paul, London, 1961. Contains: 'Aisteoirí faoi dhá Sholas' and part of Ceo Meala Lá Seaca.'

**One-Man Shows**

*The Importance of Being Oscar*, Dolmen, London, and O.U.P., London, 1963. 2nd, Revised Edition, Dolmen, Dublin, 1978. Report Colin Smythe, Gerrards Cross, 1995.

## Unpublished Plays

*Dancing Shadow*, performed, Dublin, 1941.
*Portrait of Miriam*, performed, Dublin, 1947.
*The Mountains Look Different*, performed, Dublin, 1948.
*Home for Christmas*, performed, Dublin, 1950.
*A Slipper for the Moon*, performed, Dublin, 1954.
*The Liar*, performed, Dublin, 1969.
*Prelude in Kazbek Street*, performed, Dublin, 1973.

## Unpublished Plays – Adaptations of Others' Work

*Hollywood Pirate* (Le Corsaire) performed, Dublin, August 1938.
*Juliet in the Rain* (Les Rates) performed, Dublin, September 1938.
*A Tale of Two Cities*, performed, Dublin, 1943.
*Jane Eyre*, performed, Dublin, 1944.
*The Picture of Dorian Grey*, performed, Dublin, 1945.
*Trilby,* performed, Dublin, 1946.
*Dr Knock* (An Apple a Day) performed, Dublin, 1953.
*The Informer*, performed, Dublin, 1958.

## Unpublished One-Man Shows

*I Must be Talking to My Friends*, performed, Dublin, 1963.
*Talking About Yeats*, performed, Dublin, 1965.

## Unpublished Variety Sketches

*Dublin Blues*, performed, Dublin, 1940.
*To Be Quite Frank*, performed, Dublin, 1940.
*Gertie, the Ghost of the Gate*, performed, Dublin, 1940.
*Buttery Blondes*, performed, Dublin, 1941.
*Zoo Blues*, performed, Dublin, 1942.
*Flops*, performed, Dublin, 1942.
*The Stylish Marriage*, performed, Dublin, 1942.
*Le Vache sur le Toit*, performed, Dublin, 1942.
*Last Tram to Dalkey*, performed, Dublin, 1943.
*Cinderella at the Window*, performed, Dublin, 1943.
*A la Crepe Suzette*, performed, Dublin, 1943.
*The Importance of being Pussy*, performed, Dublin, 1944.
*Portrait of a Woman with Red Hair*, performed, Dublin, 1944.
*The Decline and Fall of the Drama*, performed, Dublin, 1946.
*Proteus at the Telephone*, performed, Dublin, 1946.

## Unpublished Pageants

*The Ford of the Hurdles*, performed, Dublin, 1929.

*Easter 1916*, performed, Dublin, 1930.
*Pageant of Saint Patrick*, performed, Dublin, 1957.

**Unpublished Ballets**
*Full Moon for the Bride*, performed, Dublin, 1968.
*Red Petticoat.*

# TRANSLATIONS OF IRISH

Translation of Irish phrases used in the plays

*Ill Met by Moonlight (pages 79–165)*

*page 80*

BAIRBRE. Oh yes.

PROSPER. Go on!

BAIRBRE. Well, what they did was, a big wreath of summer flowers —

PROSPER. Wreath?

BAIRBRE. Yes, a wreath, and white salt and goat's blood scattered on it and . . . and the old nurse came then and she put it around her neck and the husband gave her a clout under the jaw . . .

PROSPER. A clout?

BAIRBRE. Under the jaw. And then she goes out again to the . . . to the fairy fort.

PROSPER. Is that all?

BAIRBRE. Then the cows began to give milk again and the rowan tree was in flower and everything was all right again. That's the adventure of the changeling from Brugh na Gealaí.

PROSPER. What's that word.

BAIRBRE. What word?

PROSPER. Iarlais?

BAIRBRE. Iarlais? God, an iarlais is an iarlais – what else!

*page 81*

BAIRBRE. Dammit, that bell! Isn't he clean out of his mind?

*page 82*

BAIRBRE. Yes, sir?

PROSPER. What . . .

LEE. What does the husband do in the story to put the changeling out of the place?

*page 82*

LEE. Off with you, Bairbre.

BAIRBRE. Good-day to ye both!

315

*page 98*

LEE. Bairbre! Bairbre Mannin – are you going home?

BAIRBRE. I'm not going home yet, certainly. I'll be staying over in Mary's house tonight. I'll be going to the lower end of the house.

*page 107*

MEN'S VOICES. 'Oh, God speed you home . . .
Now that Summer's come.'

BAIRBRE. Lee! Lee! Look!

LEE. What's that?

BAIRBRE. The red hen has laid this egg! Look!

LEE. The devil take it, look at that!

BAIRBRE. Goodday to you, sir. Look!

*page 108*

BAIRBRE. What did he say?

LEE. Blather.

BAIRBRE. Dammit, he's clean out of his mind.

*page 119*

CHARLES. How are you, Lee?

*page 120*

CHARLES. 'May you get the woman of your choice and land without rent.'

*page 125*

BAIRBRE. Arrah, I don't know. I don't know . . .

LEE. Think about it, girl. Give us a kiss now. One small little kiss.

BAIRBRE. Musha, I couldn't.

LEE. Come over to me now – come over!

BAIRBRE. I won't, you divil!

LEE. Come along – come on – closer!

BAIRBRE. Isn't this enough?

LEE. A few more steps. Ah, do!

BAIRBRE. What's that you're saying? . . . . Let me go! Aren't you the strong and bad-behaved lad? Oh Lee! The people are coming up from the lake – Miss Sukey's in front and she's crying.

LEE. Go on out quickly to the kitchen.

*page 125*

BAIRBRE. I'll do that.

LEE. Wait a moment!

BAIRBRE. What do you want?

LEE. This!

BAIRBRE. Musha, let me go, you villain!

*page 126*
SUSAN: Young Charles!

*page 157*
LEE. Bairbre I say! Bring the wreath here to me!
BAIRBRE. I have it.
CATHERINE. Small good will it do you.

*page 158*
CATHERINE. A hundred curses on you!

*page 165*
BAIRBRE. Lee! See this! The trees are in flower! Look Lee!
LEE. The devil take it!
LEE. Come on out till we see them. Let's look at them together.

*The Mountains Look Different (pages 171–224)*

*page 187*
TOM. Hora! Hora! Mickaleen! Be careful you don't set the place on fire! The flames are too close to the stables – is it that you want to roast us alive, you fool?
A MAN'S VOICE. There's little danger! Little danger!
BAIRBRE. . . .
TOM. . . . Wait a moment. Wait there.
BAIRBRE. . .
TOM. . . . In the devil's name what are you doing there?

*page 217*
THE WOMAN. He's gone from us! He's gone from us.
OTHER WOMEN'S VOICES. Ochone! Ochone! Ochone for ever!
THE WOMAN. Sorrow for his death! Sorrow for his death!
OTHER WOMEN'S VOICES. Oh, weep! Oh, weep! Ochone for ever!

# IRISH DRAMA SELECTIONS

ISSN 0260–7962

1. SELECTED PLAYS OF LENNOX ROBINSON
   Chosen and introduced by Christopher Murray
   Contains *Patriots*, *The Whiteheaded Boy*, *Crabbed Youth and Age*, *The Big House*, *Drama at Inish*, *Church Street*, Bibliographical Checklist.

2. SELECTED PLAYS OF DENIS JOHNSTON
   Chosen and introduced by Joseph Ronsley
   Contains *The Old Lady Says 'No!'*, *The Moon in the Yellow River*, *The Golden Cuckoo*, *The Dreaming Dust*, *The Scythe and the Sunset*, Bibliographical Checklist.

3. SELECTED PLAYS OF LADY GREGORY
   Foreword Sean O'Casey
   Chosen and introduced by Mary Fitzgerald
   Contains *The Travelling Man*, *Spreading the News*, *Kincora*, *Hyacinth Halvey*, *The Doctor In Spite of Himself*, *The Goal Gate*, *The Rising of the Moon*, *Dervorgilla*, *The Workhouse Ward*, *Grania*, *The Golden Apple*, *The Story Brought by Brigit*, *Dave*, Lady Gregory on Playwriting and her Plays, Bibliographical Checklist.

4. SELECTED PLAYS OF DION BOUCICAULT
   Chosen and introduced by Andrew Parkin
   Contains *London Assurance*, *The Corsican Brothers*, *The Octoroon*, *The Colleen Bawn*, *The Shaughraun*, *Robert Emmet*, Bibliographical Checklist.

5. SELECTED PLAYS OF ST JOHN ERVINE
   Chosen and introduced by John Cronin
   Contains *Mixed Marriage*, *Jane Clegg*, *John Ferguson*, *Boyd's Shop*, *Friends and Relations*, prose extracts, Bibliographical Checklist.

6. SELECTED PLAYS OF BRIAN FRIEL
   Chosen and introduced by Seamus Deane
   Contains *Philadelphia, Here I come*, *Translations*, *The Freedom of the City*, *Living Quarters*, *Faith Healer*, *Aristocrats*, Bibliographical Checklist.
   Our edition of this title is only for sale in North America

7. SELECTED PLAYS OF DOUGLAS HYDE
Chosen and introduced by Janet Egleson Dunleavy
and Gareth Dunleavy
Contains *The Twisting of the Rope, The Marriage, The Lost Saint, The Nativity, King James, The Bursting of the Bubble, The Tinker and the Sheeog, The Matchmaking, The Schoolmaster*, Bibliographical Checklist. This volume publishes the original Irish language texts with Lady Gregory's translations.

8. SELECTED PLAYS OF GEORGE MOORE
AND EDWARD MARTIN
Chosen and introduced by David B. Eakin and Michael Case
Contains *The Strike at Arlingford, The Bending of the Bough, The Coming of Gabrielle, The Passing of the Essenes;* and *The Heather Field, Maeve, The Tale of a Town.* Bibliographical Checklist.

9. SELECTED PLAYS OF HUGH LEONARD
Chosen and introduced by S. F. Gallagher
Contains *The Au Pair Man, The Patrick Pearse Motel, Da, Summer, A Life, Kill.* Bibliographical Checklist.

10. SELECTED PLAYS OF T. C. MURRAY
Chosen and introduced by Richard Allen Cave
Will contain *Autumn Fire, Sovereign Love, Maurice Harte, The Briery Gap, The Pipe in the Fields, Birthright.*
Bibliographical Checklist.

11. SELECTED PLAYS OF MICHEÁL mac LIAMMÓIR
Chosen and introduced by John Barrett
Contains *Where Stars Walk, Ill Met by Moonlight, The Mountains Look Different, The Liar, Prelude in Kazbek Street*, On Plays and Players (essay by mac Liammóir), Bibliographical Checklist.

12. SELECTED PLAYS OF M. J. MOLLOY
Chosen and introduced by Robert O'Driscoll
Will contain *The King of Friday's Men, The Paddy Pedlar, The Wood of the Whispering, Daughter from Over the Water, Petticoat Loose,* and *The Bachelor's Daughter.* Bibliographical Checklist.